R. Gupta's®

Accounting & Finance

for

BANKERS

For JAIIB and Diploma in Banking & Finance Examination

by

Abinash Kumar Mandilwar

M.Sc., MBA (Finance), M.Phil. (Management), CAIIB, Certified Credit Professional,
PGDFA, Diploma in Micro Finance, Diploma in Home Loan Advising

**Chief Manager & Faculty, Bank of India,
Staff Training College, Bhopal**

Updated Upto
MARCH 2019

Ramesh Publishing House, New Delhi

Published by
O.P. Gupta *for* Ramesh Publishing House

Admin. Office
12-H, New Daryaganj Road, Opp. Officers' Mess,
New Delhi-110002 ✆ 23261567, 23275224, 23275124

E-mail: info@rameshpublishinghouse.com
Website: www.rameshpublishinghouse.com

Showroom
● Balaji Market, Nai Sarak, Delhi-6 ✆ 23253720, 23282525
● 4457, Nai Sarak, Delhi-6, ✆ 23918938

First Edition : April, 2019

Book Code: R-2054

ISBN: 978-93-88642-64-4

HSN Code: 49011010

समर्पण

ॐ भूर्भुवः स्वः तत्सवितुर्वरेण्यं भर्गो
देवस्य धीमहि धियो यो नः प्रचोदयात्।।

मेरी यह पुस्तक वेदमाता माँ गायत्री,
हमारे परम पूज्य गुरुदेव पंडित श्रीराम
शर्मा आचार्य, परम वन्दनीया माता
भगवती देवी शर्मा, मेरे पूज्य पिताजी
स्व० विश्वनाथ प्रसाद एवं मेरी परम
आदरणीय माँ स्व० चन्द्रकान्ता देवी
के चरणों में सादर समर्पित।

Preface

Banking Sector in India is changing rapidly. To meet the requirement of this generation of bankers a need was felt to equip them with the basics of banking and baking related accounting knowledge. This book is written keeping the Young Banker in mind, who are not having commerce background. The main advantage of this book is to understand the bank related accounting process in easy language and to awaken the banker's confidence on accounting and finance. The book has been prepared with great hope and expectation that it will help the young generation of proficient bankers. Besides, for the preparation of JAIIB Examination, this book is also very useful for day to day banking and all Knowledge Based Examinations.

A combination of subjective as well as objective material has been comprehensively dealt in this book. This book titled "JAIIB—Accounting & Finance for Bankers" has many unique features to its credit & consists of all topics/syllabi required for JAIIB/DB&F examination with clear concepts & simple language with latest changes (up to March 2019). It has been experienced that students need objective type questions beside subjective matter. This has been taken care of in this book. To prepare the students well, objective questions are also incorporated after every chapter. Two mock tests (100 questions each) for self-evaluation of preparation are given at the end of the book.

During preparation of this book, I have received tremendous support from my family members, friends & colleagues of BOI Staff Training College, especially my wife Mrs. Sumita Taterway (Ruby), my daughters Miss Tanya and Miss Pragya. Special thanks to Shri Ajay Kumar Sinha, Faculty Members of Staff Training College, Bhopal for their support, vetting & compilation of this book.

Any suggestions towards its further improvement will be thankfully acknowledged and incorporated in the next edition.

Date: 28.03.2019   — **Abinash Kr. Mandilwar**

About the Author

The author, Mr. Abinash Kumar Mandilwar joined 'Bank of India' as Probationary Officer in 1995. He was born and completed his study as well as started his carrier in Patna. A highly experienced banker, has been working in the bank for more than 24 years. He has held several important assignments which include 10 years as branch head before his current posting as Chief Manager and Faculty at Bank of India Staff Training College at Bhopal. 

He is a Certified Associate of Indian Institute of Banking & Finance (CAIIB). His academics include Post Graduate in Chemistry, MBA (Finance), M. Phil. (Management), Honours Diploma in Computer Science., Post Graduate Diploma in Financial Advising, Certified Credit Professional, Diploma in Micro Finance, Diploma in Home Loan Advising, Diploma in Banking Oriented Paper in Hindi, Certificate in AML & KYC, Certificate in SME Finance, Certificate in Trade Finance, Certificate in Customer Service & Banking Codes and Standard. He was also awarded the Continuing Professional Development (CPD) Certification from IIBF in 2011.

As a faculty for more than 4 years at training college, is catering to training needs of managers in middle management/ Staff. He has vast experience of teaching on banking subject in Bank of India as well as associated Regional Rural Banks. He is also associated as a visiting faculty with other bank training institutes.

His articles have been published in different in house banking journals. His Power Point Presentations (PPTs) on various banking topics are appreciated by bankers on social media and Slideshare.net.

सुदीप रतन श्रीवास्तव
प्राचार्य
बैंक ऑफ इंडिया
स्टॉफ प्रशिक्षण महाविद्यालय, भोपाल

Sudeep Ratan Srivastava
Principal

Bank of India
Staff Training College, Bhopal

Foreword

I am glad to know that the book "JAIIB—Accounting & Finance for Bankers" is written by Shri A.K. Mandilwar. He is a practicing banker for more than 24 years and had worked in functional areas of the bank. The Book covers the basic conceptual part of the subject Accounting Aspects of Banking. This book is very useful to those new Young Bankers, who do not have commerce background. Mr. Mandilwar has explained the bank related accounting process in easy language. A quick perusal of the book reveals that it is quite comprehensive, exhaustive and suitable for the new practitioners of banking as well as for those preparing themselves for the exams conducted by IIBF. The language of the book is simple and lucid.

There is a need to publish a complete book covering all the aspects so that new recruits get updated without referring to many voluminous books. The book will be of great help to the new entrants in the banking industry especially for their orientation to the core operational areas of banking. The readers will also be introduced to the entire accounting process in banking.

I am confident that this book will be of use to all the candidates who are appearing for the JAIIB/DB&F Examination and also to those general banking personnel who desire to update their information on the subject. The book will help the new entrants who did not study such subjects in their academic life. The test papers given at the end of each chapter will immensely be beneficial to the new entrants and will help them to prepare themselves for the practical aspects of banking. In short this is a concise text book which will help the readers prepare for their JAIIB/DB&F Exams.

I am sure the book by Shri Mandilwar will serve the purpose of the book on the subject 'Accounting & Finance for Bankers' which will be quite handy for referring to the basics of banking. I wish the readers an interesting reading and a sound initiation into the world of banking.

Bhopal

Date: 15-03-2019

— **Sudeep Ratan Srivastava**

CONTENTS

MODULE A : BUSINESS MATHEMATICS AND FINANCE

1. Calculation of Interest and Annuities 3-10

• Introduction • Bank Interest • Simple Interest • Compound Interest • The Rule of 72 • Equated Monthly Instalment (EMI) • Calculation of 'Annuity' • Calculation of Present Value of Ordinary Annuity • Present Value of Annuity Due Example • Future Value of Ordinary Annuity Example • Fixed and Floating Interest Rates • Front-End and Back-End Interest Rates • Calculation of Interest using Products/Balances • Amortisation of A Debt • Repayment of a Debt • Sinking Funds.
Test Yourself

2. Calculation of YTM 11-19

• Definition of Debt • Meaning of Loans • Introduction to Bonds • Terms Associated with Bonds • Provision Available in Bonds • Types of Bonds • Valuation of Bonds • Valuation of a Coupon Bond with Annual Coupon • Valuation with Semi-annual Coupon • Calculation of the Yield of A Bond • How to Calculate Yield to Maturity of a Bond? • Yield to Maturity and Present Value of a Bond • What are the day Count Conventions used in Calculating Bond Yields? • Duration of Bond • Calculation for Duration • Bond Price Volatility.
Test Yourself

3. Capital Budgeting 20-33

• Introduction • Capital Budgeting • Importance of Capital Budgeting • Present Value (PV) and Discounting • Capital Budgeting Techniques: 1. Simple Payback Period (SPP); 2. Discounted Payback Period (DPP); 3. Accounting/Average Rate of Return (ARR); 4. Net Present Value (NPV); 5. Internal Rate of Return (IRR); 6. Profitability Index (PI); • Comparison of NPV and IRR • Sensitivity Analysis • Capital Budgeting Techniques Under Uncertainty.
Test Yourself

4. Depreciation and its Accounting 34-40

• Meaning of Depreciation • Causes of Depreciation • Need for Depreciation • Factors of Depreciation • Accounting for Depreciation • Method of Depreciation :

(ix)

1. Fixed Percentage Method or Straight-Line Method; 2. Diminishing Value or Written Down Value (WDV) Method; 3. Sum of the Years' Digits (SYD) Method of Depreciation • Replacement of a Fixed Asset and Creation of Sinking Fund.

Test Yourself

5. Foreign Exchange Arithmetic *41-46*

• Introduction • Fundamentals of Foreign Exchange • Forex (Foreign Exchange) Market • Direct and Indirect Quotation• Buy or Sell the Foreign Exchange • Some Basic Exchange Rate Arithmetic • Forward Forex Contract • Forward Exchange Rate • Arbitrage • Factors Determining Forward Exchange Rate

Test Yourself

MODULE B : PRINCIPLES OF BOOKKEEPING & ACCOUNTANCY

6. Definition, Scope and Accounting Standards *49-59*

• Introduction • Nature of Accounting • Objectives of Accounting • Types of Accounting • Origins of Accounting Principles • Accounting Standards in India and its Definition and Scope • Procedure for Issuing Accounting Standards • Generally Accepted Accounting Principles of USA (US GAAP) • These Organizations Influence the Development of GAAP in the United States • International Financial Reporting Standards (IFRS) • Difference Between GAAP & IFRS • Transfer Pricing • Types of Transfer Pricing Methods.

Test Yourself

7. Basic Accountancy Procedures *60-66*

• Introduction • Accounting Principles • Concepts and Conventions of Accountancy : A. The main accounting concepts at the recording stage; B. The main accounting concepts at the reporting stage • Accounting Conventions • Going Concern Entity • Double Entry System • Features of Double Entry System • Advantages of Double Entry System • Limitations of Double Entry System • The Principle of Conservatism • Revenue Recognition and Realisation • Accrual and Cash Basis.

Test Yourself

8. Maintenance of Cash/Subsidiary Books and Ledger *67-85*

• Introduction • Bookkeeping Basics • Account • Classification of Accounts • Journal • Advantages of Journal • Journal Entry • Voucher • Explanation of Journal • Types of Journal Entry • Ledger • Use of the words "To" and "By" • Relationship between Journal and Ledger • Utility of a Ledger • Subsidiary Books • Is the Cash Book Journal or Ledger? • Cash Book • Types of Cash Book • Simple (Single Column) Cash Book • Format of Simple Cash Book • Balancing a Single Column Cash Book • Posting entries from Single Column Cash Book to Ledger Accounts

(x)

- Two (Double) Column Cash Book • Triple Column Cash Book • Petty Cash Book • Types of Petty Cash Book • Imprest System of Petty Cash Book • Advantage of the Imprest System • Purchase Book • Sales Book

Test Yourself

9. Bank Reconciliation Statement *86-94*

- Introduction • Recording Transaction in Cash Book • Transaction Contained in the Pass Book/Bank Statement • Definition and Need of Bank Reconciliation Statement • Causes for Differences Between Cash Book and Pass Book • Preparing Reconciliation Statement • Steps in Preparing Bank Reconciliation Statement • How to Prepare a Bank Reconciliation Statement when extracts of the Cash Book and Pass Book are given • Preparation of Bank Reconciliation Statement with Adjusted Cash Book • The Advantages of Bank Reconciliation Statements.

Test Yourself

10. Trial Balance, Rectification of Errors and Adjusting & Closing Entries *95-103*

- Introduction • Meaning of a Trial Balance • Features and Purpose of a Trial Balance • Types of Trial Balance and Preparation of Trial Balance • Disagreement of a Trial Balance • Classification of Errors • Location of Errors • Rectification of Errors • Suspense Account and Rectification • Rectification of Errors when Books are Closed.

Test Yourself

11. Capital and Revenue Expenditure *104-107*

- Introduction • Expenditure • Determining Capital Nature and Revenue Nature • Receipt • Distinction between Capital Receipt and Revenue Receipt.

Test Yourself

12. Bills of Exchange *108-118*

- Introduction • Types of Instruments of Credit & NI Act • Essential conditions of a Bill of Exchange • Differences among Bill of Exchange, Promissory Note and Cheque • Parties and Certain Important Terms of Bill of Exchange • Term and Due Date of a Bill • Bills Receivable and Bills Payable • Types of Bill Finance • Discounting a Bill • Accounting Entries to be Passed • Endorsing a Bill • Dishonour of Bill • Bill Books.

Test Yourself

MODULE C : FINAL ACCOUNTS

13. Balance Sheet Equation *121-124*

- Introduction • Balance Sheet Equation • Computation of Balance Sheet Equation • Example of the Balance Sheet Equation by the various Transactions.

Test Yourself

(xi)

14. Preparation of Final Accounts *125-139*

• Introduction • Trial Balance—A Starting Point for Final Accounts • Adjustments Entries in Final Accounts • Trading Account • Preparation of Trading Account: 1. Item written on the Dr. Side of the Trading Account: 2. Items written on the Cr. Side of the Trading Account: • Closing Entries • Form of Trading Account • Profit & Loss Account • Preparation of Profit & Loss Account • Form of Profit & Loss Account • Balance Sheet • Characteristics of Balance Sheet • Grouping and Marshalling of Assets and Liabilities in Balance Sheet • Classification of Assets • Classification of Liabilities • Following Points should be noted for preparing Final Accounts • Liabilities • Assets.

Test Yourself

15. Ratio Analysis *140-152*

• Introduction • Meaning of Accounting Ratio • Classification of Accounting Ratios • Uses of Accounting Ratios • Limitations of Ratio Analysis • Calculation and Interpretation of Various Ratios • Users of Financial Ratios • Practice Set.

Test Yourself

16. Final Accounts of Banking Companies *153-163*

• Introduction • Definition of a Bank • Functions of a Bank • Requirements of Banking Companies as to Accounts & Audit • Principal Books of Accounts • Preparation and Presentation of Financial Statements of Banks • Schedules of Financial Statements • Notes and General Instructions for Compilation • General Disclosure Principle of RBI.

Test Yourself

17. Company Accounts *164-184*

• Introduction • Definition of Companies • Different Types of Companies in India • Partnership Firm • Distinction Between Partnership and Limited Liability Company • Share Capital • Classes of Share Capital • Types/Nature of Share Capital • Issue of Shares • Issue of Shares at a Discount • Sweat Equity Shares• Employee Stock Options (ESOs) • Forfeiture and Reissue of Shares • Bonus Shares • Final Accounts of Companies • General Instructions for the Preparation of Balance Sheet and Profit and Loss Account • Key Features of Balance Sheet • General Instructions for preparing the Balance Sheet of a Company • Current Assets: A. Share Capital; B. Reserves and Surplus; C. Long-term Borrowings; D. Other Long-term Liabilities; E. Long-term Provisions; F. Short-term Borrowings; G. Other Current Liabilities; H. Short-term Provisions; I. Tangible Assets; J. Intangible Assets; K. Non-current Investments; L. Long-term Loans and Advances; M. Other Non-current Assets; N. Current Investments; O. Inventories; P. Trade Receivables; Q. Cash and Cash Equivalents; R. Short-term Loans and Advances; S. Other Current Assets (Specify Nature); T. Contingencies and Commitments; • Key Features Statement of Profit and Loss • General Instructions for Preparation of Statement of Profit and Loss.

Test Yourself

18. Accounting in a Computerized Environment *185-192*

• Introduction • Requirements of the Computerized Accounting System • Accounting Framework • Operating Procedure • Features of Computerised Accounting • Terms used in Computerised Accounting • Comparison between Manual and Computerised Accounting • Advantages of Computerised Accounting • Disadvantages of Computerised Accounting • Problems faced in Computerised Accounting System • Computerisation–Scope and Experiences in Banking • Core Banking Solution • Business Components • Benefits • Information Security Policies • Data Loss Prevention • Natural Disasters • Viruses • Human Errors • Software Malfunction • Hardware Malfunction.

Test Yourself

MODULE D : BANKING OPERATIONS

19. Banking Operations *195-199*

• Introduction • Functions of a Bank • Main functions of a Bank in India • Other Functions of Banks • Para Banking Services Performed by Banks • Front Office and Back Office in a Bank • Outsourcing of Financial Services by Banks • Advantages of Outsourcing • Activities that should not be Outsourced • Operating Procedures in Banks • Banking Operations Manual.

Test Yourself

20. Operational Aspects of KYC & Customer Service *200-209*

• Introduction • Objectives • Definition of Money Laundering • Punishment for Money-Laundering • Combating the Financing of Terrorism (CFT) measures • Know Your Customer • Key Elements of KYC Policy • Customer Acceptance Policy (CAP) • Risk Management • Customer Identification Procedure (CIP) • "Officially Valid Document" (OVD) • E-KYC • Walk-in Customers: 1. Individuals; 2. Company; 3. Partnership Firm; 4. Trust Documents; 5. Association of Persons • Partial Freezing/ Closure of Non-KYC Compliance Account • Monitoring of Transactions • Financial Intelligence Unit—India • Customer Service in Banks (RBI Guidelines) • Policy for General Management of the Branches • Customer Service Committee of the Board • Board approved Policies on Customer Service • Banking Codes and Standards Board of India (Jan. 2018) • Code of Bank's Commitment to Micro and Small Enterprises • Code of Bank's Commitment to Customers.

Test Yourself

21. Operational Aspects of Accounting Entries *210-214*

• Introduction • Financial Transactions in Banks • Peculiar Features of Accounting System in Banks • Preparation of Vouchers • Preparation of Vouchers in Bank • Kinds of Vouchers • Types of Debit Vouchers • Credit Vouchers • Bankers' Books • Accounting Systems of Different Banks.

Test Yourself

(*xiii*)

22. Operational Aspects of Handling Cash & Clearing *215-218*

• Introduction • Operational Aspects of Handling Clearing • Electronic Clearing Service (ECS)• Cheque Truncation System • Collection of Instruments (RBI Guidelines) • RBI Cheque Collection Policy • Local Cheques • Outstation Cheques • Cheque Drop Box Facility • Payment of Cheques/Drafts/Pay Orders/Banker's Cheques • Cash Operations • Automated Clearing House (ACH).

Test Yourself

23. Operational Aspects of Deposit Accounts *219-227*

• Introduction • Acceptance of Deposits • Types of Deposit Accounts in Banks • Salient Features of Deposit Account : Current Account; Savings Bank Account • Fixed Deposits • Recurring Deposits • Nomination Facility in Banks • Different Types of Customers • Different Types of Companies in India.

Test Yourself

24. Operational Aspects of Loan Accounts *228-236*

• Introduction • RBI Guidelines for Lending By Banking Companies • Operational Process of Loans • Types of Credit Facilities by Bank • Different Types of Borrowers • Different Types of Companies in India • Clubs & Societies.

Test Yourself

25. Operational Aspects of CBS Environment *237-240*

• Introduction • Core Banking Solutions (CBS) • Need for Core Banking Solution • Benefits of CBS • Objectives of CBS • Flow of Transactions in CBS • Operational aspects for Password Control • Steps to be taken to ensure the integrity of the password • Transaction Control • Personnel Controls • Day End Activities • Logical Access Control • Role and Responsibilities of the Bank under CBS.

Test Yourself

26. Back Office Functions & Handling Unreconciled Entries in Banks *241-244*

• Introduction • Role of Back Office in Banks • Functions Performed by the Back Office • Reconciliation Function in Banks • Sundry/Suspense Account • RBI Guidelines on Inter Office Reconciliation in Banks • Reconciliation Set up and Process at the Banks.

Test Yourself

MOCK TEST

Accounting & Finance for Bankers

• **Mock Test 1 & 2** *1-16*

RULES & SYLLABUS

PAPER-2 : ACCOUNTING & FINANCE FOR BANKERS

OBJECTIVE

JAIIB aims at providing required level of basic knowledge in banking and financial services, banking technology, customer relations, basic accountancy and legal aspects necessary for carrying out day-to-day banking operations.

ELIGIBILITY

(i) The examination is open to the ordinary members of the Institute (Any person working in the banking and finance industry whose employer is an Institutional member of the Institute can apply for membership, for details visit IIBF website).

(ii) Candidates must have passed the 12th standard examination in any discipline or its equivalent. The Institute may, however at its discretion, allow any candidate from clerical or supervisory staff cadre of banks to appear at the examination on the recommendation of the Manager of the bank/ officer-incharge of the bank's office where the candidate is working, even if he/she is not 12th standard pass or its equivalent.

(iii) Subordinate staff of recognized Banking/Financial Institutions in India, who are members of the Institute, are eligible to appear at the examination, provided they have passed the 12th standard examination or its equivalent.

SUBJECTS OF EXAMINATION

(1) Principles & Practices of Banking

(2) Accounting & Finance for Bankers

(3) Legal & Regulatory Aspects of Banking

There is no exemption in any of the subject/s for prior qualification/s.

PASSING CRITERIA

1. Minimum marks for pass in the subject is 50 out of 100.

2. Candidates securing at least 45 marks in each subject with an aggregate of 50% marks in all subjects of examination in a single attempt will also be declared as having completed the Examination.

3. Candidates will be allowed to retain credits for the subject they have passed in an attempt till the expiry of the time limit for passing the examination as mentioned below.

TIME LIMIT FOR PASSING THE EXAMINATION

1. Candidates will be required to pass the examination within a time limit of 2 years (*i.e.,* 4 consecutive attempts).

2. Candidates not able to pass examination within stipulated time period of two years are required to re-enroll themselves afresh. Such candidates will not be granted credit/s for subjects passed, if any, earlier.

3. Time limit of 2 years will start from the date of application for First attempt.

    Attempts will be counted irrespective of whether a candidate appears at any examination or otherwise.

MEDIUM OF EXAMINATION

Candidates are allowed to attempt the examination either in Hindi or English, and should clearly fill in their choice of medium at the time of registration of application. In any case change of medium will not be allowed at a later stage.

PATTERN OF EXAMINATION

(i) Question Paper will contain approximately 120 objective type multiple choice questions for 100 marks including questions based on case studies / caselets. The Institute may however vary the number of questions to be asked for a subject.

(ii) The examination will be held in Online Mode only.

(iii) There will NOT be negative marking for wrong answers.

DURATION OF EXAMINATION:

The duration of the examination will be of 2 hours.

PERIODICITY AND EXAMINATION CENTRES

a) Examination will be conducted on pre-announced dates published on IIBF Web Site. Institute conducts examination on half yearly basis, however periodicity of the examination may be changed depending upon the requirement of banking industry.

b) List of Examination centers will be available on the website. (Institute will conduct examination in those centers where there are 20 or more candidates.)

SYLLABUS OF JAIIB / DB&F

PAPER-2 : ACCOUNTING & FINANCE FOR BANKERS

MODULE A – BUSINESS MATHEMATICS AND FINANCE

✦ Calculation of Interest and Annuities

Calculation of Simple Interest & Compound Interest; Calculation of Equated Monthly Instalments; Fixed and Floating Interest Rates; Calculation of Annuities; Interest Calculation using Products/ Balances; Amortisation of a Debt; Sinking Funds.

✦ Calculation of YTM

Debt—Definition, Meaning & Salient Features; Loans; Introduction to Bonds; Terms associated with Bonds; Cost of Debt Capital; Bond value with semi-annual Interest; Current Yield on Bond; Calculation of Yield-to- Maturity of Bond; Theorems for Bond Value; Duration of Bond; Properties of Duration; Bond Price Volatility.

✦ Capital Budgeting

Present Value and Discounting; Discounted Technique for Investment Appraisal; Internal Rate of Return (IRR); Method of Investment Appraisal; NPV and IRR compared; Investment Opportunities with Capital Rationing; Investment Decision making under condition of uncertainty; Expected NPV Rule; Risk Adjusted Discount Rate Approach for NPV Determination; Sensitivity Analysis for NPV Determination; Decision Tree Analysis for NPV Estimation; Payback Methods; ARR.

✦ Depreciation and Its Accounting

Depreciation, its types and methods; Comparing Depreciation Methods.

✦ Foreign Exchange Arithmetic

Fundamentals of Foreign Exchange, Forex Markets; Direct and Indirect Quote; Some Basic Exchange Rate Arithmetic—Cross Rate, Chain Rule, Value date, etc.; Forward Exchange Rates— Forward Points; Arbitrage; Calculating Forward Points; Premium/discount; etc.

MODULE B – PRINCIPLES OF BOOKKEEPING & ACCOUNTANCY

✦ Definition, Scope and Accounting Standards

Nature and Purpose of Accounting; Historical Perspectives; Origins of Accounting Principles; Accounting Standards in India and its Definition and Scope; Generally Accepted Accounting Principles of USA (US GAAP); Transfer Pricing; Overview of IFRS; Difference between GAAP & IFRS.

✦ Basic Accountancy Procedures

Concepts of Accountancy; Going Concern Entity; Double Entry System; Principle of Conservatism; Revenue Recognition and Realisation; Accrual and Cash Basis.

✦ Maintenance of Cash/ Subsidiary Books and Ledger

Record Keeping Basics; Account Categories; Debit and Credit Concepts; Accounting and Columnar Accounting Mechanics; Journals; Ledgers; subsidiary books; etc.

✦ **Bank Reconciliation Statement**

Need for Bank Reconciliation; Causes of Differences; Preparation of Bank Reconciliation Statement; How to prepare a Bank Reconciliation Statement when Extracts of Cash Book and Pass Book are given; Adjusting the Cash Book Balance; Advantages of Bank Reconciliation Statement.

✦ **Trial Balance, Rectification of Errors and Adjusting & Closing Entries**

Meaning of a Trial Balance; Features and Purpose of a Trial Balance; Types of Trial Balance and Preparation of a Trial Balance; Disagreement of a Trial Balance; Classification of Errors; Location of Errors; Rectification of Errors; Suspense Account and Rectification; Rectification of Errors when Books are closed; Adjusting and Closing Entries.

✦ **Capital and Revenue Expenditure**

Expenditure; Distinction between Capital and Revenue Expenditure; Deferred Revenue Expenditure; Receipts; General Illustrations.

✦ **Bills of Exchange**

Types of Instruments of Credit; Term and Due Date of a Bill; Certain Important Terms; Accounting Entries to be Passed; Accommodation Bill etc.

MODULE C – FINAL ACCOUNTS

✦ **Balance Sheet Equation**

Balance Sheet Equation; Computation of Balance Sheet Equation.

✦ **Preparation of Final Accounts**

Preparation of Trading A/C; Profit and Loss A/C; Profit & Loss Appropriation Account; Balance Sheets.

✦ **Ratio Analysis**

Meaning of Accounting Ratios; Classification of Ratios; Uses of Accounting Ratios; Limitations of Accounting Ratios; Calculation and interpretation of various Ratios; Different Users and their Use of Ratios.

✦ **Final Accounts of Banking Companies**

Definition and Functions of a Bank; Requirements of Banking Companies as to Accounts and Audit; Significant Features of Accounting Systems of Banks; Principal Books of Accounts; Preparation and Presentation of Financial Statements of Banks; CMA Format; Accounting Treatment of Specific Items; Preparation of Profit and Loss Account; Comments on Profit and Loss Account; Important Items of Balance Sheet; Disclosure Requirements of Banks; Additional Disclosures prescribed by RBI; Disclosures required under BASEL norms.

✦ **Company Accounts I & II**

Definition and Types of Companies; Distinction between Partnership and Limited Liability Company; Classes of Share Capital; Issue of Shares; General Illustrations Non-voting Shares; Form of Balance Sheet; Legal Requirements for Assets; Legal Requirements for Liabilities; Legal Requirements for Profit & Loss A/c; Preparation of Final Accounts.

✦ **Accounting in a Computerized Environment**

Meaning, Features of and Terms used in Computerized Accounting; Difference between Computerized and Manual Accounting; Advantages and Disadvantages of Computerized Accounting; Functions performed by Computerized Accounting Softwares available in the Market; Computerization —Scope and Experiences in Banking; The Core Banking Components; Information Security; Internet and World Wide Web—Influences on Banking.

MODULE D – BANKING OPERATIONS

✦ **Banking Operations & Accounting Functions**

Preparation of Vouchers, cash receipt and payment entries, clearing inward and outward entries, transfer debit and credit entries, what is KYC and what are the different documents to satisfy KYC, verify KYC and authenticity of documents, operational aspects in regard to opening of all types of accounts, scrutiny of loan applications/ documents, allowing drawals and accounting entries involved at various stages, operational aspects of CBS environment etc., Back office operations in banks, handling of unreconciled entries in banks.

MODULE–A
BUSINESS MATHEMATICS AND FINANCE

CHAPTER 1

CALCULATION OF INTEREST AND ANNUITIES

INTRODUCTION

Section 5(B) of Banking Regulation Act, 1949 defines banking as "Accepting for the purpose of lending or investment of deposits of money from the public, repayable on demand and withdrawable by cheques, drafts, and orders or otherwise". Banking Company means any company which transacts the business of banking in India. Bank pays interest to the depositor on the deposit accounts and charge in interest from the borrower in the loan accounts. The interests are calculated as per pre-agreed terms on pre-defined interval. Method of calculation of interest is done either simple interest or compound interest according to agreed term of agreement.

BANK INTEREST

When a person borrows money from the bank or financial institution, some extra amount is charged by the lending entity for the use of money, called as interest. Interest is defined as the cost of borrowing money as in the case of interest charged on a loan balance. Interest is the cost of borrowing money, where the borrower pays a fee to the bank for using the latter's money. Conversely, interest can also be the rate paid for money on deposit as in the case of a certificate of deposit. The interest, typically expressed as a percentage, can be calculated in two ways, simple interest or compound interest.

Simple Interest

Simple interest is calculated on the principal, or original amount of a loan. Simple interest is the type of interest where the interest is charged only on loaned amount.

Generally, simple interest paid or received over a certain period is a fixed percentage of the principal amount that was borrowed or lent.

Simple interest is calculated using the following formula:

Simple Interest (I) = Principal amount (P) × Interest Rate (R) × Time in years (N)

Rate of Interest is the percentage of the principal charge as interest for one year. Rate is expressed in percentage; thus, it must be divided by hundred. For example, if rate is 11%, then use 11/100 or 0.11 in the formula.

Example 1: A student Miss Tanya obtains a simple-interest loan to pay one year of her college tuition, which costs ₹ 60,000 and the annual interest rate on her loan is 9%. She repays her loan over three years. The amount of simple interest she pays ₹ 16,200 (₹ 60,000 × 0.09 × 3). The total amount she repays is ₹ 76,200 (₹ 60,000 + ₹ 16,200).

Example 2: Shivam invested ₹ 50,000 in mutual fund with an interest rate of 8% for the period of 3 years. How much interest would he earn after 3 years?

Simple Interest (I) = P × R × N

Simple Interest (I) = ₹ 50,000 × 8% × 3 years

Or 50,000 × 0.08 × 3 = ₹ 12,200

Hence, Shivam would earn ₹ 12,000 in three years.

Compound Interest

Compound Interest is the interest which is computed as a percentage of revised principal, i.e. original principal plus accumulated interest of prior periods. In other words, it includes interest on interest. In this method we sum up the interest earned in the previous years to the initial principal, thus increasing the principal amount, on which the interest for the next period is charged. Here, interest is to be paid on the principal as well as the interest accrued during the loan term.

The formula for annual compound interest, including principal sum, is:

Compound Interest = Total amount of Principal and Interest in future (or Future Value) less the Principal amount at present called Present Value (PV). PV is the current worth of a future sum of money or stream of cash flows given a specified rate of return.

$$= [P\ (1 + r)^n] - P$$
$$= P[(1 + r)^n - 1]$$

Where,

P   = Principal,

r = Annual interest rate in percentage terms,

n = Number of compounding periods for a year, and

A   = Amount of money accumulated after n years including interest.

Total amount accumulated after n years including interest can be calculated as

A = $P\ (1 + r)^n$

Example 3: If a population of a village is increasing by 10 per cent yearly. If, the present population is 20000, then calculate the population of the village after 3 years.

Solution:

Present Population (P) = 20000, Rate (r) = 10% yearly, Period (n) = 3 years,

Total Population after 3 years (A) =?

$A = P\ (1 + r)^n = 20000(1+10/100)^3 = 20000(1.10)^3 = 26620$

Formula for calculation of compound interest if interest is paid more frequently:

Annually   = $P(1 + r)$ = Annually compounding

Half yearly = $P(1 + r/2)^2$ = Half yearly compounding

Quarterly   = $P(1 + r/4)^4$ = Quarterly compounding

Monthly   = $P(1 + r/12)^{12}$ = Monthly compounding

The time interval between which the interest is added to the account is called the compound period. The interest rate together with compounding period and balance in the account determines how much interest is added in each compound period. The basic formula of compound interest for calculating total amount is:

$$A = P\ (1 + r/n)^{(nt)}$$

Where,

A = the future value of the deposited/loan, including interest (Principal + Interest)

P = the principal investment amount (the initial deposit or loan amount)

r = the annual interest rate (decimal)

n = the number of times that interest is compounded per year

t = the number of years the money is invested or borrowed for

Note that this formula gives you the future value of an investment or loan, which is compound interest plus the principal. Should you wish to calculate the compound interest only, you need this:

Total compounded interest = $P\ (1 + r/n)^{(nt)} - P$

Example 4: If an amount of ₹ 5,000 is deposited into a savings account at an annual interest rate of 5%, compounded monthly. What will be the value of the investment after 10 years?

Solution: P = ₹ 5000, r = 5% = 5/100 = 0.05 (decimal), n = 12, t = 10.

If we plug those figures into the formula, we get the following (note that ^ indicates 'to the power of'):

A   = $P\ (1 + r/n)^{(nt)}$

     = $5000\ (1 + 0.05 / 12)^{12 \times 10}$

     = 8235.05.

So, the investment balance after 10 years is ₹ 8,235.05.

The Rule of 72

The rule of 72 is a shortcut to estimate the number of years required to double your money at a given annual rate of return. The rule states that you divide the rate, expressed as a percentage, into 72:

Years required to double investment

= 72 ÷ compound annual interest rate

Example 5: For instance, if you were to invest ₹ 100 with compounding interest at a rate of 9% per annum, the rule of 72 gives 72/9 = 8 years required for the investment to be worth ₹ 200; an exact calculation as per the formula = 8.0432 years.

EQUATED MONTHLY INSTALMENT (EMI)

An Equated Monthly Installment (EMI) is a fixed payment amount made by a borrower to a lender at a specified date each calendar month. Equated monthly instalments are used to pay off both interest and principal each month so that over a specified number of years, the loan is paid off in full. With most common types of loans, such as term loan, the borrower makes fixed periodic payments to the lender over the course of several years with the goal of retiring the loan. EMIs differ from variable payment plans, in which the borrower is able to pay higher payment amounts at his or her discretion. In EMI plans, borrowers are usually only allowed one fixed payment amount each month.

The formula for EMI (in arrears) is:

$$P = A \times \frac{1-\left(1+r\right)^{-n}}{r}$$

or, equivalently,

$$A = P\frac{r\left(1+r\right)^{n}}{\left(1+r\right)^{n-1}}$$

Where, P is the principal amount borrowed, A is the periodic amortization payment, r is the periodic interest rate divided by 100 (annual interest rate also divided by 12 in case of monthly instalments), and n is the total number of payments (for a 30-year loan with monthly payments $n = 30 \times 12 = 360$).

Example 6: If you borrow ₹ 10,000,000 from the bank at 10.5% annual interest (where, 'r' is 10.5% = 10.5/100 = 0.105 (decimal) and for monthly payments = 0.105/12 = 0.00875) for a period of 10 years (i.e., 120 months),

Then,

EMI = ₹ 10,000,000 × 0.00875 × (1 + 0.00875) ^120 / ((1 + 0.00875)^120 − 1) = ₹ 134,935. i.e., you will have to pay total ₹ 134,935 for 120 months to repay the entire loan amount. The total amount payable will be 134,935 * 120 = ₹ 16,192,200 that includes ₹ 6,192,200 as interest toward the loan.

Example 7: A loan of ₹ 100,000 is given @ 9% p.a. for 12 months, EMI is ₹ 8745. The appropriation towards the interest and principal out of the EMI payments based on the above given example is given below assuming that the loan is taken in August, 2018.

Year	Principal (A)	Interest (B)	Total Payment (A + B)	Balance
Aug 2018				1,00,000
Sept 2018	7,995	750	8,745	92,005
Oct 2018	8,055	690	8,745	83,950
Nov 2018	8,116	630	8,745	75,834
Dec 2018	8,176	569	8,745	67,658
Jan 2019	8,238	507	8,745	59,420
Feb 2019	8,299	446	8,745	51,121
Mar 2019	8,362	383	8,745	42,759
Apr 2019	8,424	321	8,745	34,334
May 2019	8,488	258	8,745	25,847
Jun 2019	8,551	194	8,745	17,295
Jul 2019	8,615	130	8,745	8,680
Aug 2019	8,680	65	8,745	0

CALCULATION OF 'ANNUITY'

What is an Annuity?

An annuity is a series of payments made at equal intervals. Examples of annuities are regular deposits to a savings account, monthly home mortgage payments, monthly insurance payments and pension payments. Annuities can be classified by the frequency of payment dates. The payments (deposits) may be made weekly, monthly, quarterly, yearly, or at any other regular interval of time.

An annuity is a financial product that pays out a fixed stream of payments to an individual, primarily used as an income stream for retirees. Annuities are created and sold by financial institutions, which accept and invest funds from individuals and then, upon annuitization, issue a stream of payments at a later point in time. The period of time when an annuity is being funded and before payouts begin is referred to as the accumulation phase. Once payments commence, the contract is in the annuitization phase.

There are two types of annuities:

1. Ordinary annuity; 2. Annuity due

1. **Ordinary Annuity:** An ordinary annuity is a series of equal payments made at the end of consecutive periods over a fixed length of time. While the payments in an annuity can be made as frequently as every week, in practice, ordinary annuity payments are made monthly, quarterly, semi-annually or annually.

2. **Annuity Due:** The opposite of an ordinary annuity is an annuity due, which is when payments are made at the beginning of each period.

Calculation of Present Value of Ordinary Annuity

Examples of ordinary annuities are interest payments from bond issuers, which are generally paid semi-annually and quarterly dividends from a company that has maintained stable payout levels for years. The present value of an ordinary annuity is largely dependent on the prevailing interest rate. Because of the time value of money, rising interest rates reduce the present value of an ordinary annuity, while declining interest rates increase its present value. This is because the value of the annuity is based on the return you can get elsewhere. If you can get a higher interest rate somewhere else, the value of the annuity in question goes down.

Present Value of Ordinary Annuity Formulae

The present value formula for an ordinary annuity takes into account three variables. They are:

PMT = the period cash payment

r = the interest rate per period

n = the total number of periods

Given these variables, the present value of an ordinary annuity is:

Present Value = PMT × ((1 − (1 + r) ^ − n)/r)

Example 8: If an ordinary annuity pays ₹ 50,000 per year for five years and the interest rate is 7 per cent, the present value would be:

= ₹ 50,000 × ((1 − (1 + 0.07) ^ − 5)/0.07)

= ₹ 205,010.

Present Value of Annuity Due Example

Recall that with an ordinary annuity, the investor receives the payment at the end of the time period. This stands in contrast to an annuity due, which is when the investor receives the payment at the beginning of the

period. This impacts the value of the annuity. The formula for an annuity due is slightly different as follows: Present Value of Annuity Due

= PMT + PMT x ((1 − (1 + r) ^ − (n − 1) / r)

Example 9: If the annuity in the above example was instead an annuity due, the present value of it would be calculated as:

Present Value of Annuity Due

= ₹ 50,000 + ₹ 50,000

  × ((1 − (1 + 0.07) ^ − (5 −1) / 0.07)

= ₹ 219,360.

All else being equal, an annuity due is always worth more.

Future Value of Ordinary Annuity Example

The future value of an annuity formula is used to calculate what the value at a future date would be for a series of periodic payments. The future value of an annuity formula assumes that:

1. The rate does not change

2. The first payment is one period away

3. The periodic payment does not change

If the rate or periodic payment does change, then the sum of the future value of each individual cash flow would need to be calculated to determine the future value of the annuity. If the first cash flow, or payment, is made immediately, the future value of annuity due formula would be used.

$$\text{FV of Annuity} = P \times \frac{\left[(1+r)^n - 1\right]}{r}$$

Where,

P = Periodic Payment

r = rate per period

n = number of periods

Example 10: Future value of an annuity formula an example of the future value of an annuity formula would be an individual who decides to save by depositing ₹ 1000 into an account per year for 5 years. The first deposit would occur at the end of the first year. If a deposit was made immediately, then the future value of annuity due formula would be used. The effective annual rate on the account is 2%. If she would like to determine the balance after 5 years, she would apply the future value of an annuity formula to get the following equation:

$$₹\ 1000 = P \times \frac{\left[(1+0.02)^5 - 1\right]}{0.02}$$

The balance after the 5th year would be ₹ 5204.04

FIXED AND FLOATING INTEREST RATES

Banks and Financial Institutions are charging two different mode of interest on loan accounts. They are:

1. **Floating Interest Rate or Variable Interest Rate:** A floating or variable interest rate loan is a loan in which the interest rate charged on the outstanding balance varies as market interest rates change. As a result, your payments will vary as well (as long as your payments are blended with principal and interest). The interest rate is generally linked to a benchmark rate of the bank. It may increase or decrease depending upon the change in the benchmark rate of the lending bank.

   If a vehicle loan is taken at a variable interest rate of 9.50 percent, repayable in 7 years in August 2018 and if the benchmark rate decreases to 9.25 percent in August 2019, the interest rate of this loan will also be decreased to 9.25 percent. In this case EMI will be same but the loan will be repaid earlier.

   In EMI system under floating interest rate, depending upon the change in interest rate, the repayment period varies, but amount of EMI remains the same.

2. **Fixed Interest Rate:** Fixed interest rate loans are loans in which the interest rate charged on the loan will remain fixed for that loan's entire term, no matter what market interest rates do. This will result in your payments being the same over the entire term. Whether a fixed-rate loan is better for you will depend on the interest rate environment when the loan is taken out and on the duration of the loan.

   When a loan is fixed for its entire term, it remains at the then-prevailing market interest rate, plus or minus a spread that is unique to the borrower. Generally speaking, if interest rates are relatively low, but are about to increase, then it will be better to lock in your loan at that fixed rate. Depending on the terms of your agreement, your interest rate on the new loan will stay the same, even if interest rates climb to higher levels. On the other hand, if interest rates are on the decline, then it would be better to have a variable rate loan. As interest rates fall, so will the interest rate on your loan.

Front-End and Back-End Interest Rates

Banks calculate the interest both Front-End and Back-End Interest Rates depends upon the products and terms of agreements. In case of front-end interest calculation, the interest is deducted from the principal amount before disbursement and only the net amount is disbursed. For example, bank discounts a bill of exchange, the interest applicable for the tenure of the bill is calculated and is deducted from the bill amount along with other charges and the net amount is paid to the customer.

However, the normal practice in banking industry is to charge back-end interest rate on most of the loan accounts which means that the full amount of the loan is disbursed and the interest is charged subsequently on monthly/quarterly/half yearly/agreed basis. For example, in a term loan, the interest is calculated on the actual daily balances in the account during a period and applied at the end of the period.

Obviously, the front-end interest application results in effective interest rate being more as the borrower gets less amount for use whereas, the interest is applied on the full amount.

CALCULATION OF INTEREST USING PRODUCTS/BALANCES

Front-end interest calculation in bill discounting is easy as the amount is assumed to be constant over the entire period. For example, if the tenure of the bill of ₹ 15 lakh is 4 months and the rate of discount is 12% p.a., the interest amount will be ₹ 60,000.

Banks calculate Interest of deposit and loan accounts on the basis of daily balance in the customer's account in most of the cases. Earlier this method was used in case of the loan accounts only. After RBI instruction regarding interest calculation in Savings Account, the interest is now required to be calculated on the basis of daily balances. In this method, the closing balance in the account is multiplied by the number of days for which that balance remains unchanged.

Example 11: Following table shows date-wise closing Debit Balance of an Over Draft Account of a customer. Calculate the interest charged in the account @ 10% per annum for the month of Jan 2019:

Date	Debit	Credit	Balance (Dr.)	No. of Days	Product
01/01/2019			50000	2	100000
03/01/2019		10000	40000	7	280000
10/01/2019	30000		70000	8	560000
18/01/2019	20000		90000	13	1170000
31/01/2019		15000	75000	1	75000

The total of the products is 2185000. The interest for the month of Jan 2019 will be:

$$= \frac{2185000 \times 10}{365 \times 100} = ₹\,598.63$$

AMORTISATION OF A DEBT

Amortisation means liquidation (repayment) of an interest-bearing loan through periodic payments. With payment of each instalment, the interest liability comes down. When the loan is amortised through equal payments, the debt becomes the discounted value of an annuity. The total time period during which this repayment is made is called term of the annuity. The regular time periods, during which the repayment is affected, are called payment periods.

We discuss different methods of repaying interest-bearing loans, which is one of the most important applications of annuities in business transactions. The first and most common method is the amortisation method. By using this method to liquidate an interest-bearing debt, a series of periodic payments, usually equal, are made. Each payment pays the interest on the unpaid balance and repays a part of the outstanding principal. As time goes on, the outstanding principal is gradually reduced and interest on the unpaid balance decreases. When a debt amortises, by equal payments at equal payment intervals, the debt becomes the discounted value of an annuity. The common commercial practice is to round the payment up to the next rupee.

When a debt amortises, by equal payments at equal payment intervals, the debt becomes the discounted value of an annuity. The common commercial practice is to round the payment up to the next rupee. Thus, an annuity is a sequence of payments made at regular periods over a given time interval (e.g. loan repayments). The total time, is called the term of the annuity. The regular periods, where there payments are made, are called the payment periods. Annuities, where the payments are made at the end of the payment period, are called ordinary annuities. When the payments are made at the beginning of the payment period, the process is called an annuity due.

REPAYMENT OF A DEBT

Loans in India have become explosively popular in the past few years with financiers creating more innovative loan products each year in an attempt to lure more and more customers. Applicants must learn about various methods available to them at the time of signing a loan agreement with a bank/FI. Today, multiple schemes exist for the repayment based on the kind and degree of convenience involved.

Discussed below are six types of loan repayment methods one may choose from:

1. **Regular EMI:** This is the most common type of repayment option people avail today when it comes to retail loans in India. In this option, a fixed rate of interest is decided, based on which EMIs (equated monthly instalments) are calculated for the entire repayment tenure. Interest rates are the lowest in the regular EMI option. Instalments can either be paid in the beginning of each month, called 'monthly in advance', or at the end of month, called 'monthly in arrears'.

2. **Step-up EMI:** In this arrangement, the amount of EMI increases during the term as the repayment progresses from being lowest in the first year and increasing steadily thereafter. The interest applicable in this option is higher than that in the case of regular EMIs. Customers choose this option to have a lesser burden initially and then slowly get used to higher EMIs as their income increases.

3. **Step-down EMI:** Contrary of the step-up EMI option, here the EMI reduces gradually from being highest at first. Though the interest rate with step down EMIs is higher than that in the regular EMI mode, total cost may be lesser as the principal amount is paid back sooner.

4. **Balloon EMI:** In this method, there is provision of paying a lump-sum amount up to 20 per cent of the principal at the end of the repayment tenure. Though the rate of interest chargeable in this method is higher than in case of regular EMIs, it reduces the initial burden on the borrower.

5. **Special Tie-up:** Often referred to as 'super saver tie up' method, this option ensures maximum benefit for the borrower as the financier here has a tie-up with the bank the borrower uses. The arrangement is such that whenever there is additional or excess money in the account, the same is used for an out-of-turn payment of the loan. This helps reduce the principal earlier resulting in substantial savings in the total money paid out in the long-run.

6. **Lease and Refinancing:** This is a rarely used option where the borrower pays the financier an EMI equivalent to lease charges of the vehicle and then at the end of the repayment tenure gets the option of paying current value of the car.

Each customer has a different set of financial considerations based on which he can find the most suitable option for his loan. However, having a thorough understanding of various options available in the market makes it easier to take a more beneficial decision.

SINKING FUNDS

When a specified amount of money is needed at a specified future date, it is a good practice to accumulate systematically a fund by means of equal periodic deposits. Such a fund is called a sinking fund. Sinking funds are used to pay-off debts, to redeem bond issues, to replace worn-out equipment, to buy new equipment, or in one of the depreciation methods. Since the amount needed in the sinking fund, the time the amount is needed and the interest rate that the fund earns are known, we have an annuity problem in which the size of the payment, the sinking-fund deposit, is to be determined. A schedule showing how a sinking fund accumulates to the desired amount is called a sinking-fund schedule.

TEST YOURSELF

1. Interest that is paid on the original principal amount and also on the accumulated part of interest, is called:
   (a) Simple interest
   (b) Compound interest
   (c) Annuities
   (d) Yield to maturity

2. Formula for calculation of compound interest if interest is paid Quarterly.
   (a) $P(1 + r)$
   (b) $P(1 + r/2)^2$
   (c) $P(1 + r/4)^4$
   (d) $P(1 + r/12)^{12}$

3. A bank offers 5% compound interest calculated on half-yearly basis. A customer deposits ₹ 1600 each on 1st January and 1st July of a year. At the end of the year, the amount he would have gained by way of interest is:
   (a) ₹ 120
   (b) ₹ 121
   (c) ₹ 162
   (d) ₹ 183

4. The difference between simple and compound interests compounded annually on a certain sum of money for 2 years at 4% per annum is ₹ 1. The sum (in ₹) is:
   (a) ₹ 625
   (b) ₹ 630
   (c) ₹ 650
   (d) ₹ 680

5. There is 60% increase in an amount in 6 years at simple interest. What will be the compound interest of ₹ 12,000 after 3 years at the same rate?
   (a) ₹ 2160
   (b) ₹ 3120
   (c) ₹ 3972
   (d) ₹ 6280

6. The least number of complete years in which a sum of money put out at 20% compound interest will be more than doubled is:
   (a) 4 years
   (b) 5 years
   (c) 6 years
   (d) 7 years

7. The compound interest on ₹ 30,000 at 7% per annum is ₹ 4347. The period (in years) is:
   (a) 1 year 9 months
   (b) 2 years
   (c) 2 years 3 months
   (d) 2 years 6 months

8. An _________ is a series of equal payments made at the end of consecutive periods over a fixed length of time.
   (a) Ordinary annuity
   (b) Annuity due
   (c) Future value
   (d) Annual annuity

9. Total time during which the debt is amortized, is called:
   (a) annuity duration
   (b) annuity period
   (c) term of annuity
   (d) annuity due

10. Which of the following cannot be an objective of creation of sinking fund?
    (a) to pay off debts
    (b) to replace worn out equipment
    (c) to buy new equipment
    (d) None of these

11. Manoj wants to raise a loan of ₹ 3 lakh for purchase of a car on which interest rate is 9%. He has decided to pay the amount in 5 equal yearly instalments. What will be the amount of instalment?
    (a) ₹ 76328
    (b) ₹ 77128
    (c) ₹ 75365
    (d) ₹ 77322

12. What will be the EMI of a loan of ₹ 100,000 which is given @ 9% p.a. for 12 months?
    (a) ₹ 8745
    (b) ₹ 8845
    (c) ₹ 8620
    (d) ₹ 9215

13. The future value of an annuity formula assumes that:
    (a) The rate does not change
    (b) The first payment is one period away
    (c) The periodic payment does not change
    (d) All of the above

14. _________ loans are loans in which the interest rate charged on the loan will remain fixed for that loan's entire term, no matter what market interest rates do.
    (a) A variable interest rate
    (b) A fixed interest rate
    (c) A floating interest rate
    (d) A basic interest rate

15. In this arrangement, the amount of EMI increases during the term as the repayment progresses from being lowest in the first year and increasing steadily thereafter.
(a) Regular EMI   (b) Step-up EMI
(c) Step-down EMI   (d) Balloon EMI

16. What is the difference between the compound interests on ₹ 5000 for 1.5 years at 4% per annum compounded yearly and half-yearly?
(a) ₹ 2.04   (b) ₹ 3.06
(c) ₹ 3.04   (d) ₹ 2.06

17. When difference between compound and simple interest for three years is ₹ 122 at 5% rate per annum, the principal is ______.
(a) ₹ 15800   (b) ₹ 16000
(c) ₹ 18000   (d) ₹ 17600

18. Ramesh needs ₹ 15 lakh for the education of his daughter at the end of 5th year. Considering that the interest rate is 10% at present, what amount he will have to deposit in the bank FDR with yearly compounding? (Hint- Discounting factor is 1.61051)
(a) ₹ 951382   (b) ₹ 912283
(c) ₹ 931382   (d) ₹ 981265

19. In this method, there is provision of paying a lump-sum amount up to 20 per cent of the principal at the end of the repayment tenure. Though the rate of interest chargeable in this method is higher than in case of regular EMIs, it reduces the initial burden on the borrower.
(a) Regular EMI   (b) Step-up EMI
(c) Step-down EMI   (d) Balloon EMI

20. Pragya is investing ₹ 1 lakh every year for the coming 4 years at 8%. What is the present value of the amount, she is to receive at the end of 4 years. (Hint- Discounting factor is 3.31312)
(a) ₹ 31312   (b) ₹ 335138
(c) ₹ 331312   (d) ₹ 340250

ANSWER

1	2	3	4	5	6	7	8	9	10
(b)	(c)	(b)	(a)	(c)	(a)	(b)	(a)	(c)	(d)

11	12	13	14	15	16	17	18	19	20
(b)	(a)	(d)	(b)	(a)	(a)	(b)	(c)	(d)	(c)

CALCULATION OF YTM

DEFINITION OF DEBT

Debt is an amount of money borrowed by one party from another. A debt arrangement gives the borrowing party permission to borrow money under the condition that it is to be paid back at a later date, usually with interest.

In other words, debt is a duty or obligation to pay money, deliver goods, or render service under an express or implied agreement. Commercial debt is generally subject to contractual terms regarding the amount and timing of repayments of principal and interest. Loans, bonds, notes, and mortgages are all types of debt. One who owes, is a debtor or borrower, one to whom it is owed, is a creditor or lender.

MEANING OF LOANS

The most common forms of debt are loans, including home loan, mortgage loan, auto loans, and credit card debt. Under the terms of a loan, the borrower is required to repay the balance of the loan by a certain date, typically several years in the future. The terms of the loan also stipulate the amount of interest that the borrower is required to pay annually, expressed as a percentage of the loan amount. Interest is used as a way to ensure that the lender is compensated for taking on the risk of the loan while also encouraging the borrower to repay the loan quickly in order to limit his total interest expense.

Credit card debt operates in the same way as a loan, except that the borrowed amount changes over time according to the borrower's need, up to a predetermined limit, and has a rolling, or open-ended, repayment date.

INTRODUCTION TO BONDS

A bond is a debt instrument in which an investor loans money to an entity (typically corporate or government) which borrows the funds for a defined period of time at a variable or fixed interest rate. Bonds are used by companies, municipalities, states and sovereign governments to raise money to finance a variety of projects and activities. Owners of bonds are debt holders, or creditors, of the issuer.

Most simply, bonds represent debt obligations and therefore are a form of borrowing. If a company issues a bond, the money they receive in return is a loan, and must be repaid over time. The buyers of bonds, then are essentially lenders. For example, if you have ever bought a government savings bond, you became a lender to the government. Governments and corporations commonly use bonds in order to borrow money. Governments need to fund roads, schools, dams or other infrastructure. Similarly, corporations will often borrow to grow their business, to buy property and equipment, to undertake profitable projects, for research and development or to hire employees. The problem that large organizations run into is that they typically need far more money than the average bank can provide. Bonds provide a solution by allowing many individual investors to assume the role of lender. Indeed, public debt markets let thousands of investors each lend a portion of the capital needed. Moreover, markets allow lenders to sell their bonds to other investors or to buy bonds from other individuals long after the original issuing organization raised capital.

Of course, people wouldn't lend their hard-earned money for no compensation. There is an opportunity cost involved with any investment, which is the lost opportunity of using those same funds for another purpose. The issuer of a bond must pay the investor something extra for the privilege of using his or her money. This "extra" comes in the form of the interest payments, which are made at a predetermined rate and schedule. The date on which the issuer must repay the amount borrowed (an amount known as the face value) is called the maturity date. The interest rate associated with a bond is often referred to as the bond's yield or coupon. In the past, when bonds were issued as paper documents, there would be actual coupons that investors would clip and redeem for their interest payments.

Bonds are often referred to as fixed-income securities because the lender can anticipate the exact amount of cash they will have received if a bond is held until maturity. For example, say you buy a corporate bond with a face value of ₹ 1,000, a coupon of 5% paid annually, and a maturity of 10 years. This tells you that you will receive a total of ₹ 50 (₹ 1,000 × 0.05) of interest per year for the next 10 years. The most corporate bonds pay interest semi-annually by convention. You'd then receive two payments of ₹ 25 a year for 10 years. When the bond matures in a decade, you'd then get your ₹ 1,000 back.

If the coupon payment date falls on a Sunday or any other holiday, the coupon payment is made on the next working day. However, if the maturity date falls on a Sunday or a holiday, the redemption proceeds are paid on the previous working day.

TERMS ASSOCIATED WITH BONDS

Following terms are associated with a bond :

a) **Face Value:** The face value (also known as the par value) of a bond is the price at which the bond is sold to investors when first issued, it is also the price at which the bond is redeemed at maturity.

b) **Coupon Rate:** The periodic interest payments promised to bondholders are computed as a fixed percentage of the bond's face value, this percentage is known as the coupon rate.

c) **Coupon:** A bond's coupon is the rupee value of the periodic interest payment promised to bondholders, this equals the coupon rate times the face value of the bond. For example, if a bond issuer promises to pay an annual coupon rate of 5% to bond holders and the face value of the bond is ₹ 1,000, the bond-holders are being promised a coupon payment of (0.05) × (₹ 1,000) = ₹ 50 per year.

d) **Maturity:** A bond's maturity is issued for a specific period. It is to be repaid on maturity.

e) **Redemption value:** The value, which the bond-holder gets on maturity, is called the redemption value. A bond is generally issued at a discount (less than par value) and redeemed at par.

f) **Market Value:** A bond may be traded on a stock exchange. Market value is the price at which the bond is usually bought and sold in the market. Market value may be different from the par value or the redemption value.

g) **Day-Count Convention: The** day-count convention is the system used to calculate the amount of accrued interest or the present value when the next coupon payment is less than a full coupon period away. Each bond market and financial instrument has its own day-count convention, which varies depending on the type of instrument, whether the interest rate is fixed or floating, and the country of issuance. Among the most common conventions are 30/360 or 365, actual/360 or 365, and actual/actual.

PROVISION AVAILABLE IN BONDS

A provision is a stipulation in a contract or a legal document. Often times, a stipulation requires action by a specific date or within a specified period. Provisions protect the interests of one or both parties in a contract. Following types of provision may be stipulated in bonds.

a) **Call Provisions:** Many bonds contain a provision that enables the issuer to buy the bond back from the bondholder at a pre-specified price prior to maturity. This price is known as the call price. A bond containing a call provision is said to be callable. This provision enables issuers to reduce their interest costs if rates fall after a bond is issued, since existing bonds can then be replaced with lower yielding bonds. Since a call provision is disadvantageous to the bondholder, the bond will offer a higher yield than an otherwise identical bond with no call provision.

b) **Put Provisions:** Some bonds contain a provision that enables the buyer to sell the bond back to the issuer at a pre-specified price prior to maturity. This price is known as the put price. A bond containing such a provision is said to be putable. This provision enables bondholders to benefit from rising interest rates since the bond can be sold and the proceeds reinvested at a higher yield than the original bond. Since a put provision is advantageous to the bondholder, the bond will offer a lower yield than an otherwise identical bond with no put provision.

Types of Bonds

Bonds can be classified as the following types:

(i) Fixed Rate Bonds: These are bonds on which the coupon rate is fixed for the entire life (i.e. till maturity) of the bond. Most Government bonds in India are issued as fixed rate bonds.

For example–8.24% GS 2018 was issued on April 22, 2008 for a tenor of 10 years maturing on April 22, 2018. Coupon on this security will be paid half-yearly at 4.12% (half yearly payment being half of the annual coupon of 8.24%) of the face value on October 22 and April 22 of each year.

(ii) Floating Rate Bonds (FRB): FRBs are securities which do not have a fixed coupon rate. Instead it has a variable coupon rate which is re-set at pre-announced intervals (say every six months or one year). FRBs were first issued in September 1995 in India. For example, an FRB was issued on November 07, 2016 for a tenor of 8 years, thus maturing on November 07, 2024. The variable coupon rate for payment of interest on this FRB 2024 was decided to be the average rate rounded off up to two decimal places, of the implicit yields at the cut-off prices of the last three auctions of 182 day T- Bills, held before the date of notification. The coupon rate for payment of interest on subsequent semi-annual periods was announced to be the average rate of the implicit yields at the cut-off prices of the last three auctions of 182 day T-Bills held up to the commencement of the respective semi-annual coupon periods.

(iii) The Floating Rate Bond with fixed coupon and Zero-Coupon Bonds: The Floating Rate Bond can also carry the coupon, which will have a base rate plus a fixed spread, to be decided by way of auction mechanism. The spread will be fixed throughout the tenure of the bond. For example, FRB 2031 (auctioned on May 4, 2018) carry the coupon with base rate equivalent to Weighted Average Yield (WAY) of last 3 auctions (from the rate fixing day) of 182 Day T-Bills plus a fixed spread decided by way of auction.

Zero coupon bonds are bonds with no coupon payments. However, like T- Bills, they are issued at a discount and redeemed at face value. The Government of India had issued such securities in 1996. It has not issued zero coupon bonds after that.

(iv) Capital Indexed Bonds: These are bonds, the principal of which is linked to an accepted index of inflation with a view to protecting the principal amount of the investors from inflation. A 5-year Capital Indexed Bond, was first issued in December 1997 which matured in 2002.

(v) Inflation Indexed Bonds (IIBs): IIBs are bonds wherein both coupon flows and Principal amounts are protected against inflation. The inflation index used in IIBs may be Whole Sale Price Index (WPI) or Consumer Price Index (CPI). Globally, IIBs were first issued in 1981 in UK. In India, Government of India through RBI issued IIBs (linked to WPI) in June 2013. Since then, they were issued on monthly basis (on last Tuesday of each month) till December 2013. Based on the success of these IIBs, Government of India in consultation with RBI issued the IIBs (CPI based) exclusively for the retail customers in December 2013.

(vi) Bonds with Call/ Put Options: Bonds can also be issued with features of optionality wherein the issuer can have the option to buy-back (call option) or the investor can have the option to sell the bond (put option) to the issuer during the currency of the bond. It may be noted that such bond may have put only or call only or both options. The first G-Sec with both call and put option viz. 6.72% GS 2012 was issued on July 18, 2002 for a maturity of 10 years maturing on July 18, 2012. The optionality on the bond could be exercised after completion of five years tenure from the date of issuance on any coupon date falling thereafter. The Government has the right to buy-back the bond (call option) at par value (equal to the face value) while the investor has the right to sell the bond (put option) to the Government at par value on any of the half-yearly coupon dates starting from July 18, 2007.

(vii) Special Securities: Under the market borrowing program, the Government of India also issues, from time to time, special securities to entities like Oil Marketing Companies, Fertilizer Companies, the Food Corporation of India, etc. (popularly called oil bonds, fertiliser bonds and food bonds respectively) as compensation to these companies in lieu of cash subsidies. These securities are usually long dated securities and carry a marginally higher coupon over the yield of the dated securities of comparable maturity. These securities are, however, not eligible as SLR securities but are eligible as collateral for market repo transactions. The beneficiary entities may divest these securities in the secondary market to banks, insurance companies / Primary Dealers, etc., for raising funds.

Government of India has also issued Bank Recapitalisation Bonds to specific Public Sector Banks in 2018. These securities are named as Special GoI security and are non-transferable and are not eligible investment in pursuance of any statutory provisions or directions applicable to investing banks. These securities can be held under HTM portfolio without any limit.

(viii) STRIPS (Separate Trading of Registered Interest and Principal of Securities): STRIPS are the securities created by way of separating the cash flows associated with a regular G-Sec i.e. each semi-annual coupon payment and the final principal payment to be received from the issuer, into separate securities. They are essentially Zero Coupon Bonds (ZCBs). Stripped securities represent future cash flows (periodic interest and principal repayment) of an underlying coupon bearing bond. Being G-Secs, STRIPS are eligible for SLR.

(ix) Sovereign Gold Bond (SGB): SGBs are unique instruments, prices of which are linked to commodity price viz Gold. SGBs are also budgeted in lieu of market borrowing. The Bonds shall be denominated in units of one gram of gold and multiples thereof. Minimum investment in the Bonds shall be one gram with a maximum limit of subscription of 4 kg for individuals, 4 kg for Hindu Undivided Family (HUF) and 20 kg for trusts and similar entities notified by the Government from time to time per fiscal year (April – March), provided that;

    (a) Annual ceiling will include bonds subscribed under different tranches during initial issuance by Government and those purchased from the secondary market; and

    (b) The ceiling on investment will not include the holdings as collateral by banks and other Financial Institutions.

The tenor of the SGB is for a period of 8 years with exit option from 5th year to be exercised on the interest payment dates. The bonds under SGB Scheme may be held by a person resident in India, being an individual, in his capacity as an individual, or on behalf of minor child, or jointly with any other individual. The bonds may also be held by a Trust, Charitable Institution and University. Price of the bonds shall be fixed in Indian Rupees on the basis of simple average of closing price of gold of 999 purity published by the India Bullion and Jewelers Association Limited for the last three business days of the week preceding the subscription period. The issue price of the Gold Bonds will be ₹ 50 per gram less than the nominal value to those investors applying online and the payment against the application is made through digital mode. The Bonds shall bear interest at the rate of 2.50 per cent (fixed rate) per annum on the amount of initial investment. Interest shall be paid in half-yearly rests and the last interest shall be payable on maturity along with the principal. The redemption price shall be fixed in Indian Rupees and the redemption price shall be based on simple average of closing price of gold of 999 purity of previous 3 business days from the date of repayment, published by the India Bullion and Jewellers Association Limited. SGBs acquired by the banks through the process of invoking lien/hypothecation/pledge alone shall be counted towards Statutory Liquidity Ratio. The above subscription limits, interest rate discount etc. are as per the current scheme and are liable to change going forward.

(x) 7.75% Savings (Taxable) Bonds, 2018: Government of India has decided to issue 7.75% Savings (Taxable) Bonds, 2018 with effect from January 10, 2018 in terms of GoI notification F.No.4(28)-W&M/2017 dated January 03, 2018 and RBI issued notification vide IDMD.CDD. No.1671/13.01.299/2017-18 dated January 3, 2018. These bonds may be held by:

    (i) An individual, not being a Non-Resident Indian-in his or her individual capacity, or in individual capacity on joint basis, or in individual capacity on any one or survivor basis, or on behalf of a minor as father/mother/legal guardian and;

    (ii) A Hindu Undivided Family.

There is no maximum limit for investment in these bonds. Interest on these Bonds will be taxable under the Income Tax Act, 1961 as applicable according to the relevant tax status of the Bond holders. These Bonds will be exempt from wealth-tax under the Wealth Tax Act, 1957. These Bonds will be issued at par for a minimum amount of ₹ 1,000 (face value) and in multiples thereof.

VALUATION OF BONDS

The purchaser of the bonds gets regular interest payments as also the redemption amount on maturity. The interest on bond (also called coupon rate) is fixed at the time of its issue. But interest rate in the market keeps changing and, therefore, market price of bond also changes. The market price or intrinsic value of a bond is different from the face value if the coupon rate is different from the market interest rate at that particular time.

Valuation of the above bond involves the following steps:

i) Find the residual maturity of the bond to be valued.

ii) Find the Central G-Sec yield for the above residual maturity.

iii) Add appropriate spread to the above yield to get the yield for the security.

iv) Calculate the price of the security using the derived yield above.

Market value is equal to PV of all the coupon receipts and redemption value discounted at the prevailing market rate. Therefore, the intrinsic value or the present value of a bond is:

$$V_o = \sum_{t=1}^{n} \frac{I}{(1 + kd)^t} + \frac{F}{(1 + kd)^n}$$

Where,

V_0 = Intrinsic value of the bond

I = Annual Interest payable on the bond

F = Redeemable value of the bond

n = Maturity period of the bond

kd = Cost of Capital

It is noted that during solving problems related to bond valuation, usually Present Value Interest Factor (PVIF) and Present Value Interest Factor of Annuity (PVIFA) pertaining to the applicable interest rate are provided. PVIF represents the discount value of one rupee for the period concerned and interest rate while PVIFA represents the present value of an ordinary annuity for the period concerned and interest rate. For example, PVIF (12 per cent, 5) means present value of one rupee to be received after 5 periods at the interest rate of 12% per period. PVIFA (12 per cent, 5) means present value of an ordinary annuity one rupee per period for 5 periods at the interest rate of 12% per period.

VALUATION OF A COUPON BOND WITH ANNUAL COUPON

Example 1: A bond, whose par value is ₹ 1,000, bears a coupon rate of 12 per cent and has a maturity period of 3 years. The required rate of return on the bond is 10 per cent. What is the value of this bond?

Solution:

Annual interest payable = 1,000 x 12% = 120

Principal repayment at the end of 3 years = ₹ 1,000

The value of the bond

= 120 × (PVIFA 10%, 3 years)

    + ₹ 1,000 × (PVIF 10%, 3 years)

= 120 × (2.487) + 1,000 × (0.751)

= 298.44 + 751

= ₹ 1,049.44

VALUATION WITH SEMI-ANNUAL COUPON

Considering the same case as above, If the bond carries a semi-annual interest, as the amount of the half-yearly interest can be reinvested, the value of such bonds would be more than the value of bonds with an annual interest payment. Hence, by multiplying the numbers of years to maturity by two and dividing the (i) annual interest payment, (ii) discount rate by two we can modify bond valuation formula as follows:

$$V_o = \sum_{t=1}^{2n} \frac{{}_{2n}I/2}{(1 + kd/2)^t} + \frac{F}{(1 + kd/2)^{2n}}$$

Example 2: A bond, whose par value is ₹ 1000, bears a coupon rate of 12 per cent payable semi-annually and has a maturity period of 3 years. The required rate of return on bond is 10 per cent. What is the value of this bond?

Solution:

Semi-annual interest payable

         = 1,000 x 12 per cent/2 = 60

Principal repayment at the end of 3 years = ₹ 1,000

The value of the bond

= 60 (PVIFA 10%/2, 6 pds)

    + Rs. 1,000 (PVIF 10%/2, 6 pds)

= 60 (5.0746) + 1,000 (0.746)

= 304.48 + 746

= 1,050.48

What is the relationship between yield and price of a bond? If market interest rate levels rise, the price of a bond falls. Conversely, if interest rates or market yields decline, the price of the bond rises. In other words, the yield of a bond is inversely related to its price. The relationship between yield to maturity and coupon rate of bond may be stated as follows:

   ⭘ When the market price of the bond is less than the face value, i.e., the bond sells at a discount, YTM >> coupon yield.

❍ When the market price of the bond is more than its face value, i.e., the bond sells at a premium, coupon yield >> YTM.

❍ When the market price of the bond is equal to its face value, i.e., the bond sells at par, YTM = = coupon yield.

CALCULATION OF THE YIELD OF A BOND

An investor who purchases a bond can expect to receive a return from one or more of the following sources:

❍ The coupon interest payments made by the issuer;

❍ Any capital gain (or capital loss) when the bond is sold/matured; and

❍ Income from reinvestment of the interest payments that is interest-on-interest.

The three yield measures commonly used by investors to measure the potential return from investing in a bond are briefly described below:

i) Coupon Yield: The coupon yield is simply the coupon payment as a percentage of the face value. Coupon yield refers to nominal interest payable on a fixed income security like G-Sec. This is the fixed return the Government (i.e., the issuer) commits to pay to the investor. Coupon yield thus does not reflect the impact of interest rate movement and inflation on the nominal interest that the Government pays.

Coupon yield = Coupon Payment / Face Value

Illustration:

Coupon: 8.24

Face Value: ₹ 100

Market Value: ₹ 103.00

Coupon yield = 8.24/100 = 8.24%

ii) Current Yield: The current yield is simply the coupon payment as a percentage of the bond's purchase price; in other words, it is the return a holder of the bond gets against its purchase price which may be more or less than the face value or the par value. The current yield does not take into account the reinvestment of the interest income received periodically.

Current yield

= (Annual coupon rate / Purchase price) × 100

Example 3: The current yield for a 10 year 8.24% coupon bond selling for ₹ 103.00 per ₹100 par value is calculated below:

Annual coupon interest = 8.24% x ₹ 100 = ₹ 8.24

Current yield = (8.24/103) × 100 = 8.00%

The current yield considers only the coupon interest and ignores other sources of return that will affect an investor's return.

iii) Yield to Maturity: Yield to Maturity (YTM) is the expected rate of return on a bond if it is held until its maturity. The price of a bond is simply the sum of the present values of all its remaining cash flows. Present value is calculated by discounting each cash flow at a rate, this rate is the YTM. Thus YTM is the discount rate which equates the present value of the future cash flows from a bond to its current market price. In other words, it is the internal rate of return on the bond. The calculation of YTM involves a trial-and-error procedure. A calculator or software can be used to obtain a bond's YTM easily.

HOW TO CALCULATE YIELD TO MATURITY OF A BOND?

The expected rate of return for which bond is held by bondholder till its maturity is called Yield To Maturity (YTM) of bond. In other words it is also the overall return on bond. Yield to Maturity (YTM) for a bond is the total return, interest plus capital gain, obtained from a bond held to maturity. It is expressed as a percentage and tells investors what their return on investment will be if they purchase the bond and hold on to it until the bond issuer pays them back. It is difficult to calculate a precise YTM, but you can approximate its value by using a bond yield table or one of the many online calculators for YTM.

$$\text{Approx YTM} = \frac{C + \dfrac{F - P}{n}}{\dfrac{F + P}{2}}$$

C = Coupon/Interest Payment
F = Face Value
P = Price
n = years to maturity

The yield to maturity formula is used to calculate the yield on a bond based on its current price on the market. The yield to maturity formula looks at the effective yield of a bond based on compounding as opposed to the simple yield which is found using the dividend yield formula.

Notice that the formula shown is used to calculate the approximate yield to maturity. To calculate the actual yield to maturity requires trial and error by putting rates into the present value of a bond formula until *P*, or Price, matches the actual price of the bond. Some financial calculators and computer programs can be used to calculate the yield to maturity.

Yield to Maturity and Present Value of a Bond

The yield to maturity is found in the present value of a bond formula:

$$\frac{C}{1+r} + \frac{C}{(1+r)^2} \cdots \frac{C}{(1+r)^t} + \frac{F}{(1+r)^t}$$

For calculating yield to maturity, the price of the bond, or present value of the bond, is already known. Calculating YTM is working backwards from the present value of a bond formula and trying to determine what r is.

Example of Yield to Maturity Formula

The price of a bond is ₹ 920 with a face value of ₹ 1000 which is the face value of many bonds. Assume that the annual coupons are ₹ 100, which is a 10% coupon rate, and that there are 10 years remaining until maturity. This example using the approximate formula would be:

$$\text{Approx YTM} = \frac{100 + \dfrac{1000 + 920}{10}}{\dfrac{1000 + 920}{2}}$$

After solving this equation, the estimated yield to maturity is 11.25%.

Example 4: YTM with PV of a Bond : Using the prior example, the estimated yield to maturity is 11.25%. However, after using this rate as r in the present value of a bond formula, the present value would be ₹ 927.15 which is fairly close to the price, or present value, of ₹ 920. Other examples may have a larger difference.

A higher yield to maturity will have a lower present value or purchase price of a bond. In this example, the estimated yield to maturity shows a present value of ₹ 927.15 which is higher than the actual ₹ 920 purchase price. Therefore, the yield to maturity will be a little higher than 11.25%.

Through trial and error, the yield to maturity would be 11.38%, which is found by adjusting each estimated rate until the present value equals the price of the bond.

Excel is helpful for the trial and error method by setting the spreadsheet so that all that is required to determine the present value is adjusting a fixed cell that contains the rate.

What are the Day Count Conventions used in Calculating Bond Yields?

Day count convention refers to the method used for arriving at the holding period (number of days) of a bond to calculate the accrued interest. As the use of different day count conventions can result in different accrued interest amounts, it is appropriate that all the participants in the market follow a uniform day count convention.

For example, the conventions followed in Indian market are given below:

Bond Market: The day count convention followed is 30/360, which means that irrespective of the actual number of days in a month, the number of days in a month is taken as 30 and the number of days in a year is taken as 360.

Money Market: The day count convention followed is actual/365, which means that the actual number of days in a month is taken for number of days (numerator) whereas the number of days in a year is taken as 365 days. Hence, in the case of T-Bills, which are essentially money market instruments, money market convention is followed.

In some countries, participants use actual/actual, some countries use actual/360 while some use 30/actual. Hence the convention changes in different countries and in different markets within the same country (e.g. Money market convention is different than the bond market convention in India).

DURATION OF BOND

Duration (also known as Macaulay Duration) of a bond is a measure of the time taken to recover the initial investment in present value terms. In simplest form, duration refers to the payback period of a bond to break even, i.e., the time taken for a bond to repay its own purchase price. Duration is expressed in number of years. A step by step approach for working out duration is given below.

Calculation for Duration

First, each of the future cash flows is discounted to its respective present value for each period. Since the coupons are paid out every six months, a single period is equal to six months and a bond with two years maturity will have four time periods.

Second, the present values of future cash flows are multiplied with their respective time periods (these are the weights). That is the PV of the first coupon is multiplied by 1, PV of second coupon by 2 and so on.

Third, the above weighted PVs of all cash flows is added and the sum is divided by the current price (total of the PVs in step 1) of the bond. The resultant value is the duration in no. of periods. Since one period equals to six months, to get the duration in no. of year, divide it by two. This is the time period within which the bond is expected to pay back its own value if held till maturity.

Example 5: Taking a bond having 2 years maturity, and 10% coupon, and current price of ₹ 102, the cash flows will be (prevailing 2 year yield being 9%):

Time Period (years)	1	2	3	4	Total
Inflows (...)	5	5	5	105	
PV at an yield of 9%	4.78	4.58	4.38	88.05	101.79
PV × time	4.78	9.16	13.14	352.20	379.28

Duration in number of periods = 379.28/101.79 = 3.73

Duration in years = 3.73/2 = 1.86 years

More formally, duration refers to:

a) The weighted average term (time from now to payment) of a bond's cash flows or of any series of linked cash flows.

b) The higher the coupon rate of a bond, the shorter the duration (if the term of the bond is kept constant).

c) Duration is always less than or equal to the overall life (to maturity) of the bond.

d) Only a zero coupon bond (a bond with no coupons) will have duration equal to its maturity.

e) The sensitivity of a bond's price to interest rate (i.e., yield) movements.

Duration is useful primarily as a measure of the sensitivity of a bond's market price to interest rate (i.e., yield) movements. It is approximately equal to the percentage change in price for a given change in yield. For example, for small interest rate changes, the duration is the approximate percentage by which the value of the bond will fall for a 1% per annum increase in market interest rate. So a 15-year bond with a duration of 7 years would fall approximately 7% in value if the interest rate increased by 1% per annum. In other words, duration is the elasticity of the bond's price with respect to interest rates.

BOND PRICE VOLATILITY

The sensitivity of the bond price to changes in the interest rates is called 'Bond Volatility'. Bond prices and YTM are inversely related. The fundamental change in price is that which causes yields to increase as price decreases and vice versa. This relationship is not linear, however, it is convex. There are four properties concerning the price volatility of an option free bond:

1. Price moves in the opposite direction of a change in yields, but the percentage change is not the same for all bonds.
2. For small changes in yields, the percentage change is roughly the same no matter what direction rates move.
3. For large changes in yields, the percentage price change is not the same for an increase in yield as it is for a decrease in yield
4. For a given large change in yield, the percentage price increase is greater than the percentage price decrease.

This relationship can be depicted in the following manner:

Bonds selling at:	Relationship
Par	Coupon rate = YTM
Discount	Coupon rate < YTM
Premium	Coupon rate > YTM

TEST YOURSELF

1. A bond is a __________ that provides a periodic stream of interest payments to investors while repaying the principal sum on a specified maturity date.
   (a) Share certificate
   (b) Debt instrument
   (c) Credit facility
   (d) Debenture instrument

2. Bonds that do not pay any interest rate are considered as:
   (a) Interest free bond
   (b) Zero coupon bond
   (c) Price less coupon bond
   (d) Useless price bonds

3. A bond carries a specific rate of interest which is known as:
   (a) Discount
   (b) Commission
   (c) Coupon interest
   (d) Dividend

4. Difference between face value of bond and call price of bond is considered as:
   (a) Call premium
   (b) Call provision
   (c) Discount premium
   (d) Discount provision

5. The principal of which is linked to an accepted index of inflation with a view to protecting the principal amount of the investors from inflation. These bonds are called:
(a) Inflation Index Bonds
(b) Fixed Rate Bonds
(c) Capital Indexed Bonds
(d) Zero Coupon Bonds

6. If a 7% coupon bond is trading for ₹ 975, it has a current yield of ____ per cent.
(a) 6.63
(b) 6.85
(c) 7.03
(d) 7.18

7. If an 8% coupon bond is trading for ₹ 1025, it has a current yield of ____ per cent.
(a) 6.83
(b) 6.1
(c) 7.1
(d) 7.38

8. A coupon bond pays annual interest, has a par value of ₹ 1,000 mature in 12 years, has a coupon rate of 11%, and has a yield to maturity of 12%. The current yield of this bond is ____ per cent.
(a) 10.38
(b) 10.45
(c) 10.53
(d) 10.66

9. The value which bondholder gets on maturity is called as:
(a) Market Value
(b) Face Value
(c) Intrinsic Value
(d) Redemption Value

10. Private Sector Companies can issue ______ bonds.
(a) Secured
(b) Unsecured
(c) Any one of the above
(d) None of these

11. Rate of return earned by an investor who purchases a bond and holds it till maturity is called as:
(a) Intrinsic Value
(b) Coupon Rate
(c) YTM
(d) Redemption Value

12. The relationship between the bond prices and interest rates is one of the following:
(a) direct & linear
(b) inverse & linear
(c) direct and curvilinear
(d) no relationship

13. The yield to maturity is a rate of return which:
(a) gives the current yield
(b) is the discount rate at which the present value, of the coupons and the final payment at face value, equals the current price
(c) gives the return at maturity on the bond for the original holder
(d) (b) or (c)

14. A bond holder of a company has one of the following relationships with It. Identify:
(a) shareholder
(b) depositor
(c) creditor
(d) employee

15. A coupon bond that pays interest annually is selling at par value of ₹ 1000, maturity in five years and has a coupon rate of 9%. The yield to maturity on this bond is:
(a) 9.0%
(b) 8.1%
(c) 7.2%
(d) 9.6%

16. The face value of a bond is ₹ 10000, its coupon rate 10% and time to maturity is 4 years. If the YTM is 10% it falls by 1% what will be the percentage change in price of the bond?
(a) 2.3%
(b) 4.1%
(c) 3.2%
(d) 2.6%

17. The par value of a bond if ₹ 25000, its coupon rate 8% and maturity period 10 years. The required rate of return on the bond is 10%. What is the value of bond?
(a) ₹ 21929
(b) ₹ 22619
(c) ₹ 21635
(d) ₹ 22929

18. The par value of a bond if ₹ 25000, its coupon rate 8% and maturity period 10 years and interest is payable semi-annually The required rate of return on the bond is 10%. What is the value of bond?
(a) ₹ 22929
(b) ₹ 23012
(c) ₹ 23635
(d) ₹ 22929

19. The face value of a bond is ₹ 10000, its coupon rate 10% and time to maturity is 4 years. Calculate the duration of the bond?
(a) 3.32
(b) 3.29
(c) 3.49
(d) 3.21

20. The face value of a bond is ₹ 10000, its coupon rate 10% and time to maturity is 4 years. If the YTM is 10%, calculate the duration of the bond?
(a) 3.32
(b) 3.29
(c) 3.49
(d) 3.20

ANSWER

1	2	3	4	5	6	7	8	9	10
(b)	(b)	(c)	(a)	(c)	(d)	(c)	(d)	(d)	(c)

11	12	13	14	15	16	17	18	19	20
(c)	(b)	(d)	(c)	(a)	(c)	(a)	(b)	(c)	(d)

CAPITAL BUDGETING

INTRODUCTION

Capital is the total investment of the company and budgeting is the art of building budgets. Capital Budgeting is a project selection exercise performed by the business enterprise. Capital budgeting uses the concept of present value to select the projects. Money has a time value. In deciding whether to go ahead with the investment, the investor will be concerned with how much income generation will be there in the future. A rational investor will be unwilling to undertake the investment, if he knows that he will receive less than what he can earn as interest.

CAPITAL BUDGETING

Capital budgeting is the process in which a business determines and evaluates potential large expenses or investments. Capital budgeting is a company's formal process used for evaluating potential expenditures or investments that are significant in amount. Capital Budgeting is a tool for maximizing a company's future profits since most companies are able to manage only a limited number of large projects at any one time.

Capital budgeting usually involves calculation of each project's future accounting profit by period, the cash flow by period, the present value of cash flows after considering time value of money, the number of years it takes for a project's cash flow to pay back the initial cash investment, an assessment of risk, and various other factors.

The amount of capital available for new projects is limited, management needs to use capital budgeting techniques to determine which projects will yield the most return over an applicable period. Various methods of capital budgeting can include throughout analysis, Net Present Value, Internal Rate of Return, Discounted Cash Flow and Payback Period.

IMPORTANCE OF CAPITAL BUDGETING

Capital budgeting is a step by step process that businesses use to determine the merits of an investment project. The decision of whether to accept or deny an investment project as part of a company's growth initiatives, involves determining the investment rate of return that such a project will generate.

Capital budgeting is important because it creates accountability and measurability. Any business that seeks to invest its resources in a project, without understanding the risks and returns involved, would be held as irresponsible by its owners or shareholders. Furthermore, if a business has no way of measuring the effectiveness of its investment decisions, chances are that the business will have little chance of surviving in the competitive marketplace. Businesses exist to earn profits. The capital budgeting process is a measurable way for businesses to determine the long-term economic and financial profitability of any investment project.

Capital budgeting is also vital to a business because it creates a structured step by step process that enables a company to:

1) **Develop and Formulate Long-term Strategic Goals:** The ability to set long-term goals is essential to the growth and prosperity of any business. The ability to appraise/value investment projects via capital budgeting creates a framework for businesses to plan out future long-term direction.

2) **Seek out New Investment Projects:** Knowing how to evaluate investment projects gives a business the model to seek and evaluate new projects, an important function for all businesses as they seek to compete and profit in their industry.

3) **Estimate and Forecast Future Cash Flows:** Future cash flows are what create value for businesses overtime. Capital budgeting enables executives to take a potential project and estimate its future cash flows, which then helps determine if such a project should be accepted.

4) **Facilitate the Transfer of Information:** From the time that a project starts off as an idea to the time it is accepted or rejected, numerous decisions have to be made at various levels of authority. The capital budgeting process facilitates the transfer of information to the appropriate decision makers within a company.

5) **Monitoring and Control of Expenditures:** By definition a budget carefully identifies the necessary expenditures and R&D required for an investment project. Since a good project can turn bad if expenditures aren't carefully controlled or monitored, this step is a crucial benefit of the capital budgeting process.

6) **Creation of Decision:** When a capital budgeting process is in place, a company is then able to create a set of decision rules that can categorize which projects are acceptable and which projects are unacceptable. The result is a more efficiently run business that is better equipped to quickly ascertain whether or not to proceed further with a project or shut it down early in the process, thereby saving a company both time and money.

PRESENT VALUE (PV) AND DISCOUNTING

In finance, present value (PV), also known as present discounted value, is the value of an expected income stream determined as of the date of valuation. The present value is always less than or equal to the future value because money has interest-earning potential, a characteristic referred to as the time value of money.

Future cash flows are discounted at the discount rate. The higher the discount rate, the lower the present value of the future cash flows. Determining the appropriate discount rate is the key to properly valuing future cash flows, whether they are earnings or obligations. If you received ₹ 10,000 today, the present value would be ₹ 10,000 because present value is what your investment gives you if you were to spend it today. If you received ₹ 10,000 in a year, the present value of the amount would not be ₹ 10,000 because you do not have it in your hand now, in the present. To find the present value of the ₹ 10,000 you will receive in the future, you need to pretend that the ₹ 10,000 is the total future value of an amount that you invested today. In other words, to find the present value of the future ₹ 10,000, we need to find out how much we would have to invest today in order to receive that ₹ 10,000 in the future.

The Present Value formula has a broad range of uses and may be applied to various areas of finance including corporate finance, banking finance, and investment finance. Apart from the various areas of finance that present value analysis is used, the formula is also used as a component of other financial formulas.

$$PV = FV \times \{1/(1 + r)^n\} \quad \text{or} \quad PV = FV (1 + r)^{-n}$$
$$FV = PV (1 + r)^n$$

Example 1: Present Value Formula: An individual wish to determine how much money she would need to put into her money market account to have ₹ 1000 for two years from today if she is earning 5% simple interest on her account.

The ₹ 1000 she would like two years from present day denotes the FV portion of the formula, 5% would be r, and the number of periods would simply be 2.

Putting this into the formula, we would have

$$PV = 1000 (1 + .05)^{-2}$$
$$PV = 907.03$$

When we solve for PV, she would need ₹ 907.03 today in order to reach ₹ 1000 two years from now at a rate of 5% interest.

Example 2: Let's add a little spice to our investment knowledge. Suppose that you have to receive ₹ 15000 from a person. You have two options, either get ₹ 15000 today or get ₹ 18000 in four years. Which would you choose? The decision is now more difficult. You should find the future value of ₹ 15,000, but since we are always living in the present, let's find the present value of ₹ 18,000 if interest rates are currently 4%. Remember that the equation for present value is the following:

$$PV = FV (1 + r)^{-n}$$

In the equation above, all we are doing is discounting the future value of an investment. Using the numbers above, the present value of an ₹ 18,000 payment @4% in four years would be calculated as the following:

Present Value = 18000 (1 +.04)$^{-4}$

Present Value = ₹

From the above calculation we now know our choice is between receiving ₹ 15,000 or ₹ 15, 386.48 today. Of course we should choose to postpone payment for four years!

Financial management is concerned with the values of assets today; i.e. present values. Since capital projects provide benefits into the future and since we want to determine the present value of the project, we will discount the future cash flows of a project to the present.

Present values are calculated by referring to tables or we can use calculators and spread sheets for discounting. The discount rate we will use is the opportunity costs of the Investment; i.e. the rate of return we require on any other project with similar risks.

Discounted Value or Present Value of ₹ 1.00, year = *n*, rate = *k*					
Year (*n*)	*k* = 8%	*k* = 9%	*k* = 10%	*k* = 11%	*k* = 12%
1	.926	.917	.909	.901	.893
2	.857	.842	.826	.812	.797
3	.794	.772	.751	.731	.712
4	.735	.708	.683	.659	.636
5	.681	.650	.621	.593	.567

N.B. : This factor can be derived with the help of calculator also. Suppose, If rate is 10%, then add one with the rate (1 + 10% or 1 +.10) on the calculator 1.10 and click the divide sign (/), now click is equal to (=) sign. You will get 1 which is the value of 0 year. Now again click the equal to (=) sign to get first year factor, again click the equal to (=) sign for second year factor and so on. You have to always add one with rate and get another factor.

Present Value Annuity of ₹ 1.00, year = *n*, rate = *k*					
Year (*n*)	*K* = 8%	*K* = 9%	*k* = 10%	*k* = 11%	*k* = 12%
1	0.926	0.917	0.909	0.901	0.893
2	1.783	1.759	1.736	1.713	1.690
3	2.577	2.531	2.487	2.444	2.402
4	3.312	3.240	3.170	3.102	3.037
5	3.993	3.890	3.791	3.696	3.605

Example 3: Calculate the Present Value of Cash Flows. You will receive ₹ 500 at the end of next year. If you could invest ₹ 500 today, you estimate that you could earn 12%. What is the Present Value of this future cash inflow?

₹ 500 × .893 (Present value table) = ₹ 446.50

If we were to receive the same cash flows year after year into the future, then we could use the present value tables for an annuity.

Example 4: Calculate the Present Value of Annuity Type Cash Flows.

You will receive ₹ 500 each year for the next five years. Your opportunity costs for this investment is 10%. What is the present value of this investment?

= ₹ 500 x 3.791 (Present Value Annuity)

= ₹ 1,895.50

CAPITAL BUDGETING TECHNIQUES

Capital budgeting techniques (Investment appraisal criteria) under certainty can be calculated with the help of following methods:

1) Simple Payback Period (SPP)
2) Discounted Payback Period (DPP)
3) Accounting/Average Rate of Return (ARR)
4) Net Present Value (NPV)
5) Internal Rate of Return (IRR)
6) Profitability Index (PI)

1. SIMPLE PAYBACK PERIOD (SPP)

The simple payback period is the traditional method of capital budgeting. The most commonly used and simple technique for taking decisions on capital expenditure is payback period method. This method describes in terms of period of time the relationship between annual savings (cash inflow) and total amount of capital expenditure (investment). This method represents the period (normally in number of years) which is required to get back the original cost of investment by annual cash inflow. Thus, under this method, it is observed on basis of annual cash inflow as in how many years the total amount of capital expenditure will be recovered. To be more precise, this is simply the investment divided by annual cash inflow.

Simple Payback Period = Number of years to recover initial costs

This period may be calculated by the following formula:

Simple Payback Period = Net Investment /Annual Cash Inflow

There are two methods of calculating the simple payback period.

(a) The first method can be applied when the annual Cash Flow After Taxes (CFAT) is uniform. In such a situation the initial cost of the investment is divided by the constant annual cash flow.

Example 5: If an investment of ₹ 90000 in a machine is expected to generate cash inflow of ₹ 20,000 p.a. for 10 years. The Payback Period will be calculated using following formula:

Simple Payback Period = NI/Cash Flow

$$= 90000/20000 = 4.5 \text{ years}$$

(b) The second method is used when a project's annual Cash Flow After Taxes (CFAT) are not equal. In such a situation PBP is calculated by the process of cumulating annual cash inflow till the time when cumulative cash flow becomes equal to the original investment outlays.

6. **Example:** A firm requires an initial cash outflow of ₹ 20,000 and the annual cash inflows for 5 years are ₹ 6000, ₹ 8000, ₹ 5000, ₹ 4000 and ₹ 4000 respectively. Calculate PBP.

Here, when we cumulate the cash flows for the first three years, ₹ 19,000 is recovered. In the fourth year ₹ 4000 cash flow is generated by the project but we need to recover only ₹ 1000 so the time required recovering ₹ 1000 will be (₹ 1000/₹ 4000) × 12 months = 3 months. Thus, the SPP is 3 years and 3 months (3.25 years). This can be shown in the following table:

Initial Investment is ₹ 20000					
	1ˢᵗ year	**2ⁿᵈ year**	**3ʳᵈ year**	**4ᵗʰ year**	**5ᵗʰ year**
Annual Cash Inflows	₹ 6000	₹ 8000	₹ 5000	₹ 4000	₹ 4000
Cumulative Cash Flows	₹ 6000	₹ 14000	₹ 19000	₹ 23000	₹ 27000

Formula for Calculating Simple Payback Period (SPP)

$$\text{SPP} = \text{Completed Year} + \frac{\text{Investment} - \text{Cumulative cash inflow of completed year)}}{\text{Next year cash inflow of completed year}}$$

$$= 3 \text{ years} + (20000 - 19000)/4000$$

$$= 3 + 1000/4000$$

$$= 3.25 \text{ years or 3 years and 3 months}$$

2. DISCOUNTED PAYBACK PERIOD (DPP)

The discounted payback period is a capital budgeting procedure used to determine the profitability of a project. A discounted payback period gives the number of years it takes to break even from undertaking the initial expenditure, by discounting future cash flows and recognizing the time value of money.

In discounted payback period we have to calculate the present value of each cash inflow taking the start of

the first period as zero point. For this purpose the management has to set a suitable discount rate. The discounted cash inflow for each period is to be calculated using the formula:

Discounted Cash Inflow = Actual Cash Inflow/$(1 + i)^n$

Where,

i is the discount rate;

n is the period to which the cash inflow relates.

Example 7: A firm requires an initial cash outflow of ₹ 300,000 and the annual cash inflows for 5 years are ₹ 70000, ₹ 80000, ₹ 60000, ₹ 100000 and ₹ 110000 respectively. Calculate the discounted payback period if expected inflation is 10%.

Year	Cash flow	(Present Value Factor) PVF (10)	(Present Value) PV	(Cumulative Cash Flows) CF
0	(-300000)	1	(-300000)	
1	70000	.909	63630	63930
2	80000	.826	66080	129710
3	60000	.751	45060	174770
4	100000	.683	68300	**243070**
5	110000	.621	68310	**311380**

Formula for Calculating Discounted Payback Period (DPP)

$$\text{DPP} = \text{Completed Year} + \frac{\text{Investment} - \text{Cumulative cash inflow of completed year)}}{\text{Next year cash inflow of completed year}}$$

Discounted Payback Period = 4 years + (300000 − 243070) / 68310

= 4.833 years

Decision Rule: The PBP can be used as a decision criterion to select investment proposal.

○ If the PBP is less than the maximum acceptable payback period, accept the project.

○ If the PBP is greater than the maximum acceptable payback period, reject the project.

3. ACCOUNTING / AVERAGE RATE OF RETURN (ARR)

This method is also known as the return on investment (ROI), return on capital employed (ROCE) and is using accounting information rather than cash flow. Accounting Rate of Return (ARR) is the average net income an asset is expected to generate divided by its average capital cost, expressed as an annual percentage. The ARR is a formula used to make capital budgeting decisions. These typically include situations where companies are deciding on whether or not to proceed with a specific investment (a project, an acquisition, etc.) based on the future net earnings expected compared to the capital cost.

The ARR is the ratio of the average after tax profit divided by the average investment.

ARR = (Average Net Profit/Average Investment) ×100

Where,

Average Investment = (Book value at 1st year + Book Value at end of useful life)/2

(N.B. : Where no scrap value is available, the average investment is calculated by dividing the net investment by two.)

Example 8: An initial investment of ₹ 130,000 is expected to generate annual cash inflow of ₹ 32,000 for 6 years. Depreciation is allowed on the straight line basis. It is estimated that the project will generate scrap value of ₹ 10,500 at the end of 6th year. Calculate its accounting rate of return assuming that there are no other expenses on the project.

Solution:

Annual Depreciation

= (Initial Investment − Scrap Value) ÷ Useful Life in Years

Annual Depreciation = (₹ 130,000 − ₹ 10,500) ÷ 6 ≈ ₹ 19,917

Average Accounting Income

= ₹ 32,000 − ₹ 19,917 = ₹ 12,083

Accounting Rate of Return

= (₹ 12,083 ÷ ₹ 130,000) x 100 ≈ 9.3%

Example 9: A project requires an investment of ₹ 10,00,000. The plant & machinery required under the project will have a scrap value of ₹ 80,000 at the end of its useful life of 5 years. The profits after tax and depreciation are estimated to be as follows:

Year	1	2	3	4	5
PAT (₹)	50000	75000	125000	130000	80000

We shall calculate ARR using above formula

$$ARR = \frac{(50000 + 75000 + 125000 + 130000 + 80000)/5}{(1000000 + 80000)/2} \times 100$$

ARR = 17.04%

N.B. : If depreciation and taxes are given, then for calculation of ARR is calculated after deduction of profit. Depreciation and tax is deducted first for calculation of PAT.

Example 10: ABC Company is planning to start a project which requires the total outlay of ₹ 100000 for purchase of machine having a life of 5 years. It is expected to generate year ending profit before depreciation and taxes of ₹ 50000, ₹ 30000, ₹ 20000, ₹ 30000 and ₹ 40000 from the end of first year to end of fifth year. Assuming that company pays Income Tax @40% and use straight line method of depreciation with no salvage. You are required to compute ARR.

Solution:

Initial Outflow = ₹ 100000

Life of machine 5 years, then annual depreciation will be ₹ 20000

S. No.	Profit	Depreciation	PBT	Tax @40%	PAT
1	50000	20000	30000	12000	18000
2	30000	20000	10000	4000	6000
3	20000	20000	—	—	—
4	30000	20000	10000	4000	6000
5	40000	20000	20000	8000	12000
				Total PAT	42000

ARR = (Average Net Profit/Average Investment) x 100

$$ARR = \frac{42000/5}{100000/2} \times 100 = 16.8\%$$

Decision Rule: The ARR can be used as a decision criterion to select investment proposal.

○ If the ARR is higher than the minimum rate established by the management, accept the project.

○ If the ARR is less than the minimum rate established by the management, reject the project.

The ranking method can also be used to select or reject the proposal using ARR. It will rank a project number one if it has highest ARR and lowest rank would be given to the project with lowest ARR.

4. NET PRESENT VALUE (NPV)

The Net Present Value (NPV) is the total net present value of the project. It represents the total value added or subtracted from the organization if we invest in this project. The net present value is one of the discounted cash flow or time-adjusted technique. It recognizes that cash flow streams at different time period differs in value and can be computed only when they are expressed in terms of common denominator i.e. present value.

The NPV is the difference between the present value of future cash inflows and the present value of the initial outlay, discounted at the firm's cost of capital. The procedure for determining the present values consists of two stages. The first stage involves determination of an appropriate discount rate. With the discount rate so selected, the cash flow streams are converted into present values in the second stage.

Method to compute NPV: The important steps for calculating NPV are given below:

a) Cash flows of the investment project should be forecasted based on realistic assumptions. These cash flows are the incremental cash inflow after taxes and are inclusive of depreciation (CFAT) which is assumed to be received at the end of each year. CFAT should take into account salvage value and working capital released at the end.

b) Appropriate discount rate should be identified to discount the forecasted cash flows. The appropriate discount rate is the firm's opportunity cost of capital which is equal to the required rate of return expected by investors on investments of equivalent risk.

c) Present value (PV) of cash flows should be calculated using opportunity cost of capital as the discount rate.

d) NPV should be found out by subtracting present value of cash outflows from present value of cash inflows. The project should be accepted if NPV is positive (i.e. NPV > 0)

e) The NPV can be calculated with the help of equation.

NPV = Present value of cash inflows − Initial investment

$$W = \frac{A_1}{(1+K)^1} + \frac{A_2}{(1+K)^2} + \dots + \frac{A_n}{(1+K)^n} - C = \Sigma \frac{A_1}{(1+K)^n} - C$$

Where,

A_1, A_2 represent the stream of benefits expected to occur if a course of action is adopted,

C is the cost of that action &

K is the appropriate discount rate to measure the quality of A's.

W is the NPV or, wealth which is the difference between the present worth of the stream of benefits and the initial cost.

Decision Rule: The present value method can be used as an accept-reject criterion. The present value of the future cash streams or inflows would be compared with present value of outlays. The present value outlays are the same as the initial investment.

- If the NPV is greater than 0, accept the project.
- If the NPV is less than 0, reject the project.

Example 11: Assuming that the cost of capital is 8% for a project involving a lumpsum cash outflow of ₹ 7,500 and cash inflow of ₹ 2,000 per annum for 5 years, the Net Present Value calculations are as follows:

a) Present value of cash outflows ₹ 7500

b) Present value of cash inflows
Present value of an annuity of ₹ 1 at 8% for 5 years = 3.993
Present value of ₹ 2000 annuity for 5 years
= 3.993 × 2000 = ₹ 7986

c) Net present value = present value of cash inflows − present value of cash flows

NPV = 7986 − 7500 = ₹ 486
Since the net present value of the project is positive (₹ 486), the Project is accepted.

Example 12: Calculate NPV for a Project X initially costing ₹ 250000. It has 10% cost of capital. It generates five years cash flows ₹ 90000, 80000, 70000, 60000, 50000 respectively:

Year	Year Cash Flows	PVF @ 10%	PV
1	90000	.909	81810
2	80000	.826	66080
3	70000	.751	52570
4	60000	.683	40980
5	50000	.621	31050
		ΣPV	272490
		Initial Costing ₹	250000
		NPV ₹	22490

Here the NPV is positive with expected cost of capital, it means project can be accepted.

Example 13: A company is considering an investment proposal to install new machine. The project will cost ₹ 50000. The machine has a life expectancy of 5 years and no salvage value. The company tax rate is 35%. The firm uses straight line depreciation. The estimated profit before tax from the proposed investment proposal are ₹ 10000, ₹ 11000, ₹ 14000, ₹ 15000 and ₹ 25000 from the end of first year to end of fifth year. Calculate the NPV @10% discount rate.

Solution:

Initial Outflow = ₹ 50000, Discount Rate = 10%

Life of machine 5 years, then annual depreciation will be ₹ 10000

S. No.	Profit	Dep.	PBT	Tax @35%	PAT	Dep.	Cash Flow (CF)	PVF@10%	PV
1	10000	10000	—	—-	—	10000	10000	.909	9090
2	11000	10000	1000	350	650	10000	10650	.826	8797
3	14000	10000	4000	1400	2600	10000	12600	.751	9463
4	15000	10000	5000	1750	3250	10000	13250	.683	9050
5	25000	10000	15000	5250	9750	10000	19750	.621	12265
								ΣPV	48665
								Initial Costing ₹	50000
								NPV ₹	−1335

Here, the NPV is negative with expected cost of capital, it means project can be rejected.

Expected Net Present Value: Once the probability assignments have been made to the future cash flows, the next step is to find out the expected net present value. It can be found out by multiplying the monetary values of the possible events by their probabilities. The following equation describes the expected net present value.

$$ENPV = \Sigma ENCF_t/(1+k)^t$$

Where ENPV is the expected net present value, $ENCF_t$ expected net cash flows in period t and k are the discount rate. The expected net cash flow can be calculated as follows:

$$ENCFT = NCF_{jt} \times P_{jt}$$

Where NCF_{jt} is net cash flow for j^{th} event in period t and P_{jt} probability of net cash flow for j^{th} event in period t.

Example 14: A company is considering an investment proposal costing ₹ 7,000 and has an estimated life of three years. The possible cash flows are given below:

Expected Net Present Value

Cash Flow	Prob.	Expected Value	Cash Flow	Prob.	Expected Value	Cash flow	Prob.	Expected Value
2000	0.2	400	3000	0.4	1200	4000	0.3	1200
3000	0.5	1500	4000	0.3	1200	5000	0.5	2500
4000	0.3	1200	5000	0.3	1500	6000	0.2	1200
		3100			**3900**			**4900**

If we assume a risk-free discount rate of 10%, the expected NPV for the project will be as follows :

Year	ENCF	PV@10%	PV
1	3100	.909	2817.9
2	3900	.826	3221.4
3	4900	.751	3679.9
		ΣPV	9719.2
		Initial Costing ₹	7000
		NPV ₹	**2719.2**

Decision Tree Approach: Sometimes cash flow is estimated under different managerial options with the help of decision tree approach. A decision tree is a graphic presentation of the present decision with future events and decisions. The sequence of events is shown in a format that resembles the branches of a tree.

5. INTERNAL RATE OF RETURN (IRR)

Besides determining the Net Present Value of a project, we can calculate the rate of return earned by the project. This is called the Internal Rate of Return. Internal Rate of Return (IRR) is one of the most popular economic criteria for evaluating capital projects since managers can identify with rates of return. Internal Rate of Return is calculated by finding the discount rate whereby the Net Investment amount equals the total present value of all cash inflows; i.e. Net Present Value = 0. If we have equal cash inflows each year, we can solve for IRR easily.

This technique is also known as yield on investment, marginal productivity of capital, marginal efficiency of capital, rate of return, and time-adjusted rate of return and soon. It also considers the time value of money by discounting the cash flow streams, like NPV.

Mathematically, IRR can be determined by solving following equation for:

$$C_0 = \frac{C_1}{(1+r)^1} + \frac{C_2}{(1+r)^2} + \frac{C_3}{(1+r)^3} + \dots + \frac{C_n}{(1+r)^n}$$

$$C_0 = \sum \frac{C_t}{(1+r)^t}$$

$$IRR = \sum \frac{C_t}{(1+r)^t} - C_0 = 0$$

Where,
r = The internal rate of return
C_t = Cash inflows at t period
C_0 = Initial Investment.

Decision Rule: When IRR is used to make accept-reject decisions, the decision criteria are as follows:

○ If the IRR is greater than the cost of capital, accept the project. ($r > k$)
○ If the IRR is less than the cost of capital, reject the project. ($r < k$)

Example 15: IRR Example (Annuity Table Method)

A new machinery costs ₹ 8,200 and generates cash inflow (after tax) per annum of ₹ 2,000 during its life of 5 years.

Present Value Factor = Initial Investment/Annual Cash Flow

= 8200/2000 = 4.1

The interest factor 4.1 for a 5-year project corresponds to a discount rate of 7%. So the IRR of the project is 7%. An interest factor of 4.100 indicates that the present value of one Rupee annuity for 5 years at 7% is equivalent to 4 rupees and ten paise.

The present value of ₹ 2,000 annuity is

4.100 × 2000 = 8200

Hence 7% is the IRR of the project.

Methods to Compute IRR: When any project generates uneven cash flow, the IRR can be found out by trial and error. If the calculated present value of the expected cash inflow is lower than the present value of cash outflows a lower rate should be tried and vice versa. This process can be repeated unless the NPV becomes zero.

When Trial and error method is used to solve for the IRR, two rates are computed one that gives a small positive NPV, another that gives a small negative NPV. The IRR using the trial and error method will be:

$$IRR = \text{Lower rate} + \frac{\text{NPV at Lower Rate}}{\text{NPV at Lower Rate} - \text{NPV at Higher Rate}}$$

× Differences of Rate

Example 16: A project costs ₹ 32,000 and is expected to generate cash inflows of ₹ 16,000, ₹ 14,000 and ₹ 12,000 at the end of each year for next 3 years. Calculate IRR. Let us take first trial by taking 10% discount rate randomly. A positive NPV at 10% indicates that the project's true rate of return is higher than 10%. So, another trial is taken randomly at 18%. At 18% NPV is negative. So, the project's IRR is between 10% and 18%.

Year	Cash Flows	PV @ 10%	PV	PV @ 18%	PV
1	16000	.909	14544	.847	13552
2	14000	.826	11564	.718	10052
3	12000	.751	9012	.609	7308
		ΣPV	35120	ΣPV	30912
		NCO	32000	NCO	32000
		NPV	3120	NPV	−1088

$$IRR = \text{Lower rate} + \frac{\text{NPV at Lower Rate}}{\text{NPV at Lower Rate} - \text{NPV at higher Rate}}$$
$$\times \text{ Differences of Rate}$$

$$IRR = 10 + \frac{3120}{3120 - (-1088)} \times 8$$
$$= 10 + \frac{3120}{3120 + 1088} \times 8 \qquad \textbf{IRR = 15.93\%}$$

Example 17: A company is considering an investment proposal to install new machine. The project will cost ₹ 50000. The machine has a life expectancy of 5 years and no salvage value. The company tax rate is 35%. The firm uses straight line depreciation. The estimated profit before tax from the proposed investment proposal are ₹ 10000, ₹ 11000, ₹ 14000, ₹ 15000 and ₹ 25000 from the end of first year to end of fifth year. Calculate the Internal Rate of Return (IRR).

Solution:

In the example 13, we found that NPV at discount date 10% is negative. If the discount rate decreases the NPV increases. To calculate IRR, we need another NPV at a different rate. Thus, we assume another discount rate 8% and derive another NPV.

Initial Outflow = ₹ 50000,

Life of machine 5 years, then annual depreciation will be ₹ 10000

Profit	Dep.	PBT	Tax@35%	PAT	Dep.	Cash Flow (CF)	PVF@10%	PV	PVF@8%	PV
10000	10000	—	—-	—	10000	10000	.909	9090	.926	9260
11000	10000	1000	350	650	10000	10650	.826	8797	.857	9127
14000	10000	4000	1400	2600	10000	12600	.751	9463	.794	10004
15000	10000	5000	1750	3250	10000	13250	.683	9050	.735	9739
25000	10000	15000	5250	9750	10000	19750	.621	12265	.681	13450
						ΣPV		48665		51580
						Initial Costing		50000		50000
						NPV ₹		−1335		1580

$$IRR = \text{Lower rate} + \frac{\text{NPV at Lower Rate}}{\text{NPV at Lower Rate} - \text{NPV at Higher Rate}} \times \text{ Differences of Rate}$$

$$IRR = 8 + \frac{1580}{1580 - (-1335)} \times 2 = 8 + \frac{1580}{1580 + 1335} \times 2 \qquad \textbf{IRR = 9.08\%}$$

6. PROFITABILITY INDEX (PI)

Profitability Index (PI) or Benefit-cost ratio (B/C) is similar to the NPV approach. This is an extension of the Net Present Value Method. This is a relative valuation index and hence is comparable across different types of projects requiring different quantum of initial investments.

PI approach measures the present value of returns per rupee invested. It is observed in shortcoming of NPV that, being an absolute measure, it is not a reliable method to evaluate projects requiring different initial investments. The PI method provides solution to this kind of problem.

It is a relative measure and can be defined as the ratio which is obtained by dividing the present value of future cash inflows by the present value of cash outlays.

PI = Present value of cash Inflows / Present value of cash Outflows

Decision Rule: Using the PI ratio,

○ Accept the project when PI > 1

○ Reject the project when PI < 1

○ May or may not accept when PI = 1, the firm is indifferent to the project.

When PI is greater than, equal to or less than 1, NPV is greater than, equal to or less than 0 respectively.

Example 18: Calculate NPV and Profitability Index (PI) for a Project x initially costing ₹ 275000. It has 9% cost of capital. It generates five years cash flows ₹ 90000, 80000, 75000, 60000, 70000 respectively:

Year	Year Cash Flows	PVF @ 9%	PV
1	90000	.917	82530
2	80000	.842	67360
3	75000	.772	57900
4	60000	.708	42480
5	70000	.650	45500
		ΣPV	295770
		Initial Costing ₹	275000
		NPV ₹	20770

PI = Present value of cash Inflows / Present value of cash Outflows

PI = 295770/275000 = 1.0755

PI = 1.08%

Here, the PI is greater than 1. Hence, the project can be accepted.

Comparison of NPV and IRR

Both NPV and IRR will give the same results (i.e. acceptance or rejections) regarding an investment proposal in following two situations:

1) When the project under consideration involve conventional cash flow. i.e. when an initial cash outlays is followed by a series of cash inflows.

2) When the projects are independent of one another i.e., proposals the acceptance of which does not preclude the acceptance of others and if the firm is not facing a problem of funds constraint.

The reasons for similarity in results in the above cases are simple. In NPV method a proposal is accepted if NPV is positive. NPV will be positive only when the actual rate of return on investment is more than the cut off rate. In case of IRR method, a proposal is accepted only when the IRR is higher than the cut off rate. Thus, both methods will give consistent results since the acceptance or rejection of the proposal under both of them is based on the actual return being higher than the required rate *i.e.,*

○ NPV will be positive only if r > k,

○ NPV will be negative only if r < k,

○ NPV would be zero only if r = k.

SENSITIVITY ANALYSIS

While evaluating any capital budgeting project, there is a need to forecast cash flows. The forecasting of cash flows depends on sales forecast and costs. The sales revenue is a function of sales volume and unit selling price. Sales volume will depend on the market size and

the firm's market share. The NPV and IRR of a project are determined by analysing the after-tax cash flows arrived at by combining various variables of project cash flows, project life and discount rate. The behaviour of all these variables are very much uncertain. The sensitivity analysis helps in identifying how sensitive are the various estimated variables of the project. It shows how sensitive is a project's NPV or IRR for a given change in particular variables.

The more sensitive the NPV, the more critical is the variables.

Steps: The following three steps are involved in the use of sensitivity analysis:

1) Identify the variables which can influence the project's NPV or IRR.

2) Define the underlying relationship between the variables.

3) Analyse the impact of the change in each of the variables on the project's NPV or IRR.

The Project's NPV or IRR can be computed under following three assumptions in sensitivity analysis:

1. Pessimistic (i.e. the worst),

2. Expected (i.e. the most likely)

3. Optimistic (i.e. the best).

Example 19 : A company has two mutually exclusive projects for process improvement. The management has developed following estimates of the annual cash flows for each project having a life of fifteen years and 12% discount rate.

Sensitivity Analysis

Project - A			
Net Investment (₹)	90000		
CFAT estimates:		PVAIF$_{12\%,15\ years}$	PV	NPV
Pessimistic	10000	6.811	68110	–21890
Most likely	15000	6.811	102165	12165
Optimistic	21000	6.811	143031	53031
Project - B			
Net Investment (₹)	90000		
CFAT estimates:		PVAIF$_{12\%,15\ years}$	PV	NPV
Pessimistic	13500	6.811	91948.5	1948.5
Most likely	15000	6.811	102165	12165
Optimistic	18000	6.811	122598	32598

The NPV calculations of both the projects suggest that the projects are equally desirable on the basis of the most likely estimates of cash flows. However, Project-A is riskier than Project-B, because its NPV can be negative to the extent of ₹ 21,890 but there is no possibility of incurring any losses with project B as all the NPVs are positive. As the two projects are mutually exclusive, the actual selection of the projects depends on decision maker's attitude towards the risk. If he is ready to take risk, he will select Project-A, because it has the potential of yielding NPV much higher than (₹ 53031) Project-B. But if he is risk averse, he will select Project-B.

Capital Budgeting Techniques Under Uncertainty

Risk can be defined as the chance that the actual outcome will differ from the expected outcome. Uncertainty relates to the situation where a range of differing outcome is possible, but it is not possible to assign probabilities to this range of outcomes. The two terms are generally used interchangeably in finance literature. In investment appraisal, managers are concerned with evaluating the riskiness of a project's future cash flows. Here, they evaluate the chance that the cash flows will differ from expected cash flows, NPV will be negative or the IRR will be less than the cost of capital.

In the context of risk assessment, the decision-maker does not know exactly what the outcome will be but it is possible to assign probability weightage to the various potential outcomes. The most common measures of risk are standard deviation and coefficient of variations. There are three different types of project risk to be considered:

a) **Stand-alone Risk:** This is the risk of the project itself as measured in isolation from any effect it may have on the firm's overall corporate risk.

b) **Corporate or Within-firm Risk:** This is the total or overall risk of the firm when it is viewed as a collection or portfolio of investment projects.

c) **Market or Systematic Risk:** This defines the view taken from a well-diversified shareholders and investors. Market risk is essentially the stock market's assessment of a firm's risk, its beta, and this will affect its share price.

Due to practical difficulties of measuring corporate and market risk, the stand-alone risk has been accepted as a suitable substitute for corporate and market risk. There are many techniques, which can use to deal with risk in investment appraisal.

TEST YOURSELF

1. Capital Budgeting is a part of:
(a) Investment Decision
(b) Working Capital Management
(c) Marketing Management
(d) Capital Structure

2. Capital Budgeting deals with:
(a) Short-term Decisions
(b) Long-term Decisions
(c) Both (a) and (b)
(d) Neither (a) nor (b)

3. Present Value is defined as:
   (a) Future cash flows discounted to the present at an appropriate discount rate
   (b) Inverse of future cash flows
   (c) Present cash flows compounded into the future
   (d) Discounting of compounded future cash flows

4. Annuity is defined as:
   (a) Equal cash flows at equal intervals forever
   (b) Equal cash flows at equal intervals for a specified period
   (c) Unequal cash flows at equal intervals for specified period
   (d) Unequal cash flows at equal intervals forever

5. Which of the following investment rules does not use the time value of the money concept?
   (a) The payback periods
   (b) Internal rate of return
   (c) Net present value
   (d) All of the above use the time value concept

6. According to IRR, undertake those investments that has highest IRR, provided the IRR is ________ the cost of capital.
   (a) Less Than
   (b) Equal to
   (c) Greater than
   (d) None of these

7. A sound Capital Budgeting technique is based on:
   (a) Cash Flows
   (b) Accounting Profit
   (c) Interest Rate on Borrowings
   (d) Last Dividend Paid

8. Risk in Capital budgeting implies that the decision-maker knows ____________ of the cash flows.
   (a) Variability
   (b) Probability
   (c) Certainty
   (d) None of the above

9. Which of the following is a risk factor in capital budgeting?
   (a) Industry-specific risk factors
   (b) Competition risk factors
   (c) Project-specific risk factors
   (d) All of the above

10. Decision-tree approach is used in:
    (a) Proposals with longer life
    (b) Sequential decisions
    (c) Independent Cashflows
    (d) Accept-Reject Proposal

11. Which of the following capital budgeting techniques takes into account the incremental accounting income rather than cash flows:
    (a) Net present value
    (b) Internal rate of return
    (c) Accounting/Simple rate of return
    (d) Cash payback period

12. Which of the following techniques does not take into account the time value of money?
    (a) Internal rate of return method
    (b) Simple cash payback method
    (c) Net present value method
    (d) Discounted cash payback method

13. Find out annual cash inflow and pay-back period from the following data:
    Cost of plant: ₹ 15,00,000. Life of plant: 10 years, Salvage Value of the plant: ₹ 1,00,000. Annual earning before depreciation and tax: ₹ 2,00,000. Assume tax rate: 40%
    (a) ₹ 1,86,000 and 7.523-years
    (b) ₹ 1,76,000 and 8.523 years
    (c) ₹ 1,80,000 and 8.123 years
    (d) ₹ 1,66,000 and 7.523 years

14. Generally, a project is considered acceptable if its net present value is:
    (a) negative or zero
    (b) negative or positive
    (c) positive or zero
    (d) negative

15. Consider the following data on a proposed investment:
    Investment required: ₹ 160,000, Annual cash inflows: ₹ 40,000, Life of the investment: 6 years, Salvage value: 0 and Discount rate: 10%
    Based on the above data, what is the payback period of the proposed investment project?
    (a) 0.25 years   (b) 3 years
    (c) 4 years   (d) 5 years

16. The Tanya & Company has gathered the following data on a proposed investment:
    Initial investment required: ₹ 800,000,
    Annual incremental revenue: ₹ 180,000,
    Annual incremental expenses: ₹ 60,000,
    Discount rate: 12%, Salvage value: ₹ 0
    Based on the above information, the accounting/simple rate of return is:
    (a) 22.5%   (b) 12%
    (c) 15%   (d) 10.5%

17. A company is considering the following three investment proposals:

A. Investment required: ₹ 80,000, present value of future cash inflows: ₹ 96,000

B. Investment required: ₹ 75,000, present value of future cash inflows: ₹ 120,000

C. Investment required: ₹ 100,000, present value of future cash inflows: ₹ 150,000

How would you rank the above investment proposals using profitability index method?

(a) B, A, C   (b) C, A, B

(c) A, B, C   (d) B, C, A

18. Cost of a project is ₹ 50000 and working life is eight years. Annual cash inflow is ₹ 16000. Find out the internal rate of return.

(a) 27.41%   (b) 26.32%

(c) 28.51%   (d) 27.71%

19. Ruby & Co. Ltd think to setup a project costing ₹ 10,00,000. Cash inflow (before depreciating and after tax) for the next six years are as follows:

Year	1	2	3	4	5	6
Cash Inflow ₹	400000	300000	200000	250000	175000	150000

On the basis of above information, you are required to calculate (i) Pay-back period (ii) Post pay-back profit and (iii) Post pay-back Profitability index.

(a) 2.4 Years, ₹ 475000, 47.5%

(b) 3.4 Years, ₹ 475000, 47.5%

(c) 3.4 Years, ₹ 575000, 46.5%

(d) 3.4 Years, ₹ 475000, 46.5%

20. The cost of a project is ₹ 15,00,000. Its working life is 15 years and salvage value of ₹ 50,000. Annual income before depreciation and after tax ₹ 250,000. Assume tax rate 50%. Find out pay-back period, Post pay-back profit and Post pay-back Profitability index.

(a) 6 years, ₹ 24,00,000 and 150.33%

(b) 5 years, ₹ 25,00,000 and 153.33%

(c) 6 years, ₹ 23,00,000 and 153.33%

(d) 5 years, ₹ 25,00,000 and 150.33%

ANSWER

1	2	3	4	5	6	7	8	9	10
(a)	(b)	(a)	(b)	(a)	(c)	(a)	(b)	(d)	(b)

11	12	13	14	15	16	17	18	19	20
(c)	(b)	(b)	(c)	(c)	(c)	(d)	(a)	(b)	(c)

DEPRECIATION AND ITS ACCOUNTING

MEANING OF DEPRECIATION

Depreciation is the reduction in the value of assets due to wear and tear. It is a method of allocation of cost of the asset over its useful life. Every asset is subject to wear and tear in the normal course of its use and also with passage of time. The cost of the asset is allocated over time and considered as expense.

Depreciation is a method of reallocating the cost of a tangible asset over its useful life span of it being in motion. In accounting terms, depreciation is defined as the reduction of recorded cost of a fixed asset in a systematic manner until the value of the asset becomes zero or negligible.

Generally the cost is allocated, as depreciation expense, among the periods in which the asset is expected to be used. An example of fixed assets are buildings, furniture, office equipment, machinery etc. A land is the only exception which cannot be depreciated as the value of land generally appreciates with time.

CAUSES OF DEPRECIATION

Depreciation is a value reduction in the carrying amount of a fixed asset. Depreciation is intended to roughly reflect the actual consumption of the underlying asset, so that the carrying amount of the asset has been greatly reduced to its salvage value by the time its useful life is over.

The term depreciation represents loss or diminution in the value of an asset consequent upon wear and tear, obsolescence, effluxion of time or permanent fall in market value. The causes of depreciation are:

1. **Wear and Tear:** Some assets physically deteriorate due to wear and tear in use. When an asset is constantly used for production, the asset wears out. More and more use of an asset, the greater would be the wear and tear. Physical deterioration of an asset is caused from movement, strain, friction, erosion etc. For instance, building, machineries, furniture, vehicles, plant etc. The wear and tear is general but primary cause of depreciation.

2. **Lapse of Time:** There are certain assets like leasehold property, patents, copy-right etc. that are acquired for a particular period. After the expiry of the period, they are rendered useless i.e. their value ceases to exist. Thus, their cost is written off over their legal life.

3. **Obsolescence:** A new and improved machine performs the same function more quickly and cheaply than the existing machine. As such, existing machine may become out of date or outmoded or obsolete. The new inventions, change in fashions and taste, market condition etc. are the causes to discard the value of an asset.

4. **Exhaustion:** Some assets are of wasting nature. For instance, quarries, mines, oil-well etc. It is the reduction in the value of natural deposits as resources have been extracted year after year. As such these assets are known as wasting assets. The coal mine or oil well gets physically exhausted by the removal of its contents.

5. **Maintenance:** A good maintenance of machine will naturally increase its life. When there is no maintenance, there is more depreciated value. When there is good maintenance, there is longer life to the

machines. The long life of machine depends upon good and skilled maintenance.

When there is damage to or impairment of an asset, it can be considered a cause of depreciation, since either event changes the amount of depreciation remaining to be recognized.

Only in few cases do assets appreciate. Land, gold, antique goods and old paintings may go up in value. But usually the value of asset diminishes continuously.

NEED FOR DEPRECIATION

Depreciation is provided for the assets with a view to achieve the following results:

1. **To Ascertain the True Profit:** Asset is an important tool in earning revenues. When the value of assets decreases, this loss must be brought into account; otherwise a true working result cannot be known. Depreciation is an operating expense of a physical asset, the same should be considered in arriving the true profit earned during each year. If depreciation is ignored, the loss that is occurring in respect of fixed assets will be ignored. So, depreciation should be debited to Profit and Loss Account before profit is ascertained.

2. **To Ascertain True Value of Asset:** The function of the Balance Sheet is to show the true and correct view of the state of affairs of a business. If no depreciation is charged and when assets are shown at the original cost year after year, Balance Sheet will not disclose the correct state of affairs of a business.

3. **To Retain Funds for Replacement:** Assets used in the business need replacement after the expiry of their service. When an asset is continuously used, a time will come when the asset is to be given up and hence its replacement is essential. Therefore, it is necessary to make provision and create funds to replace such assets, in proper time.

4. **To Reduce Tax Liability:** Depreciation is a tax deductible expense. As such, it is permitted by the prevailing taxation laws to be deducted from profit. Consequently, the owner of a business may avail himself of this benefit by charging depreciation to his profit and reducing his tax liability.

5. **To Present True Position:** Financial position can be studied from the Balance Sheet and for the preparation of the Balance Sheet fixed assets are required to be shown at their true value. If assets are shown in the Balance Sheet without any charge

made for their use, (that is, depreciation) then their value must have been over-stated in the Balance Sheet and will not reflect the true financial position of the business.

Consequences of Not Providing for Depreciation: If depreciation is not accounted for, the profit of the company is overstated, in turn. It is distributed among the shareholders. Thus there is no provision for replacement of machine. It must be pointed out that depreciation by itself does not create funds; it merely draws attention to the fact that out of gross revenue receipts a certain amount should be retained to replace the asset used for carrying on activities. It is mandatory to charge depreciation in profit and loss account in companies act 2013. The Companies Act makes it compulsory to write off depreciation on fixed assets before declaring dividend.

FACTORS OF DEPRECIATION

Depreciation is an allowable expense in general accounting purposes and income tax accounting purposes. But it differs categorically from other conventional expenses because depreciation charge does not occur any outflow of business fund.

The periodical amount of depreciation is affected by the following factors:

1. **The Cost of the Asset:** Cost of asset means the basic acquisition cost of the asset plus all incidental expenses which are required to the asset into use. The incidental expenses like freight, import duty, brokerage, taxes, legal expenses and installation charges are also form a part of cost of asset.

2. **The Life of the Asset:** This is the time period over which the organisation considers the fixed asset to be productive. Beyond its useful life, the fixed asset is no longer cost-effective to continue the operation of the asset.

3. **The Salvage Value of the Asset:** Post the useful life of the fixed asset, the company may consider selling it at a reduced amount. This is known as the salvage value of the asset.

4. **Method of Depreciation:** By the method of depreciation selected for amortisation of the asset which must be systematic and rational.

ACCOUNTING FOR DEPRECIATION

Depreciation is an expense and reduces the book value of asset. Therefore, a simple journal entry is to be passed at the end of the year. Journal entry for depreciation depends on whether the provision for depreciation/ accumulated depreciation account is maintained or not.

Assets such as plant and machinery, buildings, vehicles, furniture etc. which are expected to last more than one year, but not for an infinite number of years are subject to depreciation. Below journal entry for depreciation assumes that depreciation is charged directly to the asset account.

Journal entry for depreciation:

Depreciation A/C	Debit
To Asset A/C	Credit

(Assuming no provision/accumulated depreciation account is maintained)

Golden rules of accounting applied in the above journal entry are;

○ **Depreciation** – Nominal Account > Dr. All expenses & losses

○ **Asset** – Real Account > Cr. What goes out

To Transfer Depreciation into P&L

Profit & Loss A/C	Debit
To Depreciation A/C	Credit

After the asset's useful life when all depreciation is charged throughout the years the asset approaches it scrap or residual value.

Thus, depreciation is shown as an indirect expense in the debit side of profit and loss account and asset's value is to be shown after reduction of depreciation in balance sheet.

There is also a method of accounting for depreciation, although it is rarely used. In this method rather than reducing the value of asset another account is credited named as accumulated depreciation and depreciation for all assets are transferred into it. It is then showed as negative item in fixed asset is balance sheet.

Example: Let's assume that a piece of machinery worth ₹ 1,00,000 is charged depreciation (Straight line method) at 10%. The journal entry will be;

Depreciation A/C	10,000
To Machinery A/C	10,000

To Transfer it to the Income Statement

Profit & Loss A/C	10,000
To Depreciation on Machinery A/C	10,000

METHOD OF DEPRECIATION

There three methods commonly used to calculate depreciation. They are:

1) Fixed Percentage Method or Straight-Line Method

2) Diminishing Value Method or Written Down Value (WDV) Method

3) Sum of the Years' Digits Method of Depreciation

1. Fixed Percentage Method or Straight-Line Method

Simplest, most used and popular method of charging depreciation is the straight-line method. The Straight-Line Method of depreciation is also known as the 'Original Cost Method', 'Fixed Instalment Method' and 'Fixed Percentage Method'.

Under this method, an equal amount is provided each year for depreciation of each asset until the asset has been written down to nil or its scrap value at the end of the estimated life of the asset. The name of this method is derived from the fact if the successive annual depreciation over the life of the asset are plotted on a graph, the result will be a straight line with a slope equal to the annual depreciation. This method is also called 'Fixed Instalment Method' because a uniform amount of depreciation is charging each year. Straight line depreciation can be calculated by using the following formulas:

Depreciation Amount = (Cost of Asset – Salvage Value) × Useful Life in years

The formula of the annual depreciation under the method is:

Depreciation per annum = (Cost of asset – Salvage Value) × Rate of Depreciation

Example 1: Suppose a business has bought a machine for ₹ 10,000. They have estimated the useful life of the machine to be 8 years with a salvage value of ₹ 2,000.

Solution:

Now, as per the straight-line method of depreciation:

Cost of the Asset = ₹ 10,000 and Salvage Value = ₹ 2000

Total Depreciation Cost = Cost of Asset – Salvage Value = 10000 – 2000 = ₹ 8000

Useful Life of the Asset = 8 years

Thus, annual depreciation cost = (Cost of Asset – Salvage Cost)/Useful Life = 8000/8 = ₹ 1000

Hence, the Company will depreciate the machine by ₹ 1000 every year for 8 years.

Example 2: On 1 Jan 2016, Company A purchased a vehicle costing ₹ 20,000. The company expects the vehicle to be operational for 4 years at the end of which it can be sold for ₹ 5,000. Calculate depreciation expense for the year ended 31 Dec 2016, 2017, 2018 and 2019.

Solution:

Depreciable amount of the vehicle is ₹ 15,000. (₹ 20,000 cost minus ₹ 5,000. salvage value). Useful life is 4 years.

Depreciation expense for year ended 31 Dec 2016 = ₹ 15,000 ÷ 4 = ₹ 3,750 per year.

Depreciation expense shall remain the same over the useful life. Hence, an amount of ₹ 3,750 shall be the depreciation expense for year ended 31 Dec 2017, 2018 and 2019.

Advantages of Straight-Line Method are:

a) Simple and easy to understand.

b) The book value of an asset can be reduced to Zero.

c) A fair evaluation of an asset each year on the balance sheet.

Disadvantages of Straight-Line Method are:

The depreciation is equal for all the years. However, the expenditure on repairs and renewal goes on increasing as the asset gets older, resulting in higher amount charged to profit and loss account on account of depreciation and repairs in the subsequent years.

2. Diminishing Value or Written Down Value (WDV) Method

Second types of depreciation methods is diminishing value method and is also known as 'Written down value method', 'Reducing instalment method' and 'Fixed percentage on diminishing balance'. Written down value (WDV) method of depreciation is the most commonly used method of depreciation. In income tax act, depreciation is allowed as per WDV method.

According to the diminishing value method, depreciation is charged on reducing balance & a fixed rate. Depreciation, in this case, is charged over the useful life of an asset over its written down value. The percentage, at which depreciation is charged, remains fixed, however, the amount of depreciation goes on diminishing year after year. More depreciation tends to occur earlier in asset's life.

This method is more relevant where the particular asset (viz; Vehicle, Computer, Office Equipment, etc.) is expected to give better performance in the initial periods of use as compared to the later. Thus, the charge of P&L account is higher in initial year as compared to the later year of life of such asset.

Annual Depreciation

= Previous year's value (WDV) × Percentage rate

For example: Asset is purchased at ₹ 1,00,000 and depreciation rate is 10% then first year depreciation is ₹ 10,000 (10% of ₹ 1,00,000), second year depreciation is ₹ 9,000 (10% of 90,000 [1,00,000 –10,000]) and third year depreciation is ₹ 8,100 (10% of ₹ 81,000 [90,000 – 9,000]).

Example 3: A machine was purchased for ₹ 1,00,000, the estimated useful life of which is 8 years. The estimated salvage value of the machine at the end of its useful life is ₹ 20,000. It was decided to charge depreciation at 10% every year on the written down value of the machine.

The results under the written down value method after charging depreciation for 8 years will be as shown in the table below:

Year	Cost/WDV	Depreciation @ 10% on WDV	Net Book Value (at the end of the year)
1	1,00,000	10,000	90,000
2	90,000	9,000	81,000
3	81,000	8,100	72,900
4	72,900	7,290	65,610
5	65,610	6,561	59,049
6	59,049	5,905	53,144
7	53,144	5,314	47,830
8	47,830	4,783	**43,047**

In the example we discussed in the straight-line methods of depreciation we had seen that, at the end of the 8th year, using the straight-line method, only ₹ 20,000 (that is the Salvage value) was left to be written off. However, in the present scenario when we are using the written down value method of depreciation, the net book value of the Asset at the end of the 8th year is ₹ 43,047. There is still an amount of ₹ (43047 − 20000) = 23047 left to be written off.

Hence a higher percentage rate is needed to reduce the Asset to its disposable value in a given time under the written down value method. This is because the fixed rate of depreciation is applied to the written down value or the diminishing balance of the Asset instead of the original cost of asset as it was done in the straight-line method of depreciation. It is for the same reason that the diminishing balance method or the written down value method will never reduce an asset to zero net book value.

Advantages of Written Down Value Method

The following are the advantages of this method:

a) It matches the service of the asset with the depreciation charge. When asset is more efficient in the initial years, higher depreciation is charged compared to later years. It is true about fixed assets such as motor vehicles.

b) It recognizes the risk of obsolescence by charging the major part of depreciation in the early years of the life of the asset.

c) It results in a better cash flow through tax deferral as under this method, the net income to be taxed is lower in the initial years and higher in subsequent years.

d) As and when additions are made to the asset, fresh calculations of depreciation are not necessary.

e) Income-tax authorities recognize this method.

Disadvantages of Written Down Value Method

The main drawbacks of this method are as follows:

a) In subsequent years the original cost of the asset is completely lost sight of.

b) The asset can never be reduced to zero.

c) This method does not take into consideration the interest on capital invested in the asset.

d) This method requires elaborate book-keeping. The determination of correct rate of depreciation is a complex task.

3. Sum of the Years' Digits (SYD) Method of Depreciation

Sum of the Years Digit depreciation method involves calculating depreciation based on the sum of the number of years in an asset's useful life. Sum of the years' digits method of depreciation is one of the accelerated depreciation techniques which assume that assets are generally more productive when they are new and their productivity decreases as they become old. The formula to calculate depreciation under SYD method is:

SYD Depreciation

$$= \text{Depreciable Base} \times \frac{\text{Remaining Useful Life}}{\text{Sum of the Years' Digits}}$$

In the above formula, depreciable base is the difference between cost and salvage value of the asset and sum of the years' digits is the sum of the series:

1, 2, 3, ... , n; where n is the useful life of the asset in years.

Sum of the years' digits can be calculated more conveniently using the following formula:

$$\text{Sum of the Years' Digit} = \frac{n(n+1)}{2}$$

Sum of the years' digits method can also be applied on monthly basis, in which case the above formula to calculate the sum of the years' digits becomes much useful.

Example 4: Use sum of the years' digits method of depreciation to prepare a depreciation schedule of the following asset:

Cost	₹ 45,000		Useful Life in Years	4
Salvage Value	₹ 5,000		Asset is Depreciated	Yearly

Solution:

Sum of the Years' Digits = 1 + 2 + 3 + 4 = 4(4 + 1) ÷ 2 = 10

Depreciable Base = ₹ 45,000 − ₹ 5,000 = ₹ 40,000

Year	Depreciable Base	Depreciation Factor	Depreciation Expense	Accumulated Depreciation
1	₹ 40,000	4/10	4/10 × 40,000 = 16,000	₹ 16,000
2	₹ 40,000	3/10	3/10 × 40,000 = 12,000	₹ 28,000
3	₹ 40,000	2/10	2/10 × 40,000 = 8,000	₹ 36,000
4	₹ 40,000	1/10	1/10 × 40,000 = 4,000	₹ 40,000

Advantages of the Sum Years' Digits Depreciation Method

a) The sum years' digits depreciation method as one of accelerated depreciation methods better matches costs to revenues because it takes more depreciation in the early years of an assets' useful life compare to the straight-line depreciation method.

b) This method reflects more accurately the difference in usage of different assets from one period to the other compare to the straight-line depreciation method.

Disadvantages of the sum years' Digits Depreciation Method

a) SYD depreciation method might be more confusing and harder to compute compare to the straight line one.

b) It has declining amounts of depreciation expense. Declining amounts of depreciation expense usually offsets by increasing the maintenance expense which might smooth the income over the years.

REPLACEMENT OF A FIXED ASSET AND CREATION OF SINKING FUND

The sinking fund method of depreciation is used when an organization wants to set aside a sufficient amount of cash to pay for a replacement asset when the current asset reaches the end of its useful life. As depreciation is incurred, a matching amount of cash is invested, with the interest proceeds being deposited into an asset replacement fund. The interest deposited into this fund is also invested. By the time a replacement asset is needed, the funds needed to make the acquisition have accumulated in the associated fund. This approach is most applicable in industries that have a large fixed asset base, so that they are constantly providing for future asset replacements in a highly organized manner.

TEST YOURSELF

1. The main objective of providing depreciation is:
   (a) To allocate true profit
   (b) To show the true financial position in the balance sheet
   (c) To reduce tax burden
   (d) To provide funds for replacement of fixed assets

2. Depreciation is a process of:
   (a) Valuation
   (b) Allocation
   (c) Both valuation and allocation
   (d) None of these

3. Which of the following is not true?
   (a) Depreciation is an expense charged to the P&L A/c
   (b) Depreciation is not a part of the operating costs
   (c) Assets that are depreciated are tangible assets
   (d) Depreciation is like an insurance expense

4. Under written down value method of Depreciation, the WDV of the asset is always:
   (a) equal to zero   (b) less than zero
   (c) Greater than zero   (d) None of these

5. The method in which depreciation rate is constant is:
   (a) Straight line method
   (b) Declining Balance Method
   (c) Double Declining Balance Method
   (d) Accelerated Depreciation

6. The asset lose an equal amount of value each year in case of:
   (a) Straight line method
   (b) Declining Balance Method
   (c) Double Declining Balance Method
   (d) Accelerated Depreciation

7. Which of the following depreciation methods is NOT an accelerated method?
   (a) Double-declining balance
   (b) Straight-line
   (c) Sum-of-the-years' digits
   (d) None of these

8. A capital equipment costing ₹ 200,000 today has ₹ 50,000 salvage value at the end of 5 years. If the straight-line depreciation method is used, what is the book value of the equipment at the end of 2 years?
   (a) ₹ 200,000
   (b) ₹ 170,000
   (c) ₹ 140,000
   (d) ₹ 50,000

9. Cost of Car is ₹ 300,000, Depreciation Rate is 10% on WDV. What is the book value of car after 3 years?
   (a) 210,000   (b) 220,00
   (c) 214,300   (d) 218,700

10. Depreciation is incorporated in cash flows because it:
    (a) Is unavoidable cost
    (b) Is a cash flow
    (c) Reduces Tax liability
    (d) Involves an outflow

11. The XYZ purchases a new equipment. The selected data is given below:
    Cost of equipment: ₹ 25,000, Useful life of equipment: 5 years, Tax rate: 30%.
    If equipment is depreciated using straight line method, what is the depreciation tax shield associated with the new equipment?
    (a) ₹ 5,000   (b) ₹ 1,500
    (c) ₹ 3,500   (d) ₹ 7,500

12. Which are the advantages of Straight-Line Method?
    (a) Simple and easy to understand
    (b) The book value of an asset can be reduced to Zero
    (c) A fair evaluation of an asset each year on the balance sheet
    (d) All of the above

13. Which is not a disadvantage of Written Down Value Method?
    (a) In subsequent years the original cost of the asset is completely lost sight of.
    (b) The asset can never be reduced to zero.
    (c) Income-tax authorities recognize this method.
    (d) This method requires elaborate book-keeping. The determination of correct rate of depreciation is a complex task.

14. Which is not the advantages of the sum years' digits depreciation method?
    (a) The sum years' digits depreciation method as one of accelerated depreciation methods better matches costs to revenues because it takes more depreciation in the early years of an assets' useful life compared to the straight-line depreciation method.
    (b) This method reflects more accurately the difference in usage of different assets from one period to the other compared to the straight-line depreciation method.

(c) Income-tax authorities recognize this method.
(d) None of the above

15. A firm purchased certain machinery on January 01, 2013 for ₹ 1 lac. It added more machinery on July 01, 2013 for ₹ 50000. 1/2 of the machinery purchased on January 01, 2013 was sold for ₹ 25000 on Dec 31, 2014. The rate of depreciation is to be assumed 20% and the annual closing of accounts as on Dec 31. Find the value of machinery as on Dec 31, 2014.
    (a) ₹ 65000   (b) ₹ 62000
    (c) ₹ 66000   (d) ₹ 60000

16. Machinery worth ₹ 82000 is purchased and the firm spent ₹ 8000 on its installation. Its effective commercial life is estimated as 10 years and scrap value ₹ 10000. What will be written down value at the end of 3rd year, under straight line method?
    (a) ₹ 68000   (b) ₹ 66000
    (c) ₹ 62000   (d) ₹ 70000

17. In the above question, if the method would have been written down value method, what would be the amount of depreciation for 3 years and WDV of the machinery?
    (a) ₹ 21680   (b) ₹ 22320
    (c) ₹ 22580   (d) ₹ 20680

18. A firm purchased machinery worth ₹ 76000 on January 01, 2019 and its life is expected to be 8 years, with scrap value at the end ₹ 12000. What is amount of depreciation.
    (a) ₹ 11000 per annum   (b) ₹ 9500 per annum
    (c) ₹ 9000 per annum   (d) ₹ 8000 per annum

19. The periodical amount of depreciation is affected by which of the factors?
    (a) The cost of the asset
    (b) The life of the asset:
    (c) Method of depreciation
    (d) All of the above

20. Which is not the need for depreciation?
    (a) To ascertain the true profit
    (b) To increase Tax Liability
    (c) To Ascertain True Value of Asset
    (d) To Retain Funds for Replacement

ANSWER

1	2	3	4	5	6	7	8	9	10
(a)	(b)	(b)	(c)	(b)	(a)	(b)	(c)	(d)	(c)

11	12	13	14	15	16	17	18	19	20
(b)	(d)	(c)	(c)	(a)	(b)	(a)	(d)	(d)	(b)

FOREIGN EXCHANGE ARITHMETIC

INTRODUCTION

Banks undertake foreign exchange transactions for their customers. Foreign exchange is basically associated with the foreign trade. The traders in the foreign exchange market (Authorized Dealers/brokers) rely on the two basic forms of analysis viz. fundamental analysis and technical analysis. The uses of technical analysis in forex are much like share market where price is assumed to echo all news, and the charts are the objects analysis. Ultimately, the forces of demand and supply in the local forex market drive the exchange rate of the day.

FUNDAMENTALS OF FOREIGN EXCHANGE

There are three fundamental aspects in foreign exchange mechanism:

1. Every country has its own currency (legal tender) and the useful possession of the currency, can normally be had only in that country, in which it passes.

2. The rate of exchange of currency of one country to currency of other country (like barter system) depends upon the demand and supply of specific currency at the place of conversion.

3. Almost all exchange transactions currencies are routed through banks, which will convert the currency of one country into its equivalent in the currency of another country and transfer the funds from one country to another. Normally currency of buyer's country is converted into currency of seller's country. However, many times the funds may be converted into permitted currency of third country (like USD, Euro, Sterling Pound etc. which are accepted in almost all the countries) acceptable to buyer and the seller/service provider.

FOREX (FOREIGN EXCHANGE) MARKET

Foreign exchange market is described as an OTC (Over the counter) market as there is no physical place where the participants meet to execute their deals. It is more an informal arrangement among the banks and brokers operating in a financing centre purchasing and selling currencies, connected to each other by tele communications like telex, telephone and a satellite communication network, SWIFT.

The term foreign exchange market is used to refer to the wholesale segment of the market, where the dealings take place among the banks. The retail segment refers to the dealings take place between banks and their customers.

The leading foreign exchange market in India is Mumbai, Calcutta, Chennai and Delhi is other centers accounting for bulk of the exchange dealings in India. The policy of Reserve Bank has been to decentralize exchanges operations and develop broader based exchange markets. As a result of the efforts of Reserve Bank Cochin, Bangalore, Ahmedabad and Goa have emerged as new centre of foreign exchange market.

RBI reference exchange rate refers to the benchmark foreign exchange rates for Indian Rupee against major four foreign currencies, published by Reserve Bank of India on a daily basis. The Reserve Bank of India compiles and publishes on a daily basis, reference rates for four major currencies i.e. US dollar (USD), British Pound (GBP), Japanese Yen (YEN) and Euro (EUR).

The rate for spot US Dollar against Indian Rupee will be polled from the select list of contributing banks at a randomly chosen five-minute window between 11.30 a.m. and 12.30 p.m. every week-day (excluding Saturdays, Sundays and Bank Holidays in Mumbai).The other three rates, viz. EUR/INR, GBP/INR and JPY/INR would be computed by crossing the USD/INR Reference Rate with the ruling EUR/USD, GBP/USD and USD/JPY rates.

DIRECT AND INDIRECT QUOTATION

○ **Direct Quotation:** The direct method of rate quotation is called direct quote or home currency quotation. In this quote, the home currency is quoted per unit of foreign currency. In the other words it is a quote where home currency is the variable unit.

For example: I USD = ₹ 70.35 is a direct quote for an Indian national.

○ **Indirect Quotation**: The indirect method of rate quotation is called indirect quote wherein foreign currency is the variable unit against fixed amount of home currency.

For example: ₹ 100 = USD 1.4215

Direct Quote = 1/Indirect Quote and vice versa.

Till 1st August 1993, banks in India were required to quote all rate on an indirect basis. Now, from 2nd August 1993, banks in India began quoting on a direct basis only.

Buy or Sell the Foreign Exchange

Generally, a dealer in the Interbank Market will not reveal whether he is going to buy or sell the foreign exchange. Hence, in the market the quotation made will be a two-way quotation. This means the market maker will indicate two prices. One price for buying the currency and the other price for selling the currency.

For example, a Mumbai bank may quote the rate of dollar as follows;

USD 1 = ₹ 70.1625/1750

It means, the market maker is willing to buy foreign exchange US dollar at the rate of 70.1625 rupees; and he is willing to sell at the rate of 70.1750 rupees per dollar. From this, it is evident that the market maker wants to make a profit of ₹ 0.0125 in the deal of buying and selling one dollar. This quotation is a direct quotation, and the bank will apply the rule 'Buy Low; Sell High'.

The buying rate is generally known as Bid Rate; and the selling rate is known as the Offer Rate or Ask Rate. The difference between these two rates are the gross profit for the bank and is known as the Spread.

SOME BASIC EXCHANGE RATE ARITHMETIC

a) **Cross Rates:** Exchange rate between two foreign currencies is called cross rate. When rate between two currencies is not directly available, it has to be calculated through a 3rd currency which is called cross rate. This is done by using chain rule.

For example: A dealer in Mumbai sells or buys Euro against US Dollars, he uses cross rates.

Example:

US $ 1 = ₹ 72.00 and US $ 1 = Euro 0.7500.

Euro 1 = 72 / 0.75 = ₹ 96

Example: A bank is offered to purchase an export bill of Pound 100000 and the inter-bank rates are US $ 1 = ₹ 70.00/10 and Pound 1 = US $ 1.5000/10. In this case, the bank will purchase pounds at given US $ rate of ₹ 70 and deliver rupees to exporter.

Bank will sell pounds in London in inter-bank market at US $ 1.50. The amount will be worked with chainrule. Pound 1 = 1.50 x 70 = ₹ 105.

b) **Chain Rule:** The fixing of rate of exchange between the foreign currency and Indian rupee through the medium of some other currency is done by a method known as Chain Rule. The rate thus obtained is the Cross rate between these currencies.Calculation of the cross rate is based on a commonsense approach. However, it can be reduced to a rule known as the chain rule with similar steps.

c) **Value Date:** A value date is a future date used in determining the value of a product that fluctuates in price. The value date is a date on which the exchange of currencies actually takes place. The exchange rate (Cash, TOM and Spot) to be used as per the delivery date of currency. Value date can be explained with the following table:

Date of Contract	Delivery Date/Settlement Date	Rate to be used
January 12, 2019	January 12, 2019	Cash / Ready Rate
January 12, 2019	January 13, 2019	TOM Rate
January 12, 2019	January 14, 2019	Spot Rate
January 12, 2019	After January 14, 2019	Forward Rate

Based on this concept, we have the following types of exchange rates:

 (i) **Cash/Ready:** It is the rate when an exchange of currencies takes place on the date of the deal. The transaction to be settled on the same day. It is also known as value today.

 (ii) **TOM:** When the exchange of currencies takes place on the next working day, i.e. tomorrow it is called the TOM rate. The delivery of foreign exchange to be made on the day next (tomorrow) to the date of transaction.

(iii) **SPOT:** When the exchange of currencies takes place on the second working day after the date of the deal, it is called the spot rate.

(iv) **Forward Rate:** Forward transactions are based on the same principle as TOM and SPOT transactions. If the exchange of currencies takes place after a period of spot date, it is called the forward rate. Forward rates generally are expressed by indicating a premium/discount for the forward period.

  a) **Premium:** When a currency is costlier in forward or say, for a future value date, it is said to be at a premium. In the case of the direct method of quotations, the premium is added to both the selling and buying rate.

  b) **Discount:** If currency is cheaper in the forward or for a future value date, it is said to be at a discount. In the case of a direct quotation, the discount is (deducted) subtracted from both the rates, i.e. buying and selling rates.

The forward rates are quoted in terms of forward margins or forward differentials.

For example:
Spot Euro 1 = US$ 1.1480/90
1 month forward 35-32
2 months forward 72-70
3 months forward 110-107

It is understandable that if a currency is at a premium vis-a-vis another currency, the natural consequence is that the later will be at a discount vis-a-vis the former currency.

In the above exchange rate quotations Euro is at a discount and hence US $ is at a premium. We can buy US $, one month forward at
Euro 1 = US$ 1.1490 (–) 0.0032 = 1.1458
Similarly, we can sell
Euro 1 = US$ 1.1480 (–) 0.0035 = 1.1445

FORWARD FOREX CONTRACT

In a forward contract both parties enter into a contract on a given day and lock in a fixed rate on specific future date. In such types of contract, the terms of the purchase (buy or sell) are agreed up front (trade execution date) but actual exchange take place on a date in the future (maturity date). On the maturity date, both parties exchange the pre-negotiated rate.

For example, an Indian company which is likely to earn foreign currency i.e, Euro on account of an export order after one month, may enter into a contract today (trade execution date) to sell Euro and receive Indian Rupees after 1 month (maturity date). The rate is fixed on the trade date and the rate is be known as Fwd-1 month rate.

Suppose on trade date, the Indian exporter agrees to sell EURO 1000 and receive INR 72450. On the maturity date, he delivers EURO 1000 and receives INR 72450. Such types of forward contracts are known as outright forward contracts (OFTs). The OFT exchange rate are quoted as differentials that is at a premium or discount from the spot rate.

FORWARD EXCHANGE RATE

Since the foreign exchange rate will be fluctuation, the spot rate of the currency will not be the same at a future date, i.e., after one month or so. If the forward rate and spot rate happen to be the same, then it is called at par. The difference between the spot rate and the forward rate is known as Forward Margin, otherwise called Swap Points. The forward point may be either at premium or at discount. This is done for both purchase and sale transaction.

Forward Rate Calculation: Premium is added to the spot rate to work out the forward rate. Discounted is deducted from the spot rate. This makes the transaction beneficial to the bank.

  ○ The forward premium includes interest differential.
  ○ While calculating the bills buying rate, where the forward is at a premium, the bank will round off the transit and usance period to the lower month.
  ○ While calculating the bills buying rate, where the forward is at a discount, the bank will round off the transit and usance period to the higher month.

Forward rates are quoted though forward point or forward differentials (which can be either premium or discount).

For example, Euro 1 = US $ 1.2000/10.
1 month forward 30-28,
2 months forward 60-55
3 months forward 95-90.

In this case Euro is at a discount and in that case, the US $ is at a premium.

In this case, the one-month forward US $ can be purchased at the following rate:

Spot Euro 1 =US $ 1.2010—0.0028 = 1.1982

In this case, the one-month forward Euro can be sold at the following rate:

Spot Euro 1 =US $ 1.2000—0.0030 = 1.1970

Premium or Discount on Forward Transactions: The forward rate of a currency is normally either costlier or cheaper than its spot rate. When the forward margin is at premium the forward rate will be higher/costlier than the spot rate. Similarly, if the forward margin is at a discount, the forward rate shall be lower or cheaper than the spot rate. Under a direct quotation, the premium is added to the spot rate for reaching the forward rate and discount is deducted from the spot rate to arrive at the forward rate. If US $ is quoted on a particular day as spot at US $ 1 = ₹ 48.90/49.10, this would be interpreted as buying rate of ₹48.90 and selling rate as ₹ 49.10.

Forward Premium	Forward Discount
Spot Rate 1 US $ = ₹ 48.10	*Spot Rate* 1 US $ = ₹ 48.10
Forward 1 US $ = ₹ 48.30	*Forward* 1 US $ = ₹ 48.00

Forward Points: Forward rate comprises spot rate and forward points being interest rate differentials. For example, if spot rate is Euro 1 = US $ 1.4000 and 3 months forward is 1.4300, the difference of 200 points is called forward point. The forward point is determined by:

(a) supply and demand position of the currency

(b) market expectation

(c) interest rate difference between two countries.

How to Calculate Forward Differential:

Example: Euro 1 = US $ 1.40, Euro Interest rate is 6% and US$ rate is 12%. If a person borrows Euro 100 for year and by converting these into US$ invests as deposit for one year, the flow will be as under:

(1) Euro Spot borrowing 100 + interest 6. Total outflow = 106

(2) US $ Gets 140 US$ (for 100 Euro at 1.40) + get interest of 12 for one year = 152

(3) If US $ 152 are converted into Euro at 1.40 = 108.57.

Hence, gain (1) − (3) = US$ 2.57

In this case the Euro 106 = US$ 152

Hence, Euro 1 = 1.4340

Here, the difference between the spot rate 1.40 and 1.4340 = 0.340 is the forward differential.

How to Calculate Forward Points (or the SWAP cost)

Example: Euro 1 = US $ 1.40, Interest rate differential is 6%. For 90 days forward calculate the forward points. Spot rate = 1.40. Int differential = 6% Forward period = 90 days (no. in a year to be taken 360 days).

$$= \text{Forward points} \times \frac{(\text{Spot rate} \times \text{Interest rate differential} \times \text{Forward period})}{\text{Number of days in the year}} \times 100$$

$$= (1.4000 \times 6 \times 90) / 360 \times 100 = 0.0210$$

How to Calculate Interest Differential from Forward Points:

In the above example, the calculation can be made with the help of formulae:

$$= \text{Forward points} \times \frac{(\text{Forward points} \times \text{No. of days in the year} \times 100)}{(\text{Spot rate} \times \text{Forward period})} \times 100$$

$$= (0.0210 \times 360 \times 100) / 1.40 \times 90 = 6\%$$

How to Quote Forward Rate: The forward can be at premium or forward can be at a discount. In case of direct quotation, the premium is added in the spot rate and discount is deducted from the spot rate both in the buying or selling rate.

When there is Premium: Let us take an example. Euro/US$ spot rate = 1.3200/20 and forward differential one month 20-25, 2 months 40-45 and 3 months 60-65. This shows that Euro is at a premium here.

2-month Euro buying rate (bid rate)

= 1.3200 + 0.0040 = 1.3240 and

Selling rate (offer rate) = 1.3220 + 0.0045 = 1.3265.

Hence, the bid and offer rate would be = 1.3240/65

When there is Discount: Let us take an example. Euro/US$ spot rate = 1.3200/20 and forward differential one month 25-20, 2 months 45-40 and 3 months 65-60. This shows that Euro is at a discount here.

2-month Euro buying rate (bid rate)

= 1.3200 – 0.0040 = 1.3160 and
Selling rate (offer rate) =1.3220 – 0.0045 = 1.3175.
Hence, the bid and offer rate would be = 1.3160/75

ARBITRAGE

Arbitrage is the simultaneous buying and selling of foreign currencies or an asset with intention of making profits from the difference between the exchange rate prevailing at the same time in different markets. Arbitrage occurs when a security is purchased in one market and simultaneously sold in another market at a higher price, thus considered to be risk-free profit for the trader.

Example: Assume you begin with $2 million. You see that at three different institutions the following currency exchange rates are immediately available:

- Institution 1: Euros/USD = 0.894
- Institution 2: Euros/British pound = 1.276
- Institution 3: USD/British pound = 1.432

First, you would convert the $2 million to euros at the 0.894 rate, giving you 1,788,000 euros. Next, you would take the 1,788,000 euros and convert them to pounds at the 1.276 rate, giving you 1,401,254 pounds. Next, you would take the pounds and convert them back to U.S. dollars at the 1.432 rate, giving you $2,006,596. Your total risk-free arbitrage profit would be $6,596.

Example: Suppose an asset, gold, is quoted at ₹ 27,000 per 10 gm in the Delhi bullion market and at ₹ 27,500 in the Mumbai bullion market. A trader may buy 10 gm of gold in Delhi and sell it in Mumbai, making a profit of ₹ 500 (₹ 27,500 – ₹ 27,000). However, this trade will be profitable only if the cost of transactions is less than ₹ 500 per 10 gm of gold. In this example, assuming that the total transaction cost, of executing the trades and physical delivery of gold, is ₹ 200 for 10 gm, then the net profit for the trader would reduce to ₹ 300.

FACTORS DETERMINING FORWARD EXCHANGE RATE

The following factors determine the forward foreign exchange rate:

a) **Rate of Interest:** The prevailing rate of interest at home and also in the foreign country from which we want to get foreign exchange decide the forward margin.

b) **Demand and Supply of Foreign Currency:** This is similar to the principle of demand and supply of a commodity. If a particular foreign currency is in great demand than its supply, then, naturally, it will be costlier and it will be sold at a premium. If the supply exceeds the demand, the forward rate will be at a discount.

c) **Investment Activities:** Another factor influencing forward margin will be due to the hectic activities of investments, taking advantage of differences in the rate of interest between one centre and another. The investor may borrow from low interest centre and invest the amount in the high interest centre. For example, the investor may borrow at London at the rate of 4% p.a. and invest the amount in Chennai at 7% p.a. In order to secure his position, he may cover up his transaction in the forward marker. Then, he will sell spot pound-sterling and buy forward pound-sterling.

d) **Speculative Activities Regarding Spot Rates:** The forward rates are based on spot rates. Any speculation in the movement of spot rates would also influence forward rates. If exchange dealers anticipate spot rate to appreciate, they will quote forward rate at a premium. If they expect the spot rate to depreciate, the forward rate would be quoted at a discount.

e) **Exchange Regulation:** Exchange control regulations may also put restrictions or conditions on the forward dealing, leading to change in forward margin. Such restrictions may be with respect to keeping of balances abroad, borrowing overseas etc. If the Central Bank of the country intervenes in the forward market, this will influence forward margin.

TEST YOURSELF

1. Gap between ________ and ________ dates make a forex trade as cash/TOM/spot trade.
   - (a) Value Date and Settlement date
   - (b) Trade date and T + 1
   - (c) Trade Date and T + 2
   - (d) Trade Date and value date

2. Which of the following is a direct quote in India?
   - (a) 1 Pound sterling = US $ 1.70
   - (b) 1 US $ = ₹ 48.90
   - (c) ₹ 100 = US $ 2.10
   - (d) Both (a) and (b)

3. If a company contracts today for some future date of actual currency exchange, they will be making use of a ________.
   - (a) forward rate
   - (b) stock rate
   - (c) future rate
   - (d) variable rate

4. An Indian importer with foreign currency payables enters into a forward contract. His expectation is____.
   - (a) Indian Rupee to Depreciate
   - (b) Indian Rupee to Appreciate

(c) Foreign currency to Depreciate
(d) None of the above

5. A person wants to remit Euro and there is no quotation with the bank for Euro. Bank works out the rate through ₹/$ rate and $/Euro rate. This is called:
(a) bid rate
(b) offer rate
(c) cross rate
(d) floating rate

6. Forex rate in Delhi is 1 US $ = 68.80/90. In London the 1 US $ = 0.70 Euro. What is the buying rate for Euro/Rupee rate?
(a) 48.16
(b) 98.42
(c) 98.29
(d) 98.34

7. Forward contracts:
(a) contain a commitment by the owner, and are standardized.
(b) contain a commitment by the owner, and can be tailored to the desire of the owner.
(c) contain a right but not a commitment by the owner, and can be tailored to the desire of the owner.
(d) contain a right but not a commitment by the owner, and are standardized.

8. A U.S. company is expected to receive £100,000 in 120 days. If the company wants to minimize the risk of foreign exchange, then it would:
(a) buy British pounds forward
(b) sell British pounds forward
(c) buy British pounds 120 days from now
(d) sell British pounds 120 days from now

9. Forex rate in Delhi is 1 US $ = ₹ 48.80/90. In London the 1 Euro = US $ 1.60/65. An exporter wants an export bill of Euro 50000 to be purchased by the bank. How much amount will be given to the exporter in domestic currency.
(a) 38,51,000
(b) 38,82,500
(c) 39,04,000
(d) 38,96,000

10. The spot Euro 1= US $1.4250/70. The forward premium is 30-25 for one month, 70-65 for 2 months, 110-105 for 3 months. What rate will be charged for 2 months forward sale by bank?
(a) 1.4335
(b) 1.4300
(c) 1.4200
(d) 1.4205

11. The spot Euro 1 = US $1.4200/10. The forward premium is 40-35 for one month, 75-70 for 2 months, 105-100 for 3 months. 1 month's Euro can be sold at:
(a) US $1.4235
(b) US $1.4165
(c) US $ 1.4175
(d) US $1.4240

12. The spot rate is Euro 1= US $1.3300 and 2 months Euro 1 = US $ 1.340. The forward points are equal to:
(a) 100
(b) 200
(c) 300
(d) 340

13. 1 Euro = US $ 1.3280 spot and forward rate is US $ 1.3480. The difference of 200 points in this case is called:
(a) exchange difference
(b) forward discount
(c) forward premium
(d) forward points

14. If the exchange of currencies (delivery) is to be completed after the spot date, which of the following rates will be used:
(a) cash or ready rate
(b) TOM rate
(c) Spot rate
(d) Forward

15. If the exchange of currencies (delivery) is to be completed on the 2nd working day, which of the following rates will be used:
(a) cash or ready rate
(b) TOM rate
(c) Spot rate
(d) Forward

16. 1 Euro = US $ 1.60. Interest for Euro is 4% and interest for US $ 6%. A person borrows Euro 100 one year. Assuming that there is no change in Euro and $ rate, what will be gain of the person borrowing in Euro and converting them in $ and after one-year converting $ into Euro.
(a) Euro 1
(b) Euro 2
(c) Euro 3
(d) inadequate information

17. Spot exchange rate of US $ = ₹ 45 and interest rate differential is 5%. The forward period is 180 days (number of days in a year to be taken 360 days). Calculate the forward points.
(a) 0.01125
(b) 0.01115
(c) 0.01225
(d) 0.02125

18. Forward differential is known as:
(a) arbitrage rate
(b) swap rate
(c) forward rate
(d) spot rate

19. ______ is the simultaneous buying and selling of foreign currencies or an asset with intention of making profits from the difference between the exchange rate prevailing at the same time in different markets.
(a) Swap
(b) Cross rate
(c) Forward
(d) Arbitrage

20. The forward points = 0.011500 and spot rate 1US $ = 44.00. If the forward period is 180 days and number of days in a year are assumed at 360, calculate the interest differential.
(a) 5.23%
(b) 5.43%
(c) 5.85%
(d) 6.23%

ANSWER

1	2	3	4	5	6	7	8	9	10
(d)	(b)	(a)	(a)	(c)	(c)	(b)	(d)	(c)	(c)

11	12	13	14	15	16	17	18	19	20
(a)	(a)	(d)	(d)	(c)	(b)	(a)	(b)	(d)	(a)

MODULE–B
PRINCIPLES OF BOOKKEEPING & ACCOUNTANCY

DEFINITION, SCOPE AND ACCOUNTING STANDARDS

INTRODUCTION

Accounting is the process of systematically recording, measuring, and communicating information about financial transactions. Accounting is often called the language of business because the purpose of accounting is to communicate or report the results of business operations and its various aspects to various users of accounting information. Accounting is tremendously important because it is the language of business, and it is at the root of making informed business decisions. Without accounting, managers would not know which products were successful, which business decisions were the right ones, and whether the company was earning money.

The American Institute of Certified Public Accountants has defined the Financial Accounting as "the art of recording, classifying and summarising in as significant manner and in terms of money transactions and events which in part, at least of a financial character, and interpreting the results thereof".

Bookkeeping and accountancy seems to be the same, but these two are different. Bookkeeping is a part of accounting and is concerned with the recording of transactions which is often routine and clerical in nature, whereas accounting performs other functions as well, viz., measurement and communication, besides recording. An accountant designs the accounting system, supervises and checks the work of the book-keeper, prepares the reports based on the recorded data and interprets the reports. Nowadays, he is required to take part in matters of management, control and planning of economic resources.

Financial statements, normally, mean the balance sheet, profit and loss account, statement of changes in the financial position (which may be either a fund flow statement or a cash flow statement), explanatory statements, notes and schedules forming part of the financial statement. The objective of a financial statement is to provide information about the financial position, performance and changes in the financial position of an enterprise.

NATURE OF ACCOUNTING

The various definitions and explanations of accounting has been propounded by different accounting experts from time to time and the following aspects comprise the nature of accounting:

i) **Accounting as a Service Activity:** Accounting is a service activity. Its function is to provide quantitative information, primarily financial in nature, about economic entities that is intended to be useful in making economic decisions, in making reasoned choices among alternative courses of action. Accounting in itself cannot create wealth though, if it produces information which is useful to others, it may assist in wealth creation and maintenance.

ii) **Accounting as a Profession:** Accounting is very much a profession. A profession is a career that involves the acquiring of a specialised formal education before rendering any service. The accounting education is being imparted to the examinees by national and international recognised bodies like The Institute of Chartered Accountants of India (ICAI), New Delhi in India and American Institute of Certified Public Accountants (AICPA) in USA etc. In a way, accountancy as a profession has attained the stature comparable with that of lawyer, medicine or architecture.

(iii) Accounting as a Social Force: In early days, accounting was only to serve the interest of the owners. Under the changing business environment the discipline of accounting and the accountant both have to watch and protect the interests of other people who are directly or indirectly linked with the operation of modern business. Therefore, safeguarding of public interest can better be facilitated with the help of proper, adequate and reliable accounting information and as a result of it the society at large is benefited.

(iv) Accounting as a Language: Accounting is rightly referred the "language of business". It is one means of reporting and communicating information about a business. As one has to learn a new language to converse and communicate, so also accounting is to be learned and practiced to communicate business events. The expression, exhibition and presentation of accounting data such as numerals and words and debits and credit are accepted as symbols which are unique to the discipline of accounting.

(v) Accounting as Science or Art: Science is a systematised body of knowledge. It establishes a relationship of cause and effect in the various related phenomenon. It is also based on some fundamental principles. So we can say that accounting is a science. Art requires a perfect knowledge, interest and experience to do a work efficiently. Art also teaches us how to do a work in the best possible way by making the best use of the available resources. Accounting is an art as it also requires knowledge, interest and experience to maintain the books of accounts in a systematic manner. Everybody cannot become a good accountant. It can be concluded from the above discussion that accounting is an art as well as a science.

(vi) Accounting as an Information System: Accounting discipline will be the most useful one in the acquisition of all the business knowledge in the near future. Accounting generally does not generate the basic information (raw financial data), rather the raw financial data result from the day to day transactions of the business. As an information system, accounting links an information source or transmitter (generally the accountant), a channel of communication (generally the financial statements) and a set of receivers (external users).

OBJECTIVES OF ACCOUNTING

The following are the main objectives of accounting:

1. **To Keep Systematic Records:** Accounting is done to keep a systematic record of financial transactions. In the absence of accounting there would have been terrific burden on human memory which in most cases would have been impossible to bear.

2. **To Protect Business Properties:** Accounting provides protection to business properties from unjustified and unwarranted use. This is possible on account of accounting supplying the correct and proper information to the manager or the proprietor. Information about the concerned matters helps the proprietor in assuring that the funds of the business are not necessarily kept idle or underutilised.

3. **To Ascertain the Operational Profit or Loss:** Accounting helps in ascertaining the net profit earned or loss suffered on account of carrying the business. Profit and Loss Account will help the management, investors, creditors, etc. in knowing whether the business has proved to be remunerative or not. In case it has not proved to be remunerative or profitable, the cause of such a state of affairs will be investigated and necessary remedial steps will be taken.

4. **To Ascertain the Financial Position of the Business:** In addition to the Profit, a businessman must know about his financial position i.e. where he stands? what he owes and what he owns? This objective is served by the Balance Sheet or Position Statement. The Balance Sheet is a statement of assets and liabilities of the business on a particular date. It serves as barometer for ascertaining the financial health of the business.

5. **To Facilitate Rational Decision Making:** Accounting these days has taken upon itself the task of collection, analysis and reporting of information at the required points of time to the required levels of authority in order to facilitate rational decision-making.

6. **To Satisfy the Requirement of Law:** Various entities such as companies, societies, public trusts, etc., are compulsorily required to maintain accounts as per the law governing their operations, such as the Companies Act, Societies Act, Public Trust Act, etc., the maintenance of accounts is also compulsory under the Goods & Services Tax Act and Income Tax Act.

TYPES OF ACCOUNTING

The financial literature classifies accounting into two broad categories, viz, Financial Accounting and

Management Accounting. Financial accounting is primarily concerned with the preparation of financial statements whereas management accounting covers areas such as interpretation of financial statements, cost accounting, etc. The famous branches or types of accounting include: financial accounting, managerial accounting, cost accounting, auditing, taxation, inflation accounting and forensic accounting etc.

1. **Financial Accounting:** Financial accounting deals with the preparation of financial statements for the basic purpose of providing information to various interested groups like creditors, banks, share-holders, financial institutions, government, consumers, etc. Financial statements, i.e. the income statement and the balance sheet indicate the way in which the activities of the business have been conducted during a given period of time.

   Financial accounting is charged with the primary responsibility of external reporting. The users of information generated by financial accounting, like bankers, financial institutions, regulatory authorities, government, investors, etc. want the accounting information to be consistent so as to facilitate comparison. Therefore, financial accounting is based on certain concepts and conventions which include separate business entity, going concern concept, money measurement concept, cost concept, dual aspect concept, accounting period concept, matching concept, realization concept and conventions of conservatism, disclosure, consistency, etc.

   The significance of financial accounting lies in the fact that it aids the management in directing and controlling the activities of the firm and to frame relevant managerial policies related to areas like production, sales, financing, etc.

2. **Managerial Accounting:** Management accounting is 'tailor-made' accounting. It facilitates the management by providing accounting information in such a way so that it is conducive for policy making and running the day-to-day operations of the business. Its basic purpose is to communicate the facts according to the specific needs of decision-makers by presenting the information in a systematic and meaningful manner. Management accounting, therefore, specifically helps in planning and control. It helps in setting standards and in case of variances between planned and actual performances, it helps in deciding the corrective action.

An important characteristic of management accounting is that it is forward looking. Its basic focus is one future activity to be performed and not what has already happened in the past.

Since management accounting caters to the specific decision needs, it does not rest upon any well-defined and set principles. There ports generated by a management accountant can be of any duration-short or long, depending on purpose. Further, the reports can be prepared for the organisation as a whole as well as its segments.

3. **Cost Accounting:** Sometimes considered as a subset of management accounting, cost accounting refers to the recording, presentation, and analysis of manufacturing costs. Cost accounting makes elaborate cost records regarding various products, operations and functions. It is the process of determining and accumulating the cost of a particular product or activity. Any product, function, job or process for which costs are determined and accumulated, are called cost centres. Cost accounting is very useful in manufacturing businesses since they have the most complicated costing process.

Cost accountants also analyze actual and standard costs to help managers determine future courses of action regarding the company's operations.

4. **Tax Accounting:** Tax accounting helps clients follow rules set by tax authorities. It includes tax planning and preparation of tax returns. It also involves determination of income tax and other taxes, tax advisory services such as ways to minimize taxes legally, evaluation of the consequences of tax decisions, and other tax-related matters.

5. **Social Responsibility Accounting:** Social responsibility of organizations has been the most important elements of philosophy. So that, it is important to abide by organizations within the social identity theory, Satisfaction of stakeholders outside the organization to legitimate organizations will strengthen. Many of the behaviors and actions of managers and employees, was influenced by moral values rooted in ethics. Due to lack of work ethic in management, organizations, societies such as Iran, which was once rich in moral values? The advanced countries have a considerable distance, can create problems for organizations.

In addition to increasing the social expectations of organizations, societies, such issues as the environment, women, children, minorities, disabled people, equal employment and staffing reductions, are more sensitive. Organizations ignoring these rights and ethics in dealing with external stakeholders can cause problems for the organization and the organization and action of legitimacy put it, profits, and thus affects the success of the organization. Poor work ethic, the attitude of jobs, organized and effective managers, can affect the performance of individual, group and organizational influence.

6. **Human Resource Accounting:** Human Resource Accounting (HRA) is a new branch of accounting. It is based on the traditional concept that all expenditure of human capital formation is treated as a charge against the revenue of the period as it does not create any physical asset. But now-a-day this concept has changed and the cost incurred on any asset (as human resources) should be capitalised as it yields benefits measurable in monetary terms.

   Human Resource Accounting means accounting for people as the organisational resources. It is the measurement of the cost and value of people to organisations. It involves measuring costs incurred by private firms and public sectors to recruit, select, hire, train and develop employees and judge their economic value to the organisation.

7. **Internal Auditing:** This field is concerned with the examination of a company's systems and transactions to spot control weaknesses, fraud, waste, and mismanagement, and the reporting of these findings to management. The career track progresses from various internal auditor positions to the manager of internal audit. There are specialties available, such as the information systems auditor and the environmental auditor.

8. **Inflation Accounting:** Inflation accounting is a special accounting technique that can be used during periods of high inflation whereby financial statements are adjusted according to price indexes, rather than relying solely on a cost accounting basis. Companies operating in countries experiencing rapid and sustained levels of inflation or hyperinflation may be required to update their statements periodically in order to make them relevant to current economic and financial conditions.

9. **Government Accounting:** This field uses a unique accounting framework to create and manage funds, from which cash is disbursed to pay for a number of expenditures related to the provision of services by a government entity. Government accounting requires such a different skill set that accountants tend to specialize within this area for their entire careers.

10. **Forensic Accounting:** Forensic accounting involves court and litigation cases, fraud investigation, claims and dispute resolution, and other areas that involve legal matters. This is one of the popular trends in accounting today.

ORIGINS OF ACCOUNTING PRINCIPLES

Accounting is as old as money itself. However, the act of accounting was not as developed as it is today because in the early stages of civilisation, the number of transactions to be recorded were so small that each businessman was able to record and check for himself all his transactions. The Greeks, Romans, Egyptians and Babylonians had well-developed records and maintained a good system of record keeping and control. In the thirteenth and fourteenth centuries, there was a tremendous development of commerce in Italy. However, the modern system of accounting based on the principles of double entry system owes its origin to Luco Pacioli who first published the principles of Double Entry System in 1494 at Venice in Italy. Thus, the art of accounting has been practiced for centuries but it is only in the late thirties that the study of the subject 'accounting' has been taken up seriously.

The rising public status of accountants helped to transform accounting into a profession, first in the United Kingdom and then in the United States. In 1887, thirty-one accountants joined together to create the American Association of Public Accountants. The first standardized test for accountants was given a decade later, and the first CPAs were licensed in 1896.

Accounting was practiced in India twenty-three centuries ago as is clear from the book named "Arthashastra" written by Kautilya, King Chandragupta's minister. This book not only relates to politics and economics, but also explain the art of proper keeping of accounts. In India, the old method of accounting, called the 'Nama' method, is still in use. It is also called the 'Mahajani', 'Marwari' or the 'Deshi' method.

ACCOUNTING STANDARDS IN INDIA AND ITS DEFINITION AND SCOPE

ACCOUNTING STANDARDS: Accounting standards are the written statements consisting of rules and guidelines, issued by the accounting institutions, for the preparation of uniform and consistent financial statements and also for other disclosures affecting the different users of accounting information.

Accounting standards lay down the terms and conditions of accounting policies and practices by way of codes, guidelines and adjustments for making the interpretation of the items appearing in the financial statements easy and even their treatment in the books of account.

Formation of the Accounting Standards Board in India: The Institute of Chartered Accountants of India, recognizing the need to harmonies the diverse accounting policies and practices at present in use in India, constituted an Accounting Standards Board (ASB) on 21st April, 1977. The main function of ASB is to formulate accounting standards so that such standards may be established by the Council of the Institute in India. While formulating the accounting standards, ASB will take into consideration the applicable laws, customs, usages and business environment.

Procedure for Issuing Accounting Standards:

a) ASB shall determine the broad areas in which Accounting Standards need to be formulated and 'priority in regard to the selection thereof.

b) In the preparation of Accounting Standards, ASB will be assisted by Study Groups constituted to consider specific subjects. In the formation of Study Groups, provision will be made for wide participation by the members of the institute and others.

c) ASB will also hold a dialogue with the representatives of the Government, Public Sector Undertakings. Industry and other Organisations for ascertaining their views.

d) On the basis of the work of the Study Groups and the dialogue with the organisation, an exposure draft of the proposed standard will be prepared and issued for comments by members of the Institute and the public at large.

e) After taking into consideration the comments received, the exposure draft will be finalised by the ASB for submission to the council of ICAI.

f) The council of ICAI will consider the final draft and if found necessary, modify the same in consultation with ASB. The accounting standard on the relevant subject will then be issued under the authority of the council.

g) Finally, the Accounting Standard is issued. In the case of standard for non-corporate entities, the ICAI will issue the standard. And if the relevant subject relates to a corporate entity the Central Government will issue the standard.

Given below is a common size chart of IAS, IND AS and AS. A ready reference for all professional colleagues.

Sr.No.	Particulars	IAS/IFRS	Ind AS	AS
1.	Presentation of Financial Statements & Disclosure of Accounting Policies	IAS 1	Ind AS 001	AS 01
2.	Valuation of Inventories	IAS 2	Ind AS 002	AS 02
3.	Statement of Cash Flows	IAS 7	Ind AS 007	AS 03
4.	Net Profit or Loss for the period, Prior Period Items and Changes in Accounting Policies	IAS 8	Ind AS 008	AS 05
5.	Contingencies and Events Occurring after the Balance Sheet Date	IAS 10	Ind AS 010	AS 04
6.	Construction Contracts	IAS 11	Ind AS 011	AS 07
7.	Accounting for Taxes on Income	IAS 12	Ind AS 012	AS 22
8.	Property, Plant and Equipment	IAS 16	Ind AS 016	–
9.	Leases	IAS 17	Ind AS 017	AS 19
10.	Revenue Recognition	IAS 18	Ind AS 018	AS 09
11.	Employee Benefits	IAS 19	Ind AS 019	AS 15
12.	Accounting for Government Grants and Disclosure	IAS 20	Ind AS 020	AS 12
13.	The Effects of Changes in Foreign Exchange Rates	IAS 21	Ind AS 021	AS 11
14.	Borrowing Costs	IAS 23	Ind AS 023	AS 16
15.	Related Party Disclosures	IAS 24	Ind AS 024	AS 18
16.	Accounting and Reporting by Retirement Benefit Plans	IAS 26	–	–
17.	Consolidated and Separate Financial Statements	IAS 27	Ind AS 027	AS 21

Sr.No.	Particulars	IAS/IFRS	Ind AS	AS
18.	Accounting for Investments in Associates in Consolidated Financial Statements	IAS 28	Ind AS 028	AS 23
19.	Financial Reporting in Hyperinflationary Economies	IAS 29	Ind AS 029	–
20.	Financial Reporting of Interests in Joint Ventures	IAS 31	Ind AS 031	AS 27
21.	Financial Instruments: Presentation	IAS 32	Ind AS 032	AS 31
22.	Earnings per Share	IAS 33	Ind AS 033	AS 20
23.	Interim Financial Reporting	IAS 34	Ind AS 034	AS 25
24.	Impairment of Assets	IAS 36	Ind AS 036	AS 28
25.	Provisions, Contingent Liabilities and Contingent Assets	IAS 37	Ind AS 037	AS 29
26.	Intangible Assets	IAS 38	Ind AS 038	AS 26
27.	Financial Instruments: Recognition and Measurement (Accounting for Investments)	IAS 39	Ind AS 039	AS 13
28.	Investment Property	IAS 40	Ind AS 040	–
29.	Agriculture	IAS 41		
30.	First-time Adoption of Indian Accounting Standards	IFRS 1	Ind AS 101	–
31.	Share-based Payment	IFRS 2	Ind AS 102	–
32.	Business Combinations, Amalgamations	IFRS 3	Ind AS 103	AS 14
33.	Insurance Contracts	IFRS 4	Ind AS 104	–
34.	Non-current Assets Held for Sale and Discontinued (Accounting for Fixed Assets)	IFRS 5	Ind AS 105	AS 10
35.	Exploration for and Evaluation of Mineral Resources	IFRS 6	Ind AS 106	–
36.	Financial Instruments: Disclosures	IFRS 7	Ind AS 107	AS 32
37.	Operating Segments Reporting	IFRS 8	Ind AS 108	AS 17
38.	Financial Instruments	IFRS 9		

A mandatory accounting standard, if not followed, requires the auditors, who are members of ICAI, to qualify their audit reports, failing which they will be guilty of professional misconduct. Both the SEBI and Companies Act require auditors to qualify the audit reports that do not conform to mandatory accounting standards. Section 134 (5) of the Companies Act 2013 also casts a responsibility on the Board of Directors to comply with mandatory accounting standards.

Under the Section 129(5) of the Companies Act 2013, where the financial statements do not comply with the accounting standards, such companies shall disclose the following:

(a) The deviation from the accounting standards;

(b) The reasons for such a deviation;

(c) The financial effects, if any, arising out of such a deviation.

By the powers conferred to the Central Government under the Section 210A of the Companies Act, the composition of the "National Advisory Committee on Accounting Standards' had been notified on 15th June, 2001 by the Department of Company Affairs. The committee has been set up to advise the Central Government on the formulation and laying down of accounting policies and accounting standards for adoption by the corporate sector.

GENERALLY ACCEPTED ACCOUNTING PRINCIPLES OF USA (US GAAP)

Generally Accepted Accounting Principles (GAAP) of USA is a framework of accounting standards, rules and procedures defined by the professional accounting industry, which has been adopted by nearly all publicly traded U.S. companies.

Generally accepted accounting principles (GAAP) refer to a common set of accepted accounting principles, standards, and procedures that companies and their accountants must follow when they compile their financial statements. GAAP is a combination of authoritative standards (set by policy boards) and the commonly accepted ways of recording and reporting accounting information. GAAP improves the clarity of the communication of financial information.

Financial reporting should provide information that is:

❍ Useful to present to potential investors and creditors and other users in making rational investment, credit, and other financial decisions;

❍ Helpful to present to potential investors and creditors and other users in assessing the amounts, timing, and uncertainty of prospective cash receipts about economic resources, the claims to those resources, and the changes in them;

❍ Helpful for making financial decisions;

❍ Helpful in making long-term decisions;

❍ Helpful in improving the performance of the business;

❍ Useful in maintaining records.

THESE ORGANIZATIONS INFLUENCE THE DEVELOPMENT OF GAAP IN THE UNITED STATES

1. **United States Securities and Exchange Commission (SEC):** The SEC was created as a result of the Great Depression. At that time there was no structure setting accounting standards. The SEC encouraged the establishment of private standard-setting bodies through the AICPA and later the FASB, believing that the private sector had the proper knowledge, resources, and talents. The SEC works closely with various private organizations setting GAAP, but does not set GAAP itself.

2. **American Institute of Certified Public Accountants (AICPA):** In 1939, urged by the SEC, the AICPA appointed the Committee on Accounting Procedure (CAP). During the years 1939 to 1959 CAP issued 51 Accounting Research Bulletins that dealt with a variety of timely accounting problems. However, this problem-by-problem approach failed to develop the much-needed structured body of accounting principles. Thus, in 1959, the AICPA created the Accounting Principles Board (APB), whose mission it was to develop an overall conceptual framework. It issued 31 opinions and was dissolved in 1973 for lack of productivity and failure to act promptly. After the creation of the FASB, the AICPA established the Accounting Standards Executive Committee (AcSEC). It publishes:

a) Audit and Accounting Guidelines, which summarizes the accounting practices of specific industries (e.g. casinos, colleges, airlines, etc.) and provides specific guidance on matters not addressed by FASB or GASB.

b) Statements of Position, which provides guidance on financial reporting topics until the FASB or GASB sets standards on the issue.

c) Practice Bulletins, which indicate the AcSEC's views on narrow financial reporting issues not considered by the FASB or the GASB.

3. **Financial Accounting Standards Board (FASB):** Realizing the need to reform the APB, leaders in the accounting profession appointed a Study Group on the Establishment of Accounting Principles (commonly known as the Wheat Committee for its chair Francis Wheat). This group determined that the APB must be dissolved and a new standard-setting structure is created. This structure is composed of three organizations: the Financial Accounting Foundation (FAF, it selects members of the FASB, funds and oversees their activities), the Financial Accounting Standards Advisory Council (FASAC), and the major operating organization in this structure the Financial Accounting Standards Board (FASB). FASB previously had four major types of publications:

a) **Statements of Financial Accounting Standards:** the most authoritative GAAP setting publications. 168 standard has been issued before the new codification.

b) **Statements of Financial Accounting Concepts**: first issued in 1978. They are part of the FASB's conceptual framework project and set forth fundamental objectives and concepts that the FASB use in developing future standards. However, they are not a part of GAAP. There have been 7 concepts published to date.

c) **Interpretations:** modify or extend existing standards. There have been around 50 interpretations published to date.

d) **Technical Bulletins or Staff Positions**: guidelines on applying standards, interpretations, and opinions. Usually solves some very specific accounting issue that will not have a significant, lasting effect.

In 1984 the FASB created the Emerging Issues Task Force (EITF) which deals with new and unusual financial transactions that have the potential to become common (e.g. accounting for Internet-based companies). It acts more like a problem filter for the FASB – the EITF deals with short-term, quickly resolvable issues, leaving long-term, more pervasive problems for the FASB.

However, now all GAAP resides in the ASC (Accounting Standards Codification) so the FASB and EITF do not issue new standards but rather updates to the Codification. The Concepts statements still exist outside of the ASC but are not authoritative.

4. **Governmental Accounting Standards Board (GASB):** Created in 1984, the GASB addresses state and local government reporting issues. Its structure is similar to that of the FASB's, and the FASB and GASB are located together and share resources.

5. **Other Influential Organizations:** The Government Finance Officers Association (GFOA) also influences financial policies for governments (disagreements between the GFOA and GASB are rare, but can continue for many years); American Accounting Association, Institute of Management Accountants, Financial Executives Institute.

INTERNATIONAL FINANCIAL REPORTING STANDARDS (IFRS)

International Financial Reporting Standards (IFRS) are a set of international accounting standards stating how particular types of transactions and other events should be reported in financial statements. IFRS are issued by the International Accounting Standards Board (IASB), and they specify exactly how accountants must maintain and report their accounts. IFRS were established in order to have a common accounting language, so business and accounts can be understood from company to company and country to country.

Standard IFRS Requirements: IFRS covers a wide range of accounting activities. There are certain aspects of business practice for which IFRS set mandatory rules.

a) **Statement of Financial Position:** This is also known as a balance sheet. IFRS influences the ways in which the components of a balance sheet are reported.

b) **Statement of Comprehensive Income:** This can take the form of one statement, or it can be separated into a profit and loss statement and a statement of other income, including property and equipment.

c) **Statement of Changes in Equity:** Also known as a statement of retained earnings, this documents the company's change in earnings or profit for the given financial period.

d) **Statement of Cash Flow:** This report summarizes the company's financial transactions in the given period, separating cash flow into Operations, Investing, and Financing.

In addition to these basic reports, a company must also give a summary of its accounting policies. The full report is often seen side by side with the previous report, to show the changes in profit and loss. A parent company must create separate account reports for each of its subsidiary companies.

DIFFERENCE BETWEEN GAAP & IFRS

GAAP is focused on the practices of US companies. The Financial Accounting Standards Board (FASB) issues GAAP. The international alternative to GAAP is the International Financial Reporting Standards (IFRS) set by the International Accounting Standards Board (IASB). The IASB and the FASB have been working on the convergence of IFRS and GAAP since 2002. Due to the progress achieved in this partnership, the SEC, in 2007, removed the requirement for non-US companies registered in America to reconcile their financial reports with GAAP if their accounts already complied with IFRS. This was a big achievement, because prior to the ruling, non-US companies trading on US exchanges had to provide GAAP-compliant financial statements.

Differences exist between IFRS and other countries' Generally Accepted Accounting Principles (GAAP) that affect the way a financial ratio is calculated. For example, IFRS is not as strict on defining revenue and allow companies to report revenue sooner, so consequently, a balance sheet under this system might show a higher stream of revenue than GAAP's. IFRS also has different requirements for expenses; for example, if a company is spending money on development or an investment for the future, it doesn't necessarily have to be reported as an expense (it can be capitalized).

Another difference between IFRS and GAAP is the specification of the way inventory is accounted for. Some differences that still exist between both accounting rules include:

LIFO Inventory: While GAAP allows companies to use the Last In First Out (LIFO) as an inventory cost method, it is prohibited under IFRS.

Costs of Development: These costs are to be charged to expense as they are incurred under GAAP. Under IFRS, the costs can be capitalized and amortized over multiple periods.

Write-Downs: GAAP specifies that the amount of write-down of an inventory or fixed asset cannot be reversed if the market value of the asset subsequently increases. The write-down can be reversed under IFRS.

As corporations increasingly need to navigate global markets and conduct operations worldwide, international standards are becoming increasingly popular at the expense of GAAP, even in the US.

TRANSFER PRICING

Transfer pricing is the setting of the price for goods and services sold between controlled (or related) legal entities within an enterprise. Transfer price is the price at which divisions of a company transact with each other, such as the trade of supplies or labor between departments. Transfer prices are used when individual entities of a larger multi-entity firm are treated and measured as separately run entities. A transfer price can also be known as a transfer cost.

A transfer price arises for accounting purposes when different divisions of a multi-entity company are in charge of their own profits. When divisions are required to transact with each other, a transfer price is used to determine costs. Transfer prices generally do not differ much from the market price. If the price does differ, then one of the entities is at a disadvantage and would ultimately start buying from the market to get a better price.

Regulations on transfer pricing ensure the fairness and accuracy of transfer pricing among related entities. Regulations enforce an arm's length transaction rule that states that companies must establish pricing based on similar transactions done between unrelated parties.

TYPES OF TRANSFER PRICING METHODS

The good thing about transfer pricing is that the principles and practices are quite similar all around the world. The OECD Transfer Pricing Guidelines (OECD Guidelines) provide 5 common transfer pricing methods that are accepted by nearly all tax authorities. The five transfer pricing methods are divided in "traditional transaction methods" and "transactional profit methods."

We list the methods below:

(a) Traditional Transaction Methods:
1. CUP method
2. Resale price method
3. Cost plus method

(b) Transactional Profit Methods:
4. Transactional net margin method (TNMM)
5. Transactional profit split method.

(a) Traditional Transaction Methods: Traditional transaction methods measure terms and conditions of actual transactions between independent enterprises and compare these with those of a controlled transaction. This comparison can be made on the basis of direct measures such as the price of a transaction but also on the basis of indirect measures such as gross margins realized on a particular transaction.

1. **Comparable Uncontrolled Price:** The Comparable Uncontrolled Price (CUP) Method compares the price charged for property or services transferred in a controlled transaction to the price charged for property or services transferred in a comparable uncontrolled transaction in comparable circumstances. The CUP Method may also sometimes be used to determine the arm's length royalty for the use of an intangible asset. CUPs may be based on either "internal" comparable transactions or on "external" comparable transactions.

2. **The Resale Price Method (RPM):** The Resale Price Method (RPM) is one of the traditional transaction methods that can be used to determine whether a transaction reflects the arm's length principle. The Resale Price Method focuses on the related sales company which performs marketing and selling functions as the tested party in the transfer pricing analysis.

3. **The Cost-Plus Method:** The Cost-Plus Method compares gross profits to the cost of sales. The first step is to determine the costs incurred by the supplier in a controlled transaction for products transferred to an associated purchaser. Secondly, an appropriate mark-up has to be added to this cost, to make an appropriate profit in light of the functions performed. After adding this (market-based) mark-up to these costs, a price can be considered at arm's length.

The application of the Cost-Plus Method requires the identification of a mark-up on costs applied for comparable transactions between independent enterprises. An arm's length mark-up can be determined based on the mark-up applied on comparable transactions among independent enterprises.

(b) Transactional Profit Methods: The transactional profit methods don't measure the terms and conditions of actual transactions. In fact, these methods measure the net operating profits realized from controlled transactions and compare that profit level to the profit level realized by independent enterprises that are engaged in comparable transactions.

The transactional profit methods are less precise than the traditional transaction methods, but much more often applied. The reason is that application of the traditional transaction methods, which is preferred, requires detailed information and in practice this information is not easy to find.

4. **The Transactional Net Margin Method:** With the Transactional Net Margin Method (TNMM), you need to determine the net profit of a controlled transaction of an associated enterprise (tested party). This net profit is then compared to the net profit realized by comparable uncontrolled transactions of independent enterprises.

5. **The Profit Split Method:** Associated enterprises sometimes engage in transactions that are very interrelated. Therefore, they cannot be examined on a separate basis. For these types of transactions, associated enterprises normally agree to split the profits. The Profit Split Method examines the terms and conditions of these types of controlled transactions by determining the division of profits that independent enterprises would have realized from engaging in those transactions.

As opposed to other transfer pricing methods, the TNMM requires transactions to be "broadly similar" to qualify as comparable. "Broadly similar" in this context means that the compared transactions don't have to be exactly like the controlled transaction. This increases the number of situations where the TNMM can be used.

TEST YOURSELF

1. The process of systematically recording, measuring, and communicating information about financial transactions, is called __________ .
   (a) Financial assessment
   (b) Accounting procedure
   (c) Book keeping
   (d) Accounting laws

2. Which is not a correct statement about the nature of accounting?
   (a) Accounting is a service activity
   (b) Accounting is very much a profession
   (c) Accounting is an Art not a Science
   (d) Accounting is the language of business

3. GAAP stands for:
   (a) Governmental Accepted Accounting Principles
   (b) Generally Accepted Accounting Principles
   (c) Governmental Adopted Accounting Principles
   (d) Generally Adopted Accounting Principles

4. The set of rules for recording of events in accounts are called as:
   (a) Accounting Rules   (b) Accounting Standards
   (c) Accounting Laws   (d) None of these

5. The modern system of accounting based on the principles of ______ owes it origin to Luco Pacioli who first published in 1494 at Venice in Italy.
   (a) Double Entry System (b) Cost Accounting
   (c) Financial Accounting (d) None of these

6. Operating Segments Reporting is mandatory disclosure under which of the following accounting standards:
   (a) AS 12   (b) AS 17
   (c) AS 22   (d) AS 26

7. Which is the main objectives of accounting?
   (a) To keep systematic records
   (b) To ascertain the operational profit or loss
   (c) To facilitate rational decision making
   (d) All of the above

8. ______________ is 'tailor-made' accounting. It facilitates the management by providing accounting information in such a way so that it is conducive for policy making and running the day-to-day operations of the business.
   (a) Management accounting
   (b) Financial accounting
   (c) Cost accounting
   (d) Inflation accounting

9. ________ involves court and litigation cases, fraud investigation, claims and dispute resolution, and other areas that involve legal matters.
   (a) Internal auditing
   (b) Forensic accounting
   (c) Cost accounting
   (d) Inflation accounting

10. Accounting was practiced in India twenty-three centuries ago as is clear from the book named "______" written by Kautilya, King Chandragupta's minister.
    (a) Arthaniti   (b) Arthashastra
    (c) Chanakya Niti   (d) Arthatantra

11. Who frames the accounting standards in India?
(a) Reserve Bank of India
(b) The Institute of Chartered Accountants of India
(c) Ministry of Company Affairs
(d) SEBI

12. The Institute of Chartered Accountants of India, recognizing the need to harmonise the diverse accounting policies and practices at present in use in India, constituted an Accounting Standards Board (ASB) on 21st April, _______.
(a) 1949   (b) 1965
(c) 1977   (d) 1981

13. _______ are a set of international accounting standards stating how particular types of transactions and other events should be reported in financial statements.
(a) International Financial Reporting Standards (IFRS)
(b) Governmental Accounting Standards Board (GASB)
(c) American Institute of Certified Public Accountants (AICPA)
(d) Financial Accounting Standards Board (FASB)

14. Financial reporting should not provide information that is:
(a) Helpful for making financial decisions
(b) Helpful in making short-term decisions
(c) Helpful in improving the performance of the business
(d) Useful in maintaining records.

15. _________ of USA is a framework of accounting standards, rules and procedures defined by the professional accounting industry, which has been adopted by nearly all publicly traded U.S. companies.
(a) International Financial Reporting Standards (IFRS)
(b) Generally Accepted Accounting Principles (GAAP)
(c) American Institute of Certified Public Accountants (AICPA)
(d) Financial Accounting Standards Board (FASB)

16. The major differences between IFRS and GAAP is the specification of the way inventory is accounted regarding for _______.
(a) LIFO Inventory
(b) Costs of Development
(c) Write-Downs
(d) All of the above

17. The ______means pricing of a goods and services within a multi divisional organisation, particularly with regard to the cross border transactions.
(a) Selling Price
(b) International transfer pricing
(c) Transfer pricing
(d) Arm's length price

18. When divisions of a company make transactions between themselves, a transfer price is used to _______.
(a) fix price   (b) determine cost
(c) purchase price   (d) calculate profit

19. Common non-traditional methods available for determining arm's length price is/are _______.
(a) Profit Spilit Method
(b) Transactional Net Margin Method
(c) Both (a) and (b)
(d) None of these

20. The unified version of cost plus method and resale price method under transfer pricing is called:
(a) Comparable Uncontrolled Price
(b) The Resale Price Method (RPM)
(c) Cost Plus Method
(d) Transactional Net Margin Method (TNMM)

ANSWER

1	2	3	4	5	6	7	8	9	10
(d)	(c)	(b)	(b)	(a)	(b)	(d)	(a)	(b)	(b)

11	12	13	14	15	16	17	18	19	20
(b)	(c)	(a)	(b)	(b)	(d)	(c)	(b)	(c)	(d)

BASIC ACCOUNTANCY PROCEDURES

INTRODUCTION

Using generally accepted accounting principles, accountants record and report financial data in similar ways for all firms. They report their findings in financial statements that summarize a company's business transactions over a specified time period. An accounting system tracks and controls the income and expenses of a business. In dealing with the framework of accounting theory, we are confronted with a serious problem arising from differences in terminology. A number of words and terms have been used by different authors to express and explain the same idea or notion.

ACCOUNTING PRINCIPLES

The basic aims of book-keeping and accountancy are to record the business transactions and events in a summarised form. Transactions are recorded in chronological order in proper books of accounts bookkeeping. Accountancy and Science are based on fundamental truth and rules or conducts or procedures which are universally accepted. It is based on certain well-defined concepts and conventions and helps in framing broad financial policies. These rules of conducts to record business transactions are called accounting principles. These principles are developed over long period of time.

CONCEPTS AND CONVENTIONS OF ACCOUNTANCY

In dealing with the framework of accounting theory, we are confronted with a serious problem arising from differences in terminology. A number of words and terms have been used by different authors to express and explain the same idea or notion. The various terms used for describing the basic ideas are: concepts, postulates, propositions, assumptions, underlying principles, fundamentals, conventions, doctrines, rules, axioms, etc. Each of these terms is capable of precise definition.

We do feel, however, that some of these terms/ideas have a better claim to be called 'concepts' while the rest should be called 'conventions'. The term 'Concept' is used to connote the accounting postulates, i.e., necessary assumptions and ideas which are fundamental to accounting practice. In other words, fundamental accounting concepts are broad general assumptions which underline the periodic financial statements of business enterprises. The reason why some of these terms should be called concepts is that they are basic assumptions and have a direct bearing on the quality of financial accounting information. The term 'convention' is used to signify customs or tradition as a guide to the preparation of accounting statements. The following are the important accounting concepts and conventions:

Accounting Concepts		Accounting Conventions
At the Recording Stage	*At the Reporting Stage*	
1. Separate Business Entity Concept 2. Money Measurement Concept 3. Cost Concept 4. Realisation Concept 5. Dual Aspect Concept 6. Historical Records Concept	1. Going Concern Concept 2. The Matching Concept 3. Accounting Period Concept	1. Convention of Materiality 2. Convention of Consistency 3. Convention of Full Disclosure 4. Convention of Conservatism

Concepts: Two types of accounting concepts are:
A. At the Recording Stage, and
B. At the Reporting Stage

A. The following are the main accounting concepts at the recording stage:

1. **Separate Business Entity Concept:** In accounting we make a distinction between business and the owner. All the books of accounts records day to day financial transactions from the view point of the business rather than from that of the owner. For the purpose of accounting, a business concern is considered to be an entity, separate from the promoters, owners, share-holders, investors etc.

    For example, when A puts in ₹ 1 lac in a business, it would be considered that he has given ₹ 1 lac to his business, which his business would show as an amount payable (or liability) to A. In other words the accounts are maintained for this entity as distinct from the person(s) connected with it.

    Although this distinction is easily understandable in case of company cases, but at times confusions get created in respect of proprietary or partnership concerns. Whatever the position, the recording of transactions has to be in terms of their effect on the business entity considering the owners, creditors, suppliers, and customers etc. as the parties transacting business with the entity.

    The overall effect of adopting this concept is:
    a) Only the business transactions are reported and not the personal transactions of the owners.
    b) Profit is the property of business unless distributed to the owners.
    c) The personal assets of the owners are not considered while recording and reporting the assets of the business entity.

2. **Money Measurement Concept:** As per this concept, only those transactions, which can be measured in terms of money are recorded. A unit of exchange and measurement is necessary to account for business transaction in a uniform manner. Money is common denominator in terms of which the exchange ability of goods and services are measured. Since money is the medium of exchange and the standard of economic value, this concept requires that those transactions alone that are capable are being measured in terms of money only to be recorded in the books of accounts.

    Non-monetary events like public political contract, location of business, and certain disputes, efficient Sales Force etc. cannot be recorded in the books of Accounts even through these have great effects.

However, a unit of money measurement over period of time has its own drawbacks. Money has time value, which cannot be considered. Time value of money is affected seriously by economic differences etc. System of accountancy treats all units of money same irrespective of time of original and settlement of it say after two years. It will be the same amount. However value of Money in true sense will be less. This is a great drawback. This leads to the introduction of inflation accounts.

3. **Cost Concept:** The term 'assets' denotes the resources land building, machinery etc. owned by a business. The money values that are assigned to assets are derived from the cost concept. According to this concept an asset is ordinarily entered on the accounting records at the price paid to acquire it.

    Assets which a business entity may acquire would generally be recorded at their cost i.e. the amount or the price at which the acquisition has been affected. This cost becomes a reference point for all subsequent accounting and a small example would clarify the matter. An asset purchased at ₹ 1 lac would be recorded in the books at ₹ 1 lac in spite of its value increasing or decreasing for any reasons, over a time period.

    The concept of cost, brings in objectivity in reckoning the value of the assets in the absence of which subjectivity can influence the accounting. For instance, in the above example, the value of the asset for A could be ₹ 90,000 and for B (depending upon his own information, perception or consideration) it may be ₹ 1.20 lac. In the preparation of accounts by A, he is likely to take into account the asset at ₹ 90,000 while by B, the value may be taken at ₹ 1.20 lac. Similarly the inflationary or deflationary conditions may create accounting problems in respect of the assets held by the business for use over a long period.

4. **Realisation Concept:** This concept speaks about recording of only those transactions which are actually realized. For example, Sale or Profit on sales will be taken into account only when money is realized i.e. either cash is received or legal ownership is transferred.

    This concept gives recognition to a particular transaction as having been complete at a particular point of time, when the benefit is actually passed on to the party to whom it is due. For instance, if Z, in order to sell goods to Y purchases raw material, the goods would not be considered to have passed on to Y unless these are actually delivered.

5. **Dual Aspect Concept:** Financial accounting records all the transactions and events involving financial element. Each of such transactions requires two aspects to be recorded. The recognition of these two aspects of every transaction is known as a dual aspect analysis.

   This concept of accounting is the most fundamental and provides the conceptual basis for accounting mechanics. Because of this concept the resources owned by an entity should be equal to the liability, since each transaction has two aspects. A simple example would clarify the matter.

   Let us assume that Z contributes ₹ 50000 as cash to his business which is placed by the business entity in a bank. The accounting records of the transaction reflect this amount as owner's equity on the liability side and the deposit in the bank, as the asset. If a sum of ₹ 10000 is spent out of the above amount to purchase stocks, the amount of ₹ 50000 would still be shown as the liability and ₹ 40000 as bank deposit and ₹ 10000 as stocks on the assets' side. If a loan of ₹ 15000 is raised to acquire fixed assets worth ₹ 35000 (and a part of bank deposit is used to purchase these fixed assets), the position would be reflected as under:

Owner's equity	₹ 50000	Fixed Assets	₹ 35000
Loan raised	₹ 15000	Stocks	₹ 10000
		Bank deposit	₹ 20000
Total	**₹ 65000**	**Total**	**₹ 65000**

This also is known as the principle of double entry, in bookkeeping.

6. **Historical Records Concept:** Business transactions are always recorded at the actual cost at which they are actually undertaken. In accounts, usually past happenings are recorded. This is based on assumption of realisations. Accounting involves the recording of business transactions that have taken place. A trader purchases a business premises for ₹ 10,00,000. The amount due is paid to the vendor and the business acquires that place. Now, this transaction can be recorded in the books. The business transactions are recorded as and when they take place, i.e. date-wise. This leads to the preparation of historical records of all transactions. The future transactions can hardly be identified and measured accurately.

B. The following are the main accounting concepts at the reporting stage:

1. **Going Concern Concept:** Business transactions are recorded on the assumption that the business will continue for a long time. There is neither the intention nor the necessity to liquidate the particular business in near future. Therefore, it would be able to meet its contractual obligation and use its resources according to the plans and predetermined goals. Therefore, Fixed Assets are recorded at cost and Depreciation is calculated on cost / written down value. Similarly prepaid expenses are treated as Assets on the presumption that the business will continue and these expenses will be utilized in future.

   When an enterprise liquidates a branch or one division or one segment of its business, the ability of the enterprise to continue as a going concern is not imparted.

   In case of enterprise going to liquidate or become insolvent. Then the enterprise cannot be considered as a going concern.

2. **Matching Concept:** This concept stipulates that all the transactions relating to a particular aspect of the business should be taken into account to reach the correct position. For instance, if we have to work out the profit or loss position, all the revenue income items and all the revenue expenditure items must be taken into account. Adjustments, if any, are required to be made for all the expenses which have not become due or for income which has not been received but has become due or has accrued.

3. **Accounting Period Concept:** Though a business continues indefinitely according to the going concern concept, but its performance measurement has to be done after a reasonable time period and not after a long or uncertain period of time, which would not be desirable since it may create a position of uncertainty. Hence, the business is segmented into appropriate parts for judging the performance shown in each such identified segment. Such segment is known as an accounting period, say of a year or a quarter or a half-year. At the close of such accounting period, financial statements are prepared.

ACCOUNTING CONVENTIONS

The term "Convention" denotes customs or traditions or practice based on general agreement between the accounting bodies which guide the accountant while preparing the financial statements. The following are the main accounting conventions:

1. **Convention of Materiality:** The term material means "relative importance". Accounting to the convention of materiality, account should report only what is material and ignore insignificant details while preparing the final accounts. According to this

concept, while preparing the accounts, all the material details must be taken into account which may influence the decision of the investor when that comes to his notice. It also needs to be taken into account that the identification of an item/information being material or non-material, is a very subjective term and needs to be used very carefully.

2. **Convention of Consistency: This** accounting convention state that one's a particular accounting practice, method or policy is adopted to prepare accounts, statements and reports. It should be continued for years together and should not change unless it is forced to change it. Accounting practices should remain the same from one year to another. The results of different years will be comparable only when accounting rules are continuously adhered to from years to years i.e. Valuation of stock in trade, method of depreciation, treatment of approval sale etc.

3. **Convention of Full Disclosure:** According to convention of full disclosure, accounting must disclose all the material facts and information so that interested parties after reading such accounting report can get a clear view of the state of affairs of the business. Adequate information must be provided for the users to get appropriate benefit from that information. It should not lead the user to draw the conclusions, which he would not accept in case he comes to know that it is not correct. Hence, a true and fair view of the accounts must be reflected by the financial statements.

4. **Convention of Conservatism:** Financial Statements are usually drawn up on a conservative basis. There are two principles which stem directly from conservatism.

   a) The accountant should not anticipate income and should provide all possible losses;

   b) Faced with the choice between two methods of valuing an asset the accountant should choose a method which leads to the lesser value.

It is also called "Principle of prudence". Therefore, provision for bad and doubtful debts is also permitted and made every year. Accounting convention must be followed continuously. If not followed continuously it would result into understatement of incomes, assets and overstatement of liabilities and provisions and expenses.

GOING CONCERN ENTITY

Accounting assumes that the business entity will continue to operate for a long time in the future unless there is good evidence to the contrary. The enterprise is viewed as a going concern, that is, as continuing in operations, at least in the foreseeable future. In other words, there is neither the intention nor the necessity to liquidate the particular business venture in the predictable future. Because of this assumption, the accountant while valuing the assets does not take into account forced sale value of them. In fact, the assumption that the business is not expected to be liquidated in the foreseeable future establishes the basis for many of the valuations and allocations in accounting.

For example, the accountant charges depreciation on fixed assets. It is this assumption which underlies the decision of investors to commit capital to enterprise. Only on the basis of this assumption accounting process can remain stable and achieve the objective of correctly reporting and recording on the capital invested, the efficiency of management, and the position of the enterprise as a going concern.

However, if the accountant has good reasons to believe that the business, or some part of it is going to be liquidated or that it will cease to operate (say within six-month or a year), then the resources could be reported at their current values. If this concept is not followed, International Accounting Standard requires the disclosure of the fact in the financial statements together with reasons.

DOUBLE ENTRY SYSTEM

The double entry system of accounting or bookkeeping means that every business transaction will involve two accounts (or more). For example, when a company borrows money from its bank, the company's Cash account will increase and its liability account—Loans Payable—will increase. If a company pays ₹ 200 for an advertisement, its Cash account will decrease and its account—Advertising Expense—will increase.

Double entry bookkeeping means that each debit in an account will have a matching credit to another account. A transaction is not complete till there is a credit based on a matching debit. For recording a transaction properly, the knowledge of the rules of 'Debit' and 'Credit' is essential. When to debit and when to credit depends upon the nature of a transaction.

Features of Double Entry System

(i) Every transaction has two-fold aspects, i.e., one party giving the benefit and the other receiving the benefit.

(ii) Every transaction is divided into two aspects, Debit and Credit. One account is to be debited and the other account is to be credited.

(iii) Every debit must have its corresponding and equal credit.

Advantages of Double Entry System

(i) Since personal and impersonal accounts are maintained under the double entry system, both the effects of the transactions are recorded.

(ii) It ensures arithmetical accuracy of the books of accounts, for every debit, there is a corresponding and equal credit. This is ascertained by preparing a trial balance periodically or at the end of the financial year.

(iii) It prevents and minimizes frauds. Moreover, frauds can be detected early.

(iv) Errors can be checked and rectified easily.

(v) The balances of receivables and payables are determined easily, since the personal accounts are maintained.

(vi) The businessman can compare the financial position of the current year with that of the past year/s.

(vii) The businessman can justify the standing of his business in comparison with the previous year's purchase, sales, and stocks, incomes and expenses with that of the current year figures.

(viii) It helps in decision making.

(ix) The net operating results can be calculated by preparing the Trading and Profit and Loss A/c for the year ended and the financial position can be ascertained by the preparation of the Balance Sheet.

(x) It becomes easy for the Government to decide the tax.

(xi) It helps the Government to decide sickness of business units and extend help accordingly.

(xii) The other stakeholders like suppliers, banks, etc take a proper decision regarding grant of credit or loans.

Limitations of Double Entry System

(i) The system does not disclose all the errors committed in the books of accounts.

(ii) The trial balance prepared under this system does not disclose certain types of errors.

(iii) It is costly as it involves maintenance of numbers of books of accounts.

THE PRINCIPLE OF CONSERVATISM

This concept requires that the accountants must follow the policy of "playing safe" while recording business transactions and events. That is why, the accountant follow the rule—anticipate no profit but provide for all possible losses—while recording the business events. This rule means that an accountant should record lowest possible value for assets and revenues, and the highest possible value for liabilities and expenses. According to this concept, revenues or gains should be recognised only when they are realised in the form of cash or assets (i.e. debts) the ultimate cash realisation of which can be assessed with reasonable certainty. Further, provision must be made for all known liabilities, expenses and losses, Probable losses regarding all contingencies should also be provided for. 'Valuing the stock in trade at market price or cost price whichever is less', 'making the provision for doubtful debts on debtors in anticipation of actual bad debts', 'adopting written down value method of depreciation as against straight line method', not providing for discount on creditors but providing for discount on debtors', are some of the examples of the application of the convention of conservatism.

The principle of conservatism may also invite criticism if not applied cautiously. For example, when the accountant create secret reserves, by creating excess provision for bad and doubtful debts, depreciation, etc. The financial statements do not present a true and fair view of state of affairs. American Institute of Certified Public Accountant have also indicated that this concept need to be applied with much more caution and care as over conservatism may result in misrepresentation.

REVENUE RECOGNITION AND REALISATION

The sales revenue denotes income earned from the main business activity or activities. The income is earned when goods or services are sold to customers. If there is any return, it should be deducted from the sales value. Accounting recognises in the sense that no profit is supposed to accrue only on the acquisition of anything, however certain it may be that it will be sold at a profit. Hence, according to this concept, revenue is recognised only when a sale is made. Unless the money has been realised, i.e., either cash has been received or a legal obligation to pay has been assumed by the customer, no sale can be said to have taken place and no profit can be said to have arisen. It prevents business firms from inflating their profits by recording incomes that are likely to accrue, i.e., expected incomes or gains are not recorded.

ACCRUAL AND CASH BASIS

It is generally accepted in accounting that the basis of reporting income is accrual. Accrual concept makes a distinction between the receipt of cash and the right to receive it, and the payment of cash and the legal obligation to pay it. This concept provides a guideline to the accountant as to how he should treat the cash receipts and the right related thereto. Accrual principle tries to evaluate every transaction in terms of its impact on the owner's equity. The essence of the accrual concept is that net income arises from events that change the owner's equity in a specified period and that these are not necessarily the same as change in the cash position of the business. Thus, it helps in proper measurement of income.

TEST YOURSELF

1. The term '______' is used to signify customs or tradition as a guide to the preparation of accounting statements.
   (a) concepts   (b) convention
   (c) Accounting Principle   (d) All of above

2. Historical cost concepts are reduced to net realisable value because of the accounting principle of ____________.
   (a) consistency   (b) conservatism
   (c) realisation   (d) None of the above

3. Accounting assumes that the business will continue to operate for a long time in future. This concept is called as:
   (a) Going concern concept
   (b) Entity going concept
   (c) Both (a) & (b)
   (d) Neither (a) nor (b)

4. While recording transactions, all possible losses must be taken into consideration but all anticipated profit should be ignored. This is called as:
   (a) Convention of Conservatism
   (b) Principle of Prudence
   (c) Both (a) & (b)
   (d) Neither (a) nor (b)

5. Under the money measurement concept the following will not be recorded in the books of account of the business. (i) Value of furniture, (ii) Quality of company goods, (iii) Bad health of managing director.
   (a) Only (i) and (ii)   (b) Only (ii) and (iii)
   (c) Only (i) and (iii)   (d) (i), (ii) and (iii)

6. The system of recording business transactions based on dual aspect concept is called ____________.
   (a) Double account system
   (b) Double entry system
   (c) Single entry system
   (d) All of the above

7. This concept speaks about recording of only those transactions which are actually realized.
   (a) Accrual concept
   (b) Entity concept
   (c) Dual aspect concept
   (d) Realisation concept

8. Which of the following investment rules does not use the time value of the money concept?
   (a) The payback period
   (b) Internal rate of return
   (c) Net present value
   (d) All of the above use the time value concept

9. Which of the following concept assumes that the business enterprise will not be sold or liquidated in the near future?
   (a) Conservatism Concept
   (b) Money Measurement Concept
   (c) Going Concern Concept
   (d) Accounting Period Concept

10. Which of the following concept distinguishes the 'business from its owners'?
    (a) Going Concern Entity
    (b) Money Measuring Entity
    (c) Accounting Period Concept
    (d) Business Entity Concept

11. Assumption of accounting entity or business entity concept is applicable for which of the following business organizations?
    (i) Societies
    (ii) Joint Stock Companies
    (iii) Corporations
    (a) Only (i) and (ii)   (b) Only (i) and (iii)
    (c) Only (ii) and (iii)   (d) (i), (ii) and (iii)

12. "Anticipate no profits and provide for all possible losses" is the essence of which of the following accounting concept/convention?
    (a) Convention of Conservatism
    (b) Materiality Convention
    (c) Convention of Consistency
    (d) Dual Aspect Concept

13. Valuation of stocks is done by a business firm at cost price or market price, whichever is lower basis, under ____________.
    (a) Convention of Full Disclosure
    (b) Convention of Materiality
    (c) Convention of Conservatism
    (d) Convection of Consistency

14. Profit is a liability for a firm and the loss is an asset under which of the following concepts __________.
(a) Business Entity Concept
(b) Materiality Concept
(c) Historical Record Concept
(d) Accounting Period Concept

15. This accounting convention states that once a particular accounting practice, method or policy is adopted to prepare accounts, statements and reports.
(a) Convention of Conservatism
(b) Materiality Convention
(c) Convention of Consistency
(d) Convention of Full Disclosure

16. The concept that recognizes the distinction between the receipt of cash and the right to receive the cash is called ______________.
(a) Accrual Concept
(b) Cash Concept
(c) Materiality Concept
(d) Full Disclosure Concept

17. The accounting equation asset = capital + liability is part of which of the following concepts?
(a) Realization Concept
(b) Materiality Concept
(c) Historical Record Concept
(d) Dual Aspect Concept

18. According to __________, accounting must disclose all the material facts and information so that interested parties after reading such accounting report can get a clear view of the state of affairs of the business.
(a) Convention of Conservatism
(b) Materiality Convention
(c) Convention of Consistency
(d) Convention of Full Disclosure

19. Accounting to the ___________, account should report only what is material and ignore insignificant details while preparing the final accounts.
(a) Convention of Conservatism
(b) Convention of Materiality
(c) Convention of Consistency
(d) Convention of Full Disclosure

20. This concept stipulates that all the transactions relating to a particular aspect of the business should be taken into account to reach the correct position.
(a) Matching Concept
(b) Materiality Concept
(c) Historical Record Concept
(d) Dual Aspect Concept

ANSWER

1	2	3	4	5	6	7	8	9	10
(b)	(b)	(c)	(c)	(b)	(a)	(d)	(a)	(c)	(d)

11	12	13	14	15	16	17	18	19	20
(d)	(a)	(c)	(a)	(c)	(a)	(d)	(d)	(b)	(a)

MAINTENANCE OF CASH/SUBSIDIARY BOOKS AND LEDGER

INTRODUCTION

One of the main parts of accounting is recordkeeping or bookkeeping. Recordkeeping is the process of recording transactions and events in an accounting system. Accounting records are key source of information and evidence used to prepare, verify and/or audit the financial statements. They also include documentation to prove asset ownership for creation of liabilities and proof of monetary and non-monetary transactions.

Accounting bodies set rules on dealing with records from a presentation of financial statements or auditing perspective. Accounting records are important for all types of accounting including financial accounting, cost accounting as well as for different types of organizations corporations, partnerships, LLPs etc.

Recordkeeping is the most basic piece of a company's financial picture. In order to do your bookkeeping and accounting, one will first need records, all of the documents that show what the company has been spending and earning over the year. This information is necessary to keep you on track, but it's also legally required in order to act as proof of all of the information that you include in your tax returns.

BOOKKEEPING BASICS

Bookkeeping is a part of accounting. The process of recording financial transactions in a systematic manner and classifying them into ledger is termed as book-keeping. Accounting cycle includes the following:

1. **Identification of Financial Transactions and events**: Accounting records only those transactions and events which are financial nature as they bring change in resources of a firm, E.g., purchase of raw materials or sale of finished good by a firm. These transactions are identified with the help of bills and receipts.

2. **Measuring of Identifying Transactions:** Accounting measures the transactions and events in terms of a common measurement of unit i.e., currency of the country.

3. **Recording**: Recording is the process of recording business transactions in the book of original entry, i.e., Journal.

4. **Classifying**: Classification is the process of collecting all entries in the journal or the subsidiary book and posted to the appropriate ledger account to find out at a glance the total effect of all similar transactions at one place by opening accounts in the ledger book.

5. **Summarising**: This involves the presenting of classifying data in a manner which is understandable and useful to internal as well as external users of accounting statements. This stage is to prepare the trail balance, a final account with view a certain of profit and loss made during a particular period and financial position of the business on a parti-cular date.

6. **Analysis and interpretation**: Financial data is analysis and interpreted so that the financial data

can make meaningful judgement of the financial performance (profit) and financial position of the business. Analysis helps in planning for the future in a better way.

7. **Communicating:** Finally, accounting function involves communicating the financial data, i.e., financial statements to the users.

ACCOUNT

Account is a summarised record of transactions at one place relating to a particular head. The account is also related to things, both tangible and intangible, e.g. land, building, equipment, brand value, trademarks etc are some of the things. An account is expressed as a statement in form of English letter 'T'. It has two sides. The left-hand side is called as "Debit' side and the right-hand side is called as "Credit' side.

Debit Account: An item recorded on the debit side of an account is said to be debited to the account. A debit entry signifies that value has flowed to the named account. e.g., payment to a creditor signifies that payment has been made for the goods purchased from him.

Credit Account: An item recorded on the credit side of an account is said to be credited to the account. A credit entry signifies that value has flown from the source indicated by the name of the account. e.g., receipt of cash from a debtor signifies that debtor has made payment for the goods purchased by him.

Note: Debit (Dr) and credit (Cr) are simply additions to or subtractions from an account.

Under Double Entry System of accounting each transaction has two aspects. One aspect is debit, it means receiving or incoming aspect. Another aspect is credit aspects, i.e., giving or outgoing aspects.

There are two approaches for deciding an account is debited or credited.

1. **American Approach or Modern Approach:** This is a modern system of classification of accounts approach.
2. **British Approach or Traditional Approach:** This is an old system of classifying accounts.

Classification of Accounts

Accounts can be broadly classified as:

1. Personal Accounts, and 2. Impersonal Accounts

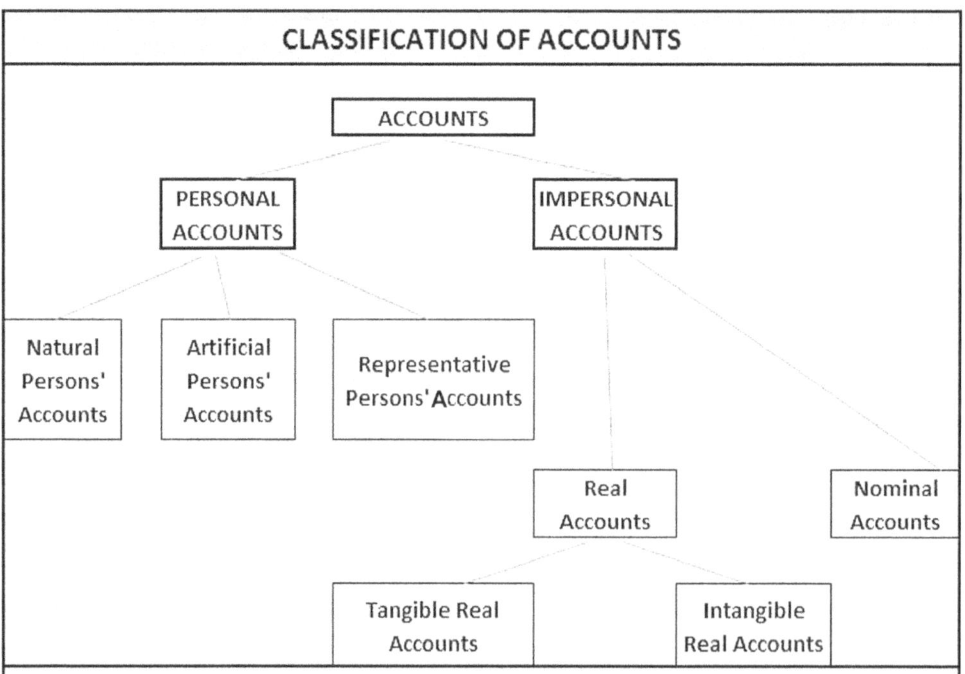

1. **Personal Accounts:** Accounts which are related to persons. e.g., Sheetal's A/c, Anil's A/c, Sunil's A/c. The persons could also be artificial persons. Bank A/c, University, School, Company, Firm etc.

A capital account is the account of the proprietor and therefore, is also personal but adjustments on account of profit and losses are made in it. Similarly, Drawings account is also a personal account.

Personal account can be further classified into three categories:

a) **Natural Personal Account:** The term 'natural persons' means persons who are creations of god. Therefore, these will include accounts in individual name, e.g., Anil's A/c, Sunil's A/c.

b) **Artificial Personal Accounts:** These accounts include accounts of corporate bodies or institutions, which are recognised as persons in business dealings, e.g., Bank A/c, University, School, Company, Firm etc.

c) **Representative Personal Account:** These are accounts which represent a certain person or a group of persons. Accounts such as wage outstanding account, prepaid insurance account, accrued interest account are considered as representative personal accounts, e.g., if rent is due to the landlord, an outstanding rent.

Personal Accounting Rules: Debit the receiver, Credit the giver i.e., Debit the account of the person who receives something and credit the account of the person who gives something.

E.g., if you purchase goods from Gopi, on credit, the two accounts involved are 'goods (purchase) account' and 'Gopi's account'. The latter account is a personal account. Since Gopi is the giver in this transaction, his account will be credited. Similarly, if cash is paid to Gopi, Gopi's account will be debited since he is the receiver. Thus, the account of a person is debited with any benefit that such person receives and is credited with any benefit that such person imparts.

2. **Impersonal Account:** Accounts which are not personal such as machinery, cash, rent etc. It can be further classified as (a) Real Account and (b) Nominal Account.

a) **Real Account:** These are accounts related to tangible and intangible assets or properties or possessions. Depending on their physical existence or otherwise, they are further classified as follows:

(i) **Tangible Real Account** – Assets that have physical existence and can be seen, and touched. e.g. Machinery A/c, Stock A/c, Cash A/c, Vehicle A/c, and the like.

(ii) **Intangible Real Account** – These represent possession of properties that have no physical existence but can be measured in terms of money and have value attached to them, e.g. Goodwill A/c, Trade mark A/c, Patents & Copy Rights A/c, Intellectual Property Rights A/c and the like.

Real Accounting Rules: Debit what comes in, Credit what goes out i.e., debit the account of the thing that comes in and credit the account of the thing that goes out, e.g., where furniture is purchased for cash, furniture account is debited while cash account is credited.

b) **Nominal Account:** These accounts are related to expenses or losses and incomes or gains e.g. Salary and Wages A/c, Rent of Rates A/c, Travelling Expenses A/c, Commission received A/c, Loss by fire A/c etc.

Nominal Accounting Rules: Debit expenses or losses, Credit Incomes and gains i.e., debit the account of expenses and losses and credit all incomes and gains, e.g., if you pay salary to your clerk, the two accounts are involved are the 'salary account' and 'cash account'. Salary account is a nominal account. Salary paid is an expense of the business and therefore, this account will be debited. Similarly, if interest is received, interest account will be credited, since interest is an income item.

Rules of Debit and Credit at a Glance

Types of Account	*Account to be Debited*	*Account to be Credited*
Personal A/c	Receiver	Giver
Real A/c	What comes in	What goes out
Nominal A/c	Expenses and loss	Income and gain

• **Illustration 1**: How will you classify the following into personal, real and nominal accounts?

(i) Investments

(ii) Freehold Premises

(iii) Accrued Interest

(iv) Punjab Agro Industries Corporation

(v) Janata Allied Mechanical Works

(vi) Salary Accounts

(vii) Loose Tools Accounts

(viii) Purchases Account

(ix) Indian Bank Ltd.

(x) Capital Account

(xi) Brokerage Account

(xii) Toll Tax Account

(xiii) Dividend Received Account

(xiv) Royalty Account

(xv) Sales Account

Solution:

Personal Account: (iii), (iv), (v), (x)

Real Account: (i), (ii), (vii), (viii), (xv).

Nominal Account: (vi), (ix), (xi), (xii), (xiii), (xiv)

• **Illustration 2:** State the names of the accounts to be debited or credited in the following transactions:

No.	Transactions	Name of Account Affected	Classification of Account	Applications of the Rules	Answers
1.	Sujit commenced business with cash	Sujit's capital A/c	Personal A/c	Credit the giver	Credit
		Cash A/c	Real A/c	Cash comes in, debit what comes in	Debit
2.	Purchased goods for cash	Purchase A/c	Real A/c	Goods come in	Debit
		Cash A/c	Real A/c	Cash goes out	Credit
3.	Sold goods on credit to Mr. Avinash	Avinash's A/c	Personal A/c	Avinash is receiver	Debit
		Cash A/c	Real A/c	Cash goes out	Credit
4.	Cash received from Mr. Avinash	Cash A/c	Real A/c	Cash comes in	Debit
		Avinash's A/c	Personal A/c	Avinash is giver	Credit
5.	Cash deposited into bank	Bank A/c	Personal A/c	Bank is receiver	Debit
		Cash A/c	Real A/c	Cash goes out	Credit

JOURNAL

Journal is a historical record of business transaction or events. The word journal comes from the French word "Jour" meaning "day". It is a book of original or prime entry. Journal is a primary book for recording the day to day transactions in a chronological order (i.e. date wise), in debit and credit form and in a systematic manner. The journal is a form of diary for business transactions. This is called the book of first entry since every transaction is recorded firstly in the journal. Journal is also known as "Prime entry" or "Original entry" book.

Advantages of Journal

The following are the advantages of a journal:

(i) **Chronological Record:** It records transactions as and when they happen. So, it is possible to get a detailed day-to-day information.

(ii) **Minimising the Possibility of Errors:** The nature of transaction and its effect on the financial position of the business is determined by recording and analysing into debit and credit aspect.

(iii) **Narration:** It means explanation of the recorded transactions.

(iv) **Helps to Finalise the Accounts:** Journal is the basis of ledger posting and the ultimate Trial Balance. The Trial balance helps to prepare the final accounts.

In connection with the Journal, the following points are to be remembered

○ For each transaction, the exact accounts should be debited and credited. For that, the two accounts involved must be identified to pass a proper journal entry.

○ Sometimes, a journal entry may have more than one debit or more than one credit. This type of journal entry is called compound journal entry. Regardless of how many debits or credits are contained in a compound journal entry, all the debits are entered before any credits are entered. The aggregate amount of debits should be equal to the aggregate amount of credits.

○ For a business, journal entries generally extend to several pages. Therefore, the total are cast at the end of each page, against the debit and credit columns, the following words are written in the particular column, which indicates, carried forward (of the amount on the next page) **"Total c/f"**.

○ The debits and credits totals of the page are then written on the next page in the amount columns; and opposite to that on the left, the following words are written in the particulars column to indicate brought forward (of the amount of the previous page) **"Total b/f"**. This process is repeated on every page and on the last page, **"Grand Total"** is casting.

Journal Entry

Journal entry means recording the business transactions in the journal. For each transaction, a separate entry is recorded. Before recording, the transaction is analysed to determine which account is to be debited and which account is to be credited.

SPECIMEN OF JOURNAL					
Date	*Particulars/Transactions*	*Voucher no.*	*L/f*	*Dr. Amt.*	*Cr. Amt.*
dd-mm-yy	Name of A/c to be debited Name of A/c to be credited (narration describing the transaction)	__________	Reference of page number of the A/c in ledger	________	________

Voucher

It is a written instrument that serves to confirm or witness (vouch) for some fact such as a transaction. A voucher is a document that shows goods have bought or services have been rendered, authorizes payment, and indicates the ledger account(s) in which these transactions have to be recorded.

Explanation of Journal

(i) **Date Column:** This column contains the date of the transaction.

(ii) **Particulars:** This column contains which account is to be debited and which account is to be credited. It is also supported by an explanation called narration.

(iii) **Voucher Number:** This Column contains the number written on the voucher of the respective transaction.

(iv) **Ledger Folio (L.F.):** This column contains the folio (i.e. page no.) of the ledger, where the transaction is posted.

(v) **Dr. Amount and Cr. Amount:** This column shows the financial value of each transaction. The amount is recorded in both the columns, since for every debit there is a corresponding and equal credit.

NOTE: All the columns are filled in at the time of entering the transaction except for the column of ledger folio. This is filled at the time of posting of the transaction to 'ledger'.

How to Journalise the Transactions

1. First find out the two accounts involved in a transaction.

2. Ascertain the types of those accounts and then decide by applying rules of Debit and Credit as to which account is to be debited and which account is to be credited.

3. The name of the account is to be debited is to be written first under "Particulars column. It is written close to the first margin line and the name of the account to be credited is to be proceeded by the word "To" and is to be written on the Second line.

4. The amount involved in the transactions is written under the "Dr" and "Cr" columns against the names of debit and credit accounts respectively.

5. A brief explanation of the entry is given in the bracket just below the entry. It is called "narration".

6. A line is drawn below each Journal Entry from first margin line to the second margin line to keep the entries of the transaction separate from one another.

7. **Ledger Folio (L.F.):** It means page number in the ledger. The page on which the particular account is opened in the "Ledger" is stated under "L.F." column to facilitate easy reference.

8. **Date:** The date of the transaction is written under the column "Date".

Example: As per voucher no. 31 of Roy Brothers, on 10.05.2018 goods of ₹ 50000 were purchased.

Cash was paid immediately. Ledger Folios of the Purchase A/c and Cash A/c are 5 and 17 respectively. Journal entry of the above transaction is given bellow:

In the books of Roy Brothers

Journal Entries

Date	Particulars	Voucher no.	L/f	Dr. Amt.	Cr. Amt.
10.05.2018	Purchase A/c Dr. To Cash A/c (Being goods purchased for Cash)	31	5 17	50,000	 50,000

- **Illustration 3 :** Let us illustrate the journal entries for the following transactions:

2018

1 April Mr. Vikas and Mrs. Vaibhavi who are husband and wife start consulting business by bringing in their personal cash of ₹ 5,00,000 and ₹ 2,50,000 respectively.

10 April Bought office furniture of ₹ 25,000 for cash. Bill No. - 2018/F/3

11 April Opened a current account with Punjab National Bank by depositing ₹ 1,00,000

15 April Paid office rent of ₹ 15,000 for the month by cheque to M/s Realtors Properties. Voucher No. 3

20 April Bought a motor car worth ₹ 4,50,000 from Millennium Motors by making a down payment of ₹ 50,000 by cheque and the balance by taking a loan from HDFC Bank. Voucher No. M/13/7 FUNDAME

25 April Vikas and Vaibhavi carried out a consulting assignment for Avon Pharmaceuticals and raise a bill for ₹ 10,00,000 as consultancy fees. Bill No. B13/4/1 raised. Avon Pharmaceuticals have immediately settled ₹ 2,50,000 by way of cheque and the balance will be paid after 30 days. The cheque received is deposited into Bank.

30 April Salary of one receptionist @ 5,000 per month and one officer @ 10,000 per month. The salary for the current month is payable to them.

Solution:

In the Books of Vikash & Vaibhavi

Journal Entries

Journal Folio-1

Date	Particulars	Voucher no.	L/f	Dr. Amt.	Cr. Amt.
01-04-2018	Cash A/c Dr. To Vikas's Capital A/c To Vaibhavi's Capital A/c **(Being capital brought in by the partners)**		1 2 3	7,50,000	 5,00,000 2,50,000
10-04-2018	Furniture A/c Dr. To Cash A/c **(Being furniture purchased in cash)**	2018/F/3	4 1	25,000	 25,000
11-04-2018	Punjab National Bank A/c Dr. To Cash A/c **(Being current account opened with Punjab National Bank by depositing cash)**		5 1	1,00,000	 1,00,000
15-04-2018	Rent A/c Dr. To Punjab National Bank A/c **(Being rent paid to Realtors Properties for the month)**	3	6 5	15,000	 15,000

Date	Particulars		Voucher no.	L/f	Dr. Amt.	Cr. Amt.
20-04-2018	Motor Car A/c	Dr.	M/13/7	7	4,50,000	
	To Punjab National Bank A/c			5		50,000
	To Loan from HDFC Bank A/c			8		4,00,000
	(Being car purchased from Millennium Motors by paying down payment and loan arrangement)					
25-04-2018	Punjab National Bank A/c	Dr.	B13/4/1	5	2,50,000	
	Avon Pharma A/c	Dr.		9	7,50,000	
	To Consultancy Fees A/c					10,00,000
	(Being amount received and revenue recognized for fees charged)					
30-04-2018	Salary A/c	Dr.		11	15,000	
	To Salary payable A/c			12		15,000
	(Being the entry to record Salary obligation for the month)					

Types of Journal Entry

Entries in a Journal are of two types:

1. **Simple Journal Entry:** Simple journal entry is an entry in which only two accounts are affected, i.e., one account is debited and another is credited with an equal amount.

2. **Compound Journal Entry:** Compound journal entry is an entry in which two or more Accounts are debited and one or more accounts are credited or vice versa.

NOTE: It should be noted that, in the compound journal entry discount received/allowed should always be written along with cash entry.

EXAMPLE: A debt of ₹ 5,000 due from Pragya (Debtor) has been discharged by receipt of ₹ 4,850 cash, ₹ 150 allowed as discount.

The transactions affect three accounts as follows:

(i) **Cash A/c**: Asset: Cash A/c (₹ 4,850) to be debited because cash, i.e., an asset. An Asset has increased when the account is debited.

(ii) **Discount Allowed**: Expense: Discount allowed A/c (₹ 150) to be debited because it is an expense or loss for business

(iii) **Pragya (Debtor)**: Asset A/c: Pragya (Debtor) (₹ 5,000) to be credited because it is an asset.

The entry for the transactions is a Compound Entry as follows:

Date	Particulars		L/f	Dr. Amt.	Cr. Amt.
	Cash A/c	Dr.		4,850	
	Discount allowed A/c	Dr		150	
	To Pragya's A/c				5,000
	(Being the amount from Pragya and allowed him discount)				

- **Illustration 4:** (Compound Journal Entry). Record the following transactions in a journal:

Date		Amount
Jan. 1	Paid to Pragya ₹ 9,500 in full settlement of his account of ₹ 10,000.	
Jan. 2	Received from Tanya ₹ 12,000 in cash and allowed discount	100
Jan. 3	Paid salaries	5,000
Jan. 3	Paid rent	3,000
Jan. 3	Paid wages	1,000
Jan. 5	Purchased goods of ₹ 20,000 out of which goods of ₹12,000 were on credit from Shyam Lal	

Solution:

In the Books of ....

Journal Entries

Date	Particulars		L/f	Dr. Amt.	Cr. Amt.
2019 Jan. 1	Pragya's A/c 　　To cash A/c 　　To discount received A/c **(Being the payment to Pragya in full settlement of his account)**	Dr.		10,000	 9,500 500
Jan. 2	Cash A/c Discount Allowed A/c 　　To Tanya A/c **(Being the receipt of money from Tanya and allowed him discount)**	Dr. Dr.		12,000 100	 12100
Jan. 3	Salaries A/c Rent A/c Wages A/c 　　To Cash A/c **(Being the payment of salaries, rent & wages)**	Dr. Dr. Dr.		5,000 3,000 1,000	 9,000
Jan. 5	Purchase A/c 　　To cash A/c 　　To Shyam lal's A/c **(Being goods purchased for cash ₹ 8,000 and on credit from Shyam Lal for ₹ 12,000)**	Dr.		20,000	 8,000 12,000

1. **Opening Entries**: The opening entry is an item which is passed in the Journal proper or General Ledger. The purpose of passing this entry is to record the opening balances of the accounts transferred from the previous year to the New Year. The accounts which are appearing on the assets side of balance sheet are debited in the opening entry while the accounts which are appearing in the liabilities side are credited.

At the end of each accounting period, the books of accounts need to be closed for preparation of final accounts. Also, in the beginning of the new accounting period, new books of accounts are to be opened. For this purpose, opening and closing entries need to be passed. These entries are passed in journal proper.

The entry can be given as:

All Asset A/cs　　　　　　　　Dr
　　To All Liabilities A/c
　　To Owners' Capital A/cs

- **Illustration 5 :** Consider the following balances in the Balance Sheet as on 31st March 2018. Pass the opening entry on 1st April 2019.

Subodh's Capital A/c	2,75,000
Loan from HDFC bank	4,25,000
Plant and machinery	3,30,000
Cash in hand	20,000
Balance at Citi bank	1,75,000
Trade Debtors	3,55,000
Closing stock	1,35,000
Trade Payables	2,95,000
Outstanding Expenses	40,000
Prepaid Insurance	20,000

Solution:

The opening entry will be as follows:

Plant and machinery A/c	Dr	3,30,000
Cash in hand A/c	Dr	20,000

Balance at Citi bank A/c	Dr	1,75,000	
Trade Debtors A/c	Dr	3,55,000	
Closing stock A/c	Dr	1,35,000	
Prepaid Insurance	Dr	20,000	
To Subodh's Capital A/c			2,75,000
To Loan from HDFC bank A/c			4,25,000
To Trade Payables A/c			2,95,000
To Outstanding Expenses A/c			40,000

2. **Closing Entries**: All the expenses and gains or income related nominal accounts must be closed at the end of the year. In order to close them, they are transferred to either Trading A/c or Profit and Loss A/c. Journal entries required for transferring them to such account is called a 'closing entry'.

   The Closing Entries are passed on the basis of trial balance for transferring the balances to Trading and profit and loss A/c. These entries are mainly for:

   a) For transferring purchases and direct expenses (goods related) to Trading A/c

Trading A/c	Dr
To Opening stock A/c	
To Purchases A/c	
To Factory expenses A/c	
To Freight & carriage inward A/c	

   b) For transferring sales and closing stocks

Sales A/c	Dr
Closing Stock A/c	Dr
To Trading A/c	

   c) For transferring gross profit or gross loss to P&L A/c

   For Gross Profit

Trading A/c	Dr
To P&L A/c	

   For Gross Loss

P&L A/c	Dr
To Trading A/c	

   d) For transferring expenses

P&L A/c	Dr
To Respective expense A/c	

   e) For transferring Incomes

Respective income A/cs	Dr
To P & L A/c	

   f) For transferring Net profit or Net loss

   For Net Profit:

P&L A/c	Dr
To Capital A/c	

   For Net Loss:

Capital A/c	Dr
To P & L A/c	

LEDGER

Ledger contains a classified summary of all transactions recorded in cash book and journal. All Personal, Real and Nominal Accounts are prepared into the ledger.

A Ledger may be defined as a "book or register which contains, in a summarised and classified form, a permanent record of all transactions". It is the most important book of accounts, since the trial balance is drawn from it and from the trial balance, finance statements are prepared. Hence, the ledger is called the principle book.

The Ledger Folio (L.F.) column in the Journal is used at the time when debits and credits are posted to the Ledger. The page number of the Ledger on which the posting has been done is mentioned in the L.F. Column of the Journal.

In the Book of ABC

Journal

Date	Particulars		L/f	Dr. Amt.	Cr. Amt.
	Salaries A/c	Dr.		10,000	
	To cash A/c				10,000

Specimen of Ledger

Dr.   **Cr.**

Date	Particulars	J/f	Amount	Date	Particulars	J/f	Amount
	To Cash A/c		10,000		By Salaries		10,000

Use of the Words "To" and "By"

It is customary to use words 'To' and 'By' while making posting in the Ledger. The word 'To' be used with the accounts which appear on the debit side of a Ledger Account.

For example, in the Salaries Account, instead of writing only "Cash" as shown above, the words "To Cash" will appear on the debit side of the account. Similarly, the word "By" is used with accounts which appear on the credit side of a Ledger Account. For example, in the above case, the words "By Salaries A/c" will appear on the credit side of the Cash Account instead of only "Salaries A/c". The words 'To' and 'By' do not have any specific meanings.

Relationship between Journal and Ledger

Journal and Ledger are the most useful books kept by a business entity. The points of distinction between the two are given below:

1. The journal is a book of original entry whereas the ledger is the main book of account.

2. In the journal business transactions are recorded as and when they occur i.e. date-wise. However, posting from the journal is done periodically, maybe weekly, fortnightly as per the convenience of the business.

3. The journal does not disclose the complete position of an account. On the other hand, the ledger indicates the position of each account debit wise or credit wise, as the case may be. In this way, the net position of each account is known immediately.

4. The record of transactions in the journal is in the form of journal entries whereas the record in the ledger is in the form of an account.

Utility of a Ledger

The main utilities of a ledger are summarised as under:

a) It provides complete information about all accounts in one book.

b) It enables the ascertainment of the main items of revenues and expenses

c) It enables the ascertainment of the value of assets and liabilities.

d) It facilitates the preparation of Final Accounts.

SUBSIDIARY BOOKS

When number of transactions is large, it is practically impossible to record all the transactions through one journal because of the following reasons:

a) The system of recording all transactions in a journal requires;

   i) Writing down of the name of the account involved as many times as the transactions occur; and

   ii) An individual posting of each account debited and credited and hence, involves the repetitive journalizing and posting labour.

b) Such a system does not provide the information on a prompt basis.

c) Such a system does not facilitate the installation of an internal check system since only one person can handle the journal.

d) The journal becomes bulky and voluminous.

Is the Cash Book Journal or Ledger?

- Cash Book is a book of original entry since transactions are recorded for the first time from the source documents.

- The cash book is ledger in the sense that it is designed in the form of a Cash Account and records cash receipts on the debit side and cash payments on the credit side.

- Thus, the cash Book is both a journal and a ledger.

CASH BOOK

A Cash Book is a special journal which is used for recording all cash receipts and all cash payments. Cash Book is a book of original entry since transactions are recorded for the first time from the source documents. The Cash Book is larger in the sense that it is designed in the form of a Cash Account and records cash receipts on the debit side and cash payments on the credit side. If a cash book is maintained, there is no need for preparing a cash account in the ledger.

Features

- Only cash transactions are recorded in the Cash Book.

- It performs the functions of both journal and the ledger at the same time.

- All cash receipts are recorded on the debit side and all cash payments are recorded on the credit side.

- The Cash Book, recording only cash transactions can never show a credit balance.

- **Illustration 6 :** Write up a Cash Book of Mr. Y for the month of April 2019, which serves as the only book of original entry.

Date	Particulars
April 2019	
1	Balance in hand ₹ 15,000
4	Sold goods on credit to Mrs. Pragya on credit ₹ 3,000
6	Sold goods for cash ₹ 10,000
8	Purchased goods on credit from Mrs. Tanya for ₹ 3,000
12	Paid to Mrs. Tanya ₹ 2,000 and received discount ₹ 200
15	Return goods to Mrs. Tanya ₹ 800
20	Goods returned by Mrs Pragya ₹ 300
25	Pragya settled his account for ₹ 2,500
26	Paid salary by cheque for ₹ 2,000
30	Received interest for ₹ 4,000

Solution:

In the books of Mr. Y Cash Book (as the only Book of Single Entry)

Date	Particulars	L/f	Amount	Date	Particulars	L/f	Amount
2019				2019			
April 1	To balance b/d		15,000	April 4	By Pragya's A/c (goods sold on credit)		3,000
4	To sales A/c (goods sold on Mrs. Pragya)		3,000	8	By purchase A/c (goods purchased on credit)		3,000
6	To sales A/c (goods sold for cash)		10,000	12	By Tanya's A/c By Tanya's A/c (Paid to Tanya & discount received)		2,000 200
8	To Tanya's A/c (goods purchased on credit)		3,000	15	By Tanya's A/c (goods returned)		800
12	To discount received A/c		200	20	By Return inwards A/c (goods returned by Mrs Pragya)		300
				April 30	By bal. C/d		21,900
			31,200				**31,200**
2019							
May 1	To Bal. B/d		21,900				

TYPES OF CASH BOOK

Cash Book can be of several kinds:

1. **Simple (Single column) Cash Book:** For recording cash transactions only.
2. **Two (Double) Column Cash Book:** For recording cash transactions involving gain or loss on account of discount.
3. **Three Column Cash Books:** For recording cash and bank transactions involving gain or loss on account of discount.
4. **Petty Cash Book:** For recording petty expenses.

Simple (Single Column) Cash Book

This cash book has one amount column on each side. All cash receipts are recorded on the receipt side and all cash payments on the payment side. In fact, this book is nothing but a Cash Account. Hence, there is no need to open this account in the ledger.

Format of Simple Cash Book

Date	Particulars	V.No.	J/f	Amount	Date	Particulars	V.No.	J/f	Amount
(1)	(2)	(3)	(4)	(5)	(1)	(2)	(3)	(4)	(5)

The purpose of five columns used on both sides of a single column cash book is briefly explained below:

a) **Date:** The date column of the cash book is used to record the year, month and actual date of each cash transaction. This column ensures the chronological record of each business transaction involving receipt or payment of cash.

b) **Description:** The description column is used to record the account titles to be debited or credited as a result of each cash transaction. A short explanation (also known as narration) of each cash transaction may also be written in this column. This column is sometime titled as "particulars".

c) **Voucher No:** Voucher is a document that supports a business transaction. This column is used to record the serial number of a receipt voucher or payment voucher.

d) **Posting Reference:** This column is used to write the page number of each ledger account named in the description column of the cash book.

e) **Amount:** The amount column of single column cash book is used to record the money value of each cash transaction.

Balancing a Single Column Cash Book

The single column cash book has only one money column which is totalled and balanced like a traditional T-account. At the end of each month or another appropriate period, the amount column of both sides are totalled. The difference between totals is written on the lighter side below all other entries. This difference is the closing cash balance for the current period and is usually termed as balance carried down (balance c/d). In next period, it becomes the opening cash balance and is usually termed as balance brought down (balance b/d).

Note: The debit side (receipt side) of a single column cash book is always heavier than the credit side (payment side) because we cannot pay more cash than we receive during a period.

Posting Entries from Single Column Cash Book to Ledger Accounts

All entries in the cash book are periodically posted to appropriate accounts in general ledger and relevant subsidiary ledgers. The posting procedure is given below:

1. The balance b/d and balance c/d (i.e., opening and closing balances) of the cash book are not posted.

2. The entries on the debit side (or receipt side) of the cash book are posted to the credit side of relevant accounts in the ledger.

3. The entries on the credit side (or payment side) of the cash book are posted to the debit side of relevant accounts in the ledger.

4. The page numbers of the ledger accounts (i.e., account numbers) to which the entries have been posted are written in the posting reference column of the single column cash book. It makes easy to locate an account in the ledger to which an entry has been posted.

Example: The Harper Company uses a single column cash book to record all cash transactions. It engaged in the following cash transactions during the month of September 2018.

- Sep.01: Cash in hand at start of the month ₹ 4,654.
- Sep.02: Paid salaries to employees for the last month ₹ 3,000.
- Sep.05: Cash received from S & Co. for a previous credit sale ₹ 2,720.
- Sep.06: Merchandise purchased for cash ₹ 1,400.
- Sep.07: Merchandise sold for cash ₹ 4,700.
- Sep.10: Office furniture purchased for cash ₹ 3,080.
- Sep.12: Stationery purchased for cash ₹ 170.
- Sep.15: Merchandise sold for cash ₹ 9,000.
- Sep.17: Cash paid to A & Co. for a previous credit purchase ₹ 1,780.
- Sep.20: Merchandise purchased for cash ₹ 2,460.

- Sep.21: Merchandise sold for cash ₹ 4,680.
- Sep.24: Cash received from S & Co. for a previous credit sale ₹ 2,400.
- Sep.28: Cash paid for office rent ₹ 1,600.
- Sep.30: Merchandise sold for cash ₹ 7,200

Required: Record the above transactions in a single column cash book (simple cash book) and post entries from the cash book to the relevant ledger accounts in general and subsidiary ledgers.

Solution:

Single Column Cash Book of Harper Company

Dr. (Receipt)				Cash Book		Cr. (Payments)			
Date	Description	VN	PR	Amount	Date	Description	VN	PR	Amount
2018					**2018**				
Sep.01	Balance b/d		—	4654	Sep.02	Salaries		415	3000
Sep.05	S & Co		410	2720	Sep.06	Purchase		420	1400
Sep.07	Sales		405	4700	Sep.10	Furniture		425	3080
Sep.15	Sales		405	9000	Sep.12	Stationery		430	170
Sep.21	Sales		405	4680	Sep.17	A & Co.		440	1780
Sep.24	S & Co		410	2400	Sep.20	Purchase		420	2460
Sep.30	Sales		405	7200	Sep.28	Rent		435	1600
					Sep.30	Balance c/d		—	21864
				35354					35354
Oct.01	Balance b/d			21864					

TWO (DOUBLE) COLUMN CASH BOOK

This Cash Book has two amount columns one for cash and another for discount on each side. It is customary in business to allow discount when payment is received from a customer promptly and before due date. It is equally so when payment is made to a creditor before due date. All cash receipts and discount allowed are recorded on the debit side and all cash payments and discount received are recorded on the credit side of Cash Book.

The posting from the cash columns is done in the same manner as it is done in Single Column Cash Book. Entries from discount column of the debit side of the Cash Book are posted on the credit side of every individual debtor's account to whom the business has allowed the discount. The total of the debit side of the discount column is shown on the debit side of the "Discount Allowed Account" by writing "To Sundries" in the particulars column. Entries from the discount column of the credit side of the Cash Book are posted on the debit side of every individual creditor's account by whom the discount is allowed to the business. The total of the credit side of the discount column is shown on the credit side of the "Discount Received Account" by writing "By Sundries" in the particulars column.

The cash column of the Double Column Cash Book is balanced exactly in the same manner as in case of the Single Column Cash Book. But, the discount columns are not balanced but merely totalled. These totals are posted to the respective Discount Allowed Account and Discount Received Account.

Format of Double Column Cash Book

Date	Particulars	J/f	Discount Allowed	Cash	Date	Particulars	J/f	Discount Allowed	Cash
(1)	(2)	(3)	(4)	(5)	(1)	(2)	(3)	(4)	(5)

- **Illustration 2**: From the following transactions, prepare the Two Column Cash Book and also post them in the Ledger.

Date		₹
2018		
Aug. 1	Cash in hand	25,500
Aug. 2	Received from Rakesh and	2,900
	Discount allowed to him	100
Aug. 5	Cash sales	6,000
Aug. 6	Purchased goods for cash	7,800
Aug. 8	Received from Neelam and	1,350
	Allowed her discount	50
Aug. 12	Paid to Ravinder and	3,400
	Received Discount	200
Aug. 20	Paid rent	1,000
Aug. 25	Interest received in cash	500
Aug. 26	Paid to Kamal and	1,760
	Received discount	40
Aug. 28	Machinery purchased	5,200
Aug. 30	Salaries paid	3,000

Solution :

Date	Particulars	J/f	Discount	Cash	Date	Particulars	J/f	Discount	Cash
2018 Aug.					2018 Aug.				
1	Cash in hand			25,500	6	By Purchase A/c			7,800
2	To Rakesh's A/c		100	2,900	12	By Ravinder's A/c		200	3,400
5	To Sales A/c			6,000	20	By Rent A/c			1,000
8	To Neelam's A/c		50	1,350	26	By Kamal's A/c		40	1,760
25	To Interest A/c			500	28	By Machinery A/c			5,200
					30	By Salaries A/c			3,000
					31	By Bal. C/d			14,090
			150	**36,250**				**240**	**36,250**
Sept 1	To bal. B/d			14,090					

TRIPLE COLUMN CASH BOOK

This type of Cash Book is an improvement over the Double Column Cash Book. In modern times, it is virtually impossible to imagine any business without having dealings with a bank. Most of the transactions relating to receipts and payments of money are made through cheques. So transactions through bank are also recorded in the cash book by adding one more column i.e. bank column on both sides of the cashbook. Therefore there are three columns on both sides of the cash book i.e. cash, bank and discount columns. That is why this type of cash book is known as Triple Column Cash Book.

Receipt side (Dr side) of the Triple Column Cash Book is used to record all receipts both in cash and by cheques as also to record the discount allowed to our debtors while receiving the payment. Cash receipts are entered in the cash column whereas amounts received by cheques are entered in the bank column and discount allowed in the discount column. Posting from the debit side of the cash book is made to the credit side of each account in the ledger—in case of personal accounts credit is to be given for cash or cheques received plus discount allowed.

Payment side (Cr. side) of the Cash Book is used to record all payments both in cash and through cheques as also to record the discount received or availed by us from our creditors while making payment to them. Cash payments are recorded in the cash column, payments through cheques are entered in the bank column and discount received in the discount column. Posting from the credit side of the cashbook is made on the debit side of respective accounts—in case of personal accounts debit is to be given for the total of the payments made and discount received.

After recording all the relevant transactions in the Cash Book, all the columns of the Cash Book are totalled. The difference in the cash columns is put on the credit side of Cash Book in the column by writing "By Balance c/d". The bank balance may have a debit balance or a credit balance. If the total of the debit side of the bank column is more than the total of the credit side of the bank column, it has a debit balance and if the total of the credit side is more than that of the debit side, then it has a credit balance (overdraft). However, the difference is put on the lesser side. There is no need to balance the discount columns. The discount columns of both the sides are totalled.

In the Triple Column Cash Book there will be some cross or contra entries i.e., transfer of money from cash to bank (amount deposited) and vice-versa (amount withdrawn from bank for office use). In all such cases both entries occur in the cash book and no ledger entry is required. This is indicated by a contra sign (C) in the folio column indicating there by that the double entry aspect of this transaction is complete and it requires no posting to the ledger.

- **Illustration 3:** Prepare a Triple Column Cash Book from the following particulars:

2019

Jan. 1. Cash in hand ₹ 50,000.

2. Paid into bank ₹ 10,000.

3. Bought goods from Hari for ₹ 200 for cash.

4. Bought goods for ₹ 2,000 paid cheque for them, discount allowed 1%

5. Sold goods to Mohan for cash ₹ 250.

6. Received a cheque from Shyam to whom goods were sold for ₹ 800. Discount allowed 12.5%

8. Purchased an old typewriter for ₹ 200. Spent ₹ 50 on its repairs.

9. Bank notified that Shyam's cheque has been returned dishonoured and debited to the account in respect of charges ₹ 10.

10. Received a money order for ₹ 25 from Hari.

11. Shyam settled his account by means of a cheque for ₹ 820, ₹ 20 being for interest charged.

12. Withdrew from bank ₹ 10,000.

18. Discounted a bill of exchange for ₹1,000 at 1% through bank.

20. Honoured our own acceptance by cheque ₹ 5,000.

22. Withdrew for personal use ₹ 1,000.

24. Paid trade expenses ₹ 2,000.

25. Withdrew from bank for private expenses ₹ 1,500.

26. Purchased machinery from Rajiv for ₹ 5,000 and paid him by means of a bank draft purchased for ₹ 5,005.

27. Issued cheque to Ram Saran for cash purchase of furniture ₹ 1,575.

28. Received a cheque for commission ₹ 500 from R. & Co. and deposited into bank.

29. Ramesh who owned us ₹ 500 became bankrupt and paid us 50 paisa in a rupee.

30. Received payment of a loan of ₹ 5,000 and deposited ₹ 3,000 out of it into bank.

31. Paid rent to landlord 'Mohan' by a cheque of ₹ 500.

31. Interest allowed by bank ₹ 30.

31. Half-yearly bank charges ₹

Solution :

Date	Particulars	J/f	Discount	Cash	Bank	Date	Particulars	J/f	Discount	Cash	Bank
2019						2019					
Jan 1	To Balance b/d			50,000		Jan 2	By Bank A/c	c		10,000	
Jan 2	To Cash A/c	c			10,000	Jan 3	By Purchases A/c			200	
Jan 5	To Sales A/c			250		Jan 4	By Purchases A/c		20		1,980
Jan 6	To Shyam's A/c		100		700	Jan 8	By Typewriter A/c			200	
Jan 10	To Hari's A/c			25		Jan 8	By Typewriter A/c			50	
Jan 11	To Shyam's A/c				800	Jan 9	By Shyam's A/c				700
Jan 11	To Interest A/c				20	Jan 9	By Bank charges A/c				10
Jan12	To Bank A/c	c		10,000		Jan 12	By Cash A/c	c			10,000
Jan 18	To B/R A/c		10		990	Jan 20	By B/P A/c				5,000
Jan 28	To Commission A/c				500	Jan 22	By Drawings A/c			1,000	
Jan 29	To Ramesh's A/c			250		Jan 24	By Trade Exp. A/c			2,000	
Jan 30	To Loans A/c			2,000	3,000	Jan 25	By Drawings A/c				1,500
Jan 31	To Interest A/c				30	Jan 26	By Machinery A/c				5,000
						Jan 26	By Bank charges A/c				5
						Jan 27	By Furniture A/c				1,575
						Jan 29	By Ramesh A/c			250	
						Jan 29	By Bad debts A/c			250	
						Jan 31	By Rent A/c				500
						Jan 31	By Bank charges A/c				55
Jan 31	To Balance c/d (Bank overdraft)				10,285	Jan 31	By Balance c/d		90	48,575	
			110	62,525	26,325				110	62,525	26,325

PETTY CASH BOOK

In every business organisation, there are a number of payments which involve small amounts e.g. payments for postage, telegrams, carriage, etc. If all these transactions are recorded in the Cash Book, it will increase the head cashier's work manifold and it will make the Cash Book unnecessarily bulky and uneasy. Normally, one person is handed over a small amount to meet the petty expenses of a given period (say, week, fortnight or month) and is authorised to make such payments and to record them in a separate Cash Book. Such person, amount and Cash Books are called as "Petty Cashier", 'Imprest' and 'Petty Cash Book' respectively.

Types of Petty Cash Book

1. Simple Petty Cash Book
2. Analytically Petty Cash Book

1. **Simple Petty Cash Book:** Simple petty cash book means this book is similar to single cash book where only one amount column is maintained in each side of such book. Amount received from head cashier is entered on the debit side of cash book and all petty payment are made by cashier are recorded in credit side. At last, the balance amount is found amount is found out.

2. **Analytically Petty Cash Book:** Under this system separate column is provided for each heading of petty expenses in credit side of cash book. The debit sides of petty cash book contain only one column for the cash received from the cashier. When there is large number of transactions, only most common petty expenses are assembled in the sundry expenses or miscellaneous expenses column.

Imprest System of Petty Cash Book

The Petty Cash Book may or may not be maintained on 'Imprest System'. Under both the systems (i.e. Imprest and Non-imprest), the petty cashier submits the Petty Cash Book to the Head Cashier who examines the Petty Cash Book. Under the Imprest system, the Head Cashier makes the reimbursement of the amount spent by the Petty Cashier but under Non-imprest system, the Head Cashier may handover the Cash to the Petty Cashier equal to/more than/less than the amount spent. Usually, the Petty Cash Book is maintained on the basis of imprest system.

Advantage of the Imprest System

The system of petty cash payments along with the imprest system offers the following advantages:

1) The money in the hands of the petty cashier is limited to the imprest amount.

2) As the periodical reimbursements are the actual expenses paid and not mere advances on account only, they are as such brought prominently to the notice of Chief Cashier.
3) The Chief Cashier, by handing over a fixed sum, is relieved of the cumbersome work of petty disbursements.
4) The main cash book is not unnecessarily clogged with the large number of small items. Even in the ledger, only the totals are posted.
5) At all time, the amount of cash in hand plus expenses not reimbursed must equal the imprest amount, thus, facilitating a simple check.
6) The maximum liability of the petty cashier can never exceed the imprest amount.
7) The regular check of the petty cash book creates a sense of responsibility in the petty cashier.

All the heads of expenses are totaled periodically and such periodic totals are individually posted to the debit side of the concern edledger accounts in the ledger by writing 'To Petty Cash A/c' in the particulars column. The Petty Cash Account in the ledger is credited with the total expenditure incurred during the period by writing 'By Sundriesas per Petty Cash Book' in the particulars column. The ledger folio number is written under every total amount of expense to indicate that the entry has been posted in the ledger. In the folio column of the ledger account, the page number of the petty cash book is written.

- **Illustration 4:** From the following particulars, prepare Petty Cash Book on imprest system of K.P. Singh & Co. for the month of January, 2019.

2019		
1	Opening Balance (on imprest system)	100
2	Paid for stamps	12
3	Paid cleaner's wages	15
4	Paid for fare	16
5	Paid for office tea	15
6	Paid to proprietor for personal use	10
7	Paid for advertisement	30
8	Drew imprest from ahead cashier	
9	Paid for cartage	10
10	Paid for travelling expenses	25
11	Paid for telegram sent	15
12	Paid for entertainment to travelling salesmen	20
13	Advance to peon	10
14	Paid for printing bill	5
15	Paid for stationery	3
16	Drew imprest from head cashier	

Solution:

Date	Particulars	Cash book folio	Total	Date	Particulars	V. No.	Post-age& tele-gram	Conveyance & traveling	Staff Welfare Enterta inment	Cart-age	Print-ing & Statio-nery	Misc. Item	total
2019				2019									
Jan 1	To bal. b/d		100	Jan 2	Stamps		12						12
				Jan 3	Cleaner's wages							15	15
				Jan 4	Fare			16					16
				Jan 5	Office tea				15				15
				Jan 6	Proprietor							10	10
				Jan 7	Advertis.							30	30
				Jan 7	Bal. c/d								2
			100				12	16	15			55	100
Jan 8	To bal. b/d		?	Jan 9	Cartage					10			10
Jan 8	To cash from head cashier		98	Jan 10	Travelling			25					25
				Jan 11	Telegram		15						15
				Jan 12	Entertain.				20				20
				Jan 13	Adv. to peon							10	10
				Jan 14	Printing						5		5
				Jan 15	Stationery						3		3
				Jan 15	Bal. c/d								12
			100				15	25	20	10	8	10	100
Jan 16	To bal. b/d		12										
Jan 16	To cash from head cashier		88										

Purchase Book

The purchase book records the transactions related to credit purchase of goods only. It follows that any cash purchase or purchase of things other than goods is not recorded in the purchase daybook. Periodically, the totals of Purchase book are posted to Purchase account in the ledger. The specimen Purchase book is given below:

In the Books of ABC
Purchase Book

Date	Name of the Suppliers and details of Goods purchased	Invoice No.	L. F.	Details	Amount (₹)

Sales Book

The sales book records transaction of credit sale of goods to customers. Sale of other things, even on credit, will not be entered in the sales day book but will be entered in Journal Proper. If goods are sold for cash, it will be entered in cash book. Total of sales book is periodically posted to sales account in the ledger. The specimen of a salesbook is given below:

In the Books of ABC
Sales Book

Date	Particulars	Invoice No. /reference	L. F.	Details	Amount (₹)

TEST YOURSELF

1. Under Double entry system, accounts are classified in:
   (a) Two types
   (b) Three types
   (c) Four types
   (d) None of the above

2. The language of accounting is:
   (a) Money
   (b) Transactions
   (c) Business
   (d) None of these

3. Credit balance in the bank column of cash book indicates:
   (a) Deposit
   (b) Overdraft
   (c) Both (a) & (b)
   (d) Neither (a) & ((b)

4. The book, which contains all accounts permanently, is called:
   (a) Journal
   (b) Ledger
   (c) Trial balance
   (d) Balance sheet

5. Which of the following entry is not written in the journal?
   (a) Purchase book
   (b) Creditor a/c
   (c) Debtor a/c
   (d) Capital a/c

6. Transaction is first recorded in the______ and they are posted to the______.
   (a) Ledger, journal
   (b) Journal, ledger
   (c) Any of the above
   (d) None of these

7. Following is known as the book of prime entry:
    (a) Journal   (b) Cash book
    (c) Subsidiary book   (d) All

8. Cash book records___________.
    (a) All cash receipt
    (b) All cash payment
    (c) All cash receipt & payments
    (d) All type of transactions

9. Which is not type of petty cash book are _______?
    (a) Simple petty cash book
    (b) Columnar petty cash book
    (c) Two columnar petty cash book
    (d) None of these

10. Consignee's account is a:
    (a) Real a/c
    (b) Personal a/c
    (c) Representative personal a/c
    (d) Nominal a/c

11. Debit means:
    (a) an increase in asset
    (b) an increase in liability
    (c) an increase in the proprietor's equity
    (d) a decrease in asset

12. When an entry is made in a journal:
    (a) accounts to be debited are listed first
    (b) accounts to be credited are listed first
    (c) accounts may be listed in any order
    (d) accounts may be listed in chronological order

13. A compound journal entry:
    (a) does not require narrations
    (b) generally, extends to several pages
    (c) has equal debits and credits
    (d) none of these

14. Which of the following accounts will be credited on giving cash donations?
    (a) Cash account   (b) Donation account
    (c) Purchase account   (d) None of the above

15. A ledger is called a book of:
    (a) Primary entry   (b) Secondary entry
    (c) Final entry   (d) None of the above

16. Nominal accounts relate to _______.
    (i) incomes (ii) expenses (iii) assets (iv) liabilities
    (a) (i) to (iv) all   (b) (i) and (ii) only
    (c) (ii) and (iii) only   (d) (i) and (iii) only

17. The journal entries are posted in the ledger _______.
    (a) In order of their category
    (b) In order of their dates
    (c) In order of their importance
    (d) As per discretion of the firm

18. Which of the following are not properly matched in terms of classification of accounts?
    (a) Machinery–real account
    (b) Ramesh (buyer of goods from the firm on credit)-personal account
    (c) Bank account–real account
    (d) Salary paid–nominal account

19. In a three-column cash book ...... does not exist.
    (a) Cash column   (b) Bank column
    (c) Petty cash column   (d) Discount column

20. In a business firm, the chief cashier hands over some cash to the petty cashier who submits the account of petty cash after a fixed time interval. This system is called (most appropriate):
    (a) Petty cash system
    (b) Petty cash book system
    (c) Imprest system of petty cash book
    (d) Advance system of petty cash book

ANSWER

1	2	3	4	5	6	7	8	9	10
(a)	(a)	(b)	(b)	(a)	(b)	(d)	(c)	(c)	(c)

11	12	13	14	15	16	17	18	19	20
(a)	(a)	(c)	(a)	(b)	(b)	(b)	(c)	(c)	(c)

BANK RECONCILIATION STATEMENT

INTRODUCTION

Bank reconciliation statement is a report which compares the bank balance as per company's accounting records with the balance stated in the bank statement. The statement outlines the deposits, withdrawals and other activity affecting a bank account for a specific period. A bank reconciliation statement is a useful financial internal control tool used to thwart fraud.

RECORDING TRANSACTION IN CASH BOOK

Businesses maintain cash book to record both the cash as well as bank transactions. A cashbook has a cash column which shows cash available with the business and a bank column which shows cash at bank.

In the cash book of a trader, a bank column is provided on both sides. Bank account is a personal account. When, a cheque is received and deposited in the bank, the trader debits his bank account by applying the principle of personal account, debit the receiver. The format of the cash book becomes as under:

Dr.							Cr.
Date	**Particulars**	**Cash**	**Bank**	**Date**	**Particulars**	**Cash**	**Bank**
01/12/18	To opening balance	40000	60000				
02/12/18	To cash deposit		20000	02/12/18	By deposit at bank	20000	
				03/12/18	By salary cheque		25000
04/12/18	To deposit of cheque from A		10000				

The entries, mentioned in the above illustration, represent:

1. Opening cash balance ₹ 40000 as on 01/12/18
2. Opening bank balance ₹ 60000 as on 01/12/18
3. Deposit of cash of ₹ 20000 in the bank account on 02/12/18
4. Issue of cheque of ₹ 25000 for salary on 03/12/18
5. Deposit of cheque of ₹ 10000 received from A on 04/12/18

While the principle applied to the cash account is: Debit what comes in and credit what goes out, the principle applied to bank account in the cash book is: Debit the receiver credit the giver. Thus, when any cash or cheque is deposited in the bank account, it is posted as debit entry in the cash book and whenever cash is withdrawn or cheque is issued, the bank account is credited in the cash book.

TRANSACTION CONTAINED IN THE PASS BOOK/BANK STATEMENT

Bank also keeps an account for every customer in their books. All the deposits are recorded on credit side of customer's account and withdrawals are on the debit side of their account. An account statement is sent regularly to the customers by the bank. When an individual or a firm deposits any money into a bank or withdraws money by issuing a cheque from a bank, he/it records the transaction in the debit-side of the bank columns of the Cash Book for such deposits and credit side of the bank column of the Cash book for such withdrawals.

On the other hand, bank also records such transactions in its book i.e. credit such account for deposits and debit such account for any withdrawals. The Bank issues a book to the account holder after recording such transactions. The book which is prepared by the bank for account holder is known as Pass Book. In case of Current Account, the bank issues Statements and not a Pass Book. The statement is known as Bank Statement.

A Specimen of a Bank Statement is presented below:

Bank of India
Current Account of ABC Enterprises
Bank Statement

Date	Particulars	Debit	Credit	Balance
01/12/18	B/F			60000
02/12/18	Cash deposit		20000	80000
05/12/18	Salary Cheque paid	25000		55000
06/12/18	By clearing		10000	65000

In the above statement, it is noted that all transactions related to the bank, in our cash book are also reflected in the bank statement, but the date of the some transactions related to cheques are different due to realisation or presentation of cheque in clearing. So, there is a direct correlation between our cash book and the passbook. If we deposit ₹ 20000 in the bank, we debit the bank column of our cash book. But, for the bank we become a creditor and accounting entries posted by them are –Dr Cash A/c ₹ 20000, Cr ABC ₹ 20000. So, in the passbook, this amount of ₹ 20000, deposited by us, will be reflected as a credit entry. Thus, the cash book and the passbook can be called the mirror image of each other.

DEFINITION OF BANK RECONCILIATION STATEMENT

A statement which is prepared to reconcile the causes of difference between Bank Balance as per Cash Book and Bank Balance as per Pass Book/ Bank Statement is known as a Bank Reconciliation Statement.

In other way, we can say that a bank reconciliation statement is a summary of banking and business activity that reconciles an entity's bank account with its financial records.

Features or Characteristics of Bank Reconciliation Statement

From the above, the following features of the statement emerge:
a) It is merely a statement not an account.
b) This is a periodical statement.
c) It can be prepared at any time during the financial year, as and when it is required.
d) It is prepared on a particular day or this statement is valid for the day it is prepared.
e) The preparation of bank reconciliation statement is not a part of the double entry book-keeping.
f) Since it is prepared on a particular date, it is written as Bank Reconciliation Statement as at/as on _____.
g) The causes which are responsible for the disagreement of the two balances can easily be found out.

Need of Bank Reconciliation Statement
a) It helps to understand the actual Bank balance.
b) It helps to identify the mistakes in the Cash Book and the Pass Book.

c) It helps to detect and prevent frauds and errors in recording the Banking transactions.

d) It helps to incorporate certain expenditures/income debited/credited by Bank in the books of accounts.

CAUSES FOR DIFFERENCES BETWEEN CASH BOOK AND PASS BOOK

The differences are basically of two types:

(A) Items appear in Cash Book but not appearing in Pass Book and

(B) Items appear in Pass Book but not appearing in the Cash Book

Let us understand these reasons:

(A) Items not appearing in Bank Pass Book: It can be classified into four parts.

(1) Cheques issued by business entity not debited by the Bank: This may be because they might not have been banked by the payee or it may still be under clearance. The entry in Cash Book will be made immediately when the cheque is issued thereby reducing the Bank balance in the books of entity's books of A/cs. Here, Bank balance as per Cash Book will be less, but as per Bank Pass Book it will be more. This is also termed as unpresented cheques.

(2) Cheques deposited but not credited by the Bank: The business entity may receive cheques or draft which is deposited into the Bank for collecting the payment. Again entry in Cash Book will be instant thereby increasing the balance. Here, Bank balance as per Cash Book will be more than the balance as per Bank passbook. This is also called as outstanding cheques.

(3) Errors: The Bank may by mistake miss out entering the debit or credit which results in the difference.

(4) Standing Instructions: The entity may give standing instruction to the Bank for certain regular payments like loan repayment instalment, transfer of funds etc. This may get entered in the Cash Book immediately, but Pass Book entry may be delayed.

(B) Items not appearing in the Cash Book: It can also be classified into four parts.

(1) Bank interest, Bank charges etc.: The Bank will charge interest on overdraft or also charges for services, issue of demand draft, pay orders etc. Here, being the source of transaction, the Bank will record in the Pass Book immediately and send the debit advice slips to the business entity. The entry in the Cash Book may be delayed. Similarly the Bank could credit interest on fixed deposits, which may get entered in business books at a later date.

(2) Direct Deposits in Bank Account: Sometimes customers or others may directly deposit an amount in the Bank for goods or services rendered. The Bank will enter it immediately, but entry in Cash Book will appear later.

(3) Bills for Collection: The Business Entity may send bills of exchange for collection. The Bank will collect the payment and credit the same in the passbook. The entry in Cash Book will be made only after receipt of information from the Bank.

(4) Errors: The records may be missed out by the book-keeper of the Business Entity.

PREPARING RECONCILIATION STATEMENT

It is generally experienced that when a comparison is made between the bank balance as shown in the firm's cash book, the two balances do not tally. Hence, we have to first ascertain the causes of difference thereof and then reflect them in a statement called Bank Reconciliation Statement to reconcile (tally) the two balances. In order to prepare a bank reconciliation statement, we need to have a bank balance as per the cash book and a bank statement as on a particular day along with details of both the books. If the two balances differ, the entries in both the books are compared and the items on account of which the difference has arisen are ascertained with the respective amounts involved so that the bank reconciliation statement may be prepared.

Proforma of Bank Reconciliation Statement

	Particulars	Amount (₹)
Add	Balance as per cash book	—
	Add: Cheques issued but not presented	—
	Interest credited by the bank	—
Less	Cheques deposited but not credited by the bank	—
	Bank charges not recorded in the cash book	—
	Balance as per the passbook	**XXXXX**

It can also be prepared with two amount columns one showing additions (+ column) and another showing deductions (-column). For convenience, we usually adopt this treatment.

Proforma of Bank Reconciliation Statement (table form)

	Particulars	Amount Rs. (+)	Amount Rs. (−)
	Balance as per cash book	____	
	Cheques issued but not presented '	____	
	Interest credited by the bank	____	
	Cheque deposited but not credited by the bank		____
	Bank charges not recorded in the cash book		____
	Balance as per the passbook		**XXXXX**

Steps in Preparing Bank Reconciliation Statement

One has to have a systematic approach towards preparation of the reconciliation. To avoid a lengthy reconciliation, one must ensure that the entries in the Cash Book are absolutely online. One also must obtain the Bank statements at regular intervals. Once this checking is done, Bank reconciliation could be done by following these steps:

a) Identify the balances and the character thereof. Remember, a debit balance in Cash Book means asset where as a credit balance means a Bank overdraft. In Bank passbook, it's reverse. A debit balance in Pass Book means overdraft and a credit balance is a favourable balance. This must be carefully understood.

b) Based on the above, start with the balance (or overdraft) as per one book and arrive at the balance (or overdraft) as per the other book. The items of differences will be added to or deducted from the balance (or overdraft) with which the reconciliation is started.

c) The end result should be the balance (or overdraft) as per the other book e.g. if you start with balance as per Cash Book, then after adding or deducting items of differences, you should arrive at the balance (or overdraft) as per the Pass Book.

d) One has to make sure that all the items of differences from Cash Book as well as Bank book are taken into account in the reconciliation statement.

e) Whether the items of differences should be added or deducted will depend on the sequence you follow. This is shown in the following table:

When Reconciliation is Started with	Bal. as per CB	OD as per CB	Bal. as per PB	OD as per PB
Cheques deposited in Bank, but not cleared	Less	Add	Add	Less
Cheques issued, but not presented in Bank	Add	Less	Less	Add
Bank charges debited in PB only	Less	Add	Add	Less
Interest debited in PB only	Less	Add	Add	Less
Payments by Bank debited in PB only	Less	Add	Add	Less
Direct payment by customer in PB only	Add	Less	Less	Add
Bills discounted & dishonoured in PB only	Less	Add	Add	Less
Cheques deposited, dishonoured in PB only	Less	Add	Add	Less
Interest, Dividend, Commission collected by Bank not recorded in the Cash Book	Add	Less	Less	Add
Overcasting of payment side of Cash Book or Under casting of Receipt side of Cash Book	Add	Less	Less	Add
Undercasting of Payment side of Cash Book or overcasting of Receipts side of Cash Book	Less	Add	Add	Less

- **Illustration:** From the following information ascertain the balance that would appear in the bank pass book of A on 31st March, 2018:
  - i. Bank overdraft as per cash book on 31st March, 2018 ₹ 63,400.
  - ii. Interest on overdraft for 6 months ended 31st March, 2018, ₹1,600 entered in the pass book.
  - iii. Bank charges of ₹ 300 for the above period are debited in the pass book.
  - iv. Cheques issued but not cashed prior to 31st March, 2018, amounted to ₹ 11,680.
  - v. Cheques paid into the bank but not cleared before 31st March, 2018, were for ₹ 21,700.
  - vi. Interest on investments collected by the bank and credited in the pass book, ₹ 12,000.

Solution:

Bank Reconciliation Statement as on 31st March, 2018

Particulars	Amount Details	Amount
Overdraft as per cash Book (Cr.)		63,400
Add: Interest debited in the passbook but not yet entered in the cash book	1,600	
Bank charges debited in the pass book but not yet entered in the cash book	300	23,600
Cheques paid in but not yet credited by the bank	21,700	
		87,000
Less: Cheques issued but not yet presented	11,680	
Interest collected and credited by the bank but not yet entered in the cash book	12,000	23,600
Overdraft as per pass book (Dr.)		63,320

- **Illustration:** Bank column of the cash book showed a debit balance of ₹ 49,000 on 31st May, 2018. Bank statement or pass book showed balance of ₹ 37,400. Entries in the cash book and pass book were compared and following differences were noticed:
  - i) Cheques of Shyam ₹ 9,000 and of Mohan ₹ 15,000 were deposited but were not collected up to 31st May, 2018.
  - ii) Ramesh, a debtor, deposited a cheque of ₹ 8,000 directly into the bank.
  - iii) Bank allowed an interest of ₹ 500
  - iv) Cheque for ₹ 10,000 issued to Radhey Shyam was not presented for payment.
  - v) Bank debited the account by ₹ 6,000, being insurance premium paid as per standing instruction.
  - vi) Bank debited the account by ₹ 100, being bank charges.

You are required to prepare Bank Reconciliation Statement as on 31st May, 2018.

Solution:

Bank Reconciliation Statement as on 31st May, 2018

Particulars		Amount Details	Amount
Balance as per Cash Book (Dr.)			49,000
Add: Cheques directly deposited by Ramesh		8,000	
Interest allowed by Bank		500	
Cheques issued but not presented for payment		10,000	18,500
			67,500
Less: Cheques deposited but not yet cleared:			
Shyam	9,000		
Mohan	15,000	24,000	
Insurance Premium Paid by the bank		6,000	
Bank Charges debited		100	30,100
Balance as per Pass Book (Cr.)			37,400

How to Prepare a Bank Reconciliation Statement when Extracts of the Cash Book and Pass Book are given:

When the extracts of the cash book and pass book are given, the following points should be noted:

a) Find out the period for which both the abstracts are given.

b) Compare the cash book debit side with the pass book credit side and the cash book credit side with the pass book debit side.

c) When the period for which both the abstracts are given is common, i.e. the cash book abstract relates to January and the pass book abstract is also given for January, take into account only uncommon entries.

d) When the period for which both the abstracts are given is uncommon, i.e. the cash book relates to January but the pass book relates to February, take into account only common entries.

e) Where the period is same, uncommon entries will appear in the reconciliation statement.

f) When the period is different, common entries will appear in the reconciliation statement.

- **ILLUSTRTION:** From the following entries in the bank column of cash book of Mr. Niraj, and corresponding bank pass book, prepare Bank Reconciliation Statement as on 31st March, 2018.

Cash Book

Mar. 2018	Particulars	Amount	Mar. 2018	Particulars	Amount
1	To bal. b/f	34,000	7	By Drawings	15,000
3	To Ravi & Sons	5,000	8	By Salaries	22,000
13	To Jerbai	40,000	15	By Akash & co.	30,000
18	To Tanya & Co.	12,000	28	By Vikash Bros.	15,050
28	To Pragya & Co.	22,000	29	By Raj & Sons	8,000
29	To Sheetal & Co.	57,000	30	By Shivam Radios	4,000
31	To Abhilasha	34,250	31	By Prince	16,000
			31	By bal. c/f	**94,200**
		2,04,250			**2,04,250**

Bank Pass Book

(Mr. Niraj account with "Mohan" Bank)

Apr. 2018	Particulars	Amount	Apr. 2018	Particulars	Amount
1	To bal. (overdraft)	7,500	2	By Dividend	5,000
2	To Raj & Sons	8,000	2	By Pragya & Co.	22,000
4	To Shivam Radios	4,000	3	By Anu	2,000
8	To Salary	23,000	3	By Sheetal & Co.	57,000
10	To Drawings	5,000	5	By Abhilasha	34,250
10	To Abhilasha (cheque dishonoured)	34,250	10	By Tanu	1,700

Solution:

Bank Reconciliation Statement as on 31st March, 2018

Closing balance in Bank Statement	₹ –(7,500)
Adjustment to the balance in the Bank Statement	
a. Add: Cheques deposited but not yet credited	₹ 1,13,250
b. Subtract: Cheques issued but not presented to the Bank for payment	₹ 12,000
Adjusted balance in the Bank Statement	₹ 94,200 **(A)**

Balance as per Cash Book	₹ 94,200
Adjusted made to Cash Book	
a. Add or subtract: clerical errors	NIL
b. Add: credit entries shown in the Bank Statement but not appearing in Cash Book	NIL
c. Subtract: Debit entries shown in the Bank Statement but not appearing in Cash Book	NIL
Adjusted (corrected) Cash Book balance	₹ 94,200 **(B)**

Preparation of Bank Reconciliation Statement with Adjusted Cash Book

When we look at the various items that normally cause the difference between the passbook balance and the cash book balance, we find a number of items, which appear only in the passbook. Why not first record such items in the cash book to work out the adjusted balance (also known as amended balance)of the cash book and then prepare the bank reconciliation statement. This shall reduce the number of items responsible for the difference and have the correct figure of balance at bank in the balance sheet. In fact, this is exactly what is done in practice whereby only those items which cause the difference on account of the time gap in recording appear in bank reconciliation statement. These are as :

(i) cheques issued but not yet presented,

(ii) cheques deposited but not yet collected, and

(iii) due to an error in the passbook.

The Advantages of Bank Reconciliation Statements

Making mistakes with your accounting can lead to more than just embarrassing situations when cheque bounce or collection calls are made to companies that have already paid their bills. Performing bank reconciliations helps you spot fraud and reduce the risk of transactions that can cause late fees and penalties. The main advantages are :

1) **Error Detection:** A bank reconciliation helps you spot accounting errors common to any business. These mistakes can include addition and subtraction errors, double payments, lost cheques and missed payments. You might have recorded an invoice as paid in your general ledger, but a bank reconciliation might reveal you forgot to write the cheque. At times, your bank might make an error in your favour. You will be liable for returning that money, even if you've already spent it.

2) **Fee and Interest Tracking:** Each month, your bank adds any fees, penalties or interest payments it has applied to your account. You might have overdraft fees, go under your account balance requirement or earn interest on your checking account balance. If you order cheques or stop payment on a cheque, you might incur a fee, depending on the features of your account. A monthly bank reconciliation lets you add or subtract these amounts in your general ledger.

3) **Fraud Detection:** You might not be able to stop an employee from stealing your money once, but you might be able to prevent a second theft. Bank reconciliations help you spot ongoing fraudulent transactions. Have an independent party perform your reconciliations to prevent an accounting employee from continuing to falsify your general ledger and reconciliations.

4) **Receivables Tracking:** Payments due one month might not appear on your bank statement until the next month if you receive the payments near the end of the month. In other instances, you might accidentally leave one cheque off a deposit slip if you are filling out a slip with many entries. As you perform a review of last month's receivables, you might not see a payment that was made and contact a customer to ask where the payment is. Bank reconciliations confirm all of your receipts, helping you avoid awkward situations or identifying the entry for a receipt you didn't deposit.

5) **Transaction Status Updates:** Just because you've sent a payment doesn't mean the payee has cashed the cheque or even received it. A bank reconciliation statement might reveal that a cheque you wrote months ago still hasn't been cashed. Uncashed cheques can cause you to believe you have more money to spend than you do. Bank reconciliations allow you to spot cheques that haven't been paid and contact the payee to urge her to cash the cheque. In some instances, the payee will ask you to stop payment on—and reissue —a cheque that didn't arrive or was lost or stolen.

TEST YOURSELF

1. A Bank reconciliation statement is:
 (a) A part of Cash Book
 (b) A part of Pass Book
 (c) A statement prepared by the Bank
 (d) A statement prepared by a Customer

2. Bank reconciliation is a statement prepared to reconcile:
 (a) Trial balance
 (b) Cash book
 (c) Bank A/c
 (d) Cash as per cash book with bank balance as per bank pass book

3. Bank reconciliation statement is:
 (a) Ledger account
 (b) Part of the cash book
 (c) A statement showing difference between the balance in the pass book and cash book
 (d) A statement of position of balance of two books

4. From the books of Mr. Niraj it was observed that cheques amounting to ₹ 2,40,000 were deposited in the bank, out of which cheques worth ₹ 20,000 were dishonoured and cheques worth ₹ 40,000 are still in the process of collection. The treatment of this while preparing Bank Reconciliation Statement is:
 (a) Deduct ₹ 60,000 from overdraft balance as per pass book
 (b) Add ₹ 20,000 and deduct ₹ 40,000 from overdraft balance as per cash book
 (c) Deduct ₹ 60,000 from bank balance as per pass book
 (d) Add ₹ 60,000 from overdraft balance as per pass book

5. Benefits of preparing Bank Reconciliation Statement include:
 (i) It brings out any errors committed in preparation of Cash book/Bank Pass Book
 (ii) Highlights the delay in clearance of cheques deposited but not credited
 (iii) Help know actual bank balance
 (a) Only (i) and (ii) (b) Only (i) and (iii)
 (c) Only (ii) and (iii) (d) (i), (ii) and (iii)

6. Bank Reconciliation Statement is prepared by:
 (a) Creditor (b) Debtor
 (c) Customer (d) Bank

7. A Bank Reconciliation is prepared, so that the difference in the under noted balances is reconciled:
 (a) The difference in the balance in the cash column and bank column of the cash book
 (b) The difference in the balance in the pass book at the beginning and at the end
 (c) The difference in the cash book and pass book balances as on the date
 (d) The differences in the bank ledger and pass book

8. Bank Reconciliation Statement is:
 (a) Part of the cash book
 (b) A statement prepared to know the cause for the difference between balance as per bank column of cash book and passbook
 (c) A ledger account
 (d) All the above

9. Bank Reconciliation Statement is prepared with the help of:
 (a) Bank Passbook
 (b) Bank Passbook and bank column of cash book
 (c) Cash column of cash book
 (d) Bank Passbook and cash column of cash book

10. To know the cause for the difference between balance as per bank column of cash book and passbook, _______ is prepared.
 (a) Balance Sheet
 (b) Trial Balance
 (c) Bank Reconciliation Statement
 (d) All the above

11. A Bank Passbook is a copy of:
 (a) A customer's A/c in the bank's book
 (b) Bank column of cash book
 (c) Cash column of cash book
 (d) Copy of receipts and payments

12. As per bank pass book there is a bank overdraft of ₹ 65,000, a cheque is issued for ₹ 30,000 but it has not been presented. What shall be the the balance as per Cash Book?
 (a) ₹ 35,000 (b) ₹ 95,000
 (c) ₹ 25,000 (d) ₹ 85,000

13. A firm had deposited with a bank ₹ 30,000 cash but bank credited this amount to another account. A cheque issued by the firm for ₹ 25,000 has dishonoured due to the above reason. The balance as per cash book is ₹ 6,035. What is the balance as per pass book?
 (a) ₹ 1,135 (b) ₹ 5,035
 (c) ₹ 1,035 (d) ₹ 30,135

14. There is overdraft of ₹ 5,800 as per cash book of the customer and a cheque is deposited with the bank of ₹ 600 which is not credited by the bank. What will be the balance of pass book in the bank?
(a) ₹ 5,200
(b) ₹ 6,400
(c) ₹ 5,800
(d) ₹ 5,600

15. As per cash book there is overdraft of ₹ 520 so bank recovers interest of ₹ 50. What shall be the balance in the pass book?
(a) ₹ 520
(b) ₹ 50
(c) ₹ 570
(d) ₹ 470

16. As per the cash book there is an overdraft for ₹ 16,000 so bank charges interest of ₹ 800 and a commission of ₹ 250. What shall be the balance in the pass book?
(a) ₹ 16,800
(b) ₹ 16,250
(c) ₹ 17,050
(d) ₹ 16,550

17. In a current A/c there is a balance of ₹ 8,000 so bank recovers folio charges of ₹ 150. What shall be the balance in the pass book?
(a) ₹ 8,150
(b) ₹ 7,750
(c) ₹ 7,850
(d) none of these

18. Overdraft balance as per cash book of the customer is ₹ 5,500. Bank charges an interest of ₹ 60 and a cheque has been issued for ₹ 1,350 but it is not presented for payment. What will be the balance in the bank pass book?
(a) ₹ 4,210
(b) ₹ 4,150
(c) ₹ 4,090
(d) ₹ 5,440

19. Which is not the correct statement regarding Need of Bank Reconciliation Statement?
(a) It does not help to understand the actual Bank balance.
(b) It helps to identify the mistakes in the Cash Book and the Pass Book.
(c) It helps to detect and prevent frauds and errors in recording the Banking transactions.
(d) It helps to incorporate certain expenditures/income debited/credited by Bank in the books of accounts.

20. A statement which is prepared to reconcile the causes of difference between Bank Balance as per ________ and Bank Balance as per ________ /Bank Statement is known as a Bank Reconciliation Statement.
(a) Ledger, Trail balance
(b) Cash Book, Petty Cash Book
(c) Cash Book, Pass Book
(d) Trending A/c, Profit and Loss A/c

ANSWER

1	2	3	4	5	6	7	8	9	10
(d)	(d)	(c)	(a)	(d)	(c)	(c)	(b)	(b)	(c)

11	12	13	14	15	16	17	18	19	20
(a)	(b)	(c)	(b)	(c)	(c)	(c)	(a)	(a)	(c)

TRIAL BALANCE, RECTIFICATION OF ERRORS AND ADJUSTING & CLOSING ENTRIES

INTRODUCTION

Whenever you attempt a question in arithmetic you try to verify whether your answer is correct or not. If you attempt to solve any other type of problem you want to ensure that it has been correctly solved. For this you try to find out some ways or means. Similarly, an accountant also wants to be sure that the ledger accounts he/she has prepared are correct in respect of amount, side, balance, etc. To check the accuracy of posting in the ledger a statement is prepared. This statement is called Trial Balance.

MEANING OF A TRIAL BALANCE

A Trial Balance is a two-column schedule listing the titles and balances of all the accounts in the order in which they appear in the ledger. Trial balance may be defined as a statement or a list of all ledgers' account balances taken from various ledger books on a particular date to check the arithmetical accuracy.

According to the Dictionary for Accountants by Eric. L. Kohler, Trial Balance is defined as "a list or abstract of the balances or of total debits and total credits of the accounts in a ledger, the purpose being to determine the equality of posted debits and credits and to establish a basic summary for financial statements".

As this is merely a listing of balances, this will always be as on a particular date. Further it must be understood that Trial Balance does not form part of books of account, but it is a report prepared by extracting balances of accounts maintained in the books of accounts.

When this list with tallied debit and credit balances is drawn up, the arithmetical accuracy of basic entries, ledger posting and balancing is ensured. However, it does not guarantee that the entries are correct in all respect. Although it is supposed to be prepared at the end of accounting period, computerized accounting packages are capable of providing instant Trial Balance reports even on daily basis, as the transactions are recorded almost online.

FEATURES AND PURPOSE OF A TRIAL BALANCE

1) It is a list of debit and credit balances which are extracted from various ledger accounts.
2) Closing balances of the various ledger accounts are brought to this statement.
3) It is a tabular statement having separate sides/ columns for debit balances and credit balances.
4) The purpose is to establish arithmetical accuracy of the transactions recorded in the Books of Accounts.
5) It does not prove arithmetical accuracy which can be determined by audit.
6) It is not a part of the final statements.
7) Trial balance is not an account. It is only a statement.
8) It can be prepared at any date on which accounts are closed and balanced. But it is usually prepared at the end of the accounting year.
9) It is a link between Books of Accounts and the Profit and Loss Account and Balance sheet.

TYPES OF TRIAL BALANCE AND PREPARATION OF TRIAL BALANCE

Trial balances are of two types:

1. **Total Method or Gross Trial Balance**
2. **Balance Method or Net Trial Balance**

1. **Total Method or Gross Trial Balance:** Under this method the two sides of all the ledger accounts are totalled up. The total of the debit side is called the "debit total" and the total of the credit side is called the "credit total". Thereafter, a list of all the accounts is prepared in a separate sheet of paper with two "amount" columns on the right hand side. The first one for debit amounts and the second one for credit amounts. The total of debit side and credit side of each account is then placed on "debit amount" column and "credit amount" column respectively of the list. Finally the two columns are added separately to see whether they agree or not. This method is generally not followed in practice.

Advantages:

(a) It facilitates arithmetical accuracy of the accounts.

(b) Extraction of ledger balances is not required at the time of preparation of Trial Balance.

Disadvantages: Preparation of final accounts is not possible.

- **Illustration:** On 31st March 2018, the total debit and credit sides of various ledger accounts, receipt and payments sides of cash and bank columns of cash book of M/s V. C. Enterprises are as under:

Total Debit Side (₹)	Name of Account	Total Credit Side (₹)
5,000	M/s V. C. Enterprise's Capital	76000
10,000	Opening Stock	-
2,10,000	Purchases	2,000
2,000	Sales	3,05,000
18,000	Sales Return	-
27,000	Expenses	-
1,20,000	Customers	26,000
12,000	Suppliers	80,000
6,000	Cash	-
96,000	Uco Bank	17,000

A Trial Balance of M/s V. C. Enterprise's as on 31st March 2018

Sr. No.	Name of Account	Total Debit Side (₹)	Total Credit Side (₹)
1	M/s V. C. Enterprise's Capital	5,000	76000
2	Opening Stock	10,000	-
3	Purchases	2,10,000	2,000
4	Sales	2,000	3,05,000
5	Sales Return	18,000	-
6	Expenses	27,000	-
7	Customers	1,20,000	26,000
8	Suppliers	12,000	80,000
9	Cash	6,000	-
10	Uco Bank	96,000	17,000
	5,06,000	**5,06,000**	

2. **Balance Method or Net Trial Balance:** Under this method, all the ledger accounts are balanced. The balances may be either "debit-balance" or "credit balance".

   Advantages:

   (a) It helps in the easy preparation of final accounts.

   (b) It saves time and labour in constructing a Trial Balance.

   Disadvantages: Errors may remain undisclosed irrespective of the agreement of Trial Balance. Add up the debit and credit column and record the totals.

   Illustration: From the above illustration, the Net Trial Balance of M/s V. C. Enterprises as on 31st March 2018 can be drawn as under:

Net Trial Balance of M/s V. C. Enterprise's as on 31st March 2018

Sr. No.	Name of Account	Total Debit Side (₹)	Total Credit Side (₹)
1	M/s V. C. Enterprises Capital	-	71000
2	Opening Stock	10,000	-
3	Purchases	2,10,000	2,000
4	Sales	-	3,03,000
5	Sales Return	18,000	-
6	Expenses	27,000	-
7	Customers	94,000	
8	Suppliers	-	68,000
9	Cash	6,000	-
10	Uco Bank	79,000	-
		4,04,000	**4,04,000**

DISAGREEMENT OF A TRIAL BALANCE

The debit total of trial balance should be equal to credit total. Sometimes, they are not equal and it is assumed that there are some errors in books of account. Some of the reasons of errors may be as follows:

1. Trial balance will disagree if a transaction is posted in one side of an account and omitted to post it in another side of another account.

2. If wrong amount is posted in ledger accounts, the trial balance will not agree.

3. When an amount is posted wrong side, say in debit side instead of credit side, the trial balance will not agree.

4. Sometimes, a transaction may be posted twice in the ledger accounts. As a result, the total of a trial balance will not be equal.

5. Disagreement of a trial balance may be caused by the wrong totalling or balancing of ledger accounts.

6. While totalling the figure of subsidiary books there may arise some errors that will cause disagreement of trial balance.

7. Omission to post a ledger balance also causes the disagreement of a trial balance.

8. If there is error in totalling of trial balance, a trial balance will disagree.

9. Another cause of disagreement of a trial balance may be the error made in carrying forward the total from one page to another.

CLASSIFICATION OF ERRORS

The undetected errors of this type are generally divided into two groups:

1. Clerical Errors, and 2. Errors of Principles.

1. **Clerical Errors in Trial Balance:** The errors occurred due to the negligence of employees of accounts department are clerical errors. These errors are of four types:

   a) Errors of Omissions,

   b) Errors of Commission,

   c) Compensating Errors.

a) **Errors of Omissions:** If any transaction is completely or partially omitted from being recorded in journal and ledger, it is called the error of omission. For example, Goods purchased from Karan for ₹ 5,000. If this transaction is not accounted for, still the trial balance may agree. Because an equal sum of money has been omitted from records of debit and credit accounts.

b) **Errors of Commissions:** Recording incorrect figure in a journal and posting the same amount in the correct sides of ledger accounts is called errors of commission and this does not hamper the agreement of trial balance. For example, merchandise purchases for ₹ 1,100 but recorded ₹ 1,000 both in journal and ledger.

c) **Compensating Errors:** If a short or excess amount is posted on one side of an account and if the equal sum of short or excess amount is posted in another side of another account, it is called compensating errors. This is called so because the wrong posting of one account is compensated by the wrong posting of the same amount in another account and this does not hamper equalizing totals of trial balance. For example, Anil's account is debited to ₹ 400 wrongly instead of ₹ 500. On the other hand, Sunil's account is credited by ₹ 800 instead of ₹ 900. As a result ₹ 100 short has been written on both sides of accounts and thereby agreement of trial balance is not hampered. But actually, there lie mistakes in the accounts.

2. **Errors of Principle in Trial Balance:** If a revenue expense is recorded as a capital expenditure or vice-versa it is called the error of principle. For example, Installation cost of a new machine is accounted for debiting wage expense account instead of debiting machinery account.

LOCATION OF ERRORS

Some errors are disclosed by a Trial Balance while some errors are not. If the Trial Balance does not agree, it is an indication of some error or errors in the books of account. The checking usually begins from the Trial Balance itself.

The following steps should be taken to locate the errors and the step may be taken one after another until the errors that cause the difference are located:

1) Re-total the debit and credit columns of the Trial Balance. Find out the amount of difference by the two columns, divide by 2 and see if similar amount appears in the Trial Balance. If similar figure exists, see whether it is in the correct column. It is also possible that such a balance might have been recorded on the wrong side, causing a difference of double the amount.

2) See that Cash balance and Bank balance are properly listed in the Trial Balance.

3) If still the difference exists, divide the difference by 9. If the difference is evenly divisible by 9, the error is likely to occur from the transposition or trans-placement of figures. Disarrangement of figures is transposition and trans-placement means the digits of the numbers are moved to the left or right. If such a difference exists, search the figures, where such errors might have been made.

4) Confirm that the opening balances have been correctly brought forward in the current year, from the previous year.

5) Recheck the amounts listed in the Trial balance and confirm that all the ledger balances have been copied down.

6) Check the totals in the lists of Sundry Debtors and Sundry Creditors.

7) Re-compute the Account balances.

8) Check the casting and carry forward of all subsidiary books.

9) Verify the postings of individual items from the subsidiary books.

10) After making complete checking of journal, ledger and subsidiary books, if the errors cannot be located, then transfer the difference to a Suspense Account and when the mistake is found out the Suspense Account is closed.

RECTIFICATION OF ERRORS

From the point of view of rectification of errors, these can be divided into two groups:

a) Errors affecting one account only.

b) Errors affecting two or more accounts.

a) **Errors affecting One Account or one-sided errors:** Errors which affect the agreement of the trial balance, i.e., because of which Trial Balance does not agree, are called one-sided errors.

The following errors affect only one account:

(a) Errors of posting

(b) Carry forward

(c) Balancing

(d) Omission from trial balance

(e) Casting

Such errors should first of all be located and rectified. These are rectified either with the help of journal entry or by giving an explanatory note in the account concerned and not by simply crossing the wrong amount and inserting the right one.

ILLUSTRATION: Rectify the following errors located before preparing trial balance.

1. Rent paid ₹ 80 posted as ₹ 800
2. Sales register undercast by ₹ 1000
3. Amount received from Shivam ₹ 2000 posted to his debit.
4. Cash sale to Raj of ₹10,000 posted as ₹ 1,000

Solution:

While rectifying the errors, first show the correct then wrong entry shown in the books, compare wrong entry with the correct and then rectify the same.

1) Correct posting

Dr.	₹	Cr.
To Cash	80	

Wrong posting

Dr.	₹	Cr.
To Cash	800	

Here rent A/c is debited in excess. The excess debited of ₹ 720 is to be reserved.

No entry is passed as it is one sided error. Credit rent account with the words 'By excess debit ₹ 720'.

2) Let us suppose there are two entries in the sales register of ₹ 5,000 and ₹ 1,000; correct entry and wrong entry will appear as under:

Correct posting		
Dr. Sales a/c By Sale Register	Cr. 6,000	Sales register Amt. 5,000 1,000
		6,000
Wrong posting		
Dr. Sales a/c By Sale Register	Cr. 5,000	Sales register Amt. 5,000 1,000
		5,000

Total of sales register is posted to the credited of sales a/c. Since there is an under casting of ₹ 1,000, sales account will show less credit to the extent of ₹ 1,000.

No entry is necessary as it is one sided error. Credited sales account with the words 'By under casting ₹ 1,000'.

3) Correct posting

Dr.	Shivam a/c	Cr.
	By Cash	2,000

Wrong posting

Dr.	Shivam a/c	Cr.
	To Cash	2000

Here Shivam a/c is wrongly debited with ₹ 2,000 instead of being credited. When figure is posted to the opposite side, by mistake, difference will be double the amount.

4) Cash sales recorded in the cash book with the amount. However, posting is short by ₹ 9,000. Since the sale is against cash, 'Sales a/c' will be credited.

b) **Errors affecting Two or More Accounts:** Under two-sided errors, two or more accounts are affected and in most of the cases, the debit and credit are equally affected. While rectifying these errors, first pass the correct entry, then show wrong entry which is already passed in the books and by comparing wrong entry with the correct one, rectification entry can be passed.

The following errors affect two or more accounts:

(a) Errors of omission
(b) Posting to wrong account
(c) Principles

ILLUSTRATION: Rectify the following errors:

1. Goods purchased from Sheetal wrongly recorded in sales register ₹ 1,000
2. Salary paid to Vikas, accountant, wrongly debited to his personal account ₹ 2,000
3. Wages paid for installation of machinery ₹ 5,000 were debited to wages account.
4. Rent paid ₹ 2,000 wrongly debited to postage account.

Solution:

1) **Correct entry**

Purchase a/c	dr. 1000	
To Sheetal		1000

Wrong entry

Sheetal's a/c	dr. 1000	
To sales a/c		1000

In the above case, sales account is wrongly credited and purchase account is not debited. Therefore, both these accounts required to be debited. Sheetal's account is wrongly debited instead of credited. Therefore, her account will be credited with double the amount of ₹ 1,000 (i.e., ₹ 2,000)

Sales a/c	dr. 1,000	
Purchase a/c	dr. 1,000	
To Sheetal		2,000

(Being purchase of goods wrongly recorded in sales register now rectified)

2) Correct entry

Salary a/c	dr. 2000	
To Cash a/c		2000

Wrong entry

Vikas's a/c	dr. 2000	
To Cash a/c		2000

In the above entry, Vikas's a/c is wrongly debited and salary a/c is not debited. therefore, rectification entry will affect these two accounts.

sales a/c	dr. 2,000	
To Vikas's a/c		2,000

(Being salary paid wrongly debited to personal a/c now rectified)

3) Correct entry

Machinery a/c	dr. 5000	
To Cash a/c		5,000

Wrong entry

Wages a/c	dr. 5,000	
To Cash a/c		5,000

In the above entry, Wages account is wrongly debited instead of Machinery a/c

Machinery a/c	dr. 5,000	
To Wages a/c		5,000

(Being wages paid for installation of machinery wrongly debited to Wages a/c now rectified)

4) Correct entry

Rent a/c	dr. 2,000	
To Cash a/c		2,000

Wrong entry

Postage a/c	dr. 2,000	
To Cash a/c		2,000

In the above case, entry is correctly recorded in the cash book but while posting it into ledger, it has been wrongly debited to Postage a/c instead of Rent a/c

Rent a/c	dr. 2,000	
To Postage a/c		2,000

(Being payment of rent wrongly debited to Postage A/c now rectified.)

As these errors affect two or more accounts, rectification of such errors is done with the help of a journal entry.

SUSPENSE ACCOUNT AND RECTIFICATION

Suspense a/c is the account to which the amount being the difference in trial balance is placed. If the total debit side is short, Suspense a/c will show debit balance. And if, the total of credit side is short, suspense account will show credit balance.

In the earlier paragraphs, we have learnt to rectify one-sided and two-sided errors. After preparation of a trial balance, if there is a difference, it may be temporarily transferred to a new account called 'Suspense'.

ILLUSTRATION:

i. Sales book has been totalled ₹ 1,000 short.

ii. Goods worth ₹ 1,500 returned by Green & Co., have not been recorded anywhere.

iii. Goods purchased of ₹ 2,500 have been posted to the debit of the supplier, Gupta & Co.

iv. Furniture purchased from Gulab & Co., of ₹ 10,000 has been entered in purchase book.

v. Cash received from A ₹ 2,500 has not been posted in his account.

Correct the following errors:

(A) Without Opening a Suspense Account

(B) By Opening a Suspense Account.

SOLUTION:

A) Without Opening a Suspense Account:

i) Since Sales book has been casted (totalled) short by ₹ 1,000, Sales account has been credited short by ₹ 1,000. The correcting entry is to credit the Sales account by ₹ 1,000 as "By wrong totalling of the Sales book ₹ 1,000"

ii) To rectify the omission, returns inward account has to be debited and the account of Green & Co. credited. The entry:

Returns inward A/c	dr. 1,500	
To Green & Co.		1,500

(Being the goods returned by the firm, previously omitted from the returns inward book)

iii) Gupta & Co. have been debited ₹ 2,500 instead of being credited. This account should now be credited by ₹ 5,000 to remove the wrong debit and to give the correct credit. The entry will be on the credit side "By error in posting ₹ 5,000".

iv) By this error, Purchase account has been debited by ₹ 10,000 whereas the debit should have been to the Furniture account. The correcting entry will be:

Furniture A/c   dr. 10,000
     To Purchase A/c   ₹ 10,000

(Being the correction of the mistake, by which Purchase account was debited instead of the Furniture account)

v) Cash received from A of ₹ 2,500 has not been credited to his account. For the rectification of this error, A's account should be credited as follows:

By omission of posting   ₹ 2,500

B) When Suspense Account is opened:

Errors	Particulars		L/f	(Dr.) Amt.	(Cr.) Amt.
i)	Suspense A/c To Sales A/c (being the correction arising from under casting of Sales book)	Dr;		1,000	1,000
ii)	Returns inward A/c To Green & Co. (being the recording of goods returned by Green & Co. a customer)	Dr.		1,500	1,500
iii)	Suspense a/c To Gupta & Co. (being the correction of the error by which Gupta & Co. were debited instead of being credited by ₹ 2,500)	Dr.		5,000	5,000
iv)	Furniture a/c To Purchase a/c (being the correction of recording purchase of furniture as ordinary purchases)	Dr.		10,000	10,000
v)	Suspense a/c To A's a/c (being the cash received from A, now posted to his account)	Dr.		2,500	2,500

Suspense Account

Date	Particulars	J/f	Amount	Date	Particulars	J/f	Amount
	To Sales a/c		1,000		By difference in Trial		
	To Gupta & Co.		5,000		balance		8,500
	To A		2,500		(Balancing fig.)		
			8,500				8,500

RECTIFICATION OF ERRORS WHEN BOOKS ARE CLOSED

The rectification of errors after the preparation of final accounts depends upon the nature of error. If an error is a one-sided error, it can be corrected by passing a rectifying entry with the help of the Suspense Account and if the error is two-sided, it is rectified by passing a rectifying entry in both the affected accounts and such errors are not rectified through Suspense Account.

TEST YOURSELF

1. Trial Balance is ___________.
   (a) An Account
   (b) A Statement
   (c) A part of Final Accounts
   (d) None of these

2. A sale of ₹ 20,000 was omitted from recording in the Sales Book. The existing total of debit side of the trial balance is ₹ 15,00,000. Presently, what will be the total of credit side?
   (a) ₹ 15,20,000   (b) ₹ 14,80,000
   (c) ₹ 15,40,000   (d) ₹ 14,60,000

3. Which A/c is opened when Trial Balance doesn't tally?
   (a) Trading A/c   (b) Purchase A/c
   (c) Suspense A/c   (d) Capital A/c

4. Which of the following will not affect Trial Balance?
   (a) Goods sold on credit not recorded in books
   (b) Overstating of sales register
   (c) Rent account credited instead of debit
   (d) Salary debited to the extent ½ the amount

Directions (for Qs.Nos. 5 to 12): *What would be the impact of the following errors on the Trial Balance?*

5. A copy of a sales invoice for ₹ 10,000 is not recorded in the Sales Day Book.
   (a) Excess credit ₹ 10,000
   (b) Excess debit ₹ 10,000
   (c) No impact
   (d) None of the above

6. A supplier's invoice for ₹ 2,000 is posted to the debit of the Trade Payable's account.
   (a) Excess credit ₹ 2,000
   (b) Excess debit ₹ 4,000
   (c) Excess debit ₹ 2,000
   (d) None of the above

7. The daily total of the Sales Day Book is stated as ₹ 345,000 instead of ₹ 315,000 (i.e. overcast by ₹ 30,000).
   (a) Excess credit ₹ 30,000
   (b) Excess debit ₹ 30,000
   (c) No impact
   (d) None of the above

8. A purchase invoice is recorded in the Purchases Day Book as ₹ 14,500, without taking account of 10% of that amount offered as trade discount.
   (a) Excess credit ₹ 1,450
   (b) Excess debit ₹ 1,450
   (c) No impact
   (d) None of the above

9. A sales invoice for ₹ 21,000 has been posted to the Customer's account as ₹ 12,000.
   (a) Excess credit ₹ 9,000
   (b) Excess debit ₹ 12,000
   (c) Excess credit ₹ 12,000
   (d) None of the above

10. A Credit Note for ₹ 2,400 received from a supplier has been posted to the credit of the supplier's account.
    (a) Excess credit ₹ 2,400
    (b) Excess credit ₹ 4,800
    (c) Excess debit ₹ 2,400
    (d) None of the above

11. The year-end balance in a Trade Receivable's account has been carried down as ₹ 14,800, instead of ₹ 18,400.
    (a) Excess debit ₹ 3,600
    (b) Excess credit ₹ 3,600
    (c) No impact
    (d) None of the above

12. The total of the Returns Outwards Day Book, amounting to ₹ 9,800, has been posted to the debit of the Purchases Returns account.
    (a) No impact
    (b) Excess debit ₹ 9,800
    (c) Excess debit ₹ 19,600
    (d) None of the above

13. Errors of part omission do not permit ____________.
    (a) Correct totalling of the Balance sheet
    (b) Correct totalling of the Trial Balance
    (c) The Trial Balance to agree
    (d) Preparation of Final Accounts

14. Trial Balance remains untallied due to errors. Various types of errors can be:
    1. Error of omission
    2. Error of commission
    3. Errors of principle
    4. Intentional errors
    (a) 1, 2 and 3 only
    (b) 1, 3 and 4 only
    (c) 2, 3 and 4 only
    (d) 1 to 4 all

15. XYZ had purchased certain goods from ABC firm, but these were not recorded in the purchase journal. This is error of _________. It will (affect / not affect) the trial balance.
(a) Omission, affect
(b) Compensating, not affect
(c) Principle, affect
(d) Omission, not affect

16. The closing stock given in the Trial Balance is transferred to which of the following accounts _____________.
(a) Trading account
(b) Profit and loss account
(c) Manufacturing account
(d) Balance sheet

17. Which of the following is not true?
(a) Wrong balance in an account affect the trial Balance
(b) Closing stock does not appear in the Trial Balance
(c) Trial Balance is prepared after preparation of the Final Account
(d) Sales are shown on the credit side of the Trial Balance

18. Which of the following will not affect Trial Balance?
(a) Goods sold on credit not recorded in books.
(b) Overstating of sales register.
(c) Rent account credited instead of debit.
(d) Salary debited to the extent ½ the amount.

19. Functions of a Trial Balance is:
(a) To act as a device to check the arithmetical accuracy of the accounting process
(b) To provide summary position of each account and accounts in general
(c) To act as a starting point for preparation of Final accounts
(d) All the above

20. Freight expenses for carrying Machinery is carried to Travel a/c, then rectification in Trial Balance is _____________.
(a) Debit Machinery a/c and credit Travel a/c.
(b) Credit Machinery a/c and debit Travel a/c
(c) Credit Profit and Loss account and debit Travel a/c.
(d) Debit Profit and Loss a/c (P&L) a/c and credit Travel a/c.

ANSWER

1	2	3	4	5	6	7	8	9	10
(b)	(b)	(c)	(a)	(c)	(b)	(a)	(c)	(a)	(c)

11	12	13	14	15	16	17	18	19	20
(a)	(c)	(c)	(a)	(d)	(d)	(c)	(a)	(d)	(a)

____

CAPITAL AND REVENUE EXPENDITURE

INTRODUCTION

The aim of accounting is to ascertain the financial performance of a firm. To do so the transactions have to be identified as capital or revenue in nature. This will determine whether they are placed in the Profit and Loss Account or the Balance Sheet. Let us study about capital and revenue expenditure and receipts.

EXPENDITURE

Expenditure means spending on something. This can be a payment in cash or can also be the exchange of some valuable item in exchange for goods or services. It is the process of causing of a liability by a commodity. Receipts and invoices keep the records of expenditures. An expense is a word very similar to expenditure but expense shows the deduction in the value of the asset while expenditure simply denotes the obtaining of assets.

Determining Capital Nature and Revenue Nature

There are certain basic considerations when we are determining the nature of a financial transaction, i.e. capital nature or revenue nature. Some such considerations are as follows:

1. Nature of Business: The capital or revenue nature is dependent on the type of business a person does. It is different for different types for business. For instance, a business that provides car insurance to people comes under the revenue nature but the manufacturer buying the machinery for his factory is capital expenditure.

2. Recurring Nature of Expenditure: As stated earlier, revenue nature expenditures are recurring in nature and capital nature expenditures are non-recurring in nature.

3. Purpose of Expenditure: The manufacturing process is an illustration of capital nature while renovation and repairing processes are expenses of revenue nature.

Two types of expenditures are present on the basis of time durations, That is:
1. Capital Expenditures
2. Revenue Expenditures

1. **Capital Expenditure:** Whenever a business spends money it receives some form of value representing goods or services, but the items which are purchased will be of benefit to the business for varying lengths of time. The fixed assets purchased by a firm are primarily intended for long-term use in the business, and will usually be retained by the business for some considerable time. Fixed assets consist of land, buildings, plant and machinery, furniture and fittings, office equipment, motor vehicles and all other assets which are purchased for use in the business. The assets possessed by a firm will generally be used in the business over long periods of time, and will permanently increase the profit-making capacity of the business.

Capital expenditure, therefore, can be defined as: "Expenditure on the purchase of fixed assets, or expenditure to increase the value of an existing fixed asset. Capital expenditure will increase the assets possessed by a firm and will appear on the balance sheet".

2. **Revenue Expenditure:** These are the costs incurred during the day-to-day running of a business. They include all such items as salaries, wages, telephone, lighting and heating, rent, interest rates, insurance, discounts allowed, carriage costs and so on. These are costs for the services received, and the payments made for expenses incurred by the business, and form part of the expenditure involved in the daily routine operation of running a business; they will only be of benefit for a short period of time. The costs involved are 'used up', usually in less than a year, and they will only be of a temporary nature.

Difference between Capital Expenditure and Revenue Expenditure

	Capital Expenditure		*Revenue Expenditure*
1.	Its effect is long-term, i.e. it is not exhausted within the current accounting year—its benefit is received for a number of years in future.	1.	Its effect is temporary, i.e. the benefit is received within the accounting year.
2.	An asset is acquired or the value of an existing asset is increased.	2.	Neither an asset is acquired nor is the value of an asset increased.
3.	Generally it has physical existence except intangible assets.	3.	It has no physical existence because it is incurred on items which are used by the business.
4.	It does not occur again and again. It is nonrecurring and irregular.	4.	It is recurring and regular and it occurs repeatedly.
5.	This expenditure improves the position of the business.	5.	This expenditure helps to maintain the business.
6.	A portion of this expenditure (depreciation on assets) is shown in Trading & P&L A/c and the balance is shown in the Balance Sheet on asset side.	6.	The whole amount of this expenditure is shown in Trading P & L A/c or Income Statement.
7.	It appears in the Balance Sheet until its benefit is fully exhausted.	7.	It does not appear in the Balance Sheet.
8.	It does not reduce the revenue of the concern. Purchase of fixed asset does not affect revenue.	8.	It reduces revenue (profit) of the business.

Deferred Revenue Expenditure:

Deferred revenue expenditure is the expenditure which is originally revenue in nature but the amount spent is so large that the benefit is received for not a year but for many years. A proportionate amount is charged to Profit and Loss Account of each year and balance is carried forward to subsequent years as deferred revenue expenditure. It is shown as an asset in the Balance Sheet, e.g., heavy expenditure incurred on advertisements.

RECEIPT

Capital receipt and revenue receipt, both are the very important components of accounting. It is important to correctly differentiate between the two. Classification of these transactions reflects in the final statements of the company.

- **Capital Receipts:** Capital receipts are the receipts which are not received in the ordinary course of business. These are non-recurring receipts. Money obtained from the sale of fixed assets or investments, issue of shares or debentures, loans taken are some of the examples of capital receipts. Capital receipts are shown as liability reduced from assets appearing in the Balance Sheet.

- **Revenue Receipts:** Revenue receipts are receipts obtained in the normal course of business. It is a receipt against supply of goods or services. The money obtained from sales, interest, dividend, transfer fees etc. are examples of revenue receipts. Revenue receipts are credited to Profit and Loss Account.

Distinction between Capital Receipt and Revenue Receipt

	Capital Receipt		*Revenue Receipt*
1.	It has long-term effect. The benefit is enjoyed for many years in future.	1.	It has short-term effect. The benefit is enjoyed within one accounting period.
2.	It does not occur again and again. It is non-recurring and irregular.	2.	It occurs repeatedly. It is recurring and regular.
3.	It is shown in the Balance Sheet on the liability side.	3.	It is shown in Profit and Loss Account on the credit side.
4.	Capital receipt, when invested, produces revenue receipt e.g. when capital is invested by the owner, business gets revenue receipt (i.e. sale proceeds of goods etc.).	4.	It does not produce capital receipt.
5.	The capital receipt decreases the value of asset or increases the value of liability e.g. sale of a fixed asset, loan from bank etc.	5.	This does not increase or decrease the value of asset or liability.
6.	Sometimes expenses of revenue nature are to be incurred for such receipt e.g. on obtaining loan (a capital receipt) interest is paid until its repayment.	6.	Sometimes, expenses of capital nature are to be incurred for revenue receipt, e.g. purchase of shares of a company is capital expenditure but dividend received on shares is a revenue receipt.

TEST YOURSELF

1. Freight expenses for moving new machinery to factory is ______________.
   (a) Revenue expenses
   (b) Deferred revenue expenditure
   (c) Capital expenditure
   (d) None of the above

2. For an expense to be classified as revenue or capital depends on:
   (a) Kind of expense
   (b) Duration of the benefit of the expenditure
   (c) Effect on revenue earning capacity
   (d) All of the above

3. Which of the following is not a deferred revenue expenditure?
   (a) Preliminary expenses for setting up a company.
   (b) Amount raised through Rights issue.
   (c) Huge sales promotion expenditure in launch of new product
   (d) Cost of preparing project report

4. Cost of replacement of defective parts of the machinery is __________.
   (a) Capital expenditure
   (b) Revenue expenditure
   (c) Deferred revenue expenditure
   (d) None of these

5. Which transaction is a capital receipt?
   (a) Cash received from sale of inventory
   (b) Bank interest received on deposits
   (c) Premises rent received from the tenant
   (d) Proceeds of sale of equipment

6. The difference between selling price and present book value of machinery is called:
   (a) Capital income
   (b) Revenue income
   (c) Revenue receipt
   (d) Capital receipt

7. On the last date of his food truck business, A food truck owner sold snacks worth ₹ 2,500 and sold his truck for ₹ 20,000. How should these receipts be treated in his business books?
   (a) Capital Receipt - 0, Revenue Receipt - 22500
   (b) Capital Receipt - 2500, Revenue Receipt - 20000

(c) Capital Receipt - 20000, Revenue Receipt - 2500
(d) Capital Receipt - 22500, Revenue Receipt - 0

8. Which is a capital receipt for the owner of the bicycle shop?
   (a) Purchase of bicycle delivery vehicle by cheque
   (b) Sale of old bicycle delivery vehicle for cash
   (c) Sale of bicycles for cash
   (d) Purchase of bicycles by cheque

9. Sale of machine of machine merchandising business __________.
   (a) Capital receipt
   (b) Capital income
   (c) Revenue income
   (d) Revenue receipt

10. For a bookshop owner, which of the following item is a capital receipt?
   (a) Receipt of sales commission from the publisher
   (b) Cash discount from a supplier of stationery
   (c) Proceeds from the disposal of old bookshelf
   (d) Cash from sale of notebooks

11. An expenditure charged to P&L a/c over a period of 5 to 6 years is an example of:
   (a) Revenue expenditure
   (b) Capital expenditure

   (c) Deferred revenue expenditure
   (d) All of the above

12. Maintenance of fixed assets is a ______________.
   (a) Capital Expenditure
   (b) Revenue Expenditure
   (c) Deferred Revenue Expenditure
   (d) None of the above

13. Cost of replacement of defective parts of the machinery is ______________.
   (a) Capital expenditure
   (b) Revenue expenditure
   (c) Deferred revenue expenditure
   (d) None of these

14. Loss of goods due to fire for ₹ 50000 is __________.
   (a) Capital expenditure
   (b) Revenue expenditure
   (c) Deferred revenue expenditure
   (d) None of these

15. Acquisition of Fixed assets is a ________.
   (a) Capital Expenditure
   (b) Revenue Expenditure
   (c) Deferred Revenue Expenditure
   (d) None of the above

ANSWER

1	2	3	4	5	6	7	8	9	10
(c)	(d)	(b)	(b)	(d)	(a)	(c)	(b)	(d)	(b)

11	12	13	14	15
(c)	(b)	(b)	(b)	(a)

CHAPTER 12

BILLS OF EXCHANGE

INTRODUCTION

Bill finance is one of the major activities of the Banks. Under this type of lending, Bank takes the bill drawn by borrower on his (borrower's) customer and pays him immediately deducting some amount as discount/commission. The Bank then presents the Bill to the borrower's customer on the due date of the Bill and collects the proceeds. If the bill is delayed, the borrower or his customer pays the Bank a pre-determined interest depending upon the terms of transaction. The transaction is practically an advance against the security of the bill which is due for payment.

TYPES OF INSTRUMENTS OF CREDIT & NEGOTIABLE INSTRUMENTS ACT

In India, the Negotiable Instruments Act (NI) was passed during 1881 which came into force from March 01, 1882. At present it has 147 sections and 17 chapters. It extends to the whole of India. According to Section 13 (a) of the Act, Negotiable Instruments means Promissory Note (PN), Bill of Exchange (BOE) and Cheque.

Bill of exchange is one of the payment mechanism in the business transaction. Bill of exchange was first time used in 12th century for payment in business transaction. In a business, credit transactions play very important role. Credit may also be granted by a moneylender, a banker or a financial institution. Credit is, generally, provided by obtaining, a written document called 'Instrument of Credit'. This serves as a proof of existence of credit. The most commonly used instruments of credit are:

1. Bills of Exchange 2. Promissory Notes 3. Cheque

1. **Bill of Exchange:** Section 5 of the Negotiable Instrument Act defines, "A bill of exchange is an instrument in writing containing an unconditional order, signed by the maker, directing a certain person to pay a certain sum of money only to, or to the order of a certain person or to the bearer of the instrument". A bill of exchange, therefore, is a written acknow-ledgement of the debt, written by the creditor and accepted by the debtor. There are usually three parties to a bill of exchange drawer, acceptor or drawee and payee. Drawer himself may be the payee.

Specimen of Bills of Exchange

STAMP	Mr. Alpha (Drawer) 576, Gurugram Feb 17, 2018
₹ 1,00,000	
Three months after date, pay to Mr. Beta (payee) a sum of rupees one lakh, for the value received.	
To, Mr. Gamma (drawee) 268, Noida	Mr. Alpha Sd/-

Essential Conditions of a Bill of Exchange

(i) It must be in writing.

(ii) It must be signed by the drawer.

(iii) The drawer, drawee and payee must be certain.

(iv) The sum payable must also be certain.

(v) It should be properly stamped.

(vi) It must contain an express order to pay money and money alone.

(vii) The order must be unconditional.

2. **Promissory Notes:** Section 4 of the Act defines, "A promissory note is an instrument in writing (note being a bank-note or a currency note) containing an unconditional undertaking, signed by the maker, to pay a certain sum of money to or to the order of a certain person, or to the bearer of the instruments."

   Example: If A writes "I promise to pay B or order ₹ 5000".

   An instrument to be a promissory note must possess the following elements:

   (i) It must be in writing,

   (ii) It must certainly an express promise or clear understanding to pay a certain sum of money,

   (iii) The promise should be to pay money and money only,

   (iv) Promise to pay must be unconditional,

   (v) It should be signed by the maker,

   (vi) The maker & payee must be certain.

SPECIMEN OF PROMISSORY NOTE   ____________ स्थान / *Place*

____________ *20*

₹ ____________

मांग पर   ___________________________________
On Demand

बैंक ऑफ़ **XYZ** को या उनके आदेश पर प्राप्त मूल्य के लिए रुपये
Promise to pay Bank of **XYZ** *or order, the sum of Rupees*

____

की राशि और इस राशि पर इस तारीख से
together with interest on such sum from this date, at the rate of

__________________________ प्रतिशत वार्षिक की दर से मासिक / त्रैमासिक अंतराल पर
percent per annum with Monthly / Quarterly

परिकलित ब्याज का भुगतान करने का वचन देता हूँ.
rests for value received

स्टेम्प
STAMP

SIGNATURE OF BORROWER

3. **Cheques:** Section 6 of the Act defines "A cheque is a bill of exchange drawn on a specified banker, and not expressed to be payable otherwise than on demand". A cheque is bill of exchange with two more qualifications, namely,

   a) It is always drawn on a specified banker, and

   b) It is always payable on demand.

   Consequently, all cheques are bills of exchange, but all bills are not cheques. A cheque must satisfy all the requirements of a bill of exchange; that is, it must be signed by the drawer, and must contain an unconditional order on a specified banker to pay a certain sum of money to or to the order of a certain person or to the bearer of the cheque. It does not require acceptance.

SPECIMEN OF A CTS CHEQUE

बैंक ऑफ इंडिया
BANK OF INDIA
CHAKALA Branch
MUMBAI, MAHARASHTRA, 400 093
IFSC : BKID0000067

D D M M Y Y Y Y

Pay _________________________ या धारक को Or Bearer

रुपये Rupees _________________________

अदा करें ₹ _______

खा. सं.
A/c No. _________________________

PAYABLE AT ALL OUR BRANCHES IN CLEARING

Please sign above

⑈003401⑈ 400013012⑈ 009989⑈ 11

DIFFERENCES AMONG BILL OF EXCHANGE, PROMISSORY NOTE AND CHEQUE

Differences Between A Bill of Exchange and A Promissory Note

Basis for Comparison	Bill of Exchange	Promissory Note
Meaning	Bill of Exchange is an instrument in writing showing the indebtedness of a buyer towards the seller of goods.	A promissory note is a written promise made by the debtor to pay a certain sum of money to the creditor at a future specified date.
Defined in	Section 5 of Negotiable Instruments Act, 1881.	Section 4 of Negotiable Instruments Act, 1881.
Parties	Three parties, i.e. drawer, drawee and payee.	Two parties, i.e. drawer and payee.
Drawn by	Creditor	Debtor
Liability of Maker	Secondary and conditional	Secondary and conditional
Can maker and payee be the same person?	Yes	No
Copies	Bill can be drawn in copies.	Promissory Note cannot be drawn in copies.
Dishonour	Notice is necessary to be given to all the parties involved.	Notice is not necessary to be given to the maker.

Differences Between A Bill of Exchange and A Cheque

Basis for Comparison	Cheque	Bill of Exchange
Meaning	A document used to make easy payments on demand and can be transferred through the hand delivery is known as cheque.	A written document that shows the indebtedness of the debtor towards creditor.

Basis for Comparison	Cheque	Bill of Exchange
Defined in	Section 6 of The Negotiable Instruments Act, 1881	Section 5 of The Negotiable Instruments Act, 1881
Validity Period	3 months	Not Applicable
Payable to bearer on demand	Always	Cannot be made payable on demand as per RBI Act, 1934
Grace Days	Not Applicable, as it is always payable at the time of presentment.	3 days of grace are allowed.
Acceptance	A cheque does not require acceptance.	Bill of exchange needs to be accepted.
Stamping	No such requirement.	Must be stamped.
Crossing	Yes	No
Drawee	Bank	Person or Bank
Noting or Protesting	If the cheque is dishonoured it cannot be noted or protested	If a bill of exchange is dishonoured it can be noted or protested.

PARTIES AND CERTAIN IMPORTANT TERMS OF BILL OF EXCHANGE

Parties to a Bills of Exchange: Section 7 of the Negotiable Instruments Act defines different parties of bill of exchange.

1. **Drawer:** The maker of a bill of exchange is called the 'drawer'.
2. **Drawee:** The person directed to pay the money by the drawer is called the 'drawee',
3. **Acceptor:** The acceptor is the third party who accepts responsibility for a payment in a bill of exchange. Drawee of a bill of exchange also accepts it by signining on face of the bill. He or she thereby accepts the liability for payment of the bill on or before the bills maturity date.
4. **Payee:** The person named in the instrument, to whom or to whose order the money is directed to be paid by the instrument is called the 'payee'. He is the real beneficiary under the instrument.
5. **Endorser:** When the holder transfers or endorses the instrument to anyone else, the holder becomes the 'endorser'.
6. **Endorsee:** The person to whom the bill is endorsed is called an 'endorsee'.
7. **Holder & Holder in Due Course:** A person who is legally entitled to the possession of the negotiable instrument in his own name and to receive the amount thereof, is called a 'holder'. 'Holder in Due Course' means any person who for consideration became the possessor of the bill (that is a person to whom the bill is transferred)

8. **Acceptor for Honour:** In case the original drawee refuses to accept the bill or to furnish better security when demanded by the notary, any person who is not liable on the bill, may accept it with the consent of the holder, for the honour of any party liable on the bill. Such an acceptor is called 'acceptor for honour'.

Other important terms of bill of exchange: Other important terms related to bill of exchange are as under:

1. **Retirement of Bill:** When a drawee pays the bill before its due date, it is called retirement of bill.
2. **Renewal of Bill:** When a drawee is unable to meet the bill on due date, he requests the drawer to accept a part of the bill amount in cash and for the balance to draw on him a fresh bill together with interest.
3. **Inland Bill:** When a bill drawn and made payable in India. A bill of exchange drawn or made in India & payable in or drawn upon any persons in India.
4. **Time or Usance Bills:** A bill payable after a fixed time is termed as a time bill. In other words, bill payable "after date" is a time or usance bill.
5. **Demand Bill:** A bill payable at sight or on demand is termed as a demand bill.
6. **Accommodation of Bill:** When one party accepts the bill drawn on him by another, without any consideration, for the purpose of mutual help, the bill is said to be accommodation bill.
7. **Trade Bill:** A bill drawn and accepted for a genuine trade transaction is termed as a "trade bill".

8. **Clean Bills**: A clean bill is a bill of exchange drawn as per requirements of the NI Act and is not supported by documents of title of goods. Clean bills are drawn normally to effect discharge of a debt or claim.

9. **Documentary Bills**: A bill of exchange accompanying documents of title of goods is called documentary bill. These bills are drawn to claim price of goods supplied.

10. **Notary Public:** He is an officer appointed by the Government to exercise the powers and functions relating to a protesting of negotiable instruments after dishonour.

11. **Noting:** On dishonour of a bill, the holder in due course presents the bill to a Notary Public to make necessary entries on the bill or on a separate paper attached to the bill. This is called 'Noting'.

12. **Protest:** When a promissory note or bill of exchange has been dishonoured for non-acceptance or non-payment, the holder may cause such dishonour to be noted and certified by a notary public within a reasonable period. Such a certificate is called 'Protest'.

13. **Noting charges:** Amount paid to Notary Public for recording the fact of dishonour is called 'Noting Charges'.

14. **Rebate:** When a bill is paid by drawee before due date, some allowance is given to him. This allowance is called 'Rebate'.

TERM AND DUE DATE OF A BILL

Acceptance of Bill of Exchange: The acceptance of a bill means signing by the drawer of a bill, on face with or without the words accepted and delivery thereof or giving notice of signing, to the holder of the bill. As per Section 61, a usance bill payable after sight and bills payable on a fixed date (and not demand bills) require to be presented to drawee for acceptance to make him liable and also for calculation of due date.

Rules For Due Date Calculation:

- Demand bill is payable on demand or at sight.

- Usance bill should be presented for acceptance within a reasonable time.

- The drawee is allowed 48 hours excluding public holiday to accept the bill.

- If a usance bill is payable after date, its due date is calculated from date of the bill and if it is payable after sight, its due date is calculated from date of acceptance.

- 3 days grace period is given to every Usance Promissory Note or BOE.

- Where the due date is already given by the drawer, no grace period to be given.

- Instruments payable in installments, the days of grace are to be allowed for each installment.

- **When the maturity date is a public holiday:** As per sec 25 of NI Act, such instrument be payable on the next preceding business day i.e. the previous business day.

- **Declaration of Public Holiday:** u/s 25 of NI Act 1881 , the public holiday includes Sunday and any other day declared by the Central Govt. by notification in the Official Gazette (this power has been delegated to state government).

Due Date Calculation of A Bill of Exchange

Date of Bill	Presented on	Accepted on	Payment Terms	Due Date
26.02.16	27.02.16	28.02.16	30 days after acceptance	01.04.16
26.12.15	26.12.15	28.12.15	45 days after date	12.02.16
20.12.16	21.12.16	23.12.16	1 month after sight	25.01.17
26.02.16	27.02.16	28.02.16	3 months after acceptance	31.05.16
26.12.15	26.12.15	28.12.15	2 months after date	29.02.16

Bills Receivable and Bills Payable

For convenience of accounting, we need to classify Bills of Exchange into two classes:

1. **Bills Receivable**: When we draw a Bill on a debtor or receive a Bill via endorsement from a debtor, that bill of exchange is a Bill Receivable for us as we are supposed to receive the money mentioned in the Bill.

2. **Bills Payable**: When we accept a Bill drawn by a creditor it is a Bill Payable for us as we are supposed to pay the amount mentioned in that bill.

Thus, the same bill is both a Bill Receivable and a Bill Payable—receivable from the point of view of the creditor and payable from the point of view of the debtor.

TYPES OF BILL FINANCE

Basically, a banker offers following types of bill finance:

1. **Bill Purchase:** When a bank negotiates bills payable on demand, whether clean or documentary, the facility is known as bill purchase. The face value of the bill is immediately paid to the holder. The bank after purchasing the bill, become holder in due course of the bill and acquires all the right of ownership over the instrument. Bill purchase facility is extended generally in the case of bills payable on demand. In case of dishonour of the bill, the amount is recovered from the customer.

2. **Bill Discount:** In the case of a Usance Bill, the date of payment is certain as it becomes payable after a certain number of days after it is accepted or from the date of the bill. Hence, we may be able to calculate the exact amount of interest due on the bill and recover it upfront. Interest recovered at the time of advance is called "discount". When money is against a usance bill for collection, it is called Bill Discounting. In the case of bills purchase also interest is recovered at the time of advance. However, it is only an estimated amount and not the exact amount due. Hence it is called commission and not discount.

3. **Advance against Bill for Collection:** Banks also give advance against the bills, which are in course of collection is known as advance against bill for collection. Under this facility, a prescribed margin is kept by the bank and the amount, in consideration of this is allowed to the customer. The bill thereafter is sent for collection. In all cases, the legal effect is that the banker, who lends money, becomes holder in due course for the bill.

ACCOUNTING ENTRIES TO BE PASSED

When a bill of exchange is drawn by one party on another, it must be accepted by that person. Once it is accepted, it becomes a legal document and then entries are passed in the books of the drawer and drawee. Let us learn these entries with a simple illustration.

DISCOUNTING A BILL

- **Illustration:** Prakash received from Mohan an acceptance for ₹ 30,000 on 1st July, 2018 at 3 months. Prakash got this acceptance discounted @ 12% p.a. at his bank. On due date, Mohan paid the required amount. Give the journal entries in the book of Prakash and Mohan.

  Solution:

Journal of Prakash

Date	Particulars		L/f	Dr. Amt.	Cr. Amt.
2018 July 1	B/R A/c To Mohan's A/c (being the amount of the acceptance received from Mohan)	Dr.		30,000	30,000
July 1	Bank A/c Discounting charges A/c To B/R a/c (being the bill got discounted with the bank @ 12% p.a.)	Dr. Dr.		29,100 900	30,000

Journal of Mohan

Date	Particulars		L/f	Dr. Amt.	Cr. Amt.
2018 July 1	Prakash A/c To B/P A/c (being the amount of the acceptance given to Prakash)	Dr.		30,000	30,000
July 1	B/P A/c To cash/bank a/c (being the payment of the bill due this day)	Dr.		30,000	30,000

ENDORSING A BILL

- **Illustration:** Dev owes ₹ 10,000 to Krishna. On 1st May, 2018, he sent his promissory Note for the amount payable, after 3 months. On 1st June, 2018 Krishna endorses the promissory note in favour of Wahid to whom he owned a like amount. On the due date, Dev paid the amount. Give the journal entries in the books of Krishna, Dev and Wahid.

Journal of Krishna

Date	Particulars	L/f	Dr. Amt.	Cr. Amt.
2018 May 1	B/R A/c Dr. To Dev's A/c (being the promissory note received from Dev)		10,000	10,000
July 1	Wahid A/c Dr. To B/R a/c (being the bill from Dev endorsed in favour of Wahid)		10,000	10,000

Journal of Dev

Date	Particulars	L/f	Dr. Amt.	Cr. Amt.
2018 May 1	Krishna A/c Dr. To B/P A/c (being the promissory note given to Krishna)		10,000	10,000
Aug. 4	B/P A/c Dr. To Cash/Bank a/c (being the amount of the promissory note paid)		10,000	10,000

Journal of Wahid

Date	Particulars	L/f	Dr. Amt.	Cr. Amt.
2018 June 1	B/R A/c Dr. To Krishna's A/c (being the acceptance of Dev received from Krishna)		10,000	10,000
Aug. 4	Cash/Bank a/c Dr. To B/R a/c (being the amount of Dev's acceptance received)		10,000	10,000

DISHONOUR OF BILL

A sold goods for ₹ 50,000 to B on 1st January, 2018 and on the same day he drew a bill on B at three months for the amount. The bill is duly accepted but is dishonoured on the due date. A pays ₹ 1,000 as noting charges.

Record these transactions in the journal of A&B.

A's Journal

Date	Particulars	L/f	Dr. Amt.	Cr. Amt.
2018 Jan. 1	B's A/c Dr. To Sales A/c (being the goods sold on credit)		50,000	50,000

Date	Particulars		L/f	Dr. Amt.	Cr. Amt.
Jan. 1	B/R a/c 　　　　To B's a/c (being the acceptance received)	Dr.		50,000	50,000
April 4	B's a/c 　　　　To B/R a/c 　　　　To Cash a/c (being the bill dishonoured and noting charges paid)	Dr.		51,000	50,000 1,000

B's Journal

Date	Particulars		L/f	Dr. Amt.	Cr. Amt.
2018 Jan. 1	Purchase A/c 　　　　To A's A/c (being the acceptance goods on credit)	Dr.		50,000	50,000
Jan. 1	A's a/c 　　　　To B/P A/c (being the acceptance given)	Dr.		50,000	50,000
April 4	B/P a/c Noting charges A/c 　　　　To A's A/c (being the bill dishonoured and noting charges paid by A)	Dr. Dr.		50,000 1,000	51,000

Accommodation Bills: Where a bill of exchange is drawn and accepted for providing funds to a friend in need, it is termed as accommodation bill. In this bill, the drawer and drawee are not the creditor and the debtor respectively. These are drawn for the mutual benefit of the drawer and the acceptor and are not backed by business transactions.

A bill drawn and accepted not for a genuine trade transaction but only to provide financial help to some party is termed as an "accommodation bill".

Example: A, is in need of money for three months. He induces his friend B to accept a bill of exchange drawn on him for ₹ 1,000 for three months. The bill is drawn and accepted. The bill is an "accommodation bill". A may get the bill discounted from his bankers immediately, paying a small sum as discount. Thus, he can use the funds for three months and then just before maturity he may remit the money to B, who will meet the bill on maturity. In the above example A is the "accommodated party" while B is the "accommodating party".

BILL BOOKS

Bills Receivable Book: Bills receivable book is a book where all the bills, which are received, are recorded and, posted directly to the credit of respective customer's account from there. The total amount of bills so received during the period, either at the end of the week or month, is to be posted to, in one lump sum, to the debit of the bills receivable account. The usual form of bills receivable book, with imaginary figures, is shown below:

Bills Receivable Book

No.	Date of receipt	From whom	Acceptor	Date of bill	Term	Due date	Where payable	Amt.	L/F	How disposed off	Remark
1.	1/3/18	A	A	1/3/18	1month	4/4/18	Patna	7,000	-	-	-
2.	1/4/18	B	B	1/4/18	2month	4/6/18	Patna	8,000	-	-	-
3.	1/5/18	C	C	1/5/14	1month	4/6/18	Patna	9,000	-	-	-
								24,000			

Bills Payable Book: This is a book where all particulars relating to the bills accepted are recorded and, posted from there, directly to the debit of the respective creditor's account. The total amount of the bills so accepted during the period, either at end of the week or month, is to be posted in one lump sum to the credit of bills payable account. The usual form of 'Bills Payable' book.

Bills Payable Book

No.	Date of receipt	Drawn by	Payee	Date of bill	Term	Due date	Where payable	Amt.	L/F	How disposed off	Remark
1.	1/1/18	A	A	1/1/18	1month	4/2/18	Patna	6,000	-	-	-
2.	4/2/18	X	X	4/2/18	1month	7/3/18	Patna	7,000	-	-	-
3.	10/2/18	Y	Y	10/2/18	2month	13/4/18	Patna	8,000	-	-	-
4.	1/3/18	Z	Z	1/3/18	1month	4/4/18	Patna	9,000	-	-	-
								30,000			

SUMMARY OF ACCOUNTING ENTRIES TO BE PASSED IN JOURNAL FOR BILL OF EXCHANGE

Transactions	In the book of the Drawer				In the books of the Accepter (Drawee)
	Where the B/E is Retained	Where the B/E is Discounted	Where the B/E is Endorsed	Where the B/E is sent to bank for Collection	
1. Sale of goods on credit	Debtor's a/c dr. To Sales a/c	Debtor's a/c dr. To sales a/c	Debtor's a/c dr. To sales a/c	Debtor's a/c dr. To sales a/c	Purchase a/c dr. To creditor's a/c
2. Drawing of B/E			No Entry		
3. Acceptance of a B/E by the dr.	B/R a/c dr. To Accepter's a/c (Debtor's)	B/R a/c dr. To Accepter's a/c (Debtor's)	B/R a/c dr. To Accepter's a/c (Debtor's)	B/R a/c dr. To Accepter's a/c (Debtor's)	Drawer's a/c dr. To B/P a/c
4. Treatment of bills	No Entry	Bank a/c dr. Dis. charge a/c dr. To B/R a/c	Endorsee's a/c dr. To B/R a/c	Bill sent for Collection a/c dr. To B/R a/c	No Entry
5. Honour of a bill of exchanges on due date	Cash/bank a/c dr. To B/R a/c	No Entry	No Entry	Bank a/c dr. To bill sent for Collection a/c	B/P a/c dr. To bank /cash a/c
6. Dishonour of a B/E on due date a) if nothing charges are not incurred	Accepter's a/c dr. To B/R a/c	Accepter's a/c dr. To B/R a/c	Accepter's a/c dr. To endorsee's a/c	Accepter's a/c dr. To Bill sent for collection a/c	B/P a/c dr. To drawer's a/c
b) if nothing charges are incurred	Accepter's a/c dr. (by B.R.+N.C) To B/R a/c (by B.R) To cash a/c (by N.C)	Accepter's a/c dr. (by B.R.+N.C) To Bank a/c (by B.R.+N.C)	Accepter's a/c dr. (by B.R.+N.C) To endorsee's a/c (by B.R.+N.C)	Accepter's a/c dr. (by B.R.+N.C) To Bill sent for Collection a/c (by B.R) To Bank a/c (by N.C)	B/P a/c dr. Nothing charges dr. To drawer's a/c
7. Retirement of a bill of exchanges	Cash/bank a/c dr. Rebate a/c dr. To B/R a/c	No Entry	No Entry	No Entry	B/P a/c dr. To cash/bank a/c To rebate a/c
8. Renewal of a B/E a) Cancellation of old B/E	Accepter's a/c dr. To B/R a/c	Accepter's a/c dr. To bank a/c	Accepter's a/c dr. To endorsee's a/c	Accepter's a/c dr. To bill sent for Collection a/c	B/P a/c dr. To Drawer's a/c
b) Part payment by the drawee	Cash a/c dr. To Accepter's a/c	Cash a/c dr. To Accepter's a/c	Cash a/c dr. To Accepter's a/c	Cash a/c dr. To Accepter's a/c	Drawer's a/c dr. To cash a/c
c) Interest charged to drawee	Accepter's a/c dr. To interest a/c	Accepter's a/c dr. To interest a/c	Accepter's a/c dr. To interest a/c	Accepter's a/c dr. To interest a/c	Interest a/c dr. To drawer's a/c
d) Acceptance of new B/E	B/R a/c dr. To Acceptor's a/c	B/R a/c dr. To Acceptor's a/c	B/R a/c dr. To Acceptor's a/c	B/R a/c dr. To Acceptor's a/c	Drawer's a/c dr. To B/P a/c

TEST YOURSELF

1. Bill of exchange is defined in:
   (a) Section 5 of the NI Act
   (b) Section 6 of the Indian Contract Act
   (c) Section 6 of the NI Act
   (d) Section 5 of the Indian Contract Act

2. Which is not the essential conditions of a bill of exchange?
   (a) It must be in writing
   (b) It must be signed by the drawee
   (c) The sum payable must also be certain
   (d) The order must be unconditional

3. Retiring a bill under rebate means:
   (a) Dishonouring the bill
   (b) Making payment of the bill after the due date
   (c) Making payment of the bill before the due date
   (d) Making payment of the bill on the due date

4. For a bank, Rebate on bills discounted is an item of ____________.
   (a) an income
   (b) an expenditure
   (c) an accrued income
   (d) an income received in Advance

5. Which of the following parties in a bill of exchange do match?
   (a) Drawer- the person who orders the other person to make payment
   (b) Payee- the person who is to make payment
   (c) Drawee- the person who is to receive the payment as per order of the drawer
   (d) None of the above

6. The facility to get bill of exchange discounted puts them into the category of _______.
   (a) Fixed assets
   (b) Intangible assets
   (c) Wasting assets
   (d) Current assets

7. Which of these is not an essential feature of a bill of exchange?
   (a) Conditional
   (b) The drawer, drawee and payee must be certain
   (c) In writing
   (d) It should be properly stamped

8. Early payment of a Bill of Exchange is known as:
   (a) Retirement
   (b) Renewal
   (c) Discount
   (d) Endorsement

9. The date of maturity of an "after sight" bill is calculated from the ____________.
   (a) Date of drawing the bill
   (b) Date of acceptance of the bill
   (c) Date of discounting of the bill
   (d) None of these

10. The entry regarding payment of the bill will be passed in the books of the drawer if the bill is ___________.
    (a) retained
    (b) endorsed
    (c) discounted
    (d) retained or sent to bank for collection

11. A is drawer and B is acceptor of the bill. A endorses the bill to C. The bill is dishonoured on due date. A will debit ____________.
    (a) B's a/c
    (b) C's a/c
    (c) Bills Receivable a/c
    (d) Cash a/c

12. Bill receivable for ₹ 2,600 from Navin was dishonoured and posted to debit of Allowances account.
    (i) Credit allowances account with ₹ 2,600
    (ii) Credit Navin's account with ₹ 2,600
    (iii) Debit the suspense account with ₹ 5,200
    (a) Only (i) and (ii)
    (b) Only (i) and (iii)
    (c) Only (ii) and (iii)
    (d) (i), (ii) and (iii)

13. A draws a bill on B for ₹ 50,000 for 3 months. Before the due date B sends 1/5th of the amount to A. B requested A to draw a new bill for the balance amount plus interest @ 12% p.a. for 3 months. Find the amount of the new bill.
    (a) ₹ 5,210
    (b) ₹ 4,150
    (c) ₹ 4,120
    (d) ₹ 5,820

14. On 1.3.2018 X draws a bill on Y for 3 months for ₹ 40,000. On 4.5.2018 Y pays the bill to X at 12% discount, the amount of discount will be____.
    (a) ₹ 200   (b) ₹ 400
    (c) ₹ 600   (d) ₹ 100

15. The following is (are) the current liability (ies):
(a) Bills payable
(b) Outstanding expenses
(c) Bank overdraft
(d) All of the above

16. B drew a bill of ₹ 20,000 for 2 months on A for mutual accommodation. It was decided that the proceeds would be shared equally. How much amount would be received by A if the bill was discounted @12% p.a.?
(a) ₹ 18,600   (b) ₹ 9,800
(c) ₹ 10,000   (d) ₹ 10,200

17. A draws a bill on B for ₹ 4,500 for mutual accommodation in the ratio 2:1. A got it discounted at ₹ 4,230 and remitted 1/3rd of the proceeds to B. At the time of maturity, how much amount A should remit to B such that B can pay off the bill?
(a) ₹ 3,000   (b) ₹ 2,880
(c) ₹ 2,920   (d) ₹ 3,010

18. On dishonour of a bill, the holder in due course presents the bill to a notary public to record the facts of dishonour on the bill or on paper attached to the bill, it is called:
(a) Dishonour   (b) Noting
(c) Noting charges   (d) Protesting charges

19. On the dishonour of the bill received through endorsement, debit is given to_________.
(a) Payee's a/c
(b) Acceptor's a/c
(c) Endorser's a/c
(d) Bills Receivable a/c

20. This is a book where all particulars relating to the bills accepted are recorded and, posted from there, directly to the debit of the respective creditor's account.
(a) Bills Receivable Book
(b) Bills Payable Book
(c) Bills Discounting Book
(d) Bills Return Book

ANSWER

1	2	3	4	5	6	7	8	9	10
(a)	(b)	(c)	(d)	(a)	(d)	(a)	(a)	(b)	(d)

11	12	13	14	15	16	17	18	19	20
(a)	(a)	(c)	(b)	(d)	(b)	(a)	(b)	(c)	(b)

———————————

MODULE–C
FINAL ACCOUNTS

CHAPTER 13

BALANCE SHEET EQUATION

INTRODUCTION

In its most basic form, the balance sheet equation shows what a company owns, what a company owes, and what stake the owners have in the business. The equation starts off with the company assets. These are the resources that the company has to use in the future like cash, accounts receivable, and fixed assets.

BALANCE SHEET EQUATION

The balance sheet equation or accounting equation is the most basic, fundamental part of accounting. The balance sheet equation forms the building blocks for the entire double entry accounting system. Always the total claims (those of outsiders such as creditors and of the proprietors, i.e. net worth) will equal the total assets of the business.

We can express the same as:

$$\text{Assets} = \text{Equities (total claims)}$$
$$\text{or Assets} = \text{Liabilities} + \text{Capital}$$
$$\text{or Liabilities} = \text{Assets} - \text{Capital}$$
$$\text{or Capital} = \text{Assets} - \text{Liabilities}$$

Example: Most of the time, the company doesn't own its assets outright. For instance, it might have a loan on the company car, a mortgage on the building, or even owe money to its shareholders. That is why the second part of the balance sheet equation is made up of the claims on company assets. All of these claims on the company assets are separated into two categories: liabilities and equity.

Liabilities are claims on the company assets by other firms or people. A bank loan or mortgage is a good example. The bank has a claim to the business building or land that is mortgaged. Liabilities are usually shown before equity in the balance sheet equation because liabilities must have to be repaid before owners' claims.

Equity on the other hand is the shareholders' claims on the company assets. This is the amount of money shareholders contributed to the company for an ownership stake. Equity also includes retained earnings. Once all of the claims by outside companies and claims by shareholders are added up, they will always equal the total company assets.

COMPUTATION OF BALANCE SHEET EQUATION

If there is any change in the amount of the assets or the liabilities, the owners' claim or the capital is bound to change correspondingly. If assets increase and liabilities do not, the capital will increase; a reduction in the amount of assets or an increase in the amount of liabilities will mean a reduction in the amount of capital.

a) **Capital:** It means the amount which the owner of business has invested in the firm and can claim from the firm.

b) **Liability:** It means the amount which the firm owes to outsiders. Long term liabilities are those liabilities which are payable after a long term. Current liabilities are those liabilities which are payable in near future (generally within one year).

c) **Assets:** Assets are things of value owned. Fixed assets are those assets which are purchased for the purpose of operating the business but not for resale, e.g. Land, Building, Plant and Machinery, etc. Current assets are those assets which are kept for short term for converting into cash or for resale, e.g. unsold goods, debtors, cash, bank balance, etc.

d) **Revenue:** It means the amount which, as a result of operations, is received by the business.

e) **Expense:** It is the amount spent in order to produce and sell the goods and services which produce the revenue.

f) **Income:** The difference between revenue and expense is called income (if revenue is more than expense).

g) **Debtor:** A person who owes money to the firm, mostly on account of credit sales of goods, is called a debtor.

h) **Creditor:** A person to whom money is owed by the firm is called a creditor.

Example of the Balance Sheet Equation by the Various Transactions:

Suppose Mr. Niraj starts a business and the following successive changes or transactions take place.

1. Mr. Niraj commences his business with ₹ 100,000 as capital. This means that the firm has assets totalling ₹ 100,000 in the form of cash and claims against the firm are also ₹ 100,000 in the form of capital. The balance sheet stands as follows:

Balance Sheet 1

Liabilities	₹	Assets	₹
Niraj's Capital	100,000	Cash	100,000

2. The business purchased a new machinery of ₹ 20,000. The effect of this transaction is that amount of cash in hand is lower by ₹ 20,000, but a new asset (machinery) has been acquired leaving the total assets unchanged. The balance sheet after this transaction will appear as follows:

Balance Sheet 2

Liabilities	₹	Assets	₹
Niraj's Capital	100,000	Cash	80,000
		(100,000 – 20,000)	
		Machinery	20,000
Total	**100,000**		**100,000**

3. The business purchases goods for ₹ 30,000 for cash. The effect of this transaction is that amount of cash in hand is lower by ₹ 30,000, but a new asset (stock of goods) has been acquired leaving the total assets unchanged. The balance sheet after this transaction will appear as follows:

Balance Sheet 3

Liabilities	₹	Assets	₹
Niraj's Capital	100,000	Cash	50,000
		(80,000 – 30,000)	
		Machinery	20,000
		Goods	30,000
Total	**100,000**		**100,000**

4. The business purchases goods for ₹ 25,000 on credit. Because of this transaction, the stock of goods increased by ₹ 25,000 making the total assets ₹ 125,000. Now ₹ 25,000 is payable to the supplier of goods (creditor). The balance sheet after this transaction will appear as follows:

Balance Sheet 4

Liabilities	₹	Assets	₹
Niraj's Capital	100,000	Cash (50,000 – 0)	50,000
Creditor	25,000	Machinery	20,000
		Goods (30,000 + 25,000)	55,000
Total	**125,000**		**125,000**

5. The business sells goods on credit for ₹ 25,000, the cost of the goods sold is ₹ 35,000. In this transaction, a new asset, i.e. debtor, has come into existence to the extent of ₹ 50,000. But, the stock of goods will be reduced by ₹ 35,000 (cost of goods sold). The net increase in the asset ₹ 15,000 (₹ 50,000 less ₹ 35,000) is a surplus which belongs to the owner. So his networth will now be ₹ 115,000 (Capital ₹ 100,000 plus surplus ₹ 15000). The balance sheet after this transaction will appear as follows:

Balance Sheet 5

Liabilities	₹	Assets	₹
Niraj's Capital	100,000	Cash	50,000
Reserve & Surplus	15,000	(50,000 – 0)	
		Machinery	20,000
Creditor	25,000	Goods	20,000
		(55,000 – 35,000)	
		Debtor	50,000
Total	**140,000**		**140,000**

6. The business pays ₹ 5000 for miscellaneous expenses and ₹ 6000 for wages. The cash will now be reduced by ₹ 11,000. There is no asset to show for this. These expenses will be borne by the owner and to that extent the surplus will get reduced.

Balance Sheet 6

Liabilities	₹	Assets	₹
Niraj's Capital	100,000	Cash	39,000
Reserve & Surplus	4,000	(55,000 – 11,000)	
(15,000 – 11,000)		Machinery	20,000
Creditor	25,000	Goods	20,000
		(55,000 – 35,000)	
		Debtor	50,000
Total	**129,000**		**129,000**

In the above balance sheet, ₹ 25,000 have been obtained from outsiders and ₹ 104,000 have been contributed by the owner of the business. It means, one can take any number of transactions. However, the total assets will be equal to the total of liabilities and the capital. The left-hand side shows the total liabilities of the firm or shows the sources from which the funds have been obtained. The other side of the balance sheet, which is known as the asset side, shows how the funds have been invested by the business. On the basis of the various transactions given in above example, we understand that every transaction has a double effect will always be true. On reducing or increasing an asset will have a corresponding effect on liabilities or capital.

TEST YOURSELF

1. The balance sheet equation forms the building blocks for the entire _________ system.
   - (a) Single entry accounting
   - (b) Double entry accounting
   - (c) Triple entry accounting
   - (d) All of the above

2. Find the Correct equation:
   - (a) Assets = Equities (total claims)
   - (b) Liabilities = Assets – Capital
   - (c) Capital = Assets – Liabilities
   - (d) All of the above

3. _________ means the amount which the owner of business has invested in the firm and can claim from the firm.
   - (a) Capital
   - (b) Liability
   - (c) Assets
   - (d) Revenue

4. It means the amount which the firm owes to outsiders. Long term liabilities are those liabilities which are payable after a long term. Current liabilities are those liabilities which are payable in near future (generally within one year).
   - (a) Capital
   - (b) Liability
   - (c) Assets
   - (d) Revenue

5. Which is not correct statement regarding long term liabilities?
   - (a) Long term liabilities are those liabilities which are payable after a long term
   - (b) Long term liabilities are those liabilities which are not payable within one year
   - (c) Long term liabilities are the part of Reserve and Surplus
   - (d) All of the above

6. Which is correct statement regarding Fixed assets?
   - (a) Fixed assets are those assets which are purchased for the purpose of operating the business but not for resale.
   - (b) Fixed assets are kept for short term for converting into cash or for resale.
   - (c) Fixed assets is a part of Intangible Assets.
   - (d) All are correct statements.

7. _________ means the amount which, as a result of operations, is received by the business.
   - (a) Capital
   - (b) Liability
   - (c) Assets
   - (d) Revenue

8. Which is not a Current Asset?
   - (a) Unsold goods
   - (b) Debtors,
   - (c) Profit
   - (d) Bank balance

9. Which is not an Intangible Asset?
   - (a) Loss
   - (b) Goodwill
   - (c) Patent
   - (d) Copy Right

10. A person who owes money to the firm, mostly on account of credit sales of goods, is called a________.
    - (a) Creditor
    - (b) Debtor
    - (c) Customer
    - (d) Supplier

ANSWER

1	2	3	4	5	6	7	8	9	10
(b)	(d)	(a)	(b)	(c)	(a)	(d)	(c)	(a)	(b)

PREPARATION OF FINAL ACCOUNTS

INTRODUCTION

Final accounts are statutory requirements for all type of registered organizations. They are popularly known as Financial Statements. Preparation of final accounts is governed by different Acts, Laws, Standards and Principles like Income tax law, Company Act, Partnership Act, Accounting Standards (AS), Generally Accepted Accounting Principles (GAAP) etc., used for valuation of financial transactions/events to standardize accounting information, which in turn depends upon type of organization concerned. In other words, since different types of organizations operates under different legal framework, the methodology/procedure for preparation of final accounts will change accordingly.

While the Trial Balance checks the accuracy of ledger balances, the final account reveals two facts:

1. Whether the business is in profit or loss during the period covered by the Trial Balance. A Trading and Profit & Loss Account also known as income statement is prepared for this purpose.

2. What is the financial position (financial position means picture of assets and liabilities) of the business? This is judged by preparing a Balance Sheet for the business.

Thus, Income Statement represents the summary of all the expenses and incomes occurred during the financial year whereas Balance Sheet represents the financial position of the concerned organization at a particular point of time, usually at the end of financial year i.e., 31st March (in India, financial year covers the period from 1st April to 31st March).

TRIAL BALANCE—A STARTING POINT FOR FINAL ACCOUNTS

The Trial Balance is simply a list of ledger account balances at the end of an accounting period. This summary of the ledger at the end of an accounting period, is a convenient starting point in the preparation of the final accounts i.e. Trading and Profit and Loss Account and Balance Sheet.

A Trial Balance usually contains the following types of balances:

1. Balances from expenses accounts
2. Balances from revenue accounts
3. Balances from assets accounts
4. Balances from liabilities accounts
5. Balances from capital or owner's equity account

The first two types of balances are transferred to Trading and Profit & Loss Account to find out the profit or loss. The other three types of balances are transferred to the Balance Sheet to know the financial position of the business.

Thus we prepare from the Trial Balance a Trading and Profit & Loss Account by matching revenue balance with expenses balances and by the time we have finished, we have very much smaller trial balance, which is then arranged into a Balance Sheet.

ADJUSTMENTS ENTRIES IN FINAL ACCOUNTS

Final Accounts are prepared, normally, for a complete period. It must be kept in mind that expenses and incomes for the relevant accounting period are to be taken, while preparing final accounts. If an expense has been incurred but not paid during the period, a liability for the unpaid amount should be created, before finding out the operating result and financial position of a concern. In order to prepare the final accounts on mercantile system of accounting, all expenses and incomes relating to the period, whether incurred or not, received or not, should be brought into the books. For doing this, a concern is required to pass certain entries at the end of the year to adjust the various items of incomes and expenses. Such entries are called adjusting entries.

TRADING ACCOUNT

Trading Account is prepared for calculating the gross profit or gross loss arising or incurred as a result of the trading activities of a business. In other words, it is prepared to show the result of manufacturing, buying and selling of goods. A Trading Account records the amount of purchases of goods and also the expenses which are incurred in bringing that commodity to a saleable state.

In other words, all expenses which relate to either purchase of raw material for manufacturing of goods are recorded in the Trading Account. All such expenses are called 'Direct Expenses'. According to J.R. Batliboi, "The Trading Account shows the results of buying and selling of goods. In preparing this account, the general establishment charges are ignored and only the transaction in goods are included."

PREPARATION OF TRADING ACCOUNT

Trading Account is a Nominal Account and all expenses which relate to either purchase or manufacturing of goods are written on the Dr. Side of the Trading Account.

1. Items written on the Dr. Side of Trading Account:

(a) **Opening Stock:** The stock of goods remaining unsold at the end of the previous year is termed as the opening stock of the current year. In other words, the closing stock of the last year becomes the opening stock of the current year. Opening Stock will include the following:

   I. Opening Stock of Raw Material.

   II. Opening Stock of Semi-finished goods, and

   III. Opening Stock of Finished goods.

(b) **Purchases and Purchase Returns:** Goods which have been bought for resale are termed as Purchases and goods which are returned to suppliers are termed as purchase returns or returns outwards. Purchase Account will be given on the debit side of Trial Balance and Purchase Return Account on the credit side of Trial Balance or Purchase returns will be shown as a deduction from Purchases on the debit side of Trading Account. Purchases include cash as well as credit purchases.

(c) **Direct Expenses:** All expenses incurred in purchasing the goods, bringing them to the god own and manufacture of goods are called direct expenses. Direct expenses include the Wages, Carriage or Carriage Inwards or Freight, Manufacturing Expenses etc.

2. Items written on the Cr. Side of Trading Account:

(a) **Sales and Sales Returns:** Both Cash and Credit sales will be included in sales. The sales account will be a credit balance whereas, the sales return account or returns inwards account will be a debit balance. Sales return will be deducted out of Sales on the credit side of Trading Account.

(b) **Closing Stock:** The goods remaining unsold at the end of the year is known as Closing Stock. It is valued at cost price or market price whichever is lesser. It includes the closing stock of raw material, Closing Stock of semi-finished goods and Closing Stock of finished goods.

Normally, the Closing Stock is given outside the Trail Balance. This is so because its valuation is made after the accounts have been closed. It is incorporated in the books by means of the following entry:

Closing Stock A/c   Dr.

        To Trading A/c

(Closing Stock transferred to Trading A/c)

When the above entry is passed, the Closing Stock Account is opened. On the one hand, it will be posted to the credit side of the Trading Account and on the other hand, will be shown on the Assets side of the Balance Sheet, in order to complete the double entry.

Closing Entries

At the end of each year, all accounts of expenses and incomes must be closed. The balances of these accounts are transferred to Trading Account and Profit & Loss Account. The entries passed to transfer these balances are called 'Closing Entries'.

FORM OF TRADING ACCOUNT

Trading A/c

(for the year ended................)

Dr.   Cr.

Particular	Amount	Particulars	Amount
	₹		₹

To Opening Stock
To Purchases
    Less: Purchase Returns
       or
     Returns outward
To Wages
To Wages & Salaries
To Direct Expenses
To Carriage,   or
To Carriage inwards,   or
To Carriage on Purchase
To Gas, Fuel and Power
To Freight, octroi and cartage
To Manufacturing Expenses, or
Productive Expenses
To Factory Expenses, such as:
Factory Lighting
Factory Rent etc.
To Dock Charges and Clearing charges
To Import Duty or Custom duty
To Royalty
To Gross Profit
Transferred to P&L A/c
(Balancing Figure)
		By Sales
		    Less: Sales Returns
		       or
		     Returns inwards
		By Closing Stock
		By Gross Loss
		    (if any) transferred to P&L A/c
		(Balancing Figure)	

Notes:

(1) In the heading of the Trading Account the words 'for the year ended........' are used. Because, it discloses the position of the business for the full accounting year and not at a particular point of time.

(2) No separate column for date is prepared in the Final Accounts because the date will be already mentioned in the heading itself.

(3) No column for L.F. is prepared in Final Accounts because these are prepared from Trial Balance and not from Ledger accounts directly.

- **Illustration:** Prepare a Trading Account for the year ended 31st March 2018 from the following balances:

	₹		₹
Opening Stock	4,00,000	Purchases Return	1,20,000
Purchases	20,00,000	Sales Return	2,00,000
Sales	50,00,000	Carriage on Purchase	80,000
Freight and Octroi	65,000	Carriage on Sales	1,00,000
Wages	3,00,000	Factory Rent	1,20,000
Factory Lighting	1,08,000	Office Rent	75,000
Coal, Gas and Water	22,000	Import Duty	3,20,000

Closing Stock is valued at ₹ 600,000.

Solution:

Trading A/c

(for the Financial year ended 31st March, 2018.)

Dr.   Cr.

Particular		Amount	Particulars		Amount
		₹			₹
To Opening Stock		4,00,000	By Sales	50,00,000	
To Purchases	20,00,000		*Less:* Sales Returns	2,00,000	48,00,000
Less: Purchase Returns	1,20,000	18,80,000			
or			By Closing Stock		6,00,000
Returns outward					
To Freight and Octroi		65,000	By Gross loss		
To Wages		3,00,000	(if any) transferred to P&L A/c		
To Factory Lighting		1,08,000	(Balancing Figure)		
To Coal, Gas and Water		22,000			
To Carriage on Purchase		80,000			
To Factory Rent		1,20,000			
To Import Duty		3,20,000			
To Gross Profit Transferred to P/L A/c		21,05,000			
		54,00,000			54,00,000

PROFIT & LOSS ACCOUNT

Trading account only discloses the gross profit earned as a result of buying and selling of goods. However, a businessman has to incur a number of expenses which are not taken to Trading Account. Hence, a businessman is more interested in knowing the net profit earned or net loss incurred during the year. As such, a Profit & Loss Account is prepared which contains all the items of losses and gains pertaining to the accounting period. According to Prof. Carter, "A Profit & Loss Account is an account into which all gains and losses are collected, in order to ascertain the excess gains over the losses or vice-*versa*".

PREPARATION OF PROFIT & LOSS ACCOUNT

A Profit & Loss Account is started with the amount of gross profit or gross loss brought down from the Trading Account. As such, all those expenses and losses which have not been debited to the Trading Account are now debited to Profit & Loss Account. These expenses include administrative expenses, selling expenses, distribution expenses etc. These are called 'Indirect Expenses'. Profit & Loss Account is a Nominal Account and as such, all the expenses and losses are shown on its debit side and all the incomes and gains are shown on its credit side.

Items written on the Dr. Side of Profit & Loss Account

1. **Gross Loss:** If trading account discloses Gross Loss, it is shown on the debit side first of all.
2. **Office and Administrative Expenses:** Such as salary of office employees, office rent, lighting, postage, printing, legal charges, audit fee etc.
3. **Selling and Distribution Expenses:** Such as advertisement charges, commission, carriage outwards, bad-debts, packing charges etc.
4. **Miscellaneous Expenses:** Such as interest on loan, interest on capital, repair charges, depreciation, charity etc.

Items written on the Cr. side of Profit & Loss Account

1. **Gross Profit:** The starting point of the Cr. side of Profit & Loss Account is the gross profit brought down from the Trading Account.
2. **Other Incomes and Gains:** All items of incomes and gains are shown on the credit side of the Profit & Loss Account, such as income from investments, rent received, discount received, commission earned, interest received, dividend received etc.

If the credit side of the Profit & Loss Account exceeds that of debit side, the difference is termed as net profit.

On the other hand, the excess of the debit side over the credit side is termed as net loss. Net profit is added to the capital whereas net loss is deducted from the capital.

Closing Entries Relating to Profit & loss Account

The preparation of Profit & Loss Account requires that the balances of all concerned items are transferred to it by passing the following closing entries:

1. Accounts of various items of expenses and losses are transferred to the debit side of Profit & Loss Account by means of the following entry:

   Profit & Loss A/c   Dr.
      To Salaries A/c
      To Rent, Rates and Taxes A/c
      To Printing and Stationery A/c
      To Postage and Telegrams A/c
      To General Expenses etc.

   (Transfer of nominal accounts showing Dr. balances to the Debit of P&L A/c)

2. Balances of all the accounts of incomes and gains will be transferred to the credit side of Profit & Loss Account by means of the following entry:

   Interest Received A/c   Dr.
   Commission Received A/c   Dr.
   Rent Received A/c   Dr.
      To Profit & Loss A/c

   (Transfer of nominal accounts showing Cr. balances to the Credit of P & L A/c)

3. For the transfer of credit balance of Profit & Loss A/c, known as net profit:
   Profit & loss A/c   Dr.
      To Capital A/c
   (Transfer of net profit to Capital A/c)

4. For the transfer of debit balance of Profit & Loss A/c, known as net loss:
   Capital A/c   Dr.
      To Profit & Loss A/c
   (Transfer of net loss to Capital A/c)

Form of Profit & Loss Account

Trading A/c

Dr.   *(for the year ending……………..)*   Cr.

Particular	Amount ₹	Particulars	Amount ₹
To Groos Loss b/d (if any)		By Gross Profit b/d	
(Transferred from Trading A/c)		(Transferred from Trading A/c)	
Office Expenses:		By Rent from Tenant	
To Salaries & Wages		By Rent (Cr.)	
To Rent, Rates & Taxes		By Discount received or discount (Cr.)	
To Printing & Stationery		By Commission Received	
To Lighting		By Interest on Investments	
To Insurance Premium		By Dividend on Shares	
To Telephone Charges		By Bad-Debts Recovered	
To Travelling Expenses		By Profit on Sale of Assets	
To Establishment Expenses		By Income from other Sources	
Selling and Distribution Expenses:		By Miscellaneous Receipts	
To Carriage Outwards, or		By Net Loss (if any)	
Carriage on Sales		Transferred to Capital A/c	
To Advertisement			
To Commission			
Miscellaneous Expenses:			
To Repairs			
To Depreciation			
To Interest (Dr.)			
To Bank Charges			
To Loss on Sale of Assets			
To Net Profit:			
Transferred to Capital A/c			

Notes:

(1) Those expenses which are not related to the business are not written in the Profit and Loss Account such as (i) Domestic and household expenses of the proprietor, (ii) Income-Tax, and (iii) Life Insurance Premium etc. These expenses are known as Drawings and deducted from Capital at the liabilities side of the Balance Sheet.

(2) Only those items of expenses and incomes are shown in the Profit & Loss Account which have not been shown in the Trading Account.

- **Illustration:** From the following particulars, prepare a Profit & Loss Account for the year ending 31st March, 2018.

	₹		₹
Gross Profit	21,05,000	Discount Allowed	30,000
Trade Expenses	20,000	Lighting	7,800
Carriage on Sales	1,00,000	Commission Received	8,400
Office Salaries	1,58,000	Bad-debts	12,000
Postage and Telegram	7,200	Discount (Cr.)	6,000
Office Rent	7,500	Interest on Loan	22,000
Legal Charges	4,000	Stable Expenses	14,000
Audit Fee	16,000	Export Duty	23,000
Donation	11,000	Miscellaneous Receipts	5,000
Sundry Expenses	3,600	Unproductive Expenses	41,000
Selling Expenses	53,200	Travelling Expenses	25,000

Solution:

Profit & Loss Account

(for the Financial year ended 31st March, 2018)

Dr.   Cr.

Particular	Amount	Particulars	Amount
	₹		₹
To Trade Expenses	20,000	By Gross Profit	21,05,000
To Carriage on Sales	1,00,000	By Commission Received	8,400
To Office Salaries	1,58,000	By Discount	6,000
To Postage & Telegram	7,200	By Miscellaneous Receipts	5,000
To Office Rent	75,000		
To Legal Charges	4,000		
To Audit Fee	16,000		
To Donation	11,000		
To Sundry Expenses	3,600		
To Selling Expenses	53,200		
To Discount Allowed	30,000		
To Lighting	7,800		
To Bad-Debts	12,000		
To Interest on Loan	22,000		
To Stable Expenses	14,000		
To Export Duty	23,000		
To Unproductive Expenses	41,000		
To Travelling Expenses	25,000		
To Net Profit transferred to Capital Account	15,01,600		
	21,24,400		**21,24,400**

BALANCE SHEET

After ascertaining the net profit or loss of the business enterprise, the businessman would also like to know the exact financial position of his business. For this purpose a statement is prepared which contains all the Assets and Liabilities of the business enterprise. The statement so prepared is called a Balance Sheet because it is a sheet of balances of ledger accounts which are still open after the transfer of all nominal accounts to the Trading and Profit & Loss Account. Balances of all the personal and real accounts are grouped as assets and liabilities. Liabilities are shown on the left hand side of the Balance Sheet and assets on the right hand side.

Definitions

A Balance Sheet has been defined as follows:

In the words of Karlson, "A business form showing what is owed and what the proprietor's worth, is called a Balance Sheet."

According to A. Palmer, "The Balance Sheet is a statement at a particular date showing on one side the trader's property and possessions and on the other hand the liabilities."

According to J.R. Batliboi, "A Balance Sheet is a statement prepared with a view to measure the exact financial position of a business on a certain fixed date."

Characteristics of Balance Sheet:

1. A Balance Sheet is a part of the Final Account. This is the reason that the Trading and Profit & Loss Account and the Balance Sheet are together called 'Final Accounts'. However, the Balance Sheet is a statement and not an account. It has no debit or credit side and as such the words 'To' and 'By' are not used before the names of the accounts written therein.

2. A Balance Sheet is a summary of the Personal and Real Accounts, which are still open and have not been closed by transfer to the Trading and Profit & Loss Account. Debit balances of all Personal and Real Accounts are put on the right

hand side known as Assets side, whereas the credit balances are put on the left hand side known as Liabilities side.

3. The totals of the two sides of the Balance Sheet must be equal. If the totals are not equal, there will be an error somewhere.

4. Balance Sheet is prepared on a particular date and not for a fixed period. As such, it discloses the financial position of a business on a particular date and not for a period. It is true only for the date on which it is prepared because even a single transaction would cause a change in the assets and liabilities.

5. It shows the financial position of the business according to the going concern concept.

Grouping and Marshalling of Assets and Liabilities in Balance Sheet

The Assets and Liabilities shown in the Balance Sheet are properly grouped and presented in a particular order. The term 'grouping' means showing the items of similar nature under a common heading. For example, the amount owing from various customers will be shown under the heading 'Sundry Debtors'. Similarly, under the heading 'Current Assets', the balance of Cash, bank, debtors, stock etc. will be shown.

'Marshalling' is the arrangement of various assets and liabilities in a proper order. Marshalling can be made in one of the following two ways:

1. **In the Order of Liquidity:** According to this method, an asset which is most easily convertible into Cash such as Cash in hand is written first and then will follow those assets which are comparatively less easily convertible, so that the least liquid asset such as goodwill, is shown last.

   In the same way, those liabilities which are to be paid at the earliest will be written first. In other words, current liabilities are written first of all, then fixed or long-term liabilities and lastly, the proprietor's capital. Generally, sole proprietors and partnership firms prepare their Balance Sheet in the order of liquidity. Proforma of a Balance Sheet in the order of liquidity will be as follows:

Balance Sheet

(as on ....)

Particular	Amount	Particulars	Amount
	₹		₹
Current Liabilities:		**Current Assets:**	
Bank Overdraft		Cash in Hand	
Bill Payable		Cash at Bank	

Particular	Amount	Particulars	Amount
Sundry Creditors		Bills Received	
Outstanding Expenses		Short Term Investments	
Unearned Income		Sundry Debtors	
Fixed Liabilities:		Closing Stock	
Long Term Loans		Prepaid Expenses	
Reserves:		Accured Income	
Capital:		**Fixed Assets:**	
Add: Net Profit		Furniture	
Less: Drawings		Loose Tools	
Less: Income Tax		Motor Vehicle	
Less: Life Insurance Premium		Long Term Investments	
		Plant and Machinery	
		Land and Buildings	
		Patents	
		Goodwill	

Notes:

(1) The words 'As on' are used in the heading of the Balance Sheet. Because it is true only for the date on which it is prepared.

(2) The total of both the sides of the Balance Sheet is always equal.

(3) Prepaid expenses are treated as current assets. Though Cash cannot be realised from prepaid expenses, the service will be available against these without further payment.

2. **In the Order of Permanence:** This method is exactly the reverse of the first method discussed above. Assets which are most difficult to be converted into cash such as Goodwill are written first and the assets which are most liquid such as Cash in hand are written last. Similarly, those liabilities which are to be paid last, will be written first. In other words, the proprietor's capital is written first of all, then fixed or long term liabilities and lastly, the current liabilities. Joint stock companies are required under the Companies Act to prepare their Balance Sheet in the order of permanence.

It is essential to understand the classification of various assets and liabilities before preparing a Balance Sheet.

Classification of Assets

For better understanding of Balance Sheet items, the bankers classify the Assets side of the Balance Sheet in four categories:

1. **Current Assets :** Assets which can be converted into cash in a short span generally within a period of 12 months. For Example – Cash & Bank balances, Debtors & Bills Receivables, Inventory, and Prepaid Expenses.

2. **Fixed Assets :** Those assets which take more than 12 months in realization or the assets which are fixed in their place or those assets which get depreciated due to usage. Example: Plant & Machinery, Land & Building, Furniture & Fixture, Motor Vehicles etc.

3. **Intangible or Fictitious Assets :** Assets which are shown in the Balance Sheet but actually no one can see or touch those but actually their existence cannot be denied. Example: Goodwill, Preliminary Expenses, Copyright, Patent etc.

4. **Non-Current Assets :** This includes those items which were supposed to come under Current Assets but, due to some reasons they have lost some special characteristic and came under this head. Example: Sundry Debtors above 6 months, Tools, Out of fashion/date stock, Security Deposit with Telephone Dept., Security Deposit with Electricity Department etc.

Some more classification of Current Assets is also required for academic purpose, these may be classified into the following:

1. **Liquid Assets:** Liquid assets are those which are either in the form of Cash or can be quickly

converted into cash, such as Cash, Bills Receivable, Short Term Investments, Debtors, and Accrued Income etc. In other words, if Prepaid Expenses and Closing Stock are excluded from Current Assets, the balance will be Liquid Assets.

2. **Wasting Assets:** These are the assets which are exhausted or consumed over a period of time such as mines and oil wells. Their value reduces through being worked. These also include Patents and the properties taken on lease for a definite period of time.

3. **Tangible and Intangible Assets:** Tangible assets are those which have a physical existence or which can be seen and felt like Plant and Machinery, Building, Furniture, Stock, Cash etc. Intangible assets are those which do not have any physical existence or which cannot be seen or felt such as the Goodwill, Trade Marks, Patents etc. Intangible assets are as much valuable as tangible assets because they also help the firm in earning profits. For example, Goodwill helps in attracting customers and patents are actually the know-how which help in producing the goods.

Classification of Liabilities

According to their nature, the liabilities may be classified as follows:

1. **Fixed or Long-term Liabilities:** Those liabilities which are to be repaid after one year or more are termed as long-term liabilities. These include Public Deposits, Long-term Loans, Debentures etc.

2. **Current or Short-term Liabilities:** Those liabilities which are expected to be paid within one year of the date of the Balance Sheet are termed as current or short-term liabilities. These include Bank Overdraft, Creditors, Bills Payable, Outstanding expenses etc.

3. **Contingent Liabilities:** These are the liabilities which will become payable only on the happening of some specific event, otherwise not. Such as:

   (i) **Liabilities for bill discounted:** In case a bill discounted from the bank is dishonoured by the acceptor on the due date, the firm will become liable to the bank.

   (ii) **Liability in respect of a suit pending in a court of law:** This would become an actual liability if the suit is decided against the firm.

   (iii) **Liability in respect of a guarantee given for another person:** The firm would become liable to pay the amount if the person for whom guarantee is given fails to meet his obligation.

4. **Contingent Liabilities are not shown in the Balance Sheet:** They are, however, shown as a footnote just below the balance sheet so that their existence may be revealed.

Following Points should be Noted for Preparing Final Accounts:

1. If a trial balance is not given in the question, it is better to prepare a Trial Balance first of all. If there is a difference in the Trial Balance, the difference is placed to a 'Suspense A/c' and shown in the Balance Sheet.

2. It should be remembered that all items which appear in the Trial Balance should be shown only once whereas items which appear outside the Trial Balance, known as adjustments, have to be shown at two places.

3. The items which appear on the debit side of the Trial Balance should be shown either on the debit side of the Trading or Profit & Loss A/c or on the Assets side of the Balance Sheet.

4. The items which appear on the credit side of the Trial Balance should be shown either on the credit side of the Trading or Profit & Loss A/c or on the Liabilities side of the Balance Sheet.

5. All accounts relating to Goods such as Purchases, Sales, Purchase Returns and Sales Returns are written in the Trading Account. In addition to these, the Trading Account will also be debited with all expenses which are directly related to either purchase or manufacturing of goods. All the remaining expenses or the balances of the Nominal Accounts are shown in the Profit & Loss Account.

6. The balances of Personal and Real Accounts are always shown in the Balance Sheet.

7. If the expenses in respect of 'Rent' and 'Lighting' are clearly stated as having been incurred in respect of factory, these will be shown in the Trading Account, otherwise these will be shown in Profit & Loss Account. For example, if 'Factory Rent' is given in the question, it will be shown in Trading Account. Instead, if 'Rent' is given, it will be shown in Profit & Loss Account.

8. If a trial balance is not given in the question, and it is not clearly stated whether a particular item is expense or income, it will be treated as expense such as Discount, Commission, Brokerage or Rent etc.

9. The total of both sides of the Balance Sheet will always be equal.

- **ILLUSTRATION:** Classify the Following Assets/ Liabilities in the following groups:
  1. CURRENT ASSETS
  2. FIXED ASSETS
  3. NON-CURRENT ASSETS
  4. INTANGIBLE / FICTITIOUS ASSETS
  5. CAPITAL
  6. CURRENT LIABILITIES
  7. TERM LIABILITIES
  8. RESERVES & SURPLUS
  9. CONTINGENT LIABILITIES

Land & Building	₹ 15,00,000
Preliminary Expenses	₹ 1,30,000
Promoters Contribution	₹ 59,53,000
Deposit with Tele Dept.	₹ 18,000
Cash & Bank Balance	₹ 1,67,000
Bank Guarantee	₹ 7,00,000
Bank Overdraft	₹ 4,00,000
Debenture	₹ 30,00,000
Term Loans	₹ 41,00,000
Furniture & Fittings	₹ 6,75,000
General Reserves	₹ 3,65,200
Profit & Loss Debit Balance	₹ 4,72,000
Investment for 12 months	₹ 8,00,000
Plant & Machinery	₹ 65,00,000
Depreciation on Land & Building	₹ 15,000
—Do— Plant & Machinery	₹ 18,000
—Do— Furniture & Fittings	₹ 7,800
Stock of Raw Materials	₹ 6,55,000
Semi Finished Products	₹ 3,45,000
Finished Products	₹ 5,50,000
Sundry Debtors	₹ 32,49,000
Letter of Credit	₹ 16,00,000
Bills Receivable	₹ 4,51,000
Sundry Creditors	₹ 9,60,000
Bills Payable	₹ 7,45,000
Prepaid Expenses	₹ 95,000
Outstanding Taxes	₹ 63,000
Cash Credit Account	₹ 9,00,000
12 Months Instalment of Term Loan	₹ 11,53,000
Tools	₹ 17,000
Unusable Stock	₹ 4,56,000
Goodwill	₹ 10,00,000
Letter of Undertaking	₹ 10,00,000
Drawings	₹ 6,00,000

Solution:

CURRENT ASSETS

1.	Cash & Bank Balance		₹ 1,67,000
2.	Investment for 12 months		₹ 8,00,000
3.	Inventory		
	Raw Materials	₹ 6,55,000	
	Semi-Finished	₹ 3,45,000	
	Finished Goods	₹ 5,50,000	**₹ 15,50,000**
4.	Sundry Debtors	₹ 32,49,000	
5.	Bills Receivable	₹ 4,51,000	
6.	Prepaid Expenses	₹ 95,000	**₹ 63,12,000**

FIXED ASSETS

1.	Land & Building	₹ 15,00,000	
	Less Depreciation	₹ 15,000	**₹ 14,85,000**
2.	Plant & Machinery	₹ 65,00,000	
	Less Depreciation	₹ 18,000	**₹ 64,82,000**
3.	Furniture & Fittings	₹ 6,75,000	
	Less Depreciation	₹ 7,800	**₹ 6,67,200**
			₹ 86,34,200

NON-CURRENT ASSETS

1.	Tools	₹ 17,000	
2.	Unusable Stock	₹ 4,56,000	
3.	Deposit with Telephone Dept.	₹ 18,000	**₹ 4,91,000**

INTANGIBLE / FICTITIOUS ASSETS

1.	Goodwill	₹ 10,00,000	
2.	Preliminary Expenses	₹ 1,30,000	**₹ 11,30,000**

CAPITAL & RESERVES

Promoter's Contribution		₹ 59,53,000
Less P&L Debit Balance	₹ 4,72,000	
Less Drawings	₹ 6,00,000	**₹ 10,72,000**
		₹ 48,81,000
General Reserve		₹ 3,65,200

CURRENT LIABILITIES

1.	Bank Overdraft	₹ 4,00,000	
2.	Sundry Creditors	₹ 9,60,000	
3.	Bills Payable	₹ 7,45,000	
4.	Cash Credit Account	₹ 9,00,000	
5.	12 Months Instalment of T/L	₹ 11,53,000	
6.	Outstanding Taxes	₹ 63,000	**₹ 42,21,000**

TERM LIABILITIES

1.	Term Loans	₹ 41,00,000	
2.	Debentures	₹ 30,00,000	**₹ 71,00,000**

CONTINGENT LIABILITIES

1.	Bank Guarantee	₹ 7,00,000	
2.	Letter of Credit	₹ 16,00,000	
	Letter of Undertaking	₹ 10,00,000	**₹ 33,00,000**

Balance Sheet

Capital & Liabilities	Amount (₹)	Assets & Properties	Amount (₹)
Current Liabilities	42,21,000	Fixed Assets	86,34,200
Term Liabilities	71,00,000	Current Assets	63,12,000
Capital	48,81,000	Non-Current Assets	4,91,000
Reserves	3,65,200	Intangible Assets	11,30,000
TOTAL	**1,65,67,200**	**TOTAL**	**1,65,67,200**

- **Illustration 2:** From the following balances of Siya Ram, Prepare a Balance Sheet as on 31st December, 2018.

Particulars	Amount (Dr.)	Amount (Cr.)
Plant and Machinery	8,00,000	
Land and Building	6,00,000	
Furniture	1,50,000	
Cash in Hand	20,000	
Bank Overdraft		1,80,000
Debtors and Creditors	3,20,000	2,40,000
Bills Receivable and Bills Payable	1,00,000	60,000
Closing Stock	4,00,000	
Investments (Short-term)	80,000	
Capital		15,00,000
Drawings	1,30,000	
Net Profit		6,20,000
	26,00,0000	**26,00,0000**

Solution:

Balance Sheet

(as on 31st December, 2018)

Liabilities	Amount		Assets	Amount
	₹			₹
Bank overdraft	1,80,000		Cash in Hand	20,000
B/P	60,000		B/R	1,00,000
Creditors	2,40,000		Investments (Short-term)	80,000
Capital			Debtors	3,20,000
Add: Net Profit	15,00,000		Closing Stock	4,00,000
	6,20,000		Furniture	1,50,000
	21,20,000		Plant & Machinery	8,00,000
Less: Drawings	1,30,000	19,90,000	Land & Building	6,00,000
		24,70,000		**24,70,000**

Balance Sheet: Horizontal format of Balance Sheet is also used by the business other than company.

A. Liabilities

(a) Capital: This indicates the initial amount the owner or owners of the business contributed. This contribution could be at the time of starting business or even at a later stage to satisfy requirements of funds for expansion, diversification etc. As per business entity concept, owners and business are distinct entities, and thus, any contribution by owners by way of capital is liability.

(b) Reserves and Surplus: The business is a going concern and will keep making profit or loss year by year. The accumulation of these profit or loss figures (called as surpluses) will keep on increasing or decreasing owners' equity. In case of non-corporate forms of business, the profits or losses are added to the capital A/c and not shown separately in the balance sheet of the business.

(c) Long Term or Non-Current Liabilities: These are obligations which are to be settled over a longer period of time say 5-10 years. These funds are raised by way of loans from banks and financial institutions.

Such borrowed funds are to be repaid in installments during the tenure of the loan as agreed. Such funds are usually raised to meet financial requirements to procure fixed assets. These funds should not be generally used for day-to-day business activities. Such loan are normally given on the basis of some security from the business e.g. against a charge on the fixed assets. So, long term loan are called as "Secured Loan" also.

(d) Short Term or Current Liabilities: A liability shall be classified as Current when it satisfies any of the following:

- It is expected to be settled in the organisation's normal Operating Cycle,
- It is held primarily for the purpose of being traded,
- It is due to be settled within 12 months after the Reporting Date, or
- The organization does not have an unconditional right to defer settlement of the liability for at least 12 months after the reporting date (Terms of a Liability that could, at the option of the counter party, result in its settlement by the issue of Equity Instruments do not affect its classification) Current liabilities comprise of:

(i) Sundry Creditors: Amounts payable to suppliers against purchase of goods. This is usually settled within 30-180 days.

(ii) Advances from Customers: At times customer may pay advance i.e. before they get delivery of goods. Till the business supplies goods to them, it has an obligation to pay back the advance in case of failure to supply. Hence, such advances are treated as liability till the time they get converted to sales.

(iii) Outstanding Expenses: These represent services procured but not paid for. These are usually settled within 30–60 days e.g. phone bill of Sept is normally paid in Oct.

(iv) Bills Payable: There are times when suppliers do not give clean credit. They supply goods against a promissory note to be signed as a promise to pay after or on a particular date. These are called as bills payable or notes payable.

(v) Bank Overdrafts: Banks may give fund facilities like overdraft whereby, business is permitted to issue cheques up to a certain limit. The bank will honour these cheques and will recover this money from business. This is a short term obligation.

B. Assets

In accounting language, all debit balances in personal and real accounts are called as assets. Assets are broadly classified into fixed assets and current assets.

(a) Fixed Assets: These represent the facilities or resources owned by the business for a longer period of time. The basic purpose of these resources is not to buy and sell them, but to use for future earnings. The benefit from use of these assets is spread over a very long period. The fixed assets could be in tangible form such as buildings, machinery, vehicles, computers etc, whereas some could be in intangible form viz. Patents, Trademarks, Goodwill etc. The fixed assets are subject to wear and tear which is called as depreciation. In the balance sheet, fixed assets are always shown as "original cost less depreciation".

(b) Investments: These are funds invested outside the business on a temporary basis. At times, when the business has surplus funds, and they are not immediately required for business purpose, it is prudent to invest it outside business e.g. in mutual funds or fixed deposit. The purpose is to earn a reasonable return on this money instead of keeping them idle. These are assets shown separately in balance sheet.

Investments can be classified into Current Investments and Non-current Investments.

Non-current Investments are investments which are restricted beyond the current period as to sale or disposal.

Whereas, current investments are investments that are by their nature readily realizable and is intended to be held for not more than one year from the date on which such investment is made.

(c) Current Assets: An asset shall be classified as Current when it satisfies any of the following:

- It is expected to be realised in, or is intended for sale or consumption in the organisation's normal Operating Cycle,
- It is held primarily for the purpose of being traded,
- It is due to be realised within 12 months after the Reporting Date, or
- It is Cash or Cash Equivalent unless it is restricted from being exchanged or used to settle a Liability for at least 12 months after the Reporting Date.

Current Assets Comprise of:

(i) Stocks: This includes stock of raw material, semi-finished goods or WIP, and finished goods.

Stocks are shown at lesser of the cost or market price. Provision for obsolescence, if any, is also reduced. Generally, stocks are physically counted and compared with book stocks to ensure that there are no discrepancies. In case of discre-pancies, the same are adjusted to P&L A/c and stock figures are shown as net of this adjustment.

(ii) Debtors: They represent customer balances which are not paid. The bad debts or a provision for bad debt is reduced from debtors and net figure is shown in balance sheet.

(iii) Bills Receivables: Credit to customers may be given based on a bill to be signed by them payable to the business at an agreed date in future. At the end of accounting period, the bills accepted but not yet paid are shown as bills receivables.

(iv) Cash in Hand: This represents cash actually held by the business on the balance sheet date. This cash may be held at various offices, locations or sites from where the business activity is carried out. Cash at all locations is physically counted and verified with the book balance. Discrepancies if any are adjusted.

(v) Cash at Bank: Dealing through banks is quite common. Funds held as balances with bank are also treated as current asset, as it is to be applied for paying to suppliers. The balance at bank as per books of accounts is always reconciled with the balance as per bank statement, the reasons for differences are identified and required entries are passed.

(vi) Prepaid Expenses: They represent payments made against which services are expected to be received in a very short period.

(vii) Advances to Suppliers: When amounts are paid to suppliers in advance and goods or services are not received till the balance sheet date, they are to be shown as current assets. This is because advances paid are like right to claim the business gets.

Please note that both current assets and current liabilities are used in day-to-day business activities. The current assets minus current liabilities are called as working capital or net current assets. The following report is usual horizontal form of balance sheet. Please note that the assets are normally shown in descending order of their liquidity. Also, capital, long term liabilities and short term liabilities are shown in that order.

- **Intangible Assets:** Are those Fixed Assets which cannot be seen or touched or felt, i.e., having no physical existence, e.g. Goodwill.

- **Fictitious Assets:** Are worthless assets but shown as assets in the Balance Sheet, E.g. preliminary expenses, Discount on issue of debentures.

TEST YOURSELF

1. In a Trial Balance which types of balances are transferred to the Balance Sheet to know the financial position of the business?
   (a) Balances from assets accounts
   (b) Balances from capital or owner's equity account
   (c) Balances from liabilities accounts
   (d) All of the above

2. __________ is prepared for calculating the gross profit or gross loss arising or incurred as a result of the trading activities of a business.
   (a) Trading Account
   (b) Profit & Loss A/c
   (c) Balance Sheet
   (d) Cash Book

3. Capital expenses are shown in__________.
   (a) Trading Account
   (b) Profit & Loss A/c
   (c) Balance Sheet
   (d) Cash Book

4. A ________ is an account into which all gains and losses are collected, in order to ascertain the excess gains over the losses or vice-versa.
   (a) Trading Account
   (b) Profit & Loss A/c
   (c) Balance Sheet
   (d) Cash Book

5. All expenses which relate to either purchase of raw material for manufacturing of goods are recorded in the ___________.
   (a) Trading Account
   (b) Profit & Loss A/c
   (c) Balance Sheet
   (d) Cash Book

6. Trading account is a:
   (a) Personal A/c
   (b) Real A/c
   (c) Nominal A/c
   (d) None

7. The closing stock of the last year becomes the opening stock of the current year. Opening Stock will include which of the following?
   (a) Opening Stock of Raw Material
   (b) Opening Stock of Semi-finished Goods
   (c) Opening Stock of Finished Goods
   (d) All of the above

8. Closing stock appearing in the Trial Balance is shown in __________.
   (a) Trading A/c and Balance Sheet
   (b) Profit & Loss A/c
   (c) Balance Sheet only
   (d) Trading A/c only

9. Depreciation account appearing in the Trial Balance is shown in ________.
   (a) Profit & Loss A/c
   (b) Trading A/c
   (c) Deducted from the concerned assets A/c
   (d) Shown on the liability side

10. Which of the following is a statement showing the financial status of the company at any given time?
    (a) Trading Account
    (b) Profit & Loss A/c
    (c) Balance Sheet
    (d) Cash Book

11. Which of the following is a statement of revenues and expenses for a specific period of time?
    (a) Trading Account
    (b) Profit & Loss A/c
    (c) Balance Sheet
    (d) Trial Balance

12. Balance Sheet is a statement of __________.
    (a) Assets
    (b) Liability
    (c) Capital
    (d) All of the above

13. Revenue receipts are shown in __________.
    (a) Balance Sheet
    (b) Profit & Loss appropriation A/c
    (c) Manufacturing A/c
    (d) Trading and Profit & Loss A/c

14. The term 'Financial Statement' covers:
    (a) Profit & Loss Statement
    (b) Balance Sheet and Profit & Loss Statement appropriation account
    (c) Profit & Loss Statement and Balance Sheet
    (d) All of above are false

15. Goods costing ₹ 10,000 were damaged by fire. Insurance company admitted a claim of ₹ 8,500. Profit & Loss a/c will be debited with __________.
    (a) ₹ 10,000
    (b) ₹ 8,500

(c) ₹ 5,500

(d) ₹ 1,500

16. If depreciation is not charged, Profit & Loss a/c will show:

(a) More profits

(b) Less profits

(c) Nominal profits

(d) Original profits

17. At the end of each financial year all accounts of ...... and ...... are transferred to Trading and Profit & Loss account, called closing entries.

(a) Assets, liabilities

(b) Income, liabilities

(c) Expenses, assets

(d) Income, expenses

18. The _______ are those which are either in the form of cash or can be easily converted into cash within one year of the date of Balance Sheet.

(a) Current Liabilities

(b) Current Assets

(c) Non-Current Assets

(d) Investment

19. Which is not an intangible asset?

(a) Goodwill   (b) Patent

(c) Preliminary expenses (d) Copyright

20. Which is not a Current Liability?

(a) Sundry Creditors

(b) Bills Payable

(c) Bank Overdrafts

(d) None of the above

ANSWER

1	2	3	4	5	6	7	8	9	10
(d)	(a)	(c)	(b)	(a)	(c)	(d)	(c)	(a)	(c)

11	12	13	14	15	16	17	18	19	20
(b)	(d)	(d)	(c)	(d)	(a)	(d)	(b)	(c)	(d)

RATIO ANALYSIS

INTRODUCTION

Accounting ratios, also known as financial ratios, are used to measure the efficiency and profitability of a company based on its financial reports. They provide a way of expressing the relationship between one accounting data point to another, and are the basis of ratio analysis.

MEANING OF ACCOUNTING RATIO

According to J. Batty "the term accounting ratio is used to describe significant relationships between figures shown on a Balance Sheet, in a Profit and Loss Account, in a Budgetary Control System or in any part of the accounting organisation." In simple words, it is an assessment of significance of any figure in relation to another.

An accounting ratio compares two-line items in a company's financial statements, namely made up of its income statement, balance sheet and cash flow statement. These ratios can be used to evaluate a company's fundamentals and provide information about the performance of the company over the last quarter or fiscal year. Examples of financial ratios include gross margin, operating margin, the debt-to-equity ratio, the quick ratio and the payout ratio. Each of these ratios requires the most recent data in order to be relevant.

The accounting ratios indicate a quantitative relationship which is used for analysis and decision-making. It provides basis for inter-firm as well as intra-firm comparisons. Besides, in order to make the ratios effective, they are compared with ratios of base period or with standards or with the industry average ratios.

CLASSIFICATION OF ACCOUNTING RATIOS

Accounting ratios may be classified in a number of ways to suit any particular purpose. Different kinds of ratios are selected for different types of situations. The most widely used classifications are:

(A) Traditional Classification or According to Sources

(B) Functional Classification or According to Nature

(A) Traditional Classification or According to Sources: Traditional Classification of accounting ratios can be further classified into following three groups:

1. **Balance Sheet Ratios:** These ratios are also known as financial ratios. These ratios deal with relationship between two items or group of items which are both available in Balance sheet.

   Examples of these ratios are: Current ratio, Liquid ratio, Debt-Equity ratio, Capital bearing ratio, Proprietary ratio, etc.

2. **Profit and Loss Account Ratios:** These ratios deal with the relationship between two items or group of items which are usually taken out from the Profit and Loss Account.

   Examples of these ratios are: Gross profit ratio, Net profit ratio, Operating ratio, Operating profit ratio, Interest coverage ratio, Debt service coverage ratio etc.

3. **Inter-statement Ratios or Combined Ratios:** These ratios deal with the relationship between items, one of which is drawn from Profit and Loss Account and other is from Balance Sheet.

   Examples of these ratios are: Stock turnover ratio, Debtors turnover ratio, Creditors turnover ratio, Assets turnover ratio. Return on capital employed, etc.

(B) Functional Classification or According to Nature: Functional Classification of accounting ratios can be further classified into following four groups:

1. **Liquidity Ratios:** The terms liquidity and short-term solvency are synonymously used. The liquidity ratios indicate the liquidity position of the enterprise. These ratios analyse the ability of the firm to meet its current liabilities out of current assets. Liquid ratios are of help in ascertaining the effectiveness of the working capital management.

   Examples of these ratios are: Current ratio, Quick ratio, Inventory turnover ratio, Debtors turnover ratio, Creditors turnover ratio etc.

2. **Leverage Ratios:** It refers to those financial ratios which measure the long-term solvency and capital structure of the firm. They show the mix of funds provided by the owners and lenders and also the risk involved in debt financing.

   Examples of these ratios are: Debt-Equity ratio, Capital gearing ratio, Fixed assets to Net worth ratio, Interest coverage ratio, Debt service coverage ratio etc.

3. **Turnover or Activity Ratios:** These ratios measure the efficiency with which the funds have been employed in the business. They indicate frequency of sales with respect to its assets. These are computed with reference to sales or cost of goods sold and expressed in terms of times or rates.

   Examples of these ratios are: Stock Turnover ratio, Debtors Turnover ratio, Creditors Turnover ratio, Fixed Assets Turnover ratio, etc.

4. **Profitability Ratios:** Profitability is an indication of the efficiency with which the operations of the business are carried on. Profitability ratios show the effect of business transactions on the profits. A lower profitability ratio may arise due to lack of control over business expenses.

   Examples of these ratios are: Gross profit ratio, Net profit ratio, Operating ratio, Operating profit ratio, Return in capital employed, etc.

USES OF ACCOUNTING RATIOS

Analysis of financial statements is made to assess the financial position and profitability of a concern. Analysis can be made through accounting ratios, fitting trend line, common size statements, etc. Accounting ratios calculated for a number of years show the trend of the change of position, i.e., whether the trend is upward or downward or static. The ascertainment of trend helps us in making estimates for the future. The main uses of analysis of financial statements are:

1. Ratios help to assess the profitability of the concern.

2. Ratios help in analysing the performance trends over a long period of time.

3. They also help a business to compare the financial results to those of competitors.

4. Ratios assist the management in decision making.

5. They also point out problem and weak areas along with the strength areas.

6. Ratios to help to develop relationships between different financial statement items.

7. Ratios have the advantage of controlling for differences in size. For example, two businesses may be quite different in size but can be compared in terms of profitability, liquidity, etc., by the use of ratios.

LIMITATIONS OF RATIO ANALYSIS

The technique of ratio analysis is a very useful device for making a study of the financial health of a firm. But it has some limitations which must not be lost sight of before undertaking such analysis. Some of these limitations are:

1. **Limitations of Financial Statements:** Ratios are calculated from the information recorded in the financial statements. But financial statements suffer from a number, therefore, affect the quality of ratio analysis.

2. **Historical Information:** Financial statement provides historical information. They do not reflect current conditions. Hence, it is not useful in predicting the future.

3. **Different Accounting Policies:** Different accounting policies regarding valuation of inventories, charging depreciation etc. make the accounting data and accounting ratios of two firms non-comparable.

4. **Lack of Standard of Comparison:** No fixed standards can be laid down for ideal ratios. For example, current ratio is said to be ideal if current assets are twice the current liabilities. But this conclusion may not be justifiable in case of those concerns which have adequate arrangements with their bankers for providing funds when they require, it may be perfectly ideal if current assets are equal to or slightly more than current liabilities.

5. **Quantitative Analysis:** Ratios are tools of quantitative analysis only and qualitative factors are ignored while computing the ratios. For example, a high current ratio may not necessarily mean sound liquid position when current assets include a large inventory consisting of mostly obsolete items.

6. **Window-Dressing:** The term 'window-dressing' means presenting the financial statements in such a way to show a better position than what it actually is. If, for instance, low rate of depreciation is charged, an item of revenue expense is treated as capital expenditure etc. the position of the concern may be made to appear in the balance sheet much better than what it is. Ratios computed from such balance sheet cannot be used for scanning the financial position of the business.

7. **Changes in Price Level:** Fixed assets show the position statement at cost only. Hence, it does not reflect the changes in price level. Thus, it makes comparison difficult.

8. **Causal Relationship Must:** Proper care should be taken to study only such figures as have a cause-and-effect relationship; otherwise ratios will only be misleading.

9. **Ratios Account for one Variable:** Since ratios account for only one variable, they cannot always give correct picture since several other variables such Government policy, economic conditions, availability of resources etc. should be kept in mind while interpreting ratios.

10. **Seasonal Factors Affect Financial Data:** Proper care must be taken when interpreting accounting ratios calculated for seasonal business. For example, an umbrella company maintains high inventory during rainy season and for the rest of year its inventory level becomes 25% of the seasonal inventory level. Hence, liquidity ratios and inventory turnover ratio will give biased picture.

CALCULATION AND INTERPRETATION OF VARIOUS RATIOS

(A) Leverage Ratios or Solvency or Long-term Financial Position Ratios: It refers to those financial ratios which measure the long-term solvency and capital structure of the firm. Solvency generally refers to the capacity or ability of the firm to meet its short-term and long-term obligations. The capacity to pay-off the current debts of a firm is represented by the liquidity ratios. Generally, shareholders, debenture holders and other long-term creditors like banks, financial institutions etc. are interested in these ratios. These ratios are also used to analyse the capital structure i.e., the mix of funds provided by owners and outsiders.

1. **Debt-Equity Ratio:** This ratio shows the relationship between debt capital and equity or shareholders fund in the capital structure of the firm. It is determined to measure the firm's obligations to creditors in relation to funds invested by the owners. Generally, it is calculated as:

(i) $\text{Debt-Equity Ratio} = \dfrac{\text{Long-term Debt}}{\text{Shareholders' Fund}}$

Shareholders Fund

    = Equity Share Capital + Pref. Share capital + Reserves & Surplus − Fictitious Assets

or

(ii) Debt-Equity Ratio

$$= \dfrac{\text{Long-term Debt + Short-term Debt}}{\text{Shareholders' Fund}}$$

(iii) Debt-Equity Ratio

$$= \dfrac{\text{Long-term Debt + Short-term Debt + Pref. Share Capital}}{\text{Shareholders' Fund}}$$

(iv) $\text{Debt-Equity Ratio} = \dfrac{\text{External Equities}}{\text{Internal Equities}}$

There is some controversy whether current liabilities should be included in debt or not. Argument forwarded for inclusion of current liabilities is that they are part of a company's total obligation and, like other sources of funds such as equity, long-term debts they are also not cost-free. Similarly, the modern approach is to include Redeemable Preference Shares in debt and Irredeemable Preference Shares in equity.

Significance and Interpretation: Debt-Equity ratio indicates the respective claim of creditors and owners in the assets of the firm. It shows the extent to which debt financing has been used in the business. A higher debt-equity ratio indicates higher proportion of debt content in the capital structure of the firm. There is possibility of increasing the rate of return or EPS to equity shareholders so long as the cost of debt is lower than the rate of return on investment. But financing from debt increases the financial risk of shareholders.

2. **Proprietary Ratio:** This ratio establishes the relationship between total assets and shareholders' fund. The purpose of the ratio is to indicate the percentage of owner's fund invested in fixed assets. It is calculated by dividing proprietary fund by total assets:

$$\text{Proprietary Ratio} = \dfrac{\text{Proprietary Fund}}{\text{Total Assets}}$$

Proprietary Fund

    = Equity Share Capital + Pref. Share Capital + Reserve & Surplus − Fictitious Assets

Total assets do not include fictitious assets.

Significance and Interpretation: This ratio is a test of long-term financial position of the firm. It indicates how much of the total assets have been procured with shareholders fund. Higher the ratio, lower is the dependence on external fund and hence, greater is the solvency of the firm.

3. **Fixed Assets to Proprietors' Fund:** This ratio establishes the relationship between fixed assets and shareholders fund. It is calculated as:

$$\text{Fixed Assets} - \text{Proprietrary Ratio} = \frac{\text{Fixed Assets}}{\text{Proprietary Fund}}$$

Significance and Interpretation: The ratio indicates the extent of proprietor's fund invested in acquisition of fixed assets. If it is less than 1, it will mean that a part of proprietor's fund is investment in financing working capital of the firm. For example, if the ratio is 0.75:1, it will mean that 75% of the proprietor's fund is investment in fixed assets and 25% is invested in working capital.

If the ratio is more than 1, it will mean that creditors have been used to acquire a part of fixed assets. If short-term funds are used in the purchase of fixed assets, it will adversely affect the liquidity position, as it will not be possible to liquidate fixed assets for paying short-term liabilities.

Thus, a fundamental principle of sound financing policy is that all fixed assets should be financed out of long-term funds. Short-term funds should be utilised only for working capital requirement of the firm.

4. **Interest Coverage Ratio:** This ratio relates to the fixed interest charges to the income earned by the company. It is an important test of solvency for the company. All long-term creditors are interested to know the company's ability to meet its current interest charges. The ratio between fixed interest charges and earnings before interest and taxes (EBIT) is a rough indication of the company's ability to pay fixed interest charges out of profit. Banks calculate ISCR during the financing of Working Capital.

Thus:

Interest Coverage Ratio

$$= \frac{\text{Net Profit before interest and taxes}}{\text{Fixed interest charges}}$$

Significance and Interpretation: This ratio gives an idea of the number of times that fixed interest charges are covered by earnings. It is an index of the financial strength of an enterprise and indicates the margin of safety of the long-term creditors. If the ratio is 5 times, it will mean that the company is able to pay interest five times out of its earning. A high ratio assures the lender regular and periodical interest income.

However, a too high interest coverage ratio may be the result of using a very small amount of debt in the capital structure. In this case, the firm cannot avail the full benefit of trading on equity. Again, a too low interest coverage ratio may be the result of using excessive amount of debt capital than warranted by the profitability of the firm. So, an immediate action may be taken to redeem a portion of debt to improve profitability.

5. **Debt-Services Coverage Ratio (DSCR):** The debt service coverage ratio (DSCR) compares a business's level of cash flow to its debt obligations. Lenders typically calculate DSCR by dividing the business's annual net operating income by the business's annual debt payments.

Banks or lenders don't want to lose their investments or take the trouble of chasing down a borrower who defaults. So, they look for reassurance that your business has generated—and will continue to generate—enough income to pay back the loan with interest. The formula used for calculating the debt service coverage ratio is:

DSCR = Net Operating Income / Total Debt Service

Generally, the debt service coverage ratio is calculated as:

DSCR = (Annual Net Income + Interest Expense + Depreciation + Other discretionary and non-cash items like non-contractual provided by the management)/ (Principal Repayment + Interest Payments + Lease Payments)

Thus, to calculate the debt service coverage ratio of a company or business entity, it is, at the first point, essential to calculate the net operating income of the company. Banks calculate DSCR during the financing of Term Loan. When only term loan is financing with repayment mode of EMI, it is calculated as:

DSCR =

$$\frac{\text{Net Income} + \text{Depreciation} + \text{Interest on Term Loan}}{\text{Equated Monthly Instalment (EMI)}}$$

Significance and Interpretation: Debt service coverage ratio (DSCR) is one of many financial ratios that lenders assess when considering a loan application. This ratio is especially important because the result gives some indication to the lender of whether you'll be able to pay back the loan with interest.

It provides the value in terms of the number of times the total debt service obligations consisting of interest and repayment of principal in instalments are covered by the total operating funds, available after the payment of taxes. The higher the ratio, the better it is. In general, lending financial institutions consider 2:1 as satisfactory ratio.

(B) Short term Solvency Ratios or Liquid Ratios: These ratios indicate the capacity or ability of the firm to meet the maturing or current liabilities, the efficiency of the management in utilizing the working capital and the progress attained in current financial position.

1. **Current Ratio or Working Capital Ratio:** Current ratio may be defined as the ratio of current assets and current liabilities and is obtained by dividing current assets by current liabilities. It is also known as working capital ratio. Working capital is defined as excess of current assets over current liabilities. This ratio is the indicator of short-term liquidity position of a firm. The term liquidity means the ability of the firm to meet its short-term maturing obligations.

Thus, if total current assets amount to ₹ 2,00,000 and total current liabilities ₹ 1,00,000, then,

$$\text{Current Ratio} = \frac{\text{Current Assets}}{\text{Current Liabilities}} = \frac{₹\,2,00,000}{₹\,1,00,000} = 2:1$$

Current assets mean cash or those assets convertible or expected to be converted into cash within a year.

It includes: Cash in hand and at bank, Marketable securities or readily realisable investments, Bills receivables, Book debts (excluding bad debts and provision), Inventories and Pre-paid expenses.

Current liabilities mean those liabilities which are to be paid within a year.

It includes: Sundry creditors, Bills payable, Short-term loans, Bank-overdraft, Cash credit, Outstanding expenses, Provision for taxation, Proposed dividend, Unclaimed dividend, etc.

Significance and Interpretation: Current ratio measures short-term solvency or liquidity position of the firm. It indicates the availability of current assets to meet its current liabilities. A relatively high current ratio is considered as an indication that the company is in a position to pay its current liabilities out of current assets and its liquidity position is good. But, at the same time, a higher current ratio would mean that the company may have an excessive investment in current assets that does not produce a significant return.

As a convention, current ratio 2 : 1 is taken as standard which means that for every ₹ 1 of current liabilities, current assets of the value of ₹ 2 are available for payment. The logic is that if the current assets are reduced to half i.e., ₹ 1 instead of ₹ 2, then also the creditors will be able to get their payments in full.

2. **Liquid Ratio or Add-test Ratio or Quick Ratio:** Current ratio is a crude test of liquidity. For better analysis of liquidity, the current ratio is modified. The modified version is called 'Liquid ratio' or 'Quick ratio'. Thus, current ratio is a liberal test of liquidity while quick ratio is a conservative test of liquidity.

Quick ratio or liquid ratio is the ratio between quick or liquid assets and quick or liquid liabilities. It shows the availability of funds for meeting the immediate liabilities. This ratio is obtained by dividing liquid assets by liquid liabilities. If the liquid assets amount to ₹ 1,00,000 and liquid liabilities ₹ 1,00,000, then:

$$\text{Liquid Ratio} = \frac{\text{Liquid Assets}}{\text{Liquid Liabilities}} = \frac{₹\,1,00,000}{₹\,1,00,000} = 1:1$$

Liquid Assets
= Current Assets – (Inventory + Pre-paid Expenses)

Liquid Liabilities
= Current Liabilities – Bank Overdraft

Liquid Ratio

$$= \frac{\text{Current Assets} - (\text{Inventory} + \text{Prepaid Expenses})}{\text{Current Liabilities} - \text{Bank Overdraft}}$$

Liquid assets mean those assets which are immediately convertible into cash without much loss. It includes cash, debtors-less bad debts, short-term bills receivable and temporary investments held in lieu of cash. Inventories and pre-paid expenses are excluded from liquid assets. Inventories are not included in quick assets as it takes long time for its conversion into cash. Similarly, pre-paid expenses are excluded from quick assets since no cash will be realised from it.

Liquid liabilities mean those liabilities which are payable within a short period of time. Normally, bank overdraft and cash credit facility are excluded from quick liabilities as they are used as permanent mode of financing by the firm. If bank overdraft is payable on demand, it is to be included in quick liabilities.

Significance and Interpretation: This ratio is an important indicator of financial health of a firm. As per convention, normal quick ratio should be 1: 1. It implies that every rupee of quick liabilities should be backed by quick assets of equal value. If the ratio is less than this, it means that arrangement from outside sources of funds will have to be made for meeting some portion of the immediately maturing liabilities. This is not a desirable situation and it should be avoided.

3. **Absolute Liquidity Ratio:** Absolute liquidity is represented by cash and near cash items. Hence, in computation of this ratio, only absolute liquid assets are compared with liquid liabilities. The absolute liquid assets are cash in hand, cash at Bank and marketable securities.

Absolute Liquid Ratio

$$= \frac{Cash + Bank + Marketable\ Securities}{Liquid\ Liabilities}$$

Significance and Interpretation: This ratio measures the instant capacity of the firm to meet its quick liabilities. Debtors are excluded from the list of liquid assets in order to obtain absolute liquid assets since there are some doubts relating to their liquidity. However, this ratio is not widely used in practice.

(C) Turnover Ratio: A turnover ratio represents the amount of assets or liabilities that a company replaces in relation to its sales. The concept is useful for determining the efficiency with which a business utilizes its assets.

1. **Inventory Turnover Ratio:** It is also known as Stock Turnover Ratio. Normally, it establishes a relationship between cost of goods sold during a period and average inventory held in that period. This ratio indicates whether investment in inventory is within proper limit or not.

It is an index of liquidity of a firm showing the rate at which inventories are converted into sales and then into cash. This ratio helps the financial manager to evaluate the inventory policy. This ratio is obtained by dividing cost of goods sold by average inventory or by dividing net sales by average inventory.

Thus:

Inventory Turnover Ratio

= Cost of goods sold/Average Inventory

Cost of goods sold

= Opening Stock + Purchases – Closing Stock

or Cost of goods sold = Sales – Gross profit.

Average Inventory

= 1/2 (Opening stock + Closing stock)

When number of days in a year (i.e., 365 days) are divided by the inventory turnover ratio, we get the average inventory holding period:

Average Inventory holding period

$$= \frac{365\ days}{Inventory\ Turnover}$$

$$= \frac{365\ days \times Average\ Inventory}{Cost\ of\ goods\ sold}$$

If the average inventory holding period is expressed in month, 365 days will be replaced by 12 months in the numerator. Sometime inventory turnover ratio is computed with reference to sales instead of cost of goods sold. However, the use of the first formula is more logical as, in that case, both the numerator and denominator are expressed at cost.

Significance and Interpretation: Inventory turnover ratio indicates the efficiency of inventory management. It shows how fast inventory is used/sold. It is an effective tool to measure the liquidity of inventory and thereby to avoid any danger of over-stocking.

A high inventory turnover ratio indicates brisk sales which is good from liquidity point of view. A low ratio indicates that inventories are not used/sold and lying in the warehouse for a long time. It may reflect dull business, over-investment in inventory, accumulation of huge amount of slow-moving and obsolete stock, etc. A high level of obsolete stock means blockage of capital. This will cause high interest and other inventory carrying cost. The ultimate impact is impairment of profitability.

2. **Debtors Turnover Ratio:** When a firm sells goods on credit and the realisation of credit sales is delayed, the receivable or book debt is created. Cash is received from these receivables or debtors afterwards. The speed or velocity at which these receivables are being converted into cash affects the liquidity of the firm. This ratio indicates the efficiency of the credit and collection policies of the firm.

Debtors Turnover Ratio

$$= \frac{Credit\ Sales}{Average\ Receivables}$$

When the number of days in a year (i.e., 365 days) are divided by the debtor's turnover ratio we get the average collection period i.e., the period during which fund remains blocked in the hands of customer.

Average Collection Period

$$= \frac{365 \text{ days}}{\text{Debtors Turnover Ratio}}$$

$$= \frac{365 \text{ days} \times \text{Average Receivables}}{\text{Credit Sales}}$$

If the average collection period is to be expressed in month, 365 days will be replaced by 12 months in the numerator. Receivables consist of sundry debtors and bills receivable. Average receivable may be the average of opening receivables and closing receivables.

Significance and Interpretation: The velocity or turnover of debtors gives an indication of the efficiency with which the debtors or receivables are being managed. The higher the ratio or, in other words, shorter the average collection period, better will be quality of debtors. It implies prompt payment by debtors.

3. **Creditors Turnover Ratio:** This ratio also measures the liquidity of the firm. It indicates whether the firm is making payment to the trade creditors in time or not. In other words, this ratio shows what period will be required to pay the suppliers in respect of credit purchases. This ratio is calculated by dividing the credit purchase with the figure of average accounts payable. Accounts payable include both sundry creditors and bills payable.

Creditors Turnover Ratio

$$= \frac{\text{Credit Purchase}}{\text{Average Accounts Payable}}$$

Average payment period is obtained by dividing the number of days in a year (365 days) by the creditors' turnover ratio:

Average Payment Period

$$= \frac{365 \text{ days}}{\text{Creditors Turnover Ratio}}$$

$$= \frac{\text{Average Accounts Payable}}{\text{Credit Purchase}} \times 365 \text{ days}$$

If the average payment period is expressed in months, 365 days will be replaced by 12 months in the numerator.

Significance and Interpretation: The ratio indicates the number of days the firm usually takes on an average to pay its creditors. A higher creditors turnover ratio or lower creditors payment period signifies that the creditors are being paid promptly, thus enhancing the credit-worthiness of the firm. But the firm has to invest more in working capital.

A low creditors turnover ratio is apparently favourable as, in that case the firm enjoys a lengthy credit period. Therefore, the firm has to invest less in working capital. But it will diminish the credit-worthiness of the firm. So the creditor's turnover ratio should be neither too high nor too low.

(D) Analysis of Profitability: Profitability indicates the efficiency or effectiveness with which the operations of the business is carried on. Poor operational performance may result in poor sales and, therefore, low profit. Low profitability may be due to lack of control over expenses. Profitability is the main base for liquidity as well as solvency.

Creditors, banks and financial institutions are interested in profitability ratios as they indicate liquidity or the capacity of the business to meet interest obligations. A company with sufficient profits will enhance the long-term solvency position of the business. Equity shareholders are interested in profitability ratios since they indicate the growth as well as rate of return on their investment. The major types of profitability ratios are:

1. **Gross Profit Ratio:** This is the ratio of gross profit to net sales and is expressed in percentage. Thus:

$$\text{Gross Profit Ratio} = \frac{\text{Gross Profit}}{\text{Net Sales}} \times 100$$

Significance and Interpretation: The ratio throws light on the degree of managerial efficiency in production and sales. It indicates the ability of the firm to widen the gap between sales and cost of sales. This ratio may be high due to higher selling prices in relation to costs or lower costs in relation to selling price or increased sales volume of the higher profit margin items. A low gross profit ratio should be carefully investigated.

The gross profit ratio may be low due to:

(i) Failure to control cost and to take the benefits of large scale economies,

(ii) Excessive investment in plant and machinery, and

(iii) Cut-throat competition.

2. **Net Profit Ratio:** This is the ratio of net profit after taxes to net sales. Net profit, as used here, is the balance of profit and loss account which is arrived at after considering all non-operating incomes such as interest on investment, dividend received etc. and operating expenses such as office and administrative expenses, selling and distribution expenses and non-operating expenses like loss on sale of fixed assets, provision for contingent liability,

etc. Thus:

$$\text{Net Profit Ratio} = \frac{\text{Net Profit}}{\text{Net Sales}} \times 100$$

Significance and Interpretation: This ratio is used to measure the overall profitability and is useful to owners. This ratio indicates how much of sales is left after meeting all expense. For examples, if the ratio is 10%, it will mean that 10 paise per rupee of sale belongs to the owners as their reward for taking risk in investment. So, higher this ratio, more is the return to shareholders.

3. **Operating Ratio:** This is the ratio of cost of goods sold plus operating expenses to net sales of the firm. This is closely related to the ratio of operating profit to net sales:

$$\text{Operating Ratio} = \frac{\text{Operating Cost}}{\text{Net Sales}} \times 100$$

Operating cost consists of cost of goods sold, office and administrative expenses and selling and distribution expenses. Financial charges such as interest, provision for taxation and loss on sale of investments etc. are excluded from operating expenses.

Significance and Interpretation: This ratio indicates the operational efficiency with which the business is being carried on. It reveals the percentage of net sales that is absorbed by cost of goods sold and operating expenses. Hence, the lower the operating cost, the higher will be operating profit. On the other hand, a higher operating ratio leaves a lesser margin for meeting non-operating expenses, creation of reserves and payment of interest and dividend.

4. **Operating Profit Ratio:** This is the ratio of operating profit and net sales and is expressed in percentage.

$$\text{Operating Profit Ratio} = \frac{\text{Operating Profit}}{\text{Net Sales}} \times 100$$

Operating Profit

= Net Profit + Non-operating Expenses – Non-operating Income = Sales – (Cost of goods sold + Office & Adm. Expenses + Selling & Dist. Expenses)

Significance and Interpretation: This ratio can also be computed by subtracting the operating ratio from 100. For example, if the operating ratio is 85% then the operating profit ratio would be 15% (i.e., 100 – 85). The implication of operating ratio and operating profit ratio is the same. This ratio indicates the extent of sales revenue available for interest, tax and dividend payments etc.

5. **Return on Capital Employed (ROCE):** The main objective of making investment in any business is to earn adequate return on capital invested. Hence, the return on capital employed is used as a measure of success of a business in achieving this objective. Otherwise known as return on investment, this is the barometer of overall performance of the firm. It is calculated as:

Return on Capital Employed

$$= \frac{\text{Net Profit after tax plus Interest}}{\text{Capital Employed}}$$

Capital employed may be either gross capital employed or net capital employed:

Gross Capital Employed

    = Total Assets – Fictitious Assets

    = Fixed Assets + Current Assets

Net Capital Employed

    = Total Assets – Current Liabilities

    = Fixed Assets + Current Assets – Current Liabilities

Alternatively

    = Fixed Assets + Working Capital

Net Capital Employed

    = Share Capital + Reserve & Surplus – Fictitious Assets + Long-term Loans + Short-term Loans

Significance and Interpretation: Return on capital employed is considered to be the best measure of profitability in order to assess the overall performance of the business. A comparison of the ratio with similar firms, with the industry average and over time would provide sufficient insight into how efficiently the long-term funds of owners and creditors are being used. The higher the ratio, the more efficient use of the capital employed.

So, determining a minimum rate of return on investment is very essential part of management planning and control. The investments which generate rates lower than the minimum rate of return are rejected.

However, it is very difficult to set a standard rate of return on capital employed as number of factors such as nature of business, risk involved, inflation, changes in economic conditions etc. may influence such a rate.

6. **Return on Equity Capital:** This ratio relates to the net profits finally available to equity shareholders to the amount of capital invested by them. It is obtained by dividing the profits available to equity shareholders by the equity shareholders fund.

Return on Equity Capital

$$= \frac{\text{Net Profit} - \text{Tax and Pref. Dividend}}{\text{Equity Shareholders Fund}} \times 100$$

Earning per Equity Share

$$= \frac{\text{Net Profit} - \text{Tax and Pref. Dividend}}{\text{No. of Equity Shares}}$$

Significance and Interpretation: The ratio indicates how efficiently the equity shareholders fund is being managed in the firm. Return on equity share capital or EPS helps to determine the market price of equity of the company. Therefore, this ratio is of special interest to the existing as well as prospective equity shareholders.

(E) Activity Ratios or Turnover Ratios: These ratios are used to evaluate the efficiency with which the firm uses its assets. They indicate the frequency of sales with respect to its assets. These are computed with reference to sales or cost of goods sold and expressed in terms of times or rates. Some activity ratios are:

1. **Capital Turnover Ratio:** It is the ratio of sales to capital employed. Thus,

$$\text{Capital Turnover Ratio} = \frac{\text{Sales}}{\text{Capital Employed}}$$

Alternatively,

$$\text{Capital Turnover Ratio} = \frac{\text{Cost of goods sold}}{\text{Capita Employed}}$$

Significance and Interpretation: It indicates the firm's ability to generate sales per rupee of long-term investment. The greater the ratio, the more efficient is the utilisation of long-term creditors and owners fund.

2. **Fixed Assets Turnover Ratio:** This is the ratio of net sales to net fixed assets. Thus,

Fixed Assets Turnover Ratio

$$= \frac{\text{Net Sales}}{\text{Net Fixed Assets}}$$

Significance and Interpretation: It is a measure of efficiency of utilisation of fixed assets. The ratio is calculated in determining to what extent the investment in fixed assets has been achieving its objective of generating sales. The higher the ratio, the more efficient is the utilisation of fixed assets in generating sales.

USERS OF FINANCIAL RATIOS

Financial ratio analysis is aimed to assess the financial performance and determine the financial position of an organization through its profitability, liquidity, activity, leverage and other relevant indicators. There are many groups and individuals with diverse and conflicting interests but want to know about the business performance or position. In the following major users of financial statements with their areas of interest are described.

(1) **Bankers and Lenders:** Use profitability, liquidity and investment because they want to know the ability of the borrowing business in regular scheduled interest payments and repayments of principal loan amount.

(2) **Investors:** Use profitability and investment because they are more interested in profitability performance of business and safety and security of their investment and growth potential of their investment.

(3) **Government:** Use profitability because government may use profit as a basis for taxation, grants and subsidies.

(4) **Employees:** Use profitability, liquidity and activity because employees will be concerned with job security, bonus and continuance of business and wage bargaining.

(5) **Customers:** Use liquidity because customers will seek reassurance that the business can survive in the short term and continue to supply.

(6) **Suppliers:** Use liquidity because suppliers are more interested in knowing the ability of the business to settle its short-term obligations as and when they are due.

(7) **Management:** Use all ratios because management is interested in all aspects i.e., both financial performance and financial condition of the business.

PRACTICE SET

- Classify the following assets and liabilities for balance sheet of M/s Tanya & Company for the year as on 31.3.2018.

Cash	200	Goodwill	300
Provision for expenses	200	Capital	2,000
Vehicles	1,000	Sundry debtors	1,600
Unsecured loans (long term)	800	Term loan	2,000
Investment in other firms	300	Plant & Machinery	2,500
Pre-operative expenses	200	Sundry creditors	1,200
Stocks	2,000	Reserves	1,000
Prepaid expenses	200	Expenses payable	200
Security Deposit	200	Bank Borrowing/ cash credit	1,400
Land & Building	1,500	Debentures	1,200
Sales	10,000	Net profit	500
Interest on term loan	300	Depreciation	200

Calculate Current Ratio/ Quick Ratio/ Net Working Capital/ Debt Equity Ratio / Debt Service coverage (consider that instalment during the year is 400) Ratio / Stock Turnover Ratio / Debtor Turnover Ratio / Debtor Velocity Ratio / Net Profit %.

SOLUTION:

Liabilities	Amount	Assets	Amount
OWNERS FUNDS		**FIXED ASSETS**	
Capital	2,000	Land & Building	1,500
Reserves	1,000	Plant & Machinery	2,500
		Vehicles	1,000
SUB-TOTAL (Net Worth)	**3,000**	**SUB-TOTAL (Fixed Assets)**	**5,000**
LONG TERM LIABILITIES		**NONCURRENT ASSETS (NCA)**	
Unsecured Loans	800	Investment in Firms	300
Term Loan	2,000	Security Deposit	200
Debentures	1,200		
SUB-TOTAL (Term Liabilities)	**4,000**	**SUB- TOTAL (Non-Current Assets)**	**500**
CURRENT LIABILITIES		**INTANGIBLE ASSETS**	
Provision for Expenses	200	Goodwill	300
Sundry Creditors	1,200	Pre- operative expenses	200
Expenses Payable	200		
Bank Cash Credit	1,400		
SUB-TOTAL (Current Liabilities)	3,000	**SUB-TOTAL (Total Intangible Assets)**	500
		CURRENT ASSETS	
		Cash	200
		Sunday Debtor	1,600
		Stocks	2,000
		Prepaid Expenses	200
		SUB-TOTAL (Current Assets)	**4,000**

GRAND TOTAL (Total of Liabilities)	10,000	GRAND TOTAL (Total of Assets)	10,000
Calculations:			
Net worth	Capital + reserves	2,000 + 1,000	3,000
Intangible assets			500
Tangible NW	NW – Intangible	3,000 – 500	2,500
Long term Liabilities			4,000
Long term sources	LTL + Net worth	4,000 + 3,000	7,000
Current liabilities			3,000
Short term sources	(= Current liabilities)		3,000
Outside liabilities	(= LTL + CL)	4,000 + 3,000	7,000
Long term uses	(= Fixed assets + NCA + Intangible assets)	5,000 + 500 + 500	6,000
Current Assets			4,000
Gross Working Capital	(= Total CA)		4,000
Short term uses	(CA)		4,000
Net Working Capital	CA – CL	4,000 – 3,000	1,000
Quick Asset	CA – Stocks & Prepaid Exp.	4,000 – 2,200	1,800
Current ratio	CA / CL	4,000 / 3,000	1.33:1
Quick ratio	QA / CL	1,800 / 3,000	0.66:1
Debt equity ratio	LTL / TNW	4,000 / 2,500	1.66:1
DSCR	(Profit + Depreciation + TL interest)/(TL Instalment + TL interest)		
	500 + 200 + 300 = 1,000	(1,000 / 700) = 1.43	
	400 + 300 = 700		
Stock turnover ratio	Sales / Stocks	10,000 / 2,000	5 times
Debtors turnover ratio	Sales / Sy Debtors	10,000 / 1,600	6.3 times
Debtors velocity ratio	(Sy Drs / Sales) * 12	(1,600 / 10,000) * 12	1.92 months
Net profit %	(NP / Sales) * 100	(500 / 10,000) * 100	5%

TEST YOURSELF

1. Those financial ratios which measure the long-term solvency and capital structure of the firm are called:
   (a) Turnover Ratios
   (b) Leverage Ratios
   (c) Liquidity Ratios
   (d) Profitability Ratios

2. Which one is also called as "Liquidity Ratios"?
   (a) Profitability Ratios
   (b) Turnover Ratios
   (c) Long-term Solvency Ratios
   (d) Short-term Solvency Ratios

3. Which one is not the uses of Accounting Ratios?
   (a) Facilitate Inter-Firm comparison
   (b) Facilitate Intra-Firm comparison
   (c) Help in Planning
   (d) None of these

4. Which is not a Solvency Ratio?
   (a) Debtor's Turnover Ratio (b) Current Ratio
   (c) Debt-Equity Ratio   (d) Liquidity Ratio

5. Acid test ratio is also called as
   (a) Quick Ratio   (b) Liquidity Ratio
   (c) Both a and b   (d) Neither a not b

ABC Ltd Profit and Loss Account for the year ended 31.03.2018 is given below.

Turnover - 7300	Distribution costs - 1320	Interest - 200, Dividend - 400
Cost of sales - 4234	Admin expenses - 480	Tax - 372

Balance Sheet as on 31.03.2018

Ordinary shares - 900	**Fixed Assets**
Retained profit - 2600	Plant and machinery - 3960
10% debenture - 2000	Net current assets - 1540
Financed by - 3500	
Current Liabilities = 890	**Current Assets = 2430**
Trade creditors - 200	Stocks - 1392
Proposed dividend - 400	Debtors - 800
Taxation - 170	Bank - 238
Accruals - 120	

Calculate the following based on the above details.

6. Gross profit
   (a) 1266   (b) 3066
   (c) 4234   (d) 7300

7. Operating profit
   (a) 294   (b) 694
   (c) 1066   (d) 1266

8. Profit before tax
   (a) 294   (b) 694
   (c) 1066   (d) 1266

9. Profit attributable to shareholders
   (a) 294   (b) 694
   (c) 1066   (d) 1266

10. Retained profit
    (a) 294   (b) 694
    (c) 1066   (d) 1266

11. Gross profit margin
    (a) 17.34%   (b) 23.02%
    (c) 33.33%   (d) 42%

12. Operating margin
    (a) 17.34%   (b) 23.02%
    (c) 33.33%   (d) 42%

13. Return on capital employed (ROCE) ratio
    (a) 17.34%   (b) 23.02%
    (c) 33.33%   (d) 42%

14. Current Ratio
    (a) 1.17:1   (b) 2.73:1
    (c) 1:1.17   (d) 1:2.73

15. Acid test/Quick ratio
    (a) 1.17:1   (b) 2.73:1
    (c) 1:1.17   (d) 1:2.73

ABC Limited had the following balances on 31.03.2018:

Current Liabilities = 5,00,000	Current Assets = 7,00,000
Total Liabilities = 8,00,000	Total Assets = 16,00,000
Cash provided by operations = 9,00,000	Net Income = 3,60,000
Capital Expenditures = 2,00,000	Preferred Stock Dividends = 50,000
Cash Dividends = 1,00,000	Average common shares outstanding = 100,000 shares

Calculate the following based on the above details.

16. What is the amount of working capital?
  (a) 2,00,000
  (b) 4,00,000
  (c) 6,00,000
  (d) 8,00,000

17. What is the current ratio?
  (a) 0.5   (b) 1.2
  (c) 1.4   (d) 1.8

18. What is the debt to total assets ratio?
  (a) 0.5   (b) 1.2
  (c) 1.4   (d) 1.8

19. What is the amount of free cash flow?
  (a) 2,00,000   (b) 4,00,000
  (c) 6,00,000   (d) 8,00,000

20. What is the amount of Earnings per share (EPS)?
  (a) 1.10 per share   (b) 2.10 per share
  (c) 3.10 per share   (d) 4.10 per share

ANSWER

1	2	3	4	5	6	7	8	9	10
(b)	(d)	(c)	(a)	(c)	(b)	(d)	(c)	(b)	(a)

11	12	13	14	15	16	17	18	19	20
(d)	(a)	(b)	(b)	(a)	(a)	(c)	(a)	(c)	(c)

Solution & Hints

6. Gross Profit = Turnover − Cost of sales
= 7300 − 4234 = 3066

7. Operating Profit
= Gross Profit − (Distribution costs + Admin expenses)
= 3066 − (1320 + 480) = 3066 − 1800 = 1266

8. Profit before tax
= Operating Profit − Interest = 1266 − 200 = 1066

9. Profit attributable to shareholders
= Profit before tax − Tax = 1006 − 372 = 694

10. Retained Profit
= Profit attributable to shareholders − Dividend
= 694 − 400 = 294

11. Gross Profit margin = (Gross Profit / Turnover) * 100
= (3066 / 7300) × 100 = 42 %

12. Operating margin = (Operating Profit / Turnover) * 100
= (1266 / 7300) × 100 = 17.34 %

13. Return on capital employed (ROCE) ratio
= (Earnings Before Interest and Tax (EBIT) or net operating profit) / capital employed

Capital employed
= Total Assets − Current Liabilities
= (3960 + 2430) − 890 = 6390 − 890 = 5500

ROCE = (1266/ 5500) * 100 = 23.02 %

14. Current Ratio = Current Assets / Current Liabilities
= 2430 / 890 = 2.73:1

15. Quick Ratio
= (Current Assets − Inventories − Prepayments)/Current Liabilities
= (2430 − 1392)/890 = 1038/890 = 1.17:1

16. Working Capital
= Current Assets − Current Liabilities
= 7,00,000 − 5,00,000 = 2,00,000

17. Current Ratio = Current Assets / Current Liabilities
= 7,00,000 / 5,00,000 = 1.40

18. Debt to total Assets = Total Liabilities / Total Assets
= 8,00,000 / 16,00,000 = 0.50 or 50%

19. Free cash flow
= Cash provided by operations − Capital expenditures − Cash dividends
= 9,00,000 − 2,00,000 − 1,00,000 = 6,00,000

20. Earnings per Share
= (Net income − Preferred stock dividends) / Average common shares outstanding
= (3,60,000 − 50,000) / 1,00,000 shares
= 3,10,000/100,000 shares = 3.10 per share

CHAPTER 16

FINAL ACCOUNTS OF BANKING COMPANIES

INTRODUCTION

The banking company is the most important institutional and functional vehicle for economic transformation. Finance is a bridge between the present and the future. It is the mobilisation of savings and their efficient, effective and equitable allocation for investment. It is the success with which the banking company performs its functions that sets the pace for the achievement of broader national objectives. It includes different markets, the institutions, instruments, services and mechanisms which influence the generation of savings, investment capital formation and growth.

There are various types of banks which operate in our country to meet the financial requirements of different categories of people engaged in agriculture, business, protession, etc. On the basis of functions, the banking institutions in India may be divided into the following types:

1. Public Sector Banks
2. Private Sector Banks
3. Foreign Banks
4. Regional Rural Banks
5. Co-operative Banks

DEFINITION OF A BANK

Section 5(B) of Banking Regulation Act, 1949 defines banking as "Accepting for the purpose of lending or investment of deposits of money from the public, repayable on demand and withdrawable by cheques, drafts, and orders or otherwise". Banking Company means any company which transacts the business of banking in India. Banks are governed by Reserve Bank of India Act (RBI Act) 1934 and Banking Regulation Act (BR Act) 1949. Nationalised banks are owned by Government of India and governed by directives issued by RBI.

FUNCTIONS OF A BANK

The core business of the bank is to accept deposit from the public and lending to the public or investment of such deposit. The deposit may be repayable on demand or fixed for a time as agreed by the banker and the customer. As per Sec. 6 of the Banking Regulation Act, 1949 lays down that the following business may also be carried on by a banking company, in addition to the usual banking business:

(a) Acting as agents for any governments or local authority or any other person or persons. The carrying on of agency business of any description including the clearing and forwarding of goods, giving of receipts and discharges and otherwise acting as an attorney on behalf of customers, but excluding the business of a managing agent of a company;

(b) Contracting for public and private loans and negotiating and issuing the same;

(c) Selecting, insuring, guaranteeing, underwriting, participating, in managing and carrying out of any issue, public or private, of state, municipal or other loans or of shares, stock, debentures or debenture stock of any company, corporation or association and of lending of money for the purpose of any such issue;

(d) Carrying on and transacting every kind of guarantee and indemnity business;

(e) Managing, selling and realising any property which may come into the possession of the company in satisfaction or part satisfaction of any of its claims;

(f) Acquiring or holding and generally dealing with any property, or title or interest in any such property which may form the security or part of the security for any loans or advances or which may be connected with any such security;

(g) Undertaking and executing trusts;

(h) Undertaking the administration of estates as executor, trustee or otherwise;

(i) Establishing and supporting associations, institutions, funds, trusts, and convenience for the benefit of employees, ex-employees, their dependents and the general public;

(j) Acquiring, constructing, maintaining and altering any building or works necessary for the purpose of the banking company;

(k) Selling, improving, managing, developing, exchanging, leasing, mortgaging, disposing-off or turning into account or otherwise dealing with all or any part of the property and rights of the company;

(l) Acquiring and undertaking the whole or any part of the business of any person or company when such business is of a nature enumerated or described in Sec. 6.

(m) Doing such other things as are necessary for the efficient conduct of the above-named business, such as acquisition, construction, alteration etc. of any building or works necessary or convenient for the purpose of the company; and

(n) Any other form of business which the Central Govt. may notify in the Official Gazette.

As such, other types of business are prohibited by a banking company.

REQUIREMENTS OF BANKING COMPANIES AS TO ACCOUNTS & AUDIT

○ **Annual Accounts and Balance-Sheet**: As per Section 29 of Banking Regulation Act, an expiration of each calendar year or at the expiration of a period of 12 months ending with such date as the Central Government may specify (at present being March 31 every year from March 1989), every banking company shall prepare a balance-sheet and profit and loss account as on the last working day of the year or the period, in the Forms set out in the Third Schedule (it is Form A for balance sheet and Form B for profit and loss account) or as near thereto as circumstances admit.

While preparing the accounts, the banking company should comply with the direction and instructions issued by the RBI in respect of Income Recognition and Asset Classification, Provisioning etc. norms from time to time. Central Government may amend the Forms from time to time after giving not less than 3 months' notice.

○ **Who is to Sign the Balance Sheet?** : The balance-sheet and profit and loss account shall be signed, in the case of a banking company incorporated in India, by the manager or the principal officer of the company and where there are more than three Directors of the company, by at least three of those Directors, or where there are not more than three Directors, by all the Directors, and in the case of a banking company incorporated outside India by the Manager or Agent of the principal office of the company in India.

○ **Audit of Accounts (Section 30):** The balance-sheet and profit & loss account prepared in accordance with section 29 shall be audited by a person duly qualified under any law for the time being in force to be an Auditor of companies. Every banking company shall, before appointing, reappointing or removing any Auditor or Auditors, obtain the previous approval of the Reserve Bank.

○ **Special Audit {Section 30(1B)}:** Where the Reserve Bank is of opinion that it is necessary so to do, it may direct that the special audit of the banking company's accounts, for any such transaction or class of transactions or for such period or periods, shall be conducted. It may appoint a person duly qualified, to be an Auditor of companies or direct the Auditor of the banking company himself to conduct such special audit. The Auditor shall comply with such directions and make a report of such audit to the Reserve Bank and forward a copy thereof to the company.

○ **Submission of Annual Accounts (Balance Sheet and Profit & Loss Account (Section 31):** The accounts and balance-sheet together with the Auditor's report shall be published in the prescribed manner and three copies thereof shall be furnished as returns to the Reserve Bank within three months from the end of the period to which they refer. Reserve Bank may in any case extend the said period of 3 months by a further period not exceeding 3 months.

○ **Copies of Balance-Sheets and Accounts to Registrar of Companies (Section 32):** Where a banking company in any year furnished its accounts and balance-sheet in accordance with the provisions of section 31, it shall at the same time send to the Registrar of Companies, 3 copies of such accounts and balance-sheet and of the Auditor's report.

All banks must prepare their annual balance sheet, profit & loss statements and accounts as described in Banking Regulation Act as on 31st March of every year. All those statements and returns are audited by duly qualified auditors as prescribed in the act. All the audited returns should submit to RBI and Registrar of companies. Banking company provides inspection and scrutiny of their books as stated in the act. For the inspection and scrutiny of the returns a board for financial supervision was set up.

PRINCIPAL BOOKS OF ACCOUNTS

Bank has to maintain various books and ledgers. The methods of preparation and presentation of Profit & Loss Account and a Balance Sheet of a Bank are very important and significant which include certain peculiar terms to this type of organisation. For this purpose, a short description of different books, ledgers, registers and terms which are very important are discussed hereunder.

1. Books Section: Bank maintains the different books which are as under:

a) **Cash Book:** For recording different types of cash transactions two types of cash books are recorded.

(i) **Rough Cash Book:** Rough Cash Book which deals with cash receipts and cash payments maintained by a receiving cashier and paying cashier, respectively. It records serial number, depositor's name, amount received etc. in cash, whereas, in case of cash payment, serial number, payee's name, amount paid, number of token etc. are recorded.

(ii) **A Fair Cash Book:** A Fair Cash Book, on the other hand, is one when a separate-person, after receiving the above information from the paying and receiving cashier, records the transactions in a separate book. Naturally, the transaction of the fair cash book must tally with the sum total of the above two rough cash books.

b) **Cash Balance:** The cash balance at the close of the day is written in the book which is duly signed by the cashier and the manager.

c) **Day Book:** It records day-to-day transactions of the book relating to cash transfers, dealings etc. Besides the above, Received Waste Book, Sectional Cash Book etc. are also to be maintained.

2. Ledger Section: Bank maintains the various ledgers which are as under;

a) **Current Account Ledger:** It records the transactions of those customers who open current account. Generally, the bank does not pay interest on the balance of this account but a nominal charge is taken by the bank for rendering the services.

b) **Savings Bank Ledger:** It records the transactions of those customers who open savings account in a bank. The detailed description of the customer, viz., name, address, occupation, are recorded along with an account number.

c) **Fixed Deposit Ledger:** It contains transactions of those customers who have deposited their money into the bank for a fixed period. Generally, at the top of the account, depositor's name and address, rates of interest, period of deposit, the amount so deposited etc. are to be recorded.

d) **General Ledger:** It is actually the key ledger of the accounting system of a bank. It contains a total amount in respect of total Current Accounts, total Savings Bank Account, total Loans Account, total Bills Payable Account, total Expenses and total Revenue Accounts. Each ledger is kept under self-balancing system. A trial balance can easily be prepared which helps to prepare the final account as well. Besides the above ledgers overdue fixed deposit ledger, fixed deposit interest ledger, loan ledger, investment ledger may also be prepared.

3. Register Section: The register section includes: Bills for Collection Register, Securities Register, Document Register, Standing Order Register, Cheques Dishonoured Register, Drafts Issue Register, Drafts Payable Register, D.D. Register, Foreign Letters of Credit Register etc.

The Slip System of Ledger Posting

It is a method of rapid posting in books maintained under Double Entry principle. Under this system, posting is done from various types of slips such as withdrawal slip, paying-in-slip, cheque etc. and not from journals or cash books. Slips are loose leaves of journals and these are supplied either by the customers or by the bank staff. It becomes necessary for a bank to know the position of its individual customer's account at any time and to see that the transactions are recorded as soon as they take place.

The same is not actually possible if transactions are recorded in bound books. So, original cheques and paying-in-slips are used as vouchers. Consequently, the cashier, for this purpose, credits cash account for receiving cheques and it passes on to the ledger-keeper concerned for debiting the customer' accounts.

On the contrary, for paying-in-slips the cashier debits cash account and passes on the same to the ledger-keeper concerned, for crediting the customers' accounts. In this way, the Double Entry posting is completed. The transactions which are not covered by original slips are posted by means of 'dockets' which is made out by the bank staff. These are used for posting purposes.

PREPARATION AND PRESENTATION OF FINANCIAL STATEMENTS OF BANKS

While preparing financial statements, banks have to follow various guidelines/directions given by RBI/Government of India governing the Financial Statements. It is important to go through the Director's Report, Management Discussion and Analysis Report, Corporate Governance Certificate which normally precede the Financial Statements. All together all these are incorporated in Annual Report of the Bank. The following are the highlights of Banks' Balance Sheets:

1. Balance Sheet is prepared in conformity with Form A of the Third Schedule to the Banking Regulation Act, 1949 and Profit and Loss Account in conformity with Form B ibid. They are prepared in accordance with provisions of Section 29 of the Banking Regulation Act read with Section 211 (10), (2), and 3(c) of the Companies Act 1956.

2. They are always prepared as on 31st March of every year. Listed Banks are required to publish Review financial results every quarter. But full-fledged Profit and Loss Account and Balance Sheet are prepared as on 31st March every year by all the Banks.

3. They contain 18 schedules as under:
   - **Format A:** It is the Balance Sheet of the bank. It contains twelve schedules. Schedule 1 to 5 form Liability Side of the Bank's Balance Sheet and Schedule 6 to 12 on the Asset Side of the Balance Sheet. The Assets Side of the Balance Sheet has been arranged in such a manner that liquid assets such as Cash, Balances with Banks and Investments are shown in that order. This enables the investor to quickly identify how much the Bank is liquid enough to meet its commitment towards its customers. This arrangement of Assets is from liquid to fixed assets in contrast to corporate balance sheets where the arrangement is from fixed to liquid.
   - **Format B:** It is the Profit & Loss Account of the bank. It contains four schedules. Schedule thirteen & fourteen are the income of the bank. Schedule fifteen & sixteen are the expenses of the bank.

Form A
Balance Sheet as on 31st March. 20.......

Schedules	Liabilities	As on 31.03.... (Current Year)	As on 31.03.... (Previous Year)
Schedule-1	Capital		
Schedule-2	Reserves & Surplus Schedule		
Schedule-3	Deposits Schedule		
Schedule-4	Borrowings Schedule		
Schedule-5	Other Liabilities and Provisions		
	Assets		
Schedule-6	Cash and balances with RBI		
Schedule-7	Balances with Banks and money at call and short notice		
Schedule-8	Investments		
Schedule-9	Advances		
Schedule-10	Fixed Assets		
Schedule-11	Other Assets		
Schedule-12	Contingent Liabilities: Bills for Collection Bank Guarantee issued		

Form B

Profit & Loss Account for the year ended 31st March 20....

Schedules		Year ended 31.03.... (Current year)	Year ended 31.03.... (Previous year)
Schedule-13	Interest Earned		
Schedule-14	Other Income		
Schedule-15	Interest Expended		
Schedule-16	Operating Expenses		

SCHEDULES OF FINANCIAL STATEMENTS

SCHEDULE-1 : CAPITAL & LIABILITIES

The Schedule gives details of Authorised, Issued, Subscribed and Paid up Capital of the Bank. Special mention should be made of capital held by Central Government. If calculated in percentage terms, it will give an idea of Central Government's contribution to the Capital of the bank.

For example, as on 31.3.2018, suppose in the case of Bank of India, the paid-up capital was ₹ 574.51 Cr out of which Central Government holding was ₹ 359.88 Cr. representing 62.72 %. Investor can get an idea which bank's share has velocity in the market and better traded.

SCHEDULE-2 : RESERVES & SURPLUS

This schedule consists of Statutory Reserves, Capital Reserves (revaluation reserve), Share Premium, Revenue & Other Reserves. Statutory Reserve is created by transferring of net profit earned by the Bank every year.

Capital Reserve consists of revaluation reserve created out of:

(1) Revaluation of property of the Bank,

(2) Profit on sale of investments, which are "Held to Maturity"

(3) Foreign Currency Translation Reserve and

(4) Special Reserve for Currency Swaps.

These items of capital reserve are appropriated from Net Profit of the Bank.

Share Premium is created from the premium collected by the Bank while issuing shares to the public. Revenue & other reserves are recreated by transferring balance of Net profit after making appropriations for Statutory, Capital Reserves, Dividend Payment and Special Reserves.

SCHEDULE-3 : DEPOSITS

Deposits are mainly bifurcated into Demand Deposits (which includes Current Account Deposits, Sundry Deposits and Overdue Term/Time deposits), Savings Bank Deposits and Term Deposits.

Sub-bifurcation in all these segments is Deposits from Banks and Others. It is now established that a bank should have higher percentage of Demand Deposits and Savings Bank Deposits (CASA Deposits) for better NIM (net interest margin).

In the computerized environment, Branches should not have major chunk of Overdue Term Deposits in the Demand Deposits portfolio. It will also have an impact on the Assets and Liabilities Management of the Bank (ALM).

SCHEDULE-4 : BORROWINGS

This schedule which is managed at Head Office level, consists of borrowing from RBI and other Banks. Borrowings from other Banks/other Institutions are mainly funds raised under various instruments (Innovative Perpetual Debt Instruments, Subordinated debts, Unsecured non-convertible redeemable bonds etc) which qualify for Tier I and II capital of the Bank.

Schedules 1 (Capital), Schedule 2 (Reserves & Surplus) and Schedule 4 (Borrowings) are relevant for calculation of Capital to Risk Weighted Asset Ratio (CRAR) as some balances under these schedules are considered for Calculation of CRAR.

Some important points to be noted here for calculation of Capital Adequacy under Basel I and II guidelines are given below: (Basel III guidelines are still in discussion stage and hence are not considered here)

1. Banks are required to maintain minimum capital of 9% on on-going basis for Credit Risk, Market Risk and Operational Risk.
2. The capital so calculated consists of Tier I and Tier II capital.
3. Minimum Tier I capital should be 6%
4. 80% of minimum capital to be maintained under Basel I framework.
5. Banks are required to declare the CRAR under Basel I and II frameworks in their financial statements.
6. Method of computing risk weights is different under Basel I and Basel II frameworks.

SCHEDULE-5 : OTHER LIABILITIES AND PROVISIONS

The schedule mainly consists of Bills Payable (both inward and outward Bills for collection sent to upcountry banks/branches), Interest accrued, Contingent provisions against standard assets (banks are required to maintain provisions on Standard Assets @ 0.25 % to 0.40% and in some cases 1%), Proposed Dividend and any other liabilities that have to be provided for.

The above schedules 1 to 5 form Liabilities side of the Balance Sheet. The following schedules form part of Assets side of the Balance Sheet.

SCHEDULE-6 : CASH AND BALANCES WITH RBI

Cash in Hand represents the cash held by branches of the Bank. All Branches are required to maintain cash within retention limit prescribed by the bank. Any amount beyond the limit should be transferred to RBI accounts so that the balances in RBI accounts qualify for CRR (Cash Reserve Ratio) calculations.

Keeping excess cash is fraught with security issues, and the Bank will be losing interest/other benefits on idle component of the Cash held at branches. Balances with RBI qualify for CRR calculations. Excess amount over required CRR will qualify for SLR (Statutory Liquidity Ratio). Branches should therefore maintain minimum cash with them.

SCHEDULE-7 : BALANCES WITH BANKS AND MONEY AT CALL AND SHORT NOTICE

Balances with Banks represent the balances maintained by branches with other Banks (such as SBI) for clearing purposes, etc. Any excess balance should be transferred to RBI account. Money at Call and Short Notice are entries created by Treasury of the Bank and hence should not reflect in individual branch balance sheets unless parked for any reason by the Bank.

SCHEDULE-8 : INVESTMENTS

Investments are bifurcated into six segments in Balance sheets, viz.;
  i) Government Securities;
  ii) Other approved Securities;
  iii) Shares;
  iv) Debentures and Bonds;
  v) Subsidiaries/joint ventures;
  vi) Others.

The Investments under Government Securities and Other Approved Securities qualify for SLR (Statutory Liquidity Ratio) calculations. Investments under Others include CDs/CPs etc.

All investments are to be classified into Held to Maturity, Held for Trading and Available for Sale. Depending upon the classification of the investments into these categories valuation of investments has to be made as per RBI guidelines. The valuations will have a great bearing on the profit of the bank.

SCHEDULE-9 : ADVANCES

There are three classifications under Advances, viz. first classification into Bills purchased and discounted, Cash Credit, Overdrafts and Loans repayable on demand (normally loans with repayment period less than 36 months) and Term Loans. This classification will enable the investor to know the liquidity of funds for the Bank and also how the interest streams are ensured. For example, if the balances under Cash Credit, Overdraft etc. are more than Term Loans, the Bank's liquidity position is good whereas more balances in Term Loans show steady profit by way of interest earnings.

Second classification is based on the security available in the loan portfolio. The classification is:

i) Secured by tangible assets;

ii) Covered by Bank/Government Guarantee; and

iii) Unsecured. Large number of unsecured advances and / or increase over last may indicate the Bank's vulnerability for credit risk.

Third classification is, Advances under:

i) Priority Sector;   ii) Public Sector;

iii) Banks;   iv) Others.

This classification is required as all banks are required to lend 40% of their Advances under Priority Sector.

As of now, capital requirement for Credit Risk is higher than Capital requirement for Market Risk and Operational Risk. It is therefore necessary that while undertaking Credit Risk availability and costs of additional Capital requirement need to be looked into. A realignment of portfolios and/or securing assets with collaterals will enable reduce risk weights.

SCHEDULE-10 : FIXED ASSETS

They include the following:

(I) Premises

i) At cost as on 31st March of the preceding year;

ii) Additions during the year;

iii) Deductions during the year;

iv) Depreciation to date.

Premises wholly or partly owned by the banking company for the purpose of business including residential premises should be shown against 'Premises'. In the case of premises and other fixed assets, the previous balance, additions thereto and deductions therefrom during the year, as also the total depreciation written off, should be shown. Where sums have been written off on reduction of capital or revaluation of assets, every balance sheet after the first balance sheet subsequent to the reduction or revaluation should show the revised figures for a period of five years with the date and amount of revision made.

(II) Other Fixed Assets (including Furniture and Fixtures)

i) At cost on 31st March of the preceding year;

ii) Additions during the year;

iii) Deduction during the year;

iv) Depreciation to date.

Motor vehicles and all other fixed assets other than premises but including furniture and fixtures should be shown under this head.

SCHEDULE-11 : OTHER ASSETS

They include the following:

(I) Inter/Office Adjustment (Net): The inter-office adjustment balance, if in debit, should be shown-under this head. Only net position of inter-office accounts, inland as well as foreign, should be shown here. For arriving at the net balance of inter-office accounts should be aggregated and the net balance, if in debit, only should be shown representing mostly items in transit and unadjusted items.

(II) Interest Accrued: Interest accrued but not due on investment and advances, and interest due but not collected on investments, will be the main components of this item. As bank normally debits the borrower's account with interest due on the balance sheet date, usually there may not be any amount of interest due on advances. Only such interest, as can be realised in the ordinary course, should be shown under this head.

(III) Tax Paid in Advance/deducted at Source: The amount of tax deducted at source on securities, advance tax paid, etc., the extent that these items are not set off against relative tax provisions should be shown against this item.

(IV) Stationery and Stamps: Only exceptional items of expenditure on stationery like bulk purchase of security paper, loose leaf or other ledger, etc., which are shown as quasi-assets are to be written off over a period of time should be shown here. The value should be on a realistic basis and cost escalation should not be taken into account, as these items are for internal use.

(V) Non-banking Assets Acquired in Satisfaction of Claims: Immovable properties/tangible assets acquired in satisfaction of claims are to be shown under this head.

(VI) Others: This will include items like claims which have not been met, for instance, clearing items, debit items representing additions to assets or reduction in liabilities which have not been adjusted for technical reasons, want of particulars, etc., advances given to staff by a bank as employer and not as a banker, etc. Items which are in the nature of expenses, which are pending adjustments, should be provided for and the provision netted against this item so that only the realisable value is shown under this head. Accrued income other than interest may also be included here.

SCHEDULE-12 : CONTINGENT LIABILITIES

They mainly consist of claims against the bank not acknowledge as debts, Liability on account of outstanding Forward Exchange Contracts, Derivative Contracts, Guarantees Issued etc. Notes to accounts should be referred to for any disputed liabilities that are hampering the profit of the bank in case the contingent liabilities turn out to be funded liabilities. At branches, bifurcation of guarantees into Financial and Performance should be done correctly as they carry different risk weights for CRAR calculation. Any cash collaterals available in the guarantees should be properly reduced from the outstanding amounts for CRAR calculations. The liability in respect of expired guarantees should be reversed immediately following the guidelines of their Banks.

(I) Claims against the bank not acknowledged as debts.

(II) Liability for partly paid investments: Liabilities on partly paid shares, debentures, etc., will be included in this head.

(III) Liability on account of outstanding forward exchange contracts: Outstanding forward exchange contracts may be included here.

(IV) Guarantees given on behalf of constituents:

(a) In India;

(b) Outside India;

Guarantees given for constituents in India and outside India may be shown separately.

(V) Acceptances, Endorsements and Other Obligations: This item will include letters of credit and bills accepted by the bank on behalf of customers. In such cases the bank takes upon itself the responsibility for payment.

In order to keep a proper record of such liability, the bank maintains customer acceptances endorsements and guarantee register. All obligations undertaken by the bank as a result of guarantees, endorsements, acceptances, etc., are recorded here. At the end of the accounting year, if some of these obligations remain undisbursed, they are to be shown as contingent liabilities under this head.

(VI) Other Items for which the Bank is Contingently Liable: Arrears of cumulative dividends, bills rediscounted under underwriting contracts, estimated amounts of contracts remaining to be executed on capital account and not provided for, etc., are to be included here.

SCHEDULE-13 : INTEREST EARNED

1. **Interest/Discount on Advances/Bills:** Includes interest and discount on all types of loans and advances like cash credit, demand loans, overdrafts, export loans, term loans, domestic and foreign bills purchased and discounted (including those rediscounted), overdue interest and also interest subsidy, if any, relating to such advances/bills.

2. **Income on Investments:** Includes all income derived from the investment portfolio by way of interest and dividend.

3. **Interest on balances with the Reserve Bank of India and other inter-bank funds:** Includes the interest on balances with the Reserve Bank and other banks, call loans, money market placements, etc.

4. **Others:** Includes any other interest/discount income not included in the above heads.

SCHEDULE-14 : OTHER INCOME

1. **Commission, Exchange and Brokerage:** Includes all remuneration on services such as commission on collection, commission/exchange on remittances and transfers, commission on letters of credit, letting out of lockers and guarantees, commission on Government business, commission on the other permitted agency business including consultancy and other services, brokerage, etc., on securities. It does not include foreign exchange income.

2. **Profit on Sale of Investments:** Less-loss on sale of investments;

3. **Profit on Revaluation of Investments:** Less-loss on revaluation of investments;

4. **Profit on Sale of Land, Buildings and Other Assets:** Less-loss on sale of land, buildings and other assets. Includes profit/loss on the sale of securities, furniture, land and buildings, motor vehicle, gold, silver, etc. Only the net position should be shown. If the net position is a loss, the amount should be shown as a deduction. The net profit/loss on revaluation of assets may also be shown under this item.

5. **Profit on Exchange Transaction:** Less-Loss on Exchange Transaction: Includes profit/loss on dealing in foreign exchange, all income earned by way of foreign exchange, commission and charges on foreign exchange transactions excluding interest which will be shown under interest. Only the net position should be shown. If the net position is a loss, it is to be shown as a deduction.

6. **Other Income:** Income earned by way of dividends, etc., from subsidiaries, companies, joint ventures abroad/in India.

7. **Miscellaneous Income:** Includes recoveries from constituents for godown rents, income from the bank's properties, security charges, insurance, etc., and any other miscellaneous income. In case any item under this head exceeds one percentage of the total income, particulars may be given in the notes.

SCHEDULE-15 : INTEREST EXPENDED AND

1. **Interest on Deposits:** Includes interest paid on all types of deposits from banks and other institutions.

2. **Interest on RBI/Inter-Bank Borrowings:** Include discounts/interest on all borrowings and refinance from the Reserve Bank of India and other banks.

3. **Others:** Includes discount/interest on all borrowings/ refinance, penal interest paid, etc., may also be included here.

SCHEDULE-16 : OPERATING EXPENSES

These schedules form FORM-B of Financial Statements. They are profit and loss statements of the Bank.

1. Payments to and provisions for employees include staff salaries/wages, allowances, bonus, other staff benefits like provident fund, pension, gratuity, leave fare concessions, staff welfare medical allowance to staff, etc.

2. Rent, taxes and lighting includes rent paid by the banks on buildings and municipal and other taxes paid excluding income tax and interest tax, electricity and other similar charges and levies. House rent allowance and other similar payments to staff should appear under the head 'Payments to and Provisions for Employees'.

3. Printing and stationery includes books and forms and stationery used by the bank and other printing charges which are not incurred by way of publicity expenditure.

4. Advertisement and publicity includes expenditure incurred by the bank for advertisement and publicity purposes including printing charges of publicity matter.

SCHEDULE-17 : SIGNIFICANT ACCOUNTING POLICIES

This schedule discusses various accounting policies adopted by the Bank in preparing the financial statements. The schedule mainly should be looked into to check whether Bank has made any changes in the accounting procedures which may have bearing on the profit and loss of the Bank.

SCHEDULE-18 : NOTES FORMING PART OF THE FINANCIAL STATEMENTS

RBI mandated all banks to make 53 specific disclosures in respect of preparation of financial statements. One must go through these disclosures to really understand the SWOT (Strength, Weakness, Opportunity, Threats) of the Bank. Depending upon the market analysis and requirements, RBI advises the Banks to make more disclosures in their Financial Statements. This schedule forms crux of the strength of the Financial statements. Financial Statements reflect outstanding balances in the books of the Bank on a given date. This schedule disseminates important information about the balances reflected in each schedule.

CONCLUSION: All stake holders (investors, customers, depositors, staff and Government, RBI and others) should go through all the schedules to effectively know the strength of a Bank. Employees should understand how schedules are prepared so that by realignment of some of the balances their Bank can reflect a good CRAR.

Notes and General Instructions for Compilation:

1. Formats of Balance Sheet and Profit and Loss Account cover all items likely to appear in the statements, in case a bank does not have any particular item to report, it may be omitted from the formats.

2. Corresponding comparative figures for the previous year are to be disclosed as indicated in the format. The word "current year" and "previous year" used in the format are only to indicate the order of presentation and may appear in the accounts.

3. Figures should be rounded-off to the nearest thousand rupees.

4. Unless otherwise indicated, the banks in this statement will include banking companies, nationalised banks, State Bank of India, and all other institutions including cooperatives carrying on the business of banking whether or not incorporated or operating in India. Hindi version of the Balance Sheet will be part of the annual report.

GENERAL DISCLOSURE PRINCIPLE OF RBI

RBI has issued Master Circular DBOD.No.BP.BC. 4/ 21.06.001/2015-16 dated July 1, 2015 on Basel III Capital Regulations. Banks should have a formal disclosure policy approved by the Board of directors that addresses the bank's approach for determining what disclosures it will make and the internal controls over the disclosure process. In addition, banks should implement a process for assessing the appropriateness of their disclosures, including validation and frequency.

The disclosures in this manner should be subjected to adequate validation. For example, since information in the annual financial statements would generally be audited, the additional material published with such statements must be consistent with the audited statements. In addition, supplementary material (such as Management's Discussion and Analysis) that is published should also be subjected to sufficient scrutiny (e.g. internal control assessments, etc.) to satisfy the validation issue. If material is not published under a validation regime, for instance in a stand alone report or as a section on a website, then management should ensure that appropriate verification of the information takes place, in accordance with the general disclosure principle set out below. In the light of the above, Pillar 3 disclosures will not be required to be audited by an external auditor, unless specified.

Materiality: A bank should decide which disclosures are relevant for it based on the materiality concept. Information would be regarded as material if its omission or misstatement could change or influence the assess-

ment or decision of a user relying on that information for the purpose of making economic decisions. This definition is consistent with International Accounting Standards and with the national accounting framework.

Proprietary and Confidential Information: Proprietary information encompasses information (for example on products or systems), that if shared with competitors would render a bank's investment in these products/systems less valuable, and hence would undermine its competitive position. Information about customers is often confidential, in that it is provided under the terms of a legal agreement or counter party relationship. This has an impact on what banks should reveal in terms of information about their customer base, as well as details on their internal arrangements, for instance methodologies used, parameter estimates, data etc.

TEST YOURSELF

1. Banks are governed by:
   (a) RBI Act, 1934
   (b) BR Act, 1949
   (c) Both (a) & (b)
   (d) None of the above

2. As per _______ lays down that the some other business may also be carried on by a banking company, in addition to the usual banking business.
   (a) Sec. 6 of BR Act, 1949
   (b) Sec. 5 of RBI Act, 1934
   (c) Sec. 5 of BR Act, 1949
   (d) Sec. 6 of RBI Act, 1934

3. While preparing the accounts, the banking company should comply with the directions and instructions issued by the RBI in respect of Income Recognition and Asset Classification, Provisioning etc. norms from time to time. Central Government may amend the Forms from time to time after giving not less than _______ notice.
   (a) 2 months'   (b) 3 months'
   (c) 6 months'   (d) 9 months'

4. The accounts and balance-sheet together with the Auditor's report shall be published in the prescribed manner and _______ thereof shall be furnished as returns to the Reserve Bank within three months from the end of the period to which they refer.
   (a) one copy   (b) two copies
   (c) three copies   (d) four copies

5. Section 30(1B) of BR Act, 1949 define:
   (a) Audit of accounts
   (b) Special audit
   (c) Submission of annual accounts
   (d) Copies of balance-sheets

6. Where a banking company in any year furnished its accounts and balance-sheet in accordance with the provisions of section 31, it shall at the same time send to the _______, 3 copies of such accounts and balance-sheet and of the Auditor's report.
   (a) Registrar of Companies
   (b) SEBI
   (c) Ministry of Finance
   (d) RBI

7. The ...... form of Balance Sheet and Profit and Loss account of a banking company is prescribed in Forms A and B of schedule of the Banking Regulation Act, 1949.
   (a) First   (b) Second
   (c) Third   (d) Fourth

8. _______ is actually the key ledger of the accounting system of a bank. It contains a total amount in respect of total Current Accounts, total Savings Bank Accounts, total Loans Accounts, total Bills Payable Accounts,
   (a) General Ledger
   (b) Document Register
   (c) Standing Order Register
   (d) Collection Register

9. Listed Banks are required to publish Review Financial Results every________.
   (a) month
   (b) quarter
   (c) half year
   (d) year

10. Format A is the Balance Sheet of the bank. It contains __________ schedules.
    (a) nine
    (b) ten
    (c) eleven
    (d) twelve

11. In Format A, Schedule _______ form Liability Side of the Banks Balance Sheet and Schedule _______ on the Asset side of the Balance Sheet.
    (a) 1 to 5, 6 to 12
    (b) 1 to 6, 7 to 12
    (c) 1 to 4, 5 to 12
    (d) 1 to 7, 8 to 12

12. In Form A, details of deposits are given in:
    (a) Schedule 3
    (b) Schedule 5
    (c) Schedule 8
    (d) Schedule 11

13. In Form A, details of investments are given in:
    (a) Schedule 3
    (b) Schedule 5
    (c) Schedule 8
    (d) Schedule 11

14. In Form A, details of Other Liabilities and Provisions are given in:
    (a) Schedule 3
    (b) Schedule 5
    (c) Schedule 8
    (d) Schedule 11

15. In Form A, details of Contingent Liabilities are given in:
    (a) Schedule 3
    (b) Schedule 5
    (c) Schedule 8
    (d) Schedule 11

16. In Form A, Investments are bifurcated into six segments in Balance sheets, which are not in the segments?
    (a) Government Securities
    (b) Other approved Securities
    (c) Shares
    (d) None of the above

17. Which is not covered under schedule-14 Other Income?
    (a) Commission, Exchange and Brokerage
    (b) Interest on Staff Housing Loan
    (c) Profit on Sale of Investments
    (d) Profit on Sale of Land, Buildings

18. In a Bank Balance Sheet, Figures should be rounded-off to the nearest________.
    (a) rupee
    (b) hundred rupees
    (c) thousand rupees
    (d) lakh rupees

19. Which of the following can be included in the category of voucher in a bank?
    (a) Pay-in-slip
    (b) Cheque
    (c) Withdrawal form
    (d) All of the above

20. The final accounts of a banking companies are to be prepared as per provision of:
    (a) Company Act
    (b) BR Act
    (c) RBI Act
    (d) All of the above

ANSWER

1	2	3	4	5	6	7	8	9	10
(c)	(a)	(b)	(c)	(b)	(a)	(c)	(a)	(b)	(d)

11	12	13	14	15	16	17	18	19	20
(a)	(a)	(c)	(b)	(d)	(d)	(b)	(c)	(d)	(b)

CHAPTER 17

COMPANY ACCOUNTS

INTRODUCTION

The financial statements are the end products of accounting process. Having understood how a company raises its capital, we have to learn the nature, objectives and types of financial statements. It has to prepare including their contents, format, uses and limitations. They are prepared following the consistent accounting concepts, principles, procedures and also the legal environment in which the business organisations operate. These statements are the outcome of the summarising process of accounting and are, therefore, the sources of information on the basis of which conclusions are drawn about the profitability and the financial position of a company.

DEFINITION OF COMPANIES

Companies are defined in Indian Company Act 1956. As per the provision of Company Act 2013 (implemented with effect from 1ˢᵗ April 2014), recognizes a joint Stock Company is a legal person with perpetual entity and is distinct from its members. A company or association of persons can be created at law as legal person so that the company in itself can accept limited liability for civil responsibility. Because companies are legal persons, they also may associate and register themselves as companies otherwise it will be treated as illegal. Address of the registered office is compulsory. It is the address at which all the documents and notices may be served upon the company. Cheques favouring company are not to be credited to the personal accounts of the Directors or other officers of the company.

Following documents are required for financing of a company:

a) **Certificate of Incorporation:** Issued by Registrar of Companies. It is conclusive proof for incorporation of the company and compliance of all formalities by promoters.

b) **Certificate of Commencement of Business:** A company having share capital cannot commence business until it has obtained the certificate to commence business (COB) from the concerned Registrar of Companies. Certificate of commencement of business is not required by Private Ltd. Co. as its shares are closely held and it can commence business on its incorporation.

c) **Memorandum of Association:** Company's fundamental & unalterable law. Embodies Company's name, Authorized capital, Objectives of the Company, Liability of shareholders.

d) **Article of Association:** Regulations controlling internal management of the company. Rights & powers of the Directors, rules about conduct of company meetings & business, Procedure for borrowing & limit on borrowing etc.

e) **Copy of Board Resolution:** Certified copy of Board Resolution authorizing to borrow from the Bank with details of limit, security etc., Persons who are authorized to sign the security documents & operate the bank loan account.

f) **Company Common Seal:** Common seal if any, of the company available should be embossed on bank's documents. As per Companies (Amendment) Act, 2015 and RBI instruction Company Common

Seal is not necessary, if other documents available during current account opening.

Different Types of Companies in India

I) Private Company: Private Company has shareholders with limited liability and its shares may not be offered to the general public. Shareholders of private companies limited by shares are often bound to offer the shares to their fellow shareholders prior to selling them to a third party. Private Limited Company having a no minimum paid-up share capital limitation now. (As per Companies (Amendment) Act, 2015, paid-up share capital of one lakh rupee or such higher paid-up share capital as may be prescribed is omitted now). It has minimum two members and maximum members restricted to two hundred. It has minimum two directors and no maximum number of directors is restricted.

II) Public Company: Public company means a company which is not a private company and has no minimum paid-up share capital limitation now (As per Companies (Amendment) Act, 2015, paid-up share capital of five lakh rupee or such higher paid-up share capital as may be prescribed is omitted now). Shares are offered to the public & are listed on stock exchange. Minimum seven members with no limit of maximum number. Minimum 3 directors with maximum 15 director limit. Provided that a company may appoint more than fifteen directors after passing a special resolution (As per Companies Act 2013, no Central Govt. permission required now). At least one woman director shall be on board. Certificate of commencement of business is must to do any type of business.

The public limited company can be further classified as:

a) Limited Liability Company: Liability of the member is limited to their face value of the shares purchased by them.

b) Unlimited Liability Company: An unlimited company is a company having no limit on the liability of its members.

c) Limited by Guarantee: It is a registered company in which the liability of members is limited to such amounts as they may respectively undertake by the memorandum to contribute to the assets of the company in the event of its being wound up. In the case of such companies the liability of its members is limited to the amount of guarantee undertaken by them.

III) One Person Company: The Companies Act 2013 Act introduces a new type of entity to the existing list i.e. apart from forming a public or private limited company, the 2013 act enables the formation of a new entity a 'one-person company' (OPC). An OPC means a company with only one person having a sole member [section 3(1) of 2013 Act]. OPC will be formed as a 'Private Limited Company'. Memorandum of Association of such a company will mandatorily prescribe the name of the other person, who in the event of death or disability of the subscriber shall assume his position. An OPC can be formed only by an Indian Resident and citizen.

IV) Government Company: "Government Company" means any company in which not less than fifty one per cent. Of paid-up share capital is held by the Central Government, or by any State Government, or partly by the Central Government and partly by one or more State Governments, and includes a company which is a subsidiary company of such a Government company.

V) Statutory Company: A company may be incorporated by means of a special Act of the Parliament or any state legislature. Such companies are called statutory companies; Instances of statutory companies in India are Reserve Bank of India, The Life Insurance Corporation of India, and The Food Corporation of India etc. These statutory companies are governed by the act under which they are established. The provisions of the Companies Act 1956 apply to statutory companies except where the said provisions are inconsistent with the provisions of the Act creating them. Statutory companies are mostly invested with compulsory powers.

VI) Other Companies: As per Companies act 1956, companies can be classified on the basis of time, place of incorporation and nature of working share capital as follows:

a) Foreign Company: It means a company incorporated outside India and having a place of business in India whether by itself or through an agent, physically or through electronic mode and conduct any business activity in India in any other manner.

b) Existing Company: A company which is established before the Company Act 1956 is called Existing Company.

c) Holding Company: A company is known as the holding company of another company if it has control over another company.

d) Subsidiary Company: A company is known as subsidiary of another company when control is exercised by the latter over the former. A company is deemed to be subsidiary company of another.

Partnership Firm

Partnership is the relation between persons who have agreed to share profits of business carried on by all or any one of them acting for all (Indian Partnership Act 1932). As per RBI instruction now Registration Certificate and Partnership deed to be obtained. As per Indian Companies Act 2013, Maximum number of partners can be up to 100 in a firm (Earlier number of partners was restricted to 20 for other businesses and 10 for banking business). Partnership is not a distinct legal person from the partners who have made partnership firm. HUF cannot enter into a partnership as per Supreme Court judgement of 1998. The firm should have PAN or GST Number. A partner cannot delegate his authority to operate the account.

DISTINCTION BETWEEN PARTNERSHIP AND LIMITED LIABILITY COMPANY

The special features of a limited liability company can be well understood if we compare the features of a company form of organization with that of a partnership firm. The important points of distinction between the company and partnership are given below:

1. **Definition:** Any voluntary association of persons registered as a company and formed for the purpose of any common object is called a company. But a partnership is the relation between two or more individuals who have agreed to share the profits of a business carried on by all or any of them acting for all. The partners are collectively called as a firm.

2. **Law:** A company is regulated and controlled by the Companies Act. But a partnership firm is regulated by the Partnership Act, 1932.

3. **Registration:** A company should be compulsorily registered under the Companies Act. Its formation is very difficult. But registration of a partnership firm is not compulsory under the Partnership Act. The firm is based on the partnership deed. As per RBI instruction now Registration Certificate and Partnership deed to be obtained for opening of bank account.

4. **Legal Position:** A company is a corporate body and a legal person having a corporate personality distinct from its members. The members are not liable for the acts of the company. But a partnership has no legal existence distinct from its members. Partners are liable for the acts of the firm.

5. **Liability:** The maximum liability of the shareholders, in case of a limited company, is limited to the face value of the shares purchased by them. In case of companies limited by guarantee, the liability of the shareholders will be up to the amount guaranteed by them. But in case of a partnership, the liability of the partners is unlimited. The partners are jointly and severally liable for all the debts of the partnership firm.

6. **Transferability of Shares:** Shares of a company are freely transferable unless restricted by the Articles. But a partner cannot transfer his share without the consent of all other partners.

7. **Contract:** A member of a company can enter into a contract with the same company. But a partner of a firm cannot enter into contract with the same partnership firm.

8. **Number of Members:** A private company should have a minimum of 2 members and can have a maximum of 200 members. A public company should have a minimum of 7 members and there is no maximum limit. But a partnership should have a minimum of 2 and can have a maximum of 100 persons.

9. **Management:** The management of a company is in the hands of a group of elected representatives of the shareholders. But in the case of a partnership, the management is in the hands of the partners themselves.

10. **Dissolution:** A company, being a creature of law, can only be dissolved as laid down by law. A partnership firm, on the other hand, is the result of an agreement and can be dissolved at any time by agreement. The life of a partnership ends on the death or insolvency or insanity of any one partner.

SHARE CAPITAL

The term capital usually means a particular amount of money with which a business is started. In Indian Companies Act, it has been used in different senses in various parts of the Act, but in general it means the money subscribed pursuant to Memorandum of Association of the Company. Capital, in fact, represents the assets with which the undertaking is carried on.

The sum total of nominal value of shares of a company is known as its share capital. In case of companies, the terms 'capital' and 'share capital' have been held to be synonymous. Capital to be stated in the Memorandum of Association and Articles of Association of the Company.

Classes of Share Capital

The share capital of a company limited by shares may be of the following two kinds:

1. **Preference Share Capital:** It means that part of the capital of the company which:
   (a) Carries a preferential right as to payment of dividend at fixed rate during the life time of the company.
   (b) Carries, on the winding up of the company, a preferential right to be repaid the amount of the capital paid up.
2. **Equity Share Capital:** It means with reference to a company, limited by shares, all share capital which is not preference share capital.

Types/Nature of Share Capital

The share capital of company may be of the following types:

1. **Registered, Authorised or Nominal Capital:** The Memorandum of Association of every company has to specify the amount of capital with which it wants to be registered. The capital so stated is called Registered, Authorized or Nominal Capital. The Registered Capital is the maximum amount of share capital which a company can raise by way of public subscription.
2. **Issued Capital:** The Company may not issue the entire authorised capital at once. It goes on raising the capital as and when the need for additional fund is felt. So, issued capital is that part of Authorised/Registered or Nominal Capital which is offered to the public for subscription in the form of shares. The balance of nominal capital remaining to be issued is called 'Unissued Capital'. Unissued capital may be offered for public subscription at a later date.
3. **Subscribed Capital:** It is that part of "issued capital" for which applications are received from the public. The subscribed capital is allotted to the respective subscribers as per resolution passed by the directors of the company.
4. **Called up Capital:** It is that part of subscribed capital which has been called up by the company. A company does not call at once the full amount on each of the shares it has allotted and therefore, calls up only such amount as it needs.
5. **Uncalled up Capital:** It is the uncalled portion of the allotted capital and represents contingent liability of the shareholders on the shares.
6. **Paid up Capital:** It is that part of called up capital against which payment has been received from the members on their respective shares in response to the calls made by the company.
7. **Reserve Capital:** According to Sec. 99 of the Companies Act, 1956, Reserve Capital is that part of uncalled capital of a company which can be called only in the event of its winding-up. A limited company may, by special resolution, determine that any portion of its share capital which has not been called-up, shall be called up, except in the event of the company being wound-up, such capital is known as Reserve Capital. It is available only for the creditors on the winding-up of the company.

ISSUE OF SHARES

Shares, refer to the units into which the total share capital of a company is divided. Thus, a share is a fractional part of the share capital and forms the basis of ownership interest in a company. The persons who contribute money through shares are called shareholders.

A salient characteristic of the capital of a company is that the amount on its shares can be gradually collected in easy instalments spread over a period of time depending upon its growing financial requirement. The first instalment is collected along with application and is thus, known as application money, the second on allotment (termed as allotment money), and the remaining instalment are termed as first call, second call and so on. The word final is suffixed to the last instalment. However, this in no way prevents a company from calling the full amount on shares right at the time of application. The important steps in the procedure of share issue are:

Issue of Prospectus

The Company first issues the prospectus to the public. Prospectus is an invitation to the public that a new company has come into existence and it needs funds for doing business. It contains complete information about the company and the manner in which the money is to be collected from the prospective investors.

Receipt of Applications

When prospectus is issued to the public, prospective investors intending to subscribe the share capital of the company would make an application along with the application money and deposit the same with a scheduled bank as specified in the prospectus.

Allotment of Shares

If minimum subscription has been received, the company may proceed for the allotment of shares after fulfilling certain other legal formalities. Letters of allotment are sent to those whom the shares have been allotted, and letters of regret to those to whom no allotment has been made. When allotment is made, it results in a valid contract between the company and the applicants who now became the shareholders of the company.

Shares of a company are issued either at par, at a premium or at a discount. Shares are to be issued at par when their issue price is exactly equal to their nominal value according to the terms and conditions of issue. When the shares of a company are issued more than its nominal value (face value), the excess amount is called premium. When the shares are issued at a price less than the face value of the share, it is known as shares issued at a discount. Irrespective of the fact that shares are issued at par, premium or discount, the share capital of a company as stated earlier, may be collected in instalments payable at different stages.

Accounting Treatment on Application

The amount of money paid with various instalments represents the contribution to share capital and should ultimately be credited to share capital. However, for the sake of convenience, initially individual accounts are opened for each instalment. All money received along with application is deposited with a scheduled bank in a separate account opened for the purpose. The journal entry is as follows:

Bank A/c   Dr.
     To Share Application A/c
(Amount received on application for — shares @ ₹ _______ per share)

On Allotment: When minimum subscription has been received and certain legal formalities on the allotment of

shares have been duly complied with, the directors of the company proceed to make the allotment of shares. The allotment of shares implies a contract between the company and the applicants who now become the allottees and assume the status of shareholders or members.

The journal entries with regard to allotment of shares are as follows:

1. **For Transfer of Application Money**

   Share Application A/c   Dr.
        To Share Capital A/c
   (Application money on ______ Shares allotted/ transferred to Share Capital)

2. **For Money Refunded on Rejected Application**

   Share Application A/c   Dr.
        To Bank A/c
   (Application money returned on rejected application for ___ shares)

3. **For Amount Due on Allotment**

   Share Allotment A/c   Dr.
        To Share Capital A/c

4. **For Adjustment of Excess Application Money**

   Share Application A/c   Dr.
        To Share Allotment A/c
   (Application Money on ___Shares @ ₹ __ per shares adjusted to the amount due on allotment).

5. **For Receipt of Allotment Money**

   Bank A/c   Dr.
        To Share Allotment A/c
   (Allotment money received on ___Shares @ ₹ — per share Combined Account)

   Note: The journal entries (2) and (4) can also be combined as follows:

   Share Application A/c   Dr.
        To Share Allotment A/c
        To Bank A/c
   (Excess application money adjusted to share allotment and balance refunded)

- **Illustration 1 :** Mona Earth Movers Limited decided to issue 12,000 shares of ₹100 each payable at ₹ 30 on application, ₹ 40 on allotment, ₹ 20 on first call and balance on second and final call. Applications were received for 13,000 shares. The directors decided to reject application of 1,000 shares and their application money being refunded in full. The allotment money was duly received on all the shares, and all sums due on calls are received except on 100 shares. Record the transactions in the books of Mona Earth Movers Limited.

Solution :   **Books of Mona Earth Mover Limited**

JOURNAL

Date	Particulars		L/f	Dr. Amt.	Cr. Amt.
	Bank A/c	Dr.		3,90,000	
	To Share Application A/c				3,90,000
	(Application money on 13,000 shares @ ₹ 30 per share received)				
	Share Application A/c	Dr.		3,60,000	
	To Share Capital A/c				3,60,000
	(Application money transferred to share capital)				
	Share Application A/c	Dr.		30,000	
	To Bank A/c				30,000
	(Application money on 1,000 shares returned)				
	Share Allotment A/c Dr.			30,000	
	To Share Capital A/c				30,000
	(money due on allotment of 12,000 shares @ ₹ 40 per share)				
	Bank A/c	Dr.		4,80,000	
	To Share Allotment A/c				4,80,000
	(Money received on 12,000 shares @ ₹ 40 per share on allotment)				
	Share First Call A/c Dr.			2,40,000	
	To Share Capital A/c				2,40,000
	(Money due on 12,000 shares @ ₹ 20 per share share on first call)				
	Bank A/c	Dr.		2,38,000	
	To Share First Call A/c				2,38,000
	(first call money received except for 100 shares)				
	Share Second & Final Call A/c	Dr.		1,20,000	
	To Share Capital A/c				1,20,000
	(money due on 12,000 shares @ ₹ 10 per share on second and final call)				
	Bank A/c	Dr.		1,19,000	
	To Share Second & Final Call A/c				1,19,000
	(Share second & final call money received except for 100 shares)				

Over Subscription: There are instances when applications for more shares of a company are received than the number offered to the public for subscription. This usually happens in respect of shares issue of well-managed and financially strong companies and is said to be a case of 'Over Subscription'. In such a condition, three alternatives are available to the directors to deal with the situation:

(1) They can accept some applications in full and totally reject the others;

(2) They can make a pro-rata allotment to all; and

(3) They can adopt a combination of the above two alternatives which happens to be the most common course adopted in practice.

The problem of over subscription is resolved with the allotment of shares. Therefore, from the accounting point of view, it is better to place the situation of over subscription within the total frame of application and allotment, i.e. receipt of application amount, amount due on allotment and its receipt from the shareholders, and the same has been observed in the pattern of entries.

Under Subscription: Under subscription is a situation where number of shares applied for is less than the number for which applications have been invited for subscription. For example, a company offered 2 lakh shares for subscription to the public but the applications were received for 1,90,000 shares only. In such a situation, the allotment will be confirmed to 1,90,000 shares and entries shall be made accordingly.

Issue of Shares at a Premium: It is quite common for the shares of financially strong and well-managed companies to be issued at a premium, i.e. at an amount more than the nominal or par value of shares. Thus, when a share of the nominal value of ₹ 100 is issued at ₹ 105, it is said to have been issued at a premium of 5 per cent. When the issue of shares is at a premium, the amount of premium may technically be called at any stage of the issue of shares. However, premium is generally called with the amount due on allotment, sometimes with the application money and rarely with the call money. The premium amount is credited to a separate account called 'Securities Premium Account' and is shown under the title 'Equity and Liabilities' of the company's balance sheet under the head 'Reserves and Surpluses'. It can be used only for the following four purposes as laid down by Section 78 of The Companies Act 1956:

(a) To issue fully paid bonus shares to the extent not exceeding unissued share capital of the company;

(b) To write-off preliminary expenses of the company;

(c) To write-off the expenses of, or commission paid, or discount allowed on any of the shares or debentures of the company; and

(d) To pay premium on the redemption of preference shares or debentures of the company.

The journal entries for shares issued at a premium are as follows:

1. **For Premium Amount called with Application Money**

(a) Bank A/c   Dr.
     To Share Application A/c
(Money received on application for —shares @ ₹ — per share including premium)

(b) Share Application A/c   Dr.
     To Share Capital A/c
     To Securities Premium A/c
(Transfer of Application Money to Share Capital and Securities Premium Account)

2. **Premium Amount called with Allotment Money**

(a) Share Allotment A/c   Dr.
     To Share Capital A/c
     To Securities Premium A/c
(Amount due on allotment of shares @ ₹ — per share including premium)

(b) Bank A/c   Dr.
     To Share Allotment A/c
(Allotment Money received including premium)

3. **Premium Amount called with Call Money**

(a) Share Application A/c   Dr.
     To Share Capital A/c
     To Securities Premium A/c
(Amount due on 1st/2nd call @ ₹— per share including premium)

(b) Bank A/c   Dr.
     To Share Call A/c
(Call Money received including premium)

- **Illustration 2 :** Jupiter Company Limited issued 35,000 equity shares of ₹ 10 each at a premium of ₹ 2 payable as follows:

On Application	₹ 3
On Allotment	₹ 5 (including premium)
Balance on First and Final Call	

The issue was fully subscribed. All the money was duly received.

Record journal entries in the books of the company.

Solution :   **Books of Jupiter Company Limited**

JOURNAL

Date	Particulars	L/f	Dr. Amt.	Cr. Amt.
	Bank A/c Dr. To Equity Share Application a/c (Money received on applications for 35,000 shares @ ₹ 3 per share)		1,05,000	1,05,000

Solution :   **Books of Jupiter Company Limited**

JOURNAL

Date	Particulars		L/f	Dr. Amt.	Cr. Amt.
	Equity Share Application A/c	Dr.		1,05,000	
	To Equity Share Capital A/c				1,05,000
	(Transfer of Application Money on Allotment to Share Capital)				
	Equity Share Allotment A/c	Dr.		1,75,000	
	To Equity Share Capital A/c				1,05,000
	To Securities Premium A/c				70,000
	(Amount due on Allotment of 35,000 shares @ ₹ 5 per share including premium)				
	Bank A/c	Dr.		1,75,000	
	To Equity Share Allotment A/c				1,75,000
	(Amount due on First and Final Call of ₹ 4 per share on 35,000 shares)				
	Equity share First & Final Call A/c	Dr.		1,40,000	
	To Equity Share Capital A/c				1,40,000
	(Amount due on First and Final Call of ₹ 4 per share on 35,000 shares)				
	Bank A/c	Dr.		1,40,000	
	To Equity Share First & Final Call A/c				1,40,000
	(Money received on First and Final Call)				

Issue of Shares at a Discount

There are instances when the shares of a company are issued at a discount, i.e. at an amount less than the nominal or par value of shares, the difference between the nominal value and issue price representing discount on the issue of shares. For example, when a share of the nominal value of ₹ 100 is issued at ₹ 98, it is said to have been issued at a discount of two per cent.

As a general rule, a company cannot ordinarily issue shares at a discount. It can do so only in cases such as 'reissue of forfeited shares' and in accordance with the provisions of Section 79 of the Companies Act, 1956.

Section 79 of the Companies Act, 1956 states that a company is permitted to issue shares at a discount provided the following conditions are satisfied:

(a) The issue of shares at a discount is authorised by an ordinary resolution passed by the company at its general meeting and sanctioned by the Company Law Board, now Central Government.

(b) The resolution must specify the maximum rate of discount at which the shares are to be issued but the rate of discount must not exceed 10 per cent of the nominal value of shares. The rate of discount can be more than 10 per cent if the Government is convinced that a higher rate is called for under special circumstances of a case.

(c) At least one year must have elapse since the date on which the company became entitled to commence the business.

(d) The shares are of a class which has already been issued.

(e) The shares issued within two months from the date of receiving sanction for the same from the Government or within such extended period as the Government may allow.

Whenever shares are issued at a discount, the amount of discount is brought into the books at the time of allotment by debiting an account called 'Discount on the Issue of Shares Account'.

The journal entry to be passed for the purpose is as given below:

Share Allotment A/c	Dr.
Discount on the Issue of Shares A/c	Dr.
Share Capital A/c	

(Amount due on allotment of — shares@ ₹ — per share and discount on issue brought into account)

Discount on the Issue of Shares, being a loss of capital nature to the company, will be set off from 'Securities Premium' or written-off through 'Statement of Profit and Loss, over a period of 3 to 5 years as per the guidelines of ICAI.

Sweat Equity Shares

Sweat equity shares can only be issued by a company to its Directors or Employees, at a discount or for a consideration other than cash, for their providing of know-how or creation of intellectual property rights patent, copyright or like trademark, value additions. Sweat equity shares can be issued to:

- Permanent employee of the company who has been working in India or outside India, for at least the last one year;
- Director of the company, whether a whole time Director or not;
- Employee or Director above of a subsidiary of the company, in India or outside India, or of a holding company of the company.

Sweat equity shares are issued for value additions of the Director or Employee. Value additions mean actual or anticipated economic benefits derived or to be derived by the Company from an Expert or Professional from providing know-how or making available rights in the nature of intellectual property rights. For sweat equity shares to be issued, the employee's remuneration for value addition should not have been paid or included in the normal remuneration payable, under the contract of employment or monetary consideration payable under any other contract.

Employee Stock Options (ESOs)

Employee stock options are call options on a company's common stock granted to a select group of its employees. Certain restrictions on the option provide a financial incentive for employees to align their goals with those of the company's shareholders.

Forfeiture and Reissue of Shares

If a shareholder fails to pay allotment money or a call or a part thereof by the last date fixed for payment, the Board of Directors, if Articles of Association of the company empower it to do so, proceed to forfeit the shares on which allotment money or call has become in arrears.

The Articles of Association lay down the procedure. A notice has to be served on the defaulter requiring him to pay the unpaid amount together with interest accrued by a certain date.

The notice also must state that in the event of non-payment on or before the date so named, the shares in respect of which the notice has been served will be liable to be forfeited. When shares are forfeited, the shareholder's name is removed from the register of members and the amount already paid by him on shares is forfeited to the company.

It is a capital gain and is credited to Forfeited Shares Account. A forfeited share may be reissued even at a loss. But the loss on reissue cannot exceed the gain on forfeiture of the share reissued.

Bonus Shares

The word bonus means a gift given free of charge. Bonus shares are those shares which are issued by the company free of charge as bonus to the shareholders. They are issued to the existing shareholders in proportion to their existing share holdings. It is a kind of gift to the shareholders from the company. It is bonus in the form of shares instead of cash. It is given out of accumulated profits and reserves. These shares have all types of preferences which are available to the existing shares. For example. two bonus shares for five equity shares. The issue of bonus shares is also termed as capitalization of undistributed profits.

The basic principle behind bonus shares is that the total number of shares increases with a constant ratio of number of shares held to the number of shares outstanding. For instance, if Investor A holds 200 shares of a company and a company declares 4:1 bonus, that is for every one share, he gets 4 shares for free. That is total 800 shares for free and his total holding will increase to 1000 shares.

Companies issue bonus shares to encourage retail participation and increase their equity base. When price per share of a company is high, it becomes difficult for new investors to buy shares of that particular company. Increase in the number of shares reduces the price per share. But the overall capital remains the same even if bonus shares are declared.

Conditions for Issue of Bonus Shares: Following conditions should be fulfilled for issue of bonus shares of a company.

(i) **Sufficient amount of Undistributed Profits:** There must be sufficient amount of undistributed profits for the issue of bonus shares.

(ii) **Provision in the Articles:** There must be a provision in the articles of association regarding the issue of bonus shares. If there is a provision in the articles regarding the issue of bonus shares the company can issue bonus shares if there is no provision, the company cannot issue the bonus shares.

(iii) Suitable Resolution: The Board of Directors must pass a suitable resolution in the Board meeting for the issue of bonus shares.

(iv) Shareholders Approval: The shareholders must give formal approval for the issue of bonus shares in the Annual General Meeting.

(v) When a Company can Issue: A company can issue bonus shares only twice in a period of five years.

(vi) Fully Paid up Shares: Bonus shares can be issued only when the existing shares are fully paid up.

Non-Voting Shares: These shares are like ordinary shares except that they carry no voting rights. This type of share is usually issued to employees so that part of their compensation can be paid in the form of dividends. This arrangement usually provides tax benefits for the company and the employees.

FINAL ACCOUNTS OF COMPANIES

There is no legal obligation for sole proprietorship and partnership firm to prepare final accounts, but companies have statutory obligations to keep proper books of account and to prepare its final accounts every year in the manner as prescribed in the Companies Act. Chapter IX, sections 128 to 138 of the Companies Act, 2013 deals with the legal provisions relating to the Accounts of Companies. These sections including Schedule II and III were brought into force from 1st April 2014.

GENERAL INSTRUCTIONS FOR THE PREPARATION OF BALANCE SHEET AND PROFIT & LOSS ACCOUNT

The Schedule III sets out the minimum requirements for disclosure on the face of the Balance Sheet, and the Statement of Profit & Loss (hereinafter referred to as "Financial Statements") and Notes.

Line items, sub-line items and sub-totals shall be presented as an addition or substitution on the face of the Financial Statements when such presentation is relevant to an understanding of the company's financial position or performance or to cater to industry/sector-specific disclosure requirements or when required for compliance with the amendments to the Companies Act or under the Accounting Standards.

1. Where compliance with the requirements of the Act including Accounting Standards as applicable to the companies require any change in treatment or disclosure including addition, amendment, substitution or deletion in the head or sub-head or any changes, inter se, in the financial statements or statements forming part thereof, the same shall be made and the requirements of this Schedule shall stand modified accordingly.

2. The disclosure requirements specified in this Schedule are in addition to and not in substitution of the disclosure requirements specified in the Accounting Standards prescribed under the Companies Act, 2013. Additional disclosures specified in the Accounting Standards shall be made in the notes to accounts or by way of additional statement unless required to be disclosed on the face of the Financial Statements. Similarly, all other disclosures as required by the Companies Act shall be made in the notes to accounts in addition to the requirements set out in this Schedule.

3. Notes to accounts shall contain information in addition to that presented in the Financial Statements and shall provide where required:

   a) Narrative descriptions or disaggregation's of items recognised in those statements; and

   b) Information about items that do not qualify for recognition in those statements.

4. Each item on the face of the Balance Sheet and Statement of Profit and Loss shall be cross-referenced to any related information in the notes to accounts. In preparing the Financial Statements including the notes to accounts, a balance shall be maintained between providing excessive detail that may not assist users of financial statements and not providing important information as a result of too much aggregation.

5. Depending upon the turnover of the company, the figures appearing in the Financial Statements may be rounded off as given below:

	Turnover	*Rounding off*
(a)	Less than one hundred crore rupees	To the nearest hundreds, thousands, lakhs or millions, or decimals thereof.
(b)	One hundred crore rupees or more	To the nearest lakhs, millions or crores, or decimals thereof.

Once a unit of measurement is used, it shall be used uniformly in the Financial Statements.

6. Except in the case of the first Financial Statements laid before the Company (after its incorporation) the corresponding amounts (comparatives) for the immediately preceding reporting period for all items shown in the Financial Statements including notes shall also be given.

7. For the purpose of this Schedule, the terms used herein shall be as per the applicable Accounting Standards.

KEY FEATURES OF BALANCE SHEET

1. The Schedule III permits only Vertical form of presentation.

2. It uses "Equity and Liabilities" and "Assets" as headings.

3. All assets and liabilities classified into current and non-current and presented separately on the face of the Balance Sheet.

4. Number of shares held by each shareholder holding more than 5% shares now needs to be disclosed.

5. Details pertaining to aggregate number and class of shares allotted for consideration other than cash, bonus shares and shares bought back will need to be disclosed only for a period of five years immediately preceding the Balance Sheet date.

6. Any debit balance in the Statement of Profit and Loss will be disclosed under the head "Reserves and Surplus." Earlier, any debit balance in Profit and Loss Account carried forward after deduction from uncommitted reserves was required to be shown as the last item on the asset side of the Balance Sheet.

7. Specific disclosures are prescribed for Share Application Money. The application money not exceeding the capital offered for issuance and to the extent not refundable will be shown separately on the face of the Balance Sheet. The amount in excess of subscription or if the requirements of minimum subscription are not met will be shown under "Other Current Liabilities."

8. The term "Sundry Debtors" has been replaced with the term "Trade Receivables." 'Trade Receivables' are defined as dues arising only from goods sold or services rendered in the normal course of business. Hence, amounts due on account of other contractual obligations can no longer be included in the trade receivables.

9. It requires separate disclosure of "Trade Receivables" outstanding for a period exceeding six months from the date the bill/invoice is due for payment.

10. "Capital Advances" are specifically required to be presented separately under the head "Loans & Advances" rather than including elsewhere.

11. Tangible Assets under lease are required to be separately specified under each class of asset. In the absence of any further clarification, the term "Under Lease" should be taken to mean assets given on operating lease in the case of lessor and assets held under finance lease in the case of lessee.

12. Under the Schedule III, other commitments also need to be disclosed.

Part I : BALANCE SHEET

The format of balance sheet as given in Part I of Schedule III of the Companies Act 2013 is given below :

Name of the Company: _________________________

Balance Sheet as at: _________________________ (Rupees in _____________)

	Particulars	Note No.	Figures as at the end of current reporting period	Figures as at the end of previous reporting period
	1	2	3	4
(I) (1)	**EQUITY AND LIABILITIES** **Shareholder's Funds** (a) Share Capital (b) Reserves and Surplus (c) Money received against share warrants			
(2)	**Share Application Money Pending Allotment**			
(3)	**Non-Current Liabilities** (a) Long Term Borrowings (b) Deferred Tax Liabilities (Net) (c) Other Long Term Liabilities (d) Long Term Provisions			
(4)	**Current Liabilities** (a) Short-Term Borrowings (b) Trade Payables (c) Other Current Liabilities (d) Short-Term Provisions			
	TOTAL			

	Particulars	Note No.	Figures as at the end of current reporting period	Figures as at the end of previous reporting period
	1	2	3	4
(II) (1)	**ASSETS**			
	Non-current Assets			
	(a) Fixed Assets			
	(i) Tangible Assets			
	(ii) Intangible Assets			
	(iii) Capital Work-in-progress			
	(iv) Intangible Assets Under Development			
	(b) Non-current Investments			
	(c) Deferred Tax Assets (net)			
	(d) Long Term Loans and Advances			
	(e) Other Non-current Assets			
(2)	**Current Assets**			
	(a) Current Investments			
	(b) Inventories			
	(c) Trade Receivables			
	(d) Cash and Cash Equivalents			
	(e) Short-term Loans and Advances			
	(f) Other Current Assets			
	TOTAL			

General Instructions for Preparing the Balance Sheet of a Company

Current Assets:

1. An asset shall be classified as current when it satisfies any of the following criteria:

    (a) It is expected to be realized in, or is intended for sale or consumption in, the company's normal operating cycle;

    (b) It is held primarily for the purpose of being traded;

    (c) It is expected to be realized within twelve months after the reporting date; or

    (d) It is Cash or cash equivalent unless it is restricted from being exchanged or used to settle a liability for at least twelve months after the reporting date.

    All other assets shall be classified as "**non-current**".

2. An operating cycle is the time between the acquisition of assets for processing and their realization in Cash or cash equivalents. Where the normal operating cycle cannot be identified, it is assumed to have a duration of 12 months.

3. A liability shall be classified as current when it satisfies any of the following criteria:

    (a) It is expected to be settled in the company's normal operating cycle;

    (b) It is held primarily for the purpose of being traded;

    (c) It is due to be settled within twelve months after the reporting date; or

    (d) The company does not have an unconditional right to defer settlement of the liability for at least twelve months after the reporting date. Terms of a liability that could, at the option of the counter party, result in its settlement by the issue of equity instruments do not affect its classification.

    All other liabilities shall be classified as "**non-current**."

4. A receivable shall be classified as a 'Trade Receivable' if it is in respect of the amount due on account of goods sold or services rendered in the normal course of business.

5. A payable shall be classified as a 'Trade Payable' if it is in respect of the amount due on account due on account of goods purchased or services received in the normal course of business.

6. A company shall disclose the following in the notes to accounts:

(A) Share Capital

For each class of share capital (different classes of preference shares to be treated separately):

(a) The number and amount of shares authorized;

(b) The number of shares issued, subscribed and fully paid, and subscribed but not fully paid;

(c) Par value per share;

(d) A reconciliation of the number of shares outstanding at the beginning and at the end of the period;

(e) The rights, preferences and restrictions attaching to that class including restrictions on the distribution of dividends and the repayment of capital;

(f) Shares in the company held by its holding company or its ultimate holding company or by its subsidiaries or associates;

(g) Shares in the company held by any shareholder holding more than 5 per cent shares;

(h) Shares reserved for issue under options and contracts/commitments for the sale of shares/disinvestment, including the terms and amounts;

(i) Separate particulars for a period of five years following the year in which the shares have been allotted/bought back, in respect of:

  – Aggregate number and class of shares allotted as fully paid up pursuant to contract(s) without payment being received in cash.

  – Aggregate number and class of shares allotted as fully paid up by way of bonus shares (Specify the source from which bonus shares are issued).

  – Aggregate number and class of shares bought back.

(j) Terms of any security issued along with the earliest date of conversion in descending order starting from the farthest such date.

(B) Reserves and Surplus

1. Reserves and Surplus shall be classified as:
   (a) Capital Reserves;
   (b) Capital Redemption Reserves;
   (c) Securities Premium Reserve;
   (d) Debenture Redemption Reserve;
   (e) Revaluation Reserve;
   (f) Share Options Outstanding Account:
   (g) Other Reserves–(specify the nature of each reserve and the amount in respect thereof);
   (h) Surplus i.e. balance in statement of Profit & Loss disclosing allocations and appropriations such as dividend paid, bonus shares and transfer to/from reserves; (Additions and Deductions since last Balance Sheet to be shown under each of the specified heads)

2. A reserve specifically represented by earmarked investments shall be termed as a 'Fund';

3. Debit balance of Statement of Profit and Loss shall be shown as a negative figure under the head 'Surplus' Similarly, the balance of 'Reserves and Surplus', after adjusting negative balance of surplus, if any, shall be shown under the head 'Reserves and Surplus' even if the resulting figure is in the negative.

(C) Long-term Borrowings

1. Long-term borrowings shall be classified as:
   (a) Bonds/debentures;
   (b) Term loans;
     – From banks
     – From other parties.
   (c) Deferred payment liabilities;
   (d) Deposits;
   (e) Loans and advances from related parties;
   (f) Long-term maturities of finance lease obligations;
   (g) Other loans and advances (specify nature).

2. Borrowings shall further be sub-classified as secured and unsecured. Nature of security shall be specified separately in each case.

3. Where loans have been guaranteed by directors or others, the aggregate amount of such loans under each head shall be disclosed.

4. Bonds/debentures (along with the rate of interest and particulars of redemption or conversion, as the case may be) shall be stated in descending order of maturity or conversion, starting from farthest redemption or conversion date, as the case may be. Where bonds/debentures are redeemable by instalments, the date of maturity for this purpose must be reckoned as the date on which the first instalment becomes due.

5. Particulars of any redeemed bonds/debentures which the company has power to reissue.

6. Terms of repayment of term loans and other loans shall be stated.

7. Period and amount of default in repayment of dues, providing break-up of principal and interest shall be specified separately in each case.

(D) Other Long-term Liabilities

Other Long-term Liabilities shall be classified as:

    (a) Trade payables

    (b) Others

(E) Long-term Provisions

The amounts shall be classified as:

    (a) Provision for employee benefits.

    (b) Others (specify nature).

(F) Short-term Borrowings

1. Short-term borrowings shall be classified as:

    (a) Loans Repayable on Demand
   - from Banks.
   - from Other Parties.

    (b) Loans and Advances from Subsidiaries/holding Company/associates/business ventures.

    (c) Deposits.

    (d) Other Loans and Advances (specify nature).

2. Borrowings shall further be sub-classified as secured and unsecured. Nature of security shall be specified separately in each case.

3. Where loans have been guaranteed by directors or others, a mention thereof shall be made and also the aggregate amount of loans under each head.

4. Period and amount of default in repayment of dues, providing break-up of principal and interest shall be specified separately in each case.

(G) Other Current Liabilities

The amounts shall be classified as:

(a) Current Maturities of Long-term Debt;

(b) Current Maturities of Finance Lease Obligations;

(c) Income Received in Advance;

(d) Interest Accrued but Not Due on Borrowings;

(e) Interest Accrued and Due on Borrowings;

(f) Unpaid Dividends;

(g) Application Money received for allotment of securities and due for refund and interest accrued there on. Share application money includes advances towards allotment of share capital. The terms & conditions including the number of shares proposed to be issued, the amount of premium, if any, and the period before which shares shall be allotted shall be disclosed. It shall also be disclosed whether the company has sufficient authorized capital to cover the share capital amount resulting from allotment of shares out of such share application money. Further, the period for which the share application money has been pending beyond the period for allotment as mentioned in the document inviting application for shares along with the reason for such share application money being pending shall be disclosed. Share application money not exceeding the issued capital and to the extent not refundable shall be shown under the head Equity and share application money to the extent refundable i.e., the amount in excess of subscription or in case the requirements of minimum subscription are not met, shall be separately shown under 'Other Current Liabilities';

(h) Unpaid matured deposits and interest accrued thereon;

(i) Unpaid matured debentures and interest accrued thereon;

(j) Other payables (specify nature).

(H) Short-term Provisions

The amounts shall be classified as:

    (a) Provision for employee benefits.

    (b) Others (specify nature).

(I) Tangible Assets

1. Classification shall be given as:

    (a) Land

    (b) Buildings

    (c) Plant and Equipment

    (d) Furniture and Fixtures

    (e) Vehicles

    (f) Office equipment

    (g) Others (specify nature)

2. Assets under lease shall be separately specified under each class of asset.

3. A reconciliation of the gross and net carrying amounts of each class of assets at the beginning and end of the reporting period showing additions, disposals, acquisitions and other movements and the related depreciation and impairment losses/reversals shall be disclosed separately.

4. Where sums have been written off on a reduction of capital or revaluation of assets or where sums have been added on revaluation of assets, every balance sheet subsequent to date of such write-off, or addition shall show the reduced or increased figures as applicable and shall by way of a note also show the amount of the reduction or increase as applicable together with the date therefore for the first five years subsequent to the date of such reduction or increase.

(J) Intangible Assets

Classification shall be given as:

(a) Goodwill

(b) Brands/trademarks

(c) Computer software

(d) Mastheads and publishing titles

(e) Mining rights

(f) Copyrights, and patents and other intellectual property rights, services and operating rights

(g) Recipes, formulae, models, designs and prototypes

(h) Licences and franchise

    (i) Others (specify nature)

    (ii) A reconciliation of the gross and net carrying amounts of each class of assets at the beginning and end of the reporting period showing additions, disposals, acquisitions and other movements and the related amortization and impairment losses/reversals shall be disclosed separately.

    (iii) Where sums have been written off on a reduction of capital or revaluation of assets or where sums have been added on revaluation of assets, every balance sheet subsequent to date of such write-off, or addition shall show the reduced or increased figures as applicable and shall by way of a note also show the amount of the reduction or increase as applicable together with the date therefor for the first five years subsequent to the date of such reduction or increase.

(K) Non-current Investments

1. Non-current investments shall be classified as trade investments and other investments and further classified as:

(a) Investment property;

(b) Investments in Equity Instruments;

(c) Investments in Preference shares;

(d) Investments in Government or trust securities;

(e) Investments in units, debentures or bonds;

(f) Investments in Mutual Funds;

(g) Investments in partnership firm;

(h) Other non-current investments (specify nature)

    Under each classification, details shall be given of names of the bodies corporate (indicating separately whether such bodies are: (i) subsidiaries, (ii) associates, (iii) joint ventures, or (iv) controlled special purpose entities) in whom investments have been made and the nature and extent of the investment so made in each such body corporate (showing separately investments which are partly paid). In regard to investments in the capital of partnership firms, the names of the firms (with the names of all their partners, total capital and the shares of each partner) shall be given.

2. Investments carried at other than at cost should be separately stated specifying the basis for valuation thereof.

3. The following shall also be disclosed:

(a) Aggregate amount of quoted investments and market value thereof;

(b) Aggregate amount of unquoted investments;

(c) Aggregate provision for diminution in value of investments;

(d) Aggregate amount of partly paid-up investments;

(e) The names of bodies corporate (indicating separately the names of subsidiaries, associates and other business ventures) in whose securities, investments have been made and the nature and extent of the investments so made in each such body corporate.

(L) Long-term Loans and Advances

1. Long-term loans and advances shall be classified as:

(a) Capital Advances;

(b) Security Deposits;

(c) Loans and Advances to related parties (giving details thereof);

(d) Other Loans and Advances (specify nature).

2. The above shall also be separately sub-classified as:

(a) To the extent secured, considered good;

(b) Others, considered good;

(c) Doubtful.

    (i) Allowance for bad and doubtful loans and advances shall be disclosed under the relevant heads separately.

    (ii) Loans and Advances due by directors or other officers of the company or any of them either severally or jointly with any other persons or amounts due by firms or private companies respectively in which any director is a partner or a director or a member should be separately stated.

(M) Other Non-Current Assets

Other non-current assets shall be classified as:

1. Long-term Trade Receivables (including trade receivables on deferred credit terms);

2. Others (specify nature)

3. Long-term Trade Receivables, shall be sub-classified as:
   (i) (a) secured, considered good;
       (b) unsecured, considered good;
       (c) Doubtful
   (ii) Allowance for bad and doubtful debts shall be disclosed under the relevant heads separately.
   (iii) Debts due by directors or other officers of the company or any of them either severally or jointly with any other person debts due by firms or private companies respectively in which any director is a partner or a director or a member should be separately stated.

(N) Current Investments

1. Current investments shall be classified as:
   (a) Investments in Equity Instruments;
   (b) Investments in Preference shares;
   (c) Investments in Government or trust securities;
   (d) Investments in Units, debentures or bonds;
   (e) Investments in Mutual Funds;
   (f) Investments in Partnership firm;
   (g) Other Investments (specify nature).
       Under each classification, details shall be given of names of the bodies corporate (indicating separately whether such bodies are (i) subsidiaries, (ii) associates, (iii) joint ventures, or (iv) controlled special purpose entities) in whom investments have been made and the nature and extent of the investment so made in each such body corporate (showing separately investments which are partly paid). In regard to investments in the capital of partnership firms, the names of the firms (with the names of all their partners, total capital and the shares of each partner) shall be given.

2. The following shall also be disclosed:
   (a) The basis of valuation of individual investments;
   (b) Aggregate amount of quoted investments and market value thereof;
   (c) Aggregate amount of unquoted investments;
   (d) Aggregate amount of partly paid-up investments;
   (e) Aggregate provision for diminution in value of investments.

(O) Inventories

1. Inventories shall be classified as:
   (a) Raw material;
   (b) Work-in-progress;
   (c) Finished goods;
   (d) Stock-in-trade;
   (e) Stores and spares;
   (f) Loose tools;
   (g) Others (specify nature);

2. Goods-in-transit shall be disclosed under the relevant sub-head of inventories;

3. Mode of valuation should be stated.

(P) Trade Receivables

1. Aggregate amount of Trade Receivables outstanding for a period exceeding six months from the date they are due for payment should be separately stated.

2. Trade receivables shall also be classified as:
   (a) To the extent secured, considered good;
   (b) Others, considered good;
   (c) Doubtful.

3. Allowance for bad and doubtful debts shall be disclosed under the relevant heads separately.

4. Debts due by directors or other officers of the company or any of them either severally or jointly with any other person debts due by firms or private companies respectively in which any director is a partner or a director or a member should be separately stated.

(Q) Cash and Cash Equivalents

1. Classification shall be made as:
   (a) Bank balances;
   (b) Cheques, drafts on hand;
   (c) Cash on hand;
   (d) Cash equivalents – short-term, highly liquid investments that are readily convertible into known amounts of cash and which are subject to an insignificant risk of changes in value;
   (e) Others (specify nature).

2. Earmarked bank balances (e.g., unpaid dividend) shall be separately stated.

3. Balance with banks to the extent held as security against the borrowings, guarantees, other commitments shall be disclosed separately.

4. Repatriation restrictions, if any, in respect of cash and bank balances shall be separately stated.

5. Bank deposits with more than 12 months maturity shall be disclosed separately.

(R) Short-term Loans and Advances

1. Short-term loans and advances shall be classified as:
   (a) Loans and Advances to Related parties (giving details thereof);
   (b) Others (specify nature).

2. The above shall also be sub-classified as:
   (a) To the extent secured, considered good;
   (b) Others, considered good;
   (c) Doubtful.

3. Allowance for bad and doubtful loans and advances shall be disclosed under the relevant heads separately.

4. Loans and Advances due by directors or other officers of the company or any of them either severally or jointly with any other person debts due by firms or private companies respectively in which any director is a partner or a director or a member should be separately stated.

(S) Other Current Assets (specify nature)

This is an all-inclusive heading, which incorporates current assets that do not fit into any other assets categories.

(T) Contingencies and Commitments
(to the extent not provided for)

1. Contingent liabilities shall be classified as:
   (a) Claims against the company not acknowledged as debt;
   (b) Guarantees;
   (c) Other money for which the company is contingently liable

2. Commitments shall be classified as:
   (a) Estimated amount of contracts remaining to be executed on capital account and not provided for;
   (b) Uncalled liability on shares and other investments partly paid;
   (c) Other commitments (specify nature).

(U) The amount of dividends proposed to be distributed to equity holders for the period and the related amount per share shall be disclosed separately. Arrears of fixed cumulative dividends shall also be disclosed separately.

(V) Where in respect of an issue of securities made for a specific purpose, the whole or part of the amount has not been used for the specific purpose at the Balance Sheet date, these shall be indicated by way of note how such unutilized amounts have been used or invested.

(W) If, in the opinion of the board, any of the assets other than fixed assets and non-current investments do not have a value on realization in the ordinary course of business at least equal to the amount at which they are stated, the fact that the board is of the opinion, shall be stated.

KEY FEATURES OF STATEMENT OF PROFIT AND LOSS

1) The name of 'Profit and Loss Account' has been changed to "Statement of Profit and Loss".

2) This format of Statement of Profit and Loss does not mention any appropriation item on its face. Further, 'below the line' adjustments to be presented under "Reserves and Surplus" in the Balance Sheet.

3) Any item of income or expense which exceeds one per cent of the revenue from operations or ₹ 100,000 (earlier 1 % of total revenue or ₹ 5,000), whichever is higher, needs to be disclosed separately.

4) In respect of companies other than finance companies, revenue from operations need to be disclosed separately as revenue from (a) sale of products, (b) sale of services and (c) other operating revenues.

5) Net exchange gain/loss on foreign currency borrowings to the extent considered as an adjustment to interest cost needs to be disclosed separately as finance cost.

6) Break-up in terms of quantitative disclosures for significant items of Statement of Profit and Loss, such as raw material consumption, stocks, purchases and sales have been simplified and replaced with the disclosure of "broad heads" only. The broad heads need to be decided based on materiality and presentation of true and fair view of the financial statements.

Part II : STATEMENT OF PROFIT AND LOSS

Name of the Company: ___________________________________

Profit and Loss Statement for the year ended: _____________   (Rupees in _______________)

Particulars	Note No.	Figures as at the end of current reporting period	Figures as at the end of previous reporting period
I. Revenue from Operations			
II. Other Income			
III. Total Revenue (I + II)			
IV. Expenses:			
Cost of Materials Consumed			
Purchases of Stock-in-Trade			
Changes in Inventories of Finished Goods			
Work-in-Progress and Stock-in-Trade			
Employee Benefits Expense			
Finance Costs			
Depreciation and Amortization Expense			
Other Expenses			
Total Expense			
V. Profit before Exceptional and Extraordinary Items and Tax (III-IV)			
VI. Exceptional Items			
VII. Profit before Extraordinary Items and Tax (V-VI)			
VIII. Extraordinary Items			
IX. Profit before Tax (VII-VIII)			
X. Tax Expense:			
1. Current Tax			
2. Deferred Tax			
XI. Profit (Loss) for the Period from Continuing Operations (IX-X-XIV)			
XII. Profit/(Loss) from Discountinuing Operations			
XIII. Tax Expense of Discontinuing Operaions			
XIV. Profit/(Loss) from Discontinuing Operations (after tax) (XII-XIII)			
XV. Profit/(Loss) for the Period (XI-XIV)			
XVI. Earning per Equity Share:			
1. Basic			
2. Diluted			

GENERAL INSTRUCTIONS FOR PREPARATION OF STATEMENT OF PROFIT AND LOSS

1. The Provisions of this Part shall apply to the Income and Expenditure account referred to in sub-clause (40) of Section 2, in like manner as they apply to a statement of profit and loss.

2. (A) In respect of a company other than a finance company revenue from operations shall disclose separately in the notes revenue from:

    (a) Sale of products;

    (b) Sale of services;

    (c) Other operating revenues;

    Less:

    (d) Excise duty.

    (B) In respect of a finance company, revenue from operations shall include revenue from:

(a) Interest; and

(b) Other financial services

Revenue under each of the above heads shall be disclosed separately by way of notes to accounts to the extent applicable.

3. Finance Costs

Finance costs shall be disclosed as:

(a) Interest expense;

(b) Other borrowing costs;

(c) Applicable net gain/loss on foreign currency transaction and translation.

4. Other Income

Other income shall be classified as:

(a) Interest Income (in case of a company other than a finance company);

(b) Dividend Income;

(c) Net gain/loss on sale of investments

(d) Other non-operating income (net of expenses directly attributable to such income).

5. Additional Information

A Company shall disclose by way of notes additional information regarding aggregate expenditure and income on the following items:

(a) Employee Benefits Expense [showing separately
  (i) salaries and wages
  (ii) contribution to provident and other funds,
  (iii) expense on Employee Stock Option Scheme (ESOP) and Employee Stock Purchase Plan (ESPP),
  (iv) staff welfare expense].

(b) Depreciation and amortization expense;

(c) Any item of income or expenditure which exceeds one per cent of the revenue from operations or ₹ 1,00,000, whichever is higher;

(d) Interest Income;

(e) Interest Expense;

(f) Dividend Income;

(g) Net gain/loss on sale of investments;

(h) Adjustments to the carrying amount of investments.

6. Net Gain or Loss on Foreign Currency Transaction and Translation (Other than considered as Finance Cost);

7. Payments to the Auditors as:

(a) audit,

(b) for taxation matters,

(c) for company matters,

(d) for management services,

(e) for other services,

(f) for reimbursement of expense.

8. Details of Items of Exceptional and Extraordinary Nature:

(i) Prior Period Items;

(ii) (a) In the case of manufacturing companies;
  (i) Raw materials under broad heads.
  (ii) Goods purchased under broad heads.

(b) In the case of trading companies, purchases in respect of goods traded in by company under broad heads.

(c) In the case of companies rendering or supplying services, gross income derived from services rendered or supplied under broad heads.

(d) In the case of a company, which falls under more than one of the categories mentioned in (a), (b) and (c) above, it shall be sufficient compliance with the requirements herein if purchase, sales and consumption of raw material and the gross income from services rendered is shown under broad heads.

(e) In the case of other companies gross income derived under broad heads.

(iii) In the case of all concerns having work-in-progress, work-in-progress under broad heads.

(iv) (a) The aggregate, if material, of any amounts set aside or propose to be set aside, to reserve, but not including provisions made to meet any specific liability, contingency or commitment known to exit at the date as to which the Balance Sheet is made up.

(b) The aggregate, if material, of any amounts withdrawn from such reserves.

(v) (a) The aggregate, if material, of the amounts set aside to provisions made for meeting specific liabilities, contingencies or commitment.

(b) The aggregate, if material, of the amounts with-drawn from such provisions, as no longer required.

(vi) Expenditure incurred on each of the following items, separately for each item:

(a) Consumption of stores and spare parts

(b) Power & fuel

(c) Rent

(d) Repairs to building

(e) Repairs to Machinery

(f) Insurance

(g) Rates and Taxes, excluding, taxes on income

(h) Miscellaneous expense.

(vii) (a) Dividends from subsidiary companies

(b) Provisions for losses of subsidiary companies

(viii) The profit and loss account shall also contain by way of a note the following information, namely:

(a) Value of imports calculated on C.I.F. basis by the company during the financial year in respect of:
 I. Raw materials;
 II. Components and spare parts;
 III. Capital goods.

(b) Expenditure in foreign currency during the financial year on account of royalty, know-how, professional and consultation fees, interest, and other matters.

(c) Total value if all imported raw materials, spare parts and the components consumed during the Financial year and the total value of all indigenous raw materials, spare parts and components similarly consumed and the percentage of each to the total consumption.

(d) The amount remitted during the year in foreign currencies on account of dividends with specific mention of the total number of non-resident shareholders, the total number of shares held by them on which the dividends were due and the year to which the dividends related.

(e) Earnings in foreign exchange classified under the following heads, namely:
 I. Exports of Goods calculated on F.O.B. basis;
 II. Royalty, know-how, professional and consultation fees;
 III. Interest and Dividends;
 IV. Other Income, indicating the nature thereof

Note: Broad heads shall be decided taking into account the concept of materiality and presentation of true and fair view of Financial Statements.

TEST YOURSELF

1. ______________ is called the Charter of the Company.
(a) Articles of Association
(b) Memorandum of Association
(c) Prospectus
(d) Certificate of Incorporation

2. A company comes into existence when it gets the certificate of ______________.
(a) Incorporation
(b) Commencing the business
(c) Income-tax department
(d) None of the above

3. A company incorporated outside India but has a place of business in India, is termed as:
(a) Statutory Company
(b) Foreign Company
(c) Holding Company
(d) Subsidiary Company

4. A private limited company has _______ shareholders.
(a) 2 to 200
(b) 1 to 49
(c) 7 to 51
(d) 2 to 50

5. Rights shares mean the shares which are:
(a) Issued to directors of the company
(b) Issued for a consideration other than cash
(c) Offered to the existing shareholders
(d) Issued to promoters of the company for their services.

6. Discount on issue of shares is a:
(a) Revenue loss
(b) Capital loss
(c) Deferred revenue expenditure
(d) Both Revenue and capital loss

7. The main object of permitting the company to issue non-voting equity shares is:
(a) To give higher dividend
(b) To give preference on re-payment
(c) To raise resources without losing management control
(d) All of the above

8. Shares of a limited company can be classified into:
(a) Equity
(b) Preference
(c) Equity and Preference
(d) None of the above

9. _______ capital is the amount with which Company is formed.
   (a) Authorised
   (b) Subscribed
   (c) Both (a) & (b)
   (d) All the above

10. The provisions regarding issues of shares at a discount are contained as per:
    (a) Section 56 of Companies Act 1956
    (b) Section 79 of Companies Act 1956
    (c) Section 90 of Companies Act 1956
    (d) Section 125 of Companies Act 1956

11. Paid-up Capital means amount of capital actually paid by:
    (a) Shareholders
    (b) Equity Shareholders
    (c) Preference Shareholders
    (d) All of the above

12. Discount allowed on issue of shares is shown in:
    (a) Credit side of P & L a/c
    (b) Liabilities side of Balance Sheet
    (c) Debit side of P & L a/c
    (d) Assets side of Balance Sheet

13. Profit on re-issue of forfeited shares is transferred to:
    (a) Profit and Loss a/c
    (b) Capital Reserve a/c
    (c) Share Capital a/c
    (d) General Reserve a/c

14. Rights shares mean the shares which are:
    (a) Issued to directors of the company
    (b) Issued for a consideration other than cash
    (c) Offered to the existing shareholders
    (d) Issued to promoters of the company for their services

15. Expenditure incurred on issue of equity shares is:
    (a) Revenue expenditure
    (b) Capital expenditure
    (c) Deferred capital expenditure
    (d) None

16. A public company having a share capital:
    (a) Must issue a prospectus
    (b) Cannot file a statement in lieu of prospectus
    (c) Doesn't need prospectus
    (d) May file a statement in lieu of prospectus

17. Share premium is used for:
    (a) To issue fully paid bonus shares
    (b) To write off preliminary expenses
    (c) To issue shares at discount
    (d) Both (a) & (b)

18. _______ is that part of called up capital against which payment has been received from the members on their respective shares in response to the calls made by the company.
    (a) Reserve Capital
    (b) Paid up Capital
    (c) Called up Capital
    (d) Uncalled up Capital

19. A company is known as the _______ of another company if it has control over another company.
    (a) Holding company
    (b) Existing company
    (c) Other company
    (d) Foreign company

20. Which is not a statutory company in India?
    (a) Reserve Bank of India,
    (b) Tata Iron & Steel Company
    (c) The Life Insurance Corporation of India
    (d) The Food Corporation of India

ANSWER

1	2	3	4	5	6	7	8	9	10
(b)	(a)	(b)	(a)	(c)	(b)	(c)	(c)	(a)	(b)

11	12	13	14	15	16	17	18	19	20
(a)	(d)	(b)	(c)	(c)	(d)	(d)	(b)	(a)	(b)

ACCOUNTING IN A COMPUTERISED ENVIRONMENT

INTRODUCTION

Computerised accounting system is a software that helps businesses to manage the big financial transactions, data, reports, and statements with high efficiency, speed, and better accuracy. Better quality work, lower operating costs, better efficiency, greater accuracy, minimum errors are some of the advantages of Computerized Accounting. Let us learn more about Computerized accounting environment.

REQUIREMENTS OF THE COMPUTERISED ACCOUNTING SYSTEM

Accounting Framework

A good accounting framework in terms of accounting principles, coding and grouping structure is a pre-condition. It is the application environment of the computerized accounting system.

Operating Procedure

A well-conceived and designed operating procedure blended with suitable operating environment is necessary to work with the computerized accounting system. The computer accounting is one of the database-oriented applications, wherein the transaction data is stored in well-organized database.

The user operates on such database using the required interface. And he takes the required reports by suitable transformations of stored data into information. Hence, it includes all the basic requirements of any database-oriented application in computers.

FEATURES OF COMPUTERISED ACCOUNTING

This Accounting System and its awareness among entities have become a necessity in the present environment. Businesses of whatever field and size are shifting from the practice of maintaining accounts manually. The manual process is more time-consuming and exposed to human error.

Storage and retrieval of data and generation of a report cannot be ensured in real time in the traditional system. There is a need to shift to computerized accounting systems. They have empowered business to project accurate information of financial performance.

1. **Simple and Integrated:** It helps all businesses by automating and integrating all the business activities. Such activities may be sales, finance, purchase, inventory, and manufacturing etc. It also facilitates the arrangement of accurate and up-to-date business information in a readily usable form.

2. **Accuracy & Speed:** Computerised accounting has customized templates for users which allows fast and accurate data entry. Thus, after recording the transactions it generates the information and reports automatically.

3. **Scalability:** It has the flexibility to record the transactions with the changing volume of business.

4. **Instant Reporting:** It can generate a quality report in real time because of high speed and accuracy.

5. **Security:** Secured data and information can be kept confidential as compared to the traditional accounting system.

185

6. **Quick Decision Making:** This system Generates real-time, comprehensive MIS reports and ensures access to complete and critical information, instantly.

7. **Reliability:** It generates the report with consistency and accuracy. Minimization of errors makes the system more reliable.

TERMS USED IN COMPUTERISED ACCOUNTING

The various terms used in computerised accounting and computer language are:

1. **Data:** Data mean any facts, observations, assumptions, or occurrences. In accounts, these would mean accounting entries to be passed to prepare financial statements and other related information, e.g. in sales invoices, details such as price, sales tax, date of sale, etc., are data.

2. **Record:** It consists of a group of data items related to an object of data processing, e.g. a sales register may be called record of sales invoices.

3. **Data File or File:** It is a compilation of related data records maintained in some pre-arranged order. It is similar to manual files wherein various papers are stored. An example of a computer file would be a payroll file of 1,000 employees of an entity.

4. **System:** It means various components that process the data, i.e. transactions and give outputs, i.e. results. In a manual accounting system, the components would be persons, books of account such as ledger, cash book, etc., which give results in the form of trial balance. In a computerised accounting system, it would mean the computer machine, the software programme and computer peripherals such as keyboard monitor, etc.

COMPARISON BETWEEN MANUAL AND COMPUTERISED ACCOUNTING

Accounting, by definition, is the process of identifying, recording, classifying and summarising financial transactions to produce the financial reports for their ultimate analysis. Let us understand these activities in the context of manual and computerised accounting system.

1. **Identifying:** The identification of transactions, based on application of accounting principles is common to both manual and computerised accounting system.

2. **Recording:** The recording of financial transactions, in manual accounting system is through books of original entries while the data content of such transactions is stored in a well-designed accounting database in computerised accounting system.

3. **Classification:** In a manual accounting system, transactions recorded in the books of original entry are further classified by posting into ledger accounts. This results in transaction data duplicity. In computerised accounting, no such data duplication is made to cause classification of transactions. In order to produce ledger accounts, the stored transaction data is processed to appear as classified so that the same is presented in the form of a report. Different forms of the same transaction data are made available for being presented in various reports.

4. **Summarising:** The transactions are summarised to produce trial balance in manual accounting system by ascertaining the balances of various accounts. As a result, preparation of ledger accounts becomes a prerequisite for preparing the trial balance. However, in computerised accounting, the originally stored transactions data are processed to churn out the list of balances of various accounts to be finally shown in the trial balance report. The generation of ledger accounts is not a necessary condition for producing trial balance in a computerised accounting system.

5. **Adjusting Entries:** In a manual accounting system, these entries are made to adhere to the principle of cost matching revenue. These entries are recorded to match the expenses of the accounting period with the revenues generated by them. Some other adjusting entries may be made as part of errors and rectification. However, in computerised accounting, Journal vouchers are prepared and stored to follow the principle of cost matching revenue, but there is nothing like passing adjusting entries for errors and rectification, except for rectifying an error of principle by having recorded Financial Statements. In a manual system of accounting, the preparation of financial statements pre-supposes the availability of trial balance.

   However, in computerised accounting, there is no such requirement. The generation of financial statements is independent of producing the trial balance because such statements can be prepared by direct processing of originally stored transaction data.

6. **Closing the Books:** After the preparation of financial reports, the accountants make preparations for the next accounting period. This is achieved by posting of closing and reversing journal entries. In computerised accounting, there is year-end processing to create and store opening balances of accounts in database.

It may be observed that conceptually, the accounting process is identical regardless of the technology used. Wrong voucher such as using payment voucher for a receipt transaction.

ADVANTAGES OF COMPUTERISED ACCOUNTING

1. **Better Quality Work:** The accounts prepared with the use of computers are usually uniform, neat, accurate, and more legible than manual job.

2. **Lower Operating Costs:** Computer is a labor and time saving devise. Hence, the volume of job handled with the help of computers results in economy and lower operating costs.

3. **Improved Efficiency:** Computer brings speed and accuracy in preparing the records and accounts and thus, increases the efficiency of employees.

4. **Facilitates Better Control:** From the management point of view, greater control is possible and more information may be available with the use of computer in accounting. It ensures efficient performance in accounting work.

5. **Greater Accuracy:** Computerized accounting ensures accuracy in accounting records and statements. It prevents clerical errors and omissions.

6. **Relieve Monotony:** Computerized accounting reduces the monotony of doing repetitive accounting jobs, which are tiresome and time consuming.

7. **Facilitates Standardization:** Computerized accounting facilitates standardization of accounting routines and procedures. Therefore, standardization in accounting is ensured.

8. **Minimizing Mathematical Errors:** While doing mathematics with computers, errors are virtually eliminated unless the data is entered improperly in the first instance.

DISADVANTAGES OF COMPUTERISED ACCOUNTING

1. **Reduction of Manpower:** The introduction of computers in accounting work reduces the number of employees in an organization. Thus, it leads to greater amount of unemployment.

2. **High Cost:** A small firm cannot install a computer accounting system because of its high installation and maintenance cost. To be more economical there should be large volume of work. If the system is not used to its full capacity, then it would be highly uneconomical.

3. **Require Special Skills:** Computer system calls for highly specialized operators. The availability of such skilled personnel is very scarce and very costly.

4. **Other Problems:** Frequent repair and power failure may affect the accounting work very much. Computers are prone to viruses. Often people assume the computer is doing things correctly and problems go unchecked for long period of time.

PROBLEMS FACED IN COMPUTERISED ACCOUNTING SYSTEM

1. **User Training:** The user, for using computer accounting software, needs to understand the concepts of the software. Hence, he should undergo proper training. A computer operator must learn the basics of computer, concepts of software, working with the operating system software [such as Windows/DOS] and the accounting software.

2. **System Dependency:** Using a computer solution makes the user to depend fully on the computer system and necessitates the availability of computer at all times. If the system is not available (due to hardware failure or power cut), it would be difficult to verify the accounts.

3. **Hardware Requirements:** A full-fledged computer system with a printer is required to operate the computerized accounting system. Most small organizations may not afford to have such facility with necessary software.

4. **System Failure:** When there is a system crash (hard disk crash), there is high risk of losing the data available on the hard disk drive at any point of time. It would be highly painful, if the problem occurs at end of the financial year, when the financial statements should be ready.

5. **Backups and Prints:** Backups of the data should be done regularly so that, when the data is lost, it can be restored from CD/DVD(backups). Regular print outs of the system information would be useful as manual records.

6. **Voucher Management:** Accounting software allows easy alteration of data. If a voucher is wrongly placed in a wrong head, it would be very difficult to sort out and bring back the voucher. A good voucher management is very essential.

7. **Security:** Additional security has to be provided because improper handling of the system (hardware/software) could be dangerous. Passwords, locks, etc., have to be set so that no unauthorized person can handle the system.

COMPUTERISATION – SCOPE AND EXPERIENCES IN BANKING

Computerisation has changed the banking function in all aspects. It is the basic need of modern banking systems. Computers have been installed in branches at different front office counters as well as other banking operations. Cheques are handled by the computers at clearing houses. Automated Teller Machines (ATMs) have been installed in the branch premises of various banks. Computerisation influences the following areas in the banks:

1. **Centralised Banking Operation:** Computerisation and technological innovations have enabled banks to operate on the principle of centralised banking where all the bank's branches are linked to each other online. This makes it possible for the banks to offer a customer the facility of banking at any branch/outlet of the bank as per convenience. A customer having an account with any branch of a bank can deposit and withdraw money into his account, in other branches/outlets of the banks, which are linked online.

2. **Computerised Accounting:** The accounting of bank transactions is voluminous and needs to be completed on a daily basis to know the funds position, position of borrower accounts, etc. In addition, a modern bank has various departments such as forex, treasury, merchant banking and borrowing, etc. The system software in most cases are so designed that after an error-free feeding of the initial transaction into the system and its validation by a senior executive, it also serves as the basis of the accounting entry.

3. **Deposit:** It is now possible to operate and account for all such deposit accounts more easily and conveniently with the use of computers. This transactional module offers automated, real-time posting and highly efficient deposit processing for all the balance-based liability products. It also provides back up support for opening, settling, and closing card and check account contracts.

4. **Lending:** Banks lend money in the form of loans, cash credits, overdrafts, etc. They also discount bills drawn by their customers. Like the deposit function, the lending function also is computerised in most of the banks. The work relating to charging of interest, monitoring of disbursements, inspection of the borrowing units and repayment schedule can be computerised and carried out easily and quickly.

5. **Remittances:** A bank arranges to remit money to other centres in the form of demand draft, mail transfer, or telegraphic transfer and arranges to receive in these forms from other banks. Small remittances are also effected though travellers cheques, gift cheques, etc. Facilities such as mail transfers, telegraphic transfers, use of ATMs, EFT service and Internet banking have become economical and easy with the development in communication technology.

6. **Clearing of Cheques:** The functions of the clearing house being now automated, credit to the account of the customers can be given within a shorter span of time after introduction of Truncated Cheque systems and RTGS, as compared to the system in operation a few years ago.

7. **Standing Instructions:** Customers sometimes give standing instructions to bank with respect to operation of their accounts. In case of such recurring instructions, which need to be carried out, the bank may feed the same in their computer systems to perform them automatically. This entire instruction can be fed into the system to be executed monthly and thereby eliminating the need to remember and execute the instruction manually.

8. **Automated Banking:** The concept of automated banking through Automated Teller Machines (ATMs) is the result of computerisation and technological innovation. ATMs are capable of accepting cash/cheques, disbursing cash, entertaining and an inter-bank transfer and balance enquiry on 24 hours a day and 365 days a year basis. Advance ATMs can be operated even on touch of finger rather than the keyboards used in the traditional ATMs. ATM transactions are automatically accounted on their occurrence with the help of computers.

9. **Customer Information Files Management:** This module provides centralised access to all customer-related information. This transaction allows the bank to change the information fields without modifying the underlying software.

CORE BANKING SOLUTIONS (CBS)

After the turn of consolidated databases (Back Office Application) and networks (Total Branch Automation) the next term is core banking solution. Core Banking Solution (CBS) in Banks provide the complete front-end and backend automation of banks. These applications also help the banks to achieve centralised processing of each and every service of the customer. "Core banking applications provide anywhere, anytime 24 by 7 non-stop services, which is not possible with traditional localized branch automation systems. These applications also provide automation across multiple delivery channels.

Core banking is a newly developed concept adopted by banks. It is a centralised system that provides accounting, customer information management and transaction processing functions. It provides a central operational database to bank's assets and liabilities, a transaction processing engine and a system for the financial management of the bank. In core banking, a branch will become a service outlet like an ATM booth. Thus, the importance of physical branches will be reduced. In case of core banking, customer can operate their account from various locations like—customer can open an account at one location and can deposit a cheque, check bank balance, withdraw cash, get demand draft, get account statement, transfer funds, other transactions from various locations of different cities. Implementation of core banking in banking sector allows interconnectivity of branches with the centralised data centre. Core banking is just one part of a fairly complex architecture of today's banking which takes care of the essential banking activities. The major banks in India, both in the private and public sectors are moving towards core banking solutions.

A super breed of core banking systems has emerged, which offer functionality in addition to core banking. These systems, called universal banking systems, can accommodate combinations of banking services such as retail, wholesale, private banking and securities trading. An advantage of using a universal system is that the data can be transferred easily between the different modules, so a bank can identify customer trends or selling opportunities. The following modules are offered by the Core Banking Solutions (CBS):

Customer Information Files Management: This module provides centralised access to all customer-related information. This transaction allows the bank to change the information fields without modifying the underlying software.

Deposit Management: This transactional module offers automated, real-time posting and highly efficient deposit processing for all the balance-based liability products. It also provides back up support for opening, settling, and closing card and check account contracts.

Loan Management: Loan management is an automated process for many lending products like secured and unsecured loans. It helps the bank in creating a flexible/tailormade product portfolio and streamlining the processes according to the customer's need.

Security Management: This facility helps banks to manage the following products and security processes like:

○ Security agreements such as real estate liens, registered liens, pledges, assignments, and guarantees;

○ Security amounts;

○ Encumbrances by the banking institution or a third party;

○ Declaration of purpose (specific or global);

○ Relationships between assets, transactions, and security agreements – including guarantee pools;

○ Assignment and deletion of guarantee;

○ Relevant calculations – including security cover, security distribution, loan-to-value ratios, free security and security shortfalls.

Reserve for Bad Debts: This module supports risk monitoring, provisioning, and realization of bad-debt charges.

Limit Management: This module indicates the liability limits and actual liability levels of business units and partners. Limit management checks the transactions against liability limits assigned to the borrowers.

Financial Accounting: The Financial Accounting function supports the general ledger transactions and finance management transactions at all the organizational levels, thus improving the management control and reporting.

Complementary Third-party Products: Complementary third-party products are also available to help the bank by managing the teller machines and payments.

Business Components

a) To have retail customer banking modules;

b) Deposits, loans, bills, remittances, locker, clearing, etc.;

c) Trade finance/forex modules;

d) Government business modules;

e) To have corporate finance and service branch modules;

f) To have enhanced MIS modules;

g) To have modules for business intelligence;

h) To integrate with the existing ATMs, tele-banking, debit card, kiosks and other delivery channels;

i) To have any branch banking, Internet banking and call centre;

j) To interface with existing corporate systems like treasury, IBR, centralised accounting system, HRMS, ALM, credit appraisal and management, credit monitoring and NPA management, etc.

k) To interface with systems like NDS, SFMS, RTGS, CFMS, etc.

Benefits

a) Enables the establishment of a reliable centralised data repository for the bank;

b) Facilitates data warehousing and data mining technologies for business intelligence;

c) Easy implementation of integrated customer-centric services like online ATMs, telebanking, internet banking, any branch banking, kiosk banking, cash management services, etc.;

d) Enables centralised management information, decision support and executive information systems;

e) Efficient and effective MIS, ALM, risk management, etc., using the central data pool;

f) Enables centralised management and control with centralised data;

g) Standardization of the branch automation software using a single version. Quick adoption of software changes as changes are done only at the central site;

h) Facilitates Business Process Re-engineering (BPR) to streamline the existing processes;

i) Relieves branches of jobs like data backup, MIS generation, etc.;

j) Requires infrastructure at the central location, backup location and at branches;

k) Servers are not mandatory at branch locations;

l) Attracts higher investment in the beginning;

m) Cost of implementation for further branches and delivery channels relatively cheaper;

n) Core infrastructure can be used for future expansions;

o) No extra cost for implementation of SFMS, RTGS, CFMS, etc.

INFORMATION SECURITY POLICIES

Information Security Policies are the cornerstone of information security effectiveness. The Security Policy is intended to define what is expected from an organization with respect to security of Information Systems. The overall objective is to control or guide human behavior to reduce the risk to information assets by accidental or deliberate actions. Information security policies underpin the security and well being of information resources. They are the foundation, the bottom line, of information security within an organization.

We all practice elements of data security. At home, for example, we make sure that deeds and insurance documents are kept safely so that they are available when we need them. All office information deserves to be treated in the same way. In an office, having the right information at the right time can make the difference between success and failure. Data Security will help the user to control and secure information from inadvertent or malicious changes and deletions or unauthorized disclosure. There are three aspects of data security:

Confidentiality: Protecting information from unauthorized disclosure like to the press, or through improper disposal techniques, or those who are not entitled to have the same.

Integrity: Protecting information from unauthorized modification, and ensuring that information, such as a beneficiary list, can be relied upon and is accurate and complete.

Availability: Ensuring information is available when it is required. Data can be held in many different areas, some of these are:

○ Network Servers;

○ Personal Computers and Workstations;

○ Laptop and Handheld PCs;

○ Removable Storage Media (Floppy Disks, CD-ROMS, Zip Disks, Flash Drive etc.);

○ Data Backup Media (Tapes and Optical Disks).

DATA LOSS PREVENTION

Leading Causes of Data Loss are:

○ Natural Disasters

○ Viruses

○ Human Errors

○ Software Malfunction

○ Hardware & System Malfunction

Natural Disasters

While the least probable cause of data loss, a natural disaster can have a devastating effect on the physical drive. In instances of severe housing damage, such as scored platters from fire, water emulsion due to flood, or broken or crushed platters, the drive may become unrecoverable.

The best way to prevent data loss from a natural disaster is an off-site back up. Since it is nearly impossible to predict the arrival of such an event, there should be more than one copy of the system back up kept, one onsite and one off. The type of media back up will depend on system, software, and the required frequency needed to back up. Also be sure to check backups to be certain that they have properly backed up.

Viruses

Viral infection increases at rate of nearly 200-300 new Trojans, exploits and viruses every month. With those numbers growing every day, systems are at an ever-increasing risk to become infected with a virus.

There are several ways to protect against a viral threat:

○ Install a Firewall on system to prevent hacker's access to user's data.

○ Install an anti-virus program on the system and use it regularly for scanning and remove the virus if the system has been infected. Many viruses will lie dormant or perform many minor alterations that can cumulatively disrupt system works. Be sure to check for updates for anti-virus program on a regular basis.

○ Back up and be sure to test backups from infection as well. There is no use to restore virus-infected backup.

○ Beware of any email containing an attachment. If it comes from anonymous sender or don't know from where it has come or what it is, then don't open it, just delete it and block the sender for future mail.

Human Errors

Even in today's era of highly trained, certified, and computer literate staffing there is always room for the timelessness of accidents. There are few things that might be followed:

○ Be aware. It sounds simple enough to say, but not so easy to perform. When transferring data, be sure it is going to the destination. If asked *"Would you like to replace the existing file"* make sure, before clicking "yes".

○ In case of uncertainty about a task, make sure there is a copy of the data to restore from.

○ Take extra care when using any software that may manipulate drives' data storage, such as: partition mergers, format changes, or even disk checkers.

○ Before upgrading to a new Operating System, take backup of most important files or directories in case there is a problem during the installation. Keep in mind saved data drive can also be formatted as well.

○ Never shut the system down while programs are running. The open files will, more likely, become truncated and non-functional.

Software Malfunction

Software malfunction is a necessary evil when using a computer. Even the world's top programs cannot anticipate every error that may occur on any given program. There are still few things that can lessen the risks:

○ Be sure the software used will meant ONLY for its intended purpose. Misusing a program may cause it to malfunction.

○ Using pirated copies of a program may cause the software to malfunction, resulting in a corruption of data files.

○ Be sure that the proper amount of memory installed while running multiple programs simultaneously. If a program shuts down or hangs up, data might be lost or corrupt.

○ Back up is a tedious task, but it is very useful if the software gets corrupted.

Hardware Malfunction

The most common cause of data loss, hardware malfunction or hard drive failure, is another necessary evil inherent to computing. There is usually no warning that hard drive will fail, but some steps can be taken to minimize the need for data recovery from a hard drive failure:

○ Do not stack drives on top of each other—leave space for ventilation. An overheated drive is likely to fail. Be sure to keep the computer away from heat sources and make sure it is well ventilated.

○ Use a UPS (Uninterruptible Power Supply) to lessen malfunction caused by power surges.

○ NEVER open the casing on a hard drive. Even the smallest grain of dust settling on the platters in the interior of the drive can cause it to fail.

○ If system runs the scan disk on every reboot, it shows that system is carrying high risk for future data loss. Back it up while it is still running.

○ If system makes any irregular noises such as clicking or ticking coming from the drive. Shut the system down and call Hardware Engineer for more information.

Computers are more relied upon now than ever, or more to the point the data that is contained on them. In nearly every instant the system itself can be easily repaired or replaced, but the data once lost may not be retraceable. That's why of regular system backups and the implementation of some preventative measures are always stressed upon.

TEST YOURSELF

1. _____ means accounting performed by a computer.
   - (a) Accounting
   - (b) Computerised accounting
   - (c) Manual accounting
   - (d) None of the above

2. The word Core in Core Banking Solutions (CBS) stands for:
   - (a) Central Online Real-time Environment
   - (b) Centralized Online Real-time Environment
   - (c) Centralized Online Real Environment
   - (d) Centralized Offline Real-time Environment

3. The Reserve Bank of India had appointed a Committee on Computerisation under the Chairmanship of Dr. C Rangarajan, the then Governor, RBI, in _____ to look into the modalities of drawing up phased plan of computerisation for the banking industry covering the period 1985 to 1989.
   - (a) 1981
   - (b) 1982
   - (c) 1983
   - (d) 1984

4. The major objectives of computerisation in banking are to improve:
   - (a) Customer service
   - (b) Housekeeping
   - (c) Productivity and profitability
   - (d) All of the above

5. Computerisation at the branch level can be used to:
   - (a) Provide better and speedy customer service
   - (b) Generation of various reports
   - (c) Analyze the branch-level data for decision making
   - (d) All of the above

6. Core banking applications provide anywhere, anytime _____non-stop services, which is not possible with traditional localized branch automation systems.
   - (a) 12 by 7
   - (b) 24 by 6
   - (c) 24 by 7
   - (d) 12 by 6

7. What is the meaning of UPS?
   - (a) Uniform power system
   - (b) Unchanged power system
   - (c) Uninterrupted pressure system
   - (d) Uninterrupted power supply

8. Which are the leading Causes of Data Loss:
   - (a) Natural Disasters
   - (b) Human Errors
   - (c) Software Malfunction
   - (d) All of the above

9. 'Resume' and 'Love letter' are which type of Virus?
   - (a) Dangerous
   - (b) Childish
   - (c) Ineffective
   - (d) Effective

10. _______ is a systematic and independent examination of information systems environment to ascertain whether the objectives, set out to be achieved, have been met or not.
    - (a) Controlling
    - (b) Auditing
    - (c) Protecting
    - (d) Checking

11. _____ includes the safeguarding of the information against unauthorized addition, deletion, modification or alteration.
    - (a) Data integrity
    - (b) Confidentiality
    - (c) Auditing
    - (d) Checking

12. The desired features of the data are:
    - (a) Accuracy
    - (b) Confidentiality
    - (c) Reliability
    - (d) All of the above

ANSWER

1	2	3	4	5	6	7	8	9	10
(b)	(b)	(c)	(d)	(d)	(c)	(d)	(d)	(a)	(b)

11	12
(a)	(d)

MODULE–D
BANKING OPERATIONS

BANKING OPERATIONS

INTRODUCTION

Bank is one which conducts business of banking. Banking has been defined in Section 5(b) of Banking Regulation Act. Banking means accepting deposits from public, for the purpose of lending, repayable on demand or otherwise, withdrawable by cheque, draft, order or otherwise.

Customer: There is no legal definition of a bank customer. When customer tenders an account opening form to open the a/c and banker accepts it, a contractual relationship is established. KYC definition of customer: As per RBI, for KYC policy purpose, a 'Customer may be defined as a person or entity that maintains an account with the bank and/or has a business relationship with the bank.

FUNCTIONS OF A BANK

The Banking Regulation Act, 1949 Section 5(c) defines a banker as a person, undertaking business of banking. "Banking Company" means any company which transacts the business of banking in India.

The Act further says that any company which is engaged in the manufacture of goods or carries on any trade and which accepts deposits of money from public merely for the purpose of financing its business shall not be deemed to transact the business of banking within the meaning of this clause.

As per Section 6 of the Banking Regulation Act, 1949, banks can engage in certain classes of business which are incidental to the business of banking like Lockers, Safe custody, Collection of cheques etc.

Prohibitions: As per Section 8 of B R Act, a bank is prohibited from buying, selling or dealing in goods except in connection with the realisation of a security held by it or for collection or negotiating bills of exchange.

Main functions of a Bank in India

The core functions of a bank are as follows:

(a) **Accepting Deposits:** Banks accept deposit of money from public:

1. Deposit accounts is the core activity of the bank. Deposits are major resource of the bank.

2. Banks accept demand deposits which are withdrawable on demand such as Saving Bank Accounts and Current Accounts. These deposits are also called CASA deposit and Low Cost Deposits. Because, banks provide low interest on SB Account and no interest has to provide on Current Accounts.

3. Banks also accept various types of term deposits such as RD, TDR etc. which are fixed for a fixed time period.

(b) **Granting Loans and Advances:** Bank grants advances to the public and earn interest:

1. Banks grant advance through Overdraft, Cash Credit, Demand Loan, Term Loans, Purchase or Discounting of Bills.

2. Loans are given mainly to corporates, business-men and small borrowers.

3. Loans are given against securities created from out of bank funds, personal security or goods, movable or immovable in nature.

4. **Type of Advances:** Normally, banks grant the following types of advances:

   i. Advances on the personal security of the debtor, or and for which no tangible or collateral security is taken;

   ii. Advances which are covered by tangible or collateral security;

   iii. Loans against the security of Fixed Deposit receipts;

   iv. MSME Advance, Agriculture and other business Advance;

   v. Foreign Trade;

   vi. Housing Loan;

   vii. Educational Loan;

   viii. Loans against Shares/Securities/Debentures/Insurance Policies;

   ix. Loans against National Savings Certificates, KVPs, etc;

   x. Consumer Loans, Pensioner Loan;

   xi. Securitization of Loans;

   xii. Venture Capital Advances;

   xiii. Gold loans, etc.

Other Functions of Banks

Besides accepting deposit and granting advances, other functions of banks are as follows:

1. Dealing in securities, on its own account or on behalf of its customers;

2. Opening Letters of Credit/issuing Guarantees;

3. Dealing in Foreign Exchange;

4. Remittances: through demand drafts, RTGS, NEFT, etc.;

5. Collection of cheques, drafts, pay orders, traveller's cheques, dividend and interest warrants, tax refund orders;

6. Collection of trade bills;

7. Receipt of Foreign Contribution on behalf of the registered persons/Organization;

8. Cash Management Product;

9. Automated Teller Machines (ATMs);

10. Depository Participant (DP) Services;

11. Handling Government Business;

12. Acting as trustees and executors;

13. Merchant banking, i.e. acting as managers to a public issue, etc.;

14. Safe-keeping Services;

15. Lockers;

16. Credit Cards/Debit Cards;

17. Securitisation of future lease rentals;

18. Derivatives;

19. Prepaid Payment Instruments.

Para Banking Services Performed by Banks

Banks also provide the following Para Banking Services:

1. Equipment Leasing, Hire Purchase and Factoring Services through subsidiary companies;

2. Investment in Venture Capital Funds (VCFs);

3. **Mutual Fund Business:** Sponsoring mutual funds and marketing the mutual fund units;

4. Money Market Mutual Funds (MMMFs) which come under the purview of SEBI regulations but RBI approval required before approaching SEBI for registration;

5. **Portfolio Management Services:** Though banks can not undertake Portfolio Management Services on their own, bank-sponsored NBFCs can offer PMS to their clients subject to following conditions:

   (a) Funds accepted for portfolio management from their clients, should not be entrusted to another bank for management;

   (b) 'PMS' should be in the nature of investment consultancy/management, for a fee, at the customer's risk without guaranteeing, a pre-determined return;

6. Primary Dealership Business;

7. Retailing of Government Securities;

8. Underwriting of Corporate Shares and Debentures;

9. Underwriting of bonds of Public Sector Undertakings;

10. Sponsors to Infrastructure Debt Funds (IDFs);

11. **Insurance Business:** Through risk participation or Bancassurance or Insurance broking;

12. Pension Funds Management through subsidiaries (not departmentally) with prior approval of RBI and as per eligibility criteria prescribed by Pension Fund Regulatory and Development Authority (PFRDA).

FRONT OFFICE AND BACK OFFICE IN A BANK

Front Office: Banks have generally following types of front offices:

1. Refers to bank's departments that come in contact with clients.

2. Front office include the marketing, sales, and customer relations operations of the bank.

3. The front office staff directly produces the revenue.

4. Generally, the branches of banks perform the function of the front office by receiving deposits and making loans and advances as well as providing other banking services.

5. Due to computerization in banks, many of the front office functions like fund withdrawal/transfer, accepting cheque book request, balance inquiry, statement of account have been converted into back office functions by using ATM/Internet banking/ Mobile banking. Use of technology, to replace front office activities, results in cost savings and economies of scale.

Back Office: Banks have generally following types of back offices:

1. Back office staff, perform administrative and other support functions for the front office.

2. Although the operations of a back office are not prominent, they are a major contributor to the banking business.

3. Back offices may be located other than the bank branch with cheaper rent and lower labour costs.

4. Back office functions can be outsourced to consultants and contractors, including ones in other countries.

5. The Head office and the Regional/Zonal offices do not conduct any banking business and are generally responsible for administrative and policy decisions. But, accounting for treasury functions (viz., investments, funds management, bill re-discounting) is usually carried out at the head office. Specialised activities like merchant banking are carried on by separate divisions which operate at the head office and/or at large designated branches.

6. **Specialised Branches:** Banks have set up branches exclusively for a specified segment of their clients like Personal Banking branches (catering to the needs of individual customers), Commercial or Industrial Finance branches (catering to the needs of industries in the small, medium and/or large sectors), and Recovery branches (focusing on reduction of non-performing assets of the bank).

OUTSOURCING OF FINANCIAL SERVICES BY BANKS

The world over, banks are increasingly using outsourcing as a means of both reducing cost and accessing specialist expertise, not available internally and achieving strategic aims. 'Outsourcing' may be defined as a bank's use of a third party (either an affiliated entity within a corporate group or an entity that is external to the corporate group) to perform activities on a continuing basis that would normally be undertaken by the bank itself, now or in the future. 'Continuing basis' would include agreements for a limited period.

Advantages of Outsourcing

Reduction in costs as well as use of expertise not available internally. Scope of RBI guidelines on outsourcing are as under:

(a) Activities that should not be outsourced;

(b) Bank's role and regulatory and supervisory requirements;

(c) Risk management practices for outsourced financial services;

(d) Role of Board of Directors and senior management;

(e) Evaluation of risks;

(f) Evaluating the capability of the service provider;

(g) Outsourcing agreement;

(h) Confidentiality and security.

(i) Responsibility of DSA/DMA/Recovery Agents

(j) Monitoring of outsourced activities

(k) Redressal of grievances related to outsourced services

(l) Reporting of transactions to Financial Intelligence Unit

(m) Off-shore outsourcing of financial services

Activities that should not be Outsourced

Banks which choose to outsource financial services should however not outsource core management functions including Internal Audit, Compliance function and decision-making functions like determining compliance with KYC norms for opening deposit accounts, according sanction for loans (including retail loans) and management of investment portfolio.

Operating Procedures in Banks

Banks should establish formal operating procedures, well defined limits for individual discretion and rigorous systems of internal control as banks are exposed to exceptional risks like;

a) Large number of transactions involving large amounts requiring complex accounting and internal control systems. Though manual operations replaced by technology driven processes, but checks required to avoid frauds.

b) Custody of large volumes of cash and other monetary items, like negotiable instruments requiring physical security in the storage and the transfer of these instruments with a scope for frauds.

c) Transactions are initiated, recorded and managed at different locations.

d) Geographically dispersed wide network of branches and departments, involving foreign offices also requiring greater decentralisation of authority and control functions with difficulties in maintaining uniform operating practices and accounting systems.

e) 'Off-balance sheet' items, may not involve accounting entries and may be difficult to detect.

f) Completion of transactions directly by the customers, over the Internet, mobile banking or through Automated Teller Machines (ATMs).

g) As the banks are linked to national and international settlement systems, they could pose a systemic risk.

Banking Operations Manual

To provide a ready guide to the front office functionaries in day-to-day banking operations. Used for standardizing the procedures. Provides up-to-date instructions on banking operations. Banking operations manual is prepared on the basis of extant banking law practices. It needs frequent updating to cover RBI guidelines and for implementation of Core Banking Solutions. Features of Operations Manual are as under:

1. Each bank has its own Banking Operations Manual. While the basic structure of the manual of each bank is similar, as it is based on the same legal framework and RBI guidelines, the differences are because of specialized products and policies/ practices based on the peculiar conditions of each bank. For example, activities like opening of accounts, compliance with KYC norms, handling cash, clearing, loans and advances, remittances, etc. are undertaken by every bank.

2. Mainly covers the aspects which are currently relevant to the Bank.

3. Not a document to provide any full-fledged legal framework of banking operations and not a rigorous substitute for extant circular instructions.

4. Contains important aspects of banking operations for reference of the functionaries at the delivery point of the customer services in the Bank.

5. The customer relationship policy of the Bank and also the customer service norms of the Bank.

TEST YOURSELF

1. Which is not the core functions of a bank?
   (a) Accepts Deposit
   (b) Selling Mutual Funds
   (c) Lending to Public
   (d) Investment of Funds

2. The Banking Regulation Act, 1949 _______ defines a banker as a person, undertaking business of banking. "Banking Company" means any company which transacts the business of banking in India.
   (a) Section 5(b)
   (b) Section 6(c)
   (c) Section 5(c)
   (d) Section 6(a)

3. As per Section 6 of the Banking Regulation Act, 1949, banks can engage in certain classes of business which are incidental to the business of banking like:
   (a) Lockers
   (b) Safe custody

   (c) Collection of cheques
   (d) All of the above

4. As per Section 8 of B R Act, a bank is prohibited from:
   (a) Buying, selling or dealing in goods
   (b) Realisation of a security held by it
   (c) Negotiating bills of exchange
   (d) Financing against Share

5. Banks do not grant which types of advances?
   (a) Foreign Trade
   (b) Securitization of Loans
   (c) Venture Capital Advances
   (d) None of the above

6. Besides accepting deposit and granting advances, other functions of banks are:
   (a) Depository Participant (DP) Services
   (b) Handling Government Business
   (c) Both of the above
   (d) None of the above

7. Banks also provide the following Para Banking services. Which is not categorised as Para Banking services?
   (a) Equipment Leasing, Hire Purchase and Factoring Services through subsidiary companies;
   (b) Prepaid Payment Instruments
   (c) Investment in Venture Capital Funds (VCFs)
   (d) Sponsoring mutual funds and marketing the mutual fund units

8. Which is not the correct statements regarding Front Office?
   (a) Refers to bank's departments that come in contact with clients
   (b) Front office include the marketing, sales, and customer relations operations of the bank
   (c) Front offices may be located other than the bank branch with cheaper rent and lower labour costs
   (d) The front office staff directly produces the revenue

9. Which is the correct statements regarding Back Office?
   (a) Back office staff, perform administrative and other support functions for the front office.
   (b) Although the operations of a back office are not prominent, they are a major contributor to the banking business.

   (c) Back office functions can be outsourced to consultants and contractors, including ones in other countries.
   (d) All of the above

10. Banks are increasingly using outsourcing as a means of:
    (a) Reducing cost
    (b) Accessing specialist expertise
    (c) Both of the above
    (d) None of the above

11. Scope of RBI guidelines on outsourcing are:
    (a) Activities that should not be outsourced
    (b) Evaluation of risks
    (c) Evaluating the capability of the service provider
    (d) All of the above

12. Which should be the features of Banking Operations Manual?
    (a) Mainly covers the aspects which are currently relevant to the Bank.
    (b) Contains important aspects of banking operations for reference of the functionaries at the delivery point of the customer services in the Bank.
    (c) The customer relationship policy of the Bank and also the customer service norms of the Bank.
    (d) All of the above

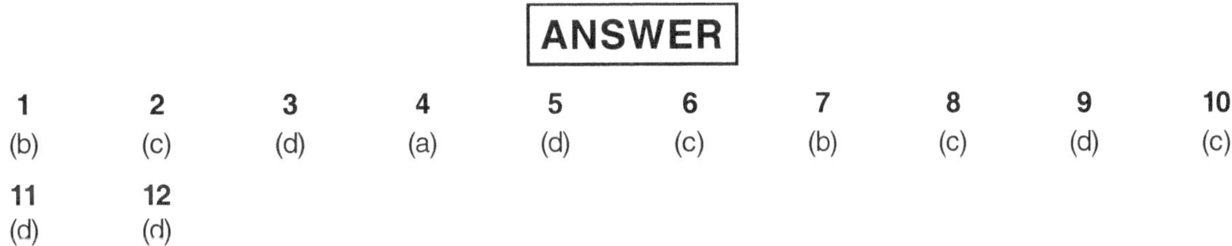

1	2	3	4	5	6	7	8	9	10
(b)	(c)	(d)	(a)	(d)	(c)	(b)	(c)	(d)	(c)

11	12
(d)	(d)

OPERATIONAL ASPECTS OF KYC & CUSTOMER SERVICE

INTRODUCTION

Banks were advised to follow certain customer identification procedure for opening of accounts and monitoring transactions of a suspicious nature for the purpose of reporting it to appropriate authority. The Prevention of Money Laundering Act (PMLA), 2002 is an Act of the Parliament of India enacted in January, 2003. The Act along with the Rules framed has come into force with effect from 1st July, 2005. These 'Know Your Customer' guidelines have been revisited in the context of the Recommendations made by the Financial Action Task Force (FATF) on Anti Money Laundering (AML) standards and on Combating of Financing of Terrorism (CFT). PMLA (Amendment) Act, 2012 as passed by Lok Sabha on 29th November, 2012 has come into force from 15th February 2013.

The Prevention of Money Laundering (Maintenance of Records) Rules 2005 have been amended vide Gazette Notification dated 1st June 2017 by Ministry of Finance.

Objective

The objectives of the Act are as under:

a) To prevent banks from being used, intentionally or unintentionally, by criminals for Money Laundering or terrorist financing activities;

b) To enable banks to know/ understand their customers and their financial dealings better;

c) To put in place a proper control mechanism for detecting and reporting suspicious transactions in accordance with the statutory and regulatory provisions;

d) To enhance method for fraud Prevention;

e) To ensure compliance with guidelines issued by the regulators including FIU-IND & RBI.

Definition of Money Laundering

Sec.3 of PML Act defines 'money laundering' as: "whosoever directly or indirectly attempts to indulge or knowingly assists or knowingly is a party or is actually involved in any process or activity connected with the proceeds of crime and projecting it as untainted property shall be guilty of the offence of money-laundering". In India AML activities are monitored by FIU-IND as per PML Act. Any act or attempted act to conceal or disguise the identity of illegally obtained proceeds so that they appear to have originated from legitimate sources.

In other words, it is the process used by criminals through which they make "dirty" money appear "clean."

Punishment for Money-Laundering

Punishment for non-adherence of the Act would be rigorous imprisonment for not less than 3 years but up to 7 years. If in case of offences done under Narcotic Drugs and Psychotropic Substance Act 1985 the maximum punishment may extend to 10 years.

Combating the Financing of Terrorism (CFT) measures

Money to fund terrorist activities moves through the global financial system via wire transfers and in and out of personal and business accounts. It can sit in the accounts of illegitimate charities and be laundered through buying and selling securities and other commodities, or purchasing and cashing out insurance policies.

Before opening of the new account branches should ensure the name is not listed in the following list available on RBI website:

I. The ISIL (Da'esh) & Al-Qaida Sanctions List

II. The 1988 Sanction List

KNOW YOUR CUSTOMER

For the purpose of this policy, according to RBI guidelines, a 'Customer' is defined as under:

I. A person or entity that maintains an account and/ or has a business relationship with the bank;

II. One, on whose behalf the account is maintained (i.e., the beneficial owner);

III. Beneficiaries of the transactions conducted by professional intermediaries, such as Stock Brokers, Chartered Accountants, Solicitors etc, as permitted by law; and

IV. Any person or firm or entity connected with a financial transaction.

KEY ELEMENTS OF KYC POLICY

The key elements of policy are:

❏ **Customer Acceptance Policy (CAP)**

❏ **Risk Management (RM)**

❏ **Customer Identification Procedure (CIP)**

❏ **Monitoring of Transactions (TM)**

Customer Acceptance Policy (CAP)

Banks should develop clear customer acceptance policies and procedures for making relationship with customers, As per RBI guideline:

a. No account is opened in anonymous or fictitious/ benami name;

b. No account is opened where the bank is unable to apply appropriate CDD measures, either due to non-cooperation of the customer or non-reliability of the documents/information furnished by the customer;

c. No transaction or account based relationship is undertaken without following the CDD procedure;

d. The mandatory information to be sought for KYC purpose while opening an account and during the periodic updation, is specified;

e. 'Optional'/additional information, is obtained with the explicit consent of the customer after the account is opened;

f. Circumstances in which, a customer is permitted to act on behalf of another person/entity, is clearly spelt out;

g. Suitable system is put in place to ensure that the identity of the customer does not match with any person or entity, whose name appears in the sanctions lists circulated by Reserve Bank of India.

Customer Acceptance Policy shall not result in denial of banking/financial facility to members of the general public, especially those, who are financially or socially disadvantaged.

Risk Management

Customers shall be categorised as low, medium and high risk category, based on the assessment and risk perception of the banks.

Risk categorisation shall be undertaken based on parameters such as customer's identity, social/financial status, nature of business activity, and information about the clients' business and their location etc. While considering customer's identity, the ability to confirm identity documents through online or other services offered by issuing authorities may also be factored in.

Low Risk Category Customers:

- Individuals (other than High Net Worth/ NRI customer) have known source of funds;

- Salaried employees, whose salary structure is well defined;

- Pensioners, benefit recipients;

- People belonging to lower economic strata of society showing small balances;

- Govt. department and govt. owned companies, Regulators, Statutory Bodies etc;

- Customer with a long term and active business relationship;

- Customer other than High & Medium risk.

Medium Risk Customer:

- NBFC;

- Builders;

- Stock Brokers.

High Risk Customer:

- Non-resident customer;

- HNI, Non-face to face customer;

- Trust, Charities, NGOs;

- Sleeping Partner firms, Investment Company;

- Donation receiving organization, Religious institution;

- Shopping malls, Jewelers;
- Petrol pump, Liquor stores;
- Antique dealers, Arms dealers, Agents, Brokers, Bullion dealers;
- Politically Exposed Persons of foreign origin;
- Customer with dubious reputation etc.;
- Companies having close family shareholding etc.;
- Person living in High Risk Countries.

Periodic updation shall be carried out at least once in every two years for high risk customers, once in every eight years for medium risk customers and once in every ten years for low risk customers.

Customer Identification Procedure (CIP)

Customer identification means undertaking client due diligence measures while commencing an account-based relationship including identifying and verifying the customer and the beneficial owner on the basis of one of the Officcially Valid Documents (OVDs). Banks/FIs need to obtain sufficient information to establish, to their satisfaction, the identity of each new customer, whether regular or occasional, and the purpose of the intended nature of the banking relationship.

Officially Valid Document (OVD)

The officially valid documents will serve the purpose for both identification of customer and also the address proof of customer.

'Officially Valid Document' (OVD) definition amended vide Gazette Notification dated 1st June 2017 by Ministry of Finance – the Permanent Account Number (PAN) Card; and the letter issued by the Unique Identification Authority of India have been removed from this definition. As per Supreme Court verdict, Aadhaar is not compulsory for opening of a bank account. Now, these five documents are considered as officially valid documents:

1. Passport (within validity)
2. Driving License (within validity)
3. Voter's Identity Card
4. Job Card issued by NREGA
5. The letter issued by the National Population Register containing details of name, address or any other document as notified by the Central Government in consultation with the Regulator.

The Government has since amended the Prevention of Money Laundering (Maintenance of Records) Rules, 2005 providing additional relaxations for the purpose of proof of address in addition to the relaxations in proof of

identity under 'simplified measures' as contained in paragraph 2(d) of PML Rules. Thus, for the limited purpose of proof of address the following additional documents are deemed to be OVDs under 'simplified measures' for 'Low Risk Customer'.

1. Utility bill which is not more than two months old of any service provider (electricity, telephone, post-paid mobile phone, piped gas, water bill);
2. Property or Municipal Tax receipt;
3. Bank account or Post Office savings bank account statement;
4. Pension or family pension payment orders (PPOs) issued to retired employees by Government Departments or Public Sector Undertakings, if they contain the address;
5. Letter of allotment of accommodation from employer issued by State or Central Government departments, statutory or regulatory bodies, and public sector undertakings, scheduled commercial banks, financial institutions and listed companies. Similarly, leave and license agreements with such employers allotting official accommodation; and
6. Documents issued by Government departments of foreign jurisdictions and letters issued by a Foreign Embassy or Mission in India.

E-KYC

In order to reduce the risk of identity fraud, document forgery & paperless KYC verification, Unique Identification Authority of India (UIDAI) has launched its E-KYC service. The E-KYC service is accepted as a valid process for KYC verification under PMLA. While using E-KYC service of UIDAI, the individual user has to authorize the UIDAI, by explicit consent, to release his/her identity/address through biometric authentication to the bank branch. The UIDAI then release the data name, age, gender, and photograph of the individual to bank. E-Aadhaar downloaded from UIDAI website may be accepted as an officially valid document.

Walk-in Customers

In case of transactions carried out by a non-account based customer, that is a walk-in customer, where the amount of transaction is equal to or exceeds ₹ 50,000 whether conducted as a single transaction or several transactions that appear to be connected, the customer's identity and address should be verified. However, if a bank has reason to believe that a customer is intentionally structuring a transaction into a series of transactions below the threshold of ₹ 50,000 the bank should verify the identity and address of the customer and also consider filing a suspicious transaction report to FIU-IND.

Banks should ensure that any remittance of funds by way of demand draft, mail/telegraphic transfer or any other mode and issue of travelers' cheques for value of ₹ 50,000 and above is effected by debit to the customer's account or against cheques and not against cash payment.

Customer Due Diligence (CDD): It means identifying and verifying the customer and the beneficial owner using 'Officially Valid Documents' as a 'proof of identity' and a 'proof of address'.

Documents needed for verification of various types of clients:

1. Individuals :

Where the client is an individual, who is eligible to be enrolled for an Aadhaar number, he shall for the purpose of sub-rule (1) submit to the reporting entity,—

(a) The Aadhaar number issued by the Unique Identification Authority of India; and

(b) The Permanent Account Number or Form No. 60 as defined in Income-tax Rules, 1962,

And such other documents including in respect of the nature of business and financial status of the client as may be required by the reporting entity:

Provided that where an Aadhaar number has not been assigned to a client, the client shall furnish proof of application of enrolment for Aadhaar and in case the Permanent Account Number is not submitted, one certified copy of an officially valid document shall be submitted. As per Supreme Court decision, Aadhaar is not mandetory now for open of a bank account.

Notwithstanding anything contained in sub-rules, an individual who desires to open a small account in a banking company may be allowed to open such an account on production of a self-attested photograph and affixation of signature or thumb print, as the case may be, on the form for opening the account:

Provided that the designated officer of the banking company, while opening the small account, certifies under his signature that the person opening the account has affixed his signature or thumb print, as the case may be, in his presence.

2. Company:

a) Certificate of incorporation;

b) Memorandum and Articles of Association;

c) A resolution from the Board of Directors

d) Aadhaar numbers; and

e) Permanent Account Numbers or Form 60 as defined in the Income-tax Rules, 1962.

3. Partnership Firm:

a) Registration certificate;

b) Partnership deed; and

c) Aadhaar numbers; and

d) Permanent Account Numbers or Form 60 as defined in the Income-tax Rules, 1962.

4. Trust Documents:

a) Registration certificate;

b) Trust deed;

c) Aadhaar numbers; and

d) Permanent Account Numbers or Form 60 as defined in the Income-tax Rules, 1962.

5. Association of Persons:

a) Resolution of the managing body of such association or body of individuals;

b) Power of attorney granted to him to transact on its behalf;

c) Aadhaar numbers; and

d) Permanent Account Numbers or Form 60 as defined in the Income-tax Rules, 1962,

e) Information as may be required by the banking company or the financial institution or the intermediary to collectively establish the legal existence of such an association or body of individuals.

Partial Freezing/Closure of Non-KYC Compliance Account

In the case of non-compliance of KYC and/or undertaking Re-KYC exercise guideline account, RBI advised the bank to take the following steps:

1. Initially, a notice of 3 months should be given for KYC compliance,

2. It should be followed by reminder for further 3 months,

3. Thereafter, Partial freeze the debit and allowing credit only,

4. If partial freeze continues for 6 months and account is still non-KYC complaint, freeze both credit and debit and may close the account.

5. Closer of account shall be approved by the Branch Manager.

6. Reason for partial freeze and closure should be communicated to account holder.

Change of Address, Transfer of Account & Close Relative Address Proof: RBI has relaxed norms of furnishing address proof. Only one documentary proof of address (either current or permanent) may be submitted. In case of address proof mentioned as per 'Proof of Address' undergoes a change, fresh address proof may be submitted within a period of six months.

In case of close relatives e.g. Wife, children & parents bank can obtain KYC documents of the relative with whom the prospective customer is living along with a declaration from the relative that the said person is staying with him/her.

Monitoring of Transactions

Bank has to monitor the transaction of its accounts and concerned report has to submit to FIU-IND periodically.

1) **Cash Transaction Report:** Cash transactions of above ₹ 10 lakhs or its equivalent in foreign currency. Series of cash transactions connected to each other, of below ₹ 10 lakhs or its equivalent in foreign currency within a month and the aggregate value of such doubtful transactions in cash or otherwise.

2) **Non-Profit Organisation:** The report of all transactions involving receipts by non-profit organizations of value more than rupees ten lakh or its equivalent in foreign currency should be submitted every month to the Director, FIU-IND by 15th of the succeeding month in the prescribed format.

3) **Suspicious Transactions Report (STR):** The Suspicious Transaction Report (STR) should be furnished within 7 days of arriving at a conclusion that any transaction, whether cash or non-cash, or a series of transactions integrally connected are of suspicious nature.

4) **Cross Boarder Wire Transfer (CBWT):** Bank has to submit to FIU-IND all Cross Boarder Wire Transfer (CBWT) for the value of more than five lakhs rupees or its equivalent in foreign currency either the origin or destination of funds in India.

5) **Counterfeit Currency Report (CCR):** Counterfeit Currency Report (CCR) to be submitted within 7 working days from the date of occurrence of transaction (Process same as STR). Branch to ZO 2 days. Up to 4 pieces FIR need not be filed. Instead a consolidated monthly statement is sent to police with counterfeit current notes. For 5 pieces and above FIR has to be filed.

Transaction Coverage	Name of Report	Period
Large Cash Transaction of above ₹ 10 lakhs/month	CTR	Within 15 days of close of each month
Suspicious Transactions	STR	Within 7 days of confirmation of suspicion
Counterfeit Currency Notes	CCR	Within 7 days of detection
Cross Boarder Wire Transfer	CBWT	Within 15 days of close of each month
Non-Profit Organization Report Receipt more than ₹ 10 lakhs	NPOTR	Within 15 days of close of each month

FINANCIAL INTELLIGENCE UNIT–INDIA

FIU-IND is a central agency. It is an independent body and report directly to the Economic Intelligence Council headed by Finance Minister. FIU-IND receives CTR, STR, CCR, NPOTR, CBWT reports. It analyzes information received by banks and suggests AML related crime. It monitors and identifies strategic key areas on AML trends, typologies & developments. The Director of FIU-IND is vested with the power of a civil court under the code of civil procedure. He has the power to seize, direct, penalize reporting entities and its employee for breach or violation of PML Act.

Money Mule: In a money mule transaction, an individual with a bank account is recruited to receive cheque deposits or wire transfers and then transfer these funds to accounts held on behalf of another person or to other individuals, minus a certain commission payment.

When caught, they face legal action for being part of such fraud. Many a times the address and contact details of such mules are found to be fake or not up to date. Which makes it difficult to locate the Account Holder. RBI has desire that banks should strictly adhere to the guidelines on KYC/AML/CFT to avoid money mules.

CKYCR: Central KYC Registry is a centralized repository of KYC records of customers in the financial sector with uniform KYC norms and inter-usability of the KYC records across the sector with an objective to reduce the burden of producing KYC documents and getting those verified every time when the customer creates a new relationship with a financial entity.

CDD Procedure and sharing KYC information with Central KYC Records Registry (CKYCR): Banks shall capture the KYC information for sharing with the CKYCR in the manner mentioned in the Rules, as required by the revised KYC templates prepared for 'individuals' and 'Legal Entities' as the case may be. Government of India has authorised the Central Registry of Securitisation Asset Reconstruction and Security Interest of India (CERSAI), to act as, and to perform the functions of the CKYCR vide Gazette Notification No. S.O. 3183(E) dated November 26, 2015.

CUSTOMER SERVICE IN BANKS (RBI GUIDELINES)

Customer service has great significance in the banking industry. The banking system in India today has perhaps the largest outreach for delivery of financial services and is also serving as an important conduit for delivery of financial services. While the coverage has been expanding day by day, the quality and content of dispensation of customer service has come under tremendous pressure mainly owing to the failure to handle the soaring demands and expectations of the customers.

Policy for General Management of the Branches

Banks' systems should be oriented towards providing better customer service and they should periodically study their systems and their impact on customer service. Banks should have a Board approved policy for general management of the branches which may include the following aspects:

(a) Providing infrastructure facilities by branches by bestowing particular attention to providing adequate space, proper furniture, drinking water facilities, with specific emphasis on pensioners, senior citizens, disabled persons, etc.

(b) Providing entirely separate enquiry counters at their large/bigger branches in addition to a regular reception counter.

(c) Displaying indicator boards at all the counters in English, Hindi as well as in the concerned regional language. Business posters at semi-urban and rural branches of banks should also be in the concerned regional languages.

(d) Posting roving officials to ensure employees' response to customers and for helping out customers in putting in their transactions.

(e) Providing customers with booklets consisting of all details of service and facilities available at the bank in Hindi, English and the concerned regional languages.

(f) Use of Hindi and regional languages in transacting business by banks with customers, including communications to customers.

(g) Reviewing and improving upon the existing security system in branches so as to instil confidence amongst the employees and the public.

(h) Wearing on person an identification badge displaying photo and name thereon by the employees.

(i) Periodic change of desk and entrustment of elementary supervisory jobs.

(j) Training of staff in line with customer service orientation. Training in Technical areas of banking to the staff at delivery points. Adopting innovative ways of training /delivery ranging from job cards to roving faculty to video conferencing.

(k) Visit by senior officials from Controlling Offices and Head Office to branches at periodical intervals for on the spot study of the quality of service rendered by the branches.

(l) Rewarding the best branches from customer service point of view by annual awards/running shield.

(m) Customer service audit, Customer surveys.

(n) Holding Customer relation programmes and periodical meetings to interact with different cross sections of customers for identifying action points to upgrade the customer service with customers.

(o) Clearly establishing a New Product and Services Approval Process which should require approval by the Board especially on issues which compromise the rights of the Common Person.

(p) Appointing Quality Assurance Officers who will ensure that the intent of policy is translated into the content and its eventual translation into proper procedures.

Customer Service Committee of the Board

Banks are required to constitute a Customer Service Committee of the Board and include experts and representatives of customers as invites to enable the bank to formulate policies and assess the compliance thereof internally with a view to strengthening the corporate governance structure in the banking system and also to bring about ongoing improvements in the quality of customer service provided by the banks.

Board Approved Policies on Customer Service

Customer service should be projected as a priority objective of banks along with profit, growth and fulfilment of social obligations. Banks should have a Board approved policy for the following:

1) **Business and Working Hours:** All customers who enter the banking hall before the close of business

hours may be attended to by the branches. The working hours of the staff should be fixed 15 minutes before the start of business hours at all branches in metropolitan and urban centres so that job can be started at commencement of Banking Hours.

2) **Display of Time Norms:** Time norms for specified business transactions should be displayed prominently in the banking hall. So that it attracts the customers' attention as well as that of the employees for adherence.

3) **Extension of Business Hours for Non-cash Transactions:** Staff at the counters may undertake the following Transactions during the extended business hours (branches to indicate the timings):

   a) **Non-voucher Generating Transactions:**
      i. Issue of passbook/statement of accounts;
      ii. Issue of cheque book;
      iii. Delivery of term deposit receipts/drafts;
      iv. Acceptance of share application form; and
      v. Acceptance of clearing cheques/bills for collection.

   b) **Voucher Generating Transactions:**
      i. Issue of term deposit receipts (TDR);
      ii. Acceptance of cheques for locker rent due;
      iii. Issue of traveller's cheques;
      iv. Issue of gift cheques;
      v. Acceptance of individual cheques for transfer credit

4) **Uninterrupted Service:** No counter remains unattended during the business hours.

5) **May I Help You Counter:** All branches, except very small ones, should have "Enquiry" or "May I help you" counters. Such counters may exclusively attend to enquiries or may be combined with other functions depending upon the requirement. Such counters should be near the entry point to the banking hall.

6) **Ramps at Automated Teller Machines (ATMs)/ Branches:** All existing ATMs/future ATMs to be provided with ramps so that wheel chair users/ persons with disabilities can easily access them. The height of the ATM should be such that it does not create an impediment in its use by a wheelchair user. Ramps to be provided at the entrance of the bank branches, so that the person with disabilities/ wheel chair users can enter the bank branches and conduct business without much difficulty.

7) **Identity Badges:** Each employee may wear on his person, identity badge with photograph and name.

8) **Complaint Box and Book:** A Complaint cum Sugg-estion Box may be kept in the bank premises at a prominent place. Complaint Book with adequate number of perforated copies in each set may also be maintained to instantly provide the complainant with an acknowledged copy of the complaint.

9) **Advisory Services on Deposit Schemes:** The banks should provide assistance/guidance to customers in the area of investment of funds in the various deposit schemes vis-a-vis the requirement of the customers.

10) **Brochures/Pamphlets for Guidance of Customers:** Banks may make available to the customers, brochures/pamphlets in regional language/Hindi/ English giving details of various schemes available and terms and conditions thereof. Such brochures may also contain, among others, dos and don'ts for smooth handling of day-to-day banking transactions.

11) **Banking Facilities to the Visually Challenged:** All the banking facilities such as cheque book facility including third party cheques, ATM facility, Net-banking facility, locker facility, retail loans, credit cards etc. to be provided to the visually challenged without any discrimination. From 1.7.2014, 100% of the new ATMs installed (earlier at least one third of new ATMs) as talking ATMs with Braille keypads.

12) **Fair Practices Code**: **Display of Bank/Service Charges:** Banks have the freedom to prescribe service charges with the approval of their Boards. However, the charges should be reasonable and not out of line with the average cost of providing these services. Banks should also take care to ensure that customers with low volume of activities are not penalized.

13) **Display of Information on Notice Board:** Banks should put-up on a notice board important aspects or indicators on 'customer service information', 'service charges', 'grievance redresser and' others'. The notice board should be updated on a periodical basis. Banks should display information relating to interest rates and service charges in their premises as well as post it on their websites, to enable the customer to obtain the desired information at a glance. The banks should display at their offices/ branches the service charges relating to the following services in the local languages:

   (a) Services rendered free of charge;
   (b) Minimum balances to be maintained in the SB account;
   (c) Charges liveable for non-maintenance of minimum balance in SB account;
   (d) Charges for collection of outstation cheques;
   (e) Charges for issue of Demand Draft;

(f) Charges for issue of cheque books, if any;

(g) Charges for account statement;

(h) Charges for account closure, if any;

(i) Charges for deposit/withdrawal at ATM locations, if any.

14) **Cheque Drop Facility and the Facility for Acknowledgement of Cheques:** No branch should refuse to give an acknowledgement on cheques being tendered by customers at their counters. Customers should be made aware of both options available to them i.e., dropping cheques in the drop box or tendering them at the counters.

15) **Infrastructure Provision:** Banks should provide adequate space, proper furniture, drinking water facilities, clean environment, (which include keeping the walls free of posters) etc., in their premises.

16) **Term Deposit Maturity Intimation in Advance:** Banks should send, as a rule, intimation for maturity dates of term deposits well in advance to their depositors in order to extend better customer service.

BANKING CODES AND STANDARDS BOARD OF INDIA (JAN. 2018)

Introduction

RBI constituted committee on Procedures and Performance Audit of Public Services in November 2003, under the chairmanship of Shri S. S. Tarapore (former Dy. Governor) to address the issues relating to availability of adequate banking services to the common man. Therefore, RBI, in its Monetary Policy Statement in April 2005 announced setting up of the Banking Codes and Standards Board of India (BCSBI) in order to ensure that comprehensive code of conduct for fair treatment of customer was evolved and adhered to. The BCSBI has been registered as a separate society under the Society Registration Act, 1860. Commercial banks, RRBs and Urban Banks are its members.

The BCSBI functions as an autonomous body to monitor and assess the compliance with codes. This is a Code of Customer Rights, which sets minimum standards of banking practices we will follow as a member of BCSBI while dealing with individual customers. It provides protection to customers and explains how a member bank is required to deal with customers in its day-to-day operations.

The Code does not replace or supersede regulatory or supervisory instructions of the Reserve Bank of India (RBI) and we will comply with such instructions/ directions issued by RBI from time to time. The Code may have set higher standards than those prescribed in the regulatory instructions and such higher standards will prevail as the Code represents the best practices voluntarily agreed to by us as our commitment to you.

Objectives of the Code: The Code has been developed to:

a) Promote good and fair banking practices by setting minimum standards in our dealings with you;

b) Increase transparency so that you can have a better understanding of what you can reasonably expect from us;

c) Encourage market forces, through competition, to achieve higher operating standards;

d) Promote a fair and cordial relationship between you and your bank;

e) Foster confidence in the banking system;

f) Promote safe and fair customer dealing in case of banking in a digitized environment;

g) Increase awareness of customers and to enhance customer protection.

Right to Transparency, Fair and Honest Dealing: We will help you to understand how our financial products and services work by:

a) Giving you timely and adequate information about them and the necessary safeguards in any one or more of the following languages - Hindi, English or the appropriate local language.

b) Ensuring that our advertising and promotional literature is clear and not misleading. We will make every effort to ensure that the contracts or agreements we frame are transparent, easily understood by and well communicated to you. The product's price, the associated risks, the terms and conditions that govern use over the product's life cycle Code of Bank's Commitment to Customers – January 2018 and mutual responsibilities will be clearly disclosed. We will ensure that you are not subjected to unfair business or marketing practices, coercive contractual terms, negative confirmations or misleading representations. For achieving this, we will be following the practices and procedures given in Chapter 3 on Information Transparency and Chapter 4 on Advertising, Marketing and Sales.

c) Ensuring that you are given complete information about our products and services, minimum balance requirements, the interest rates and service charges, besides the terms and conditions applicable to them in a transparent manner through the following methods as per your preference:

i. By sending SMS or e-mails
ii. Through electronic or print media
iii. Display on our website
iv. Display on branch notice board

[Display on website and branch notice board will be in addition to the other modes of information dissemination mentioned above.]

d) Giving you information on the facilities provided to you and how you can avail of these and whom and how you may contact for addressing your queries.

e) Displaying in our branch, for your information
   i. Services we provide.
   ii. Minimum balance requirement, if any, for Savings Bank Accounts and Current Accounts and the charges for non-maintenance thereof.
   iii. Information available in booklet form.

f) Displaying on our website our policies on:
   i. Deposits
   ii. Cheque collection
   iii. Grievance Redressal
   iv. Compensation
   v. Collection of Dues and Security Repossession
   vi. Charter of Customer Rights
   vii. Customer Protection Policy (including protection from cyber fraud)
   viii. Limited Liability in respect of unauthorized electronic banking transactions
   ix. Facilities for senior citizens and differently abled persons.

g) To increase awareness of the Code among customers we will:
   i. Provide you with a copy of the Code when you open an account with us and otherwise on request.
   ii. Make available this Code at our every branch and on our website.
   iii. Ensure that our staff are trained to provide relevant information about the Code and to effectively put the Code into practice.
   iv. Hold customer meetings on provisions of the Code periodically.

Code of Bank's Commitment to Micro and Small Enterprises

This is a Code, reflecting the bank's positive commitment to its Micro and Small Enterprise (MSE) customers to provide easy, speedy and transparent access to banking services in their day-do-day operations and in times of financial difficulty. This Code is not only a Charter of Rights of the MSE but also enshrines his obligations vis-a-vis his bank.

Code of Bank's Commitment to Customers

This is a Code of Customer Rights, which sets minimum standards of banking practices member banks have to follow while they deal with individual customer. It provides protection to customers and explains how banks are expected to deal with customers in their day-to-day operations.

TEST YOURSELF

1. The Prevention of Money Laundering Act 2002 along with the Rules framed has come into force with effect from________.
   (a) 1st July, 2002
   (b) 1st June, 2003
   (c) 1st July, 2005
   (d) 1st April, 2006

2. As per BCSBI, the interest rates and service charges, besides the terms and conditions applicable to them in a transparent manner through which of the following methods as per customer preference.
   (a) By sending SMS or e-mails
   (b) Display on our website
   (c) Display on branch notice board
   (d) All the above

3. Which is not the objectives of the BCSBI Code?
   (a) Promote good and fair banking practices by setting minimum standards in our dealings with you
   (b) Promote a fair and cordial relationship between you and your bank
   (c) Increase awareness of customers and to enhance customer protection
   (d) None

4. As per PML Act 2002, preserving bank records of tansactions for ______ from the date of each transaction between bank & clients or for 5 years after business relationship ended.
   (a) 3 years
   (b) 5 years
   (c) 8 years
   (d) 10 years

5. Which of the following is not a correct statement as per PMLA 2002?
   (a) Sec.3 of PML Act defines 'money laundering'
   (b) In India AML activities are monitored by FIU-IND
   (c) Money Laundering is the process used by criminals through which they make "clean" money appear "dirty"
   (d) Money Laundering is defined as 'Any act or attempted act to conceal or disguise the identity

of illegally obtained proceeds so that they appear to have originated from legitimate sources.'

6. Punishment for non-adherence of the Act would be rigorous imprisonment for not less than __ years but up to ___ years.
(a) 3, 5   (b) 3, 7
(c) 5, 7   (d) 5, 10

7. The BCSBI has been established on the recommendation of ___________.
(a) R V Gupta Committee
(b) S. S. Tarapore Committee
(c) Narshimham Committee
(d) V.K. Nair Committee

8. BCSBI Code does not apply to the products ________.
(a) Current accounts, savings accounts, term deposits
(b) Banking services related to Government transactions
(c) Demat accounts, Equity, Government bonds
(d) None

9. Bank's Code for Customer Service which is a voluntary code is issued by ________.
(A) RBI   (b) IBA
(c) BCSBI   (d) Central Govt.

10. All cash transactions of the value of more than ______ or its equivalent in foreign currency are covered under CTR.
(a) 5 lac   (b) 10 lac
(c) 20 lac   (d) 50 lac

11. 'Officially Valid Document' (OVD) definition amended vide Gazette Notification dated 1st June 2017 by Ministry of Finance – the _____; and the letter issued by the _____ have been removed from this definition.
(a) PAN Card, Aadhar
(b) Driving license, Passport
(c) Voter ID card, Ration card
(d) PAN card, Passport

12. Which of the documents required compulsorily for opening of a Partnership Firm account
(a) Registration certificate
(b) Partnership deed
(c) Aadhaar numbers; and Permanent Account Numbers or Form 60
(d) All of the above

13. Banks/FIs should introduce a system of maintaining proper record of transactions prescribed under Rule 3 of PML Rules, 2005. Those records are:
(a) All cash transactions of the value of more than Rupees Ten Lakhs or its equivalent in foreign currency within a month.
(b) All transactions involving receipts by non-profit organisations of value more than rupees ten lakhs or its equivalent in foreign currency.
(c) All cash transactions, where forged or counterfeit currency notes or bank notes have been used as genuine.
(d) All of the above

14. Which type of risk is not involved with money laundering?
(a) Reputational Risk   (b) Compliance Risk
(c) Credit Risk   (d) Operational Risk

15. Which are the key elements of KYC policy?
(a) Customer Acceptance Policy (CAP)
(b) Risk Management (RM)
(c) Customer Identification Procedure (CIP)
(d) All of the above

16. As per KYC policy, Bank has to open account to which of the following name?
(a) Anonymous name   (b) Fictitious name
(c) Political party   (d) Criminal background

17. Which is not categorised as Medium Risk Customer?
(a) NBFC   (b) Bullion dealers
(c) Builders   (d) Stock Brokers

18. Which is categorised as Low Risk Customer?
(a) Statutory Bodies
(b) Trust
(c) Charities
(d) Non-resident Customer

19. The Director of FIU-IND is vested with the power of a ________under the code of civil procedure.
(a) Civil Court   (b) High Court
(c) Supreme Court   (d) CBI Court

20. The Suspicious Transaction Report (STR) should be furnished within _____ of arriving at a conclusion that any transaction, whether cash or non-cash, or a series of transactions integrally connected are of suspicious nature.
(a) 3 days   (b) 7 days
(c) 15 days   (d) 30 days

ANSWER

1	2	3	4	5	6	7	8	9	10
(c)	(d)	(d)	(b)	(c)	(b)	(b)	(d)	(c)	(b)

11	12	13	14	15	16	17	18	19	20
(a)	(d)	(d)	(c)	(d)	(c)	(b)	(a)	(a)	(b)

OPERATIONAL ASPECTS OF ACCOUNTING ENTRIES

INTRODUCTION

Banks, follow the mercantile system of accounting. The system of recording classifying and summarising the transactions in a bank is in substance no different from that followed in other entities having similar volume of operations. However, in the case of banks, the need for the ledger accounts, especially those of customers, being accurate and up-to-date is much stronger than in most other types of enterprises.

In the case of banks, relatively lesser emphasis is placed on books of prime entry such as cash books or journals. This is unlike most other types of enterprises where books of prime entry are generally kept up-to-date while ledgers, including the general ledger and subsidiary ledgers for debtors, creditors, etc. are written up afterwards.

Banks follow the accounting procedure of 'voucher posting' under which the vouchers are straight away posted to the individual accounts in the subsidiary ledgers. At the end of each day, the debit and credit vouchers relating to a particular type of transactions (e.g. savings bank accounts, current accounts, demand loans, cash credit accounts, etc.) are entered on separate voucher summary sheets and the total thereof is posted to the respective control account in the general ledger. The general ledger trial balance is prepared every day.

FINANCIAL TRANSACTIONS IN BANKS

Any financial transaction is recorded in the books of the banks by way of an accounting entry and is always in terms of number of monetary units like ₹ 1000. The accounting entry could be a debit entry or a credit entry.

1. In accounting, the double entry system is used which implies that every credit/debit accounting entry should have one or more corresponding debit/credit entry.

2. Normally in accounting entries are first recorded in Journal and then posted in Ledger but in banks these are first entered in the ledger accounts concerned and then in the journal.

3. **Features of Manual Operations:** First, the entries are entered in the physical ledgers and then all the entries in a particular ledger head are entered in the journal (day book). Finally, the total is entered in the control account concerned of the General Ledger which is used in preparing the balance sheet and the P&L account. Any accounting entry in manual operations can only be made based on a physical voucher which is authenticated by the authorised officer of the branch.

4. **Features of Computerised Operations:** The accounting entry in the system is made by the staff concerned and authenticated by the official concerned. Remaining operations like day book and GL are taken care of by the system.

PECULIAR FEATURES OF ACCOUNTING SYSTEM IN BANKS

- **More Focus on Ledger Compared to Journal:** In business enterprises other than banks, books of prime entry i.e. Journals are kept up-to-date while ledgers, including the general ledger and subsidiary ledgers for debtors, creditors, etc. are written afterwards. But in case of banks, more emphasis is laid on ledger accounts and relatively lesser emphasis is placed on books of prime entry such as cash books or journals. Every transaction is entered in ledgers as soon as it takes place because in the case of banks, the need for the ledger accounts of customers, being accurate and up-to-date is much stronger.

- **Voucher Posting:** Banks follow the accounting procedure of 'voucher posting'. In this system, the vouchers are straightaway posted to the individual accounts in the subsidiary ledgers. Then, at the end of the day, the debit and credit vouchers relating to a particular type of transaction (e.g. savings bank accounts, current accounts, demand loans, cash credit accounts, etc.) are entered on separate voucher summary sheets. Total of various items of summary sheet is posted to the respective control account in the general ledger. The general ledger trial balance is prepared every day.

- **Types of Transactions:** Features of banking transactions are as under:
  1. Transactions in a bank are of two types, cash and non-cash.
  2. Non cash transactions, are also called 'Transfer Transactions'.
  3. In transfer transactions, one or both of the accounts concerned may be of the customers or the internal accounts of the bank.

PREPARATION OF VOUCHERS

Voucher preparation is very important and responsible job of an accountant. Voucher is a very primary accounting record which shows the authenticity of the transactions. In business or in banks, so many transactions take place. To record any transaction in account books, first of all a voucher is prepared by the accountant. Therefore, we call the vouchers as the base of the accounting system.

Voucher is prepared by the accountant with the help of source document. Source document means any proof relating to the business transactions. These documents include: bills, cash memos, receipts, bank deposit slips, cheque book counter foils, challans and other details which show the happening of any transaction in a business firm and bank.

Preparation of Vouchers in Bank

There are two types of transactions in a bank, cash and non-cash. The non-cash transactions also called 'Transfer Transactions'. In various transactions, one or both of the accounts concerned may be of the customers or the

internal accounts of the bank. For example, if 'X' deposits a cheque drawn in his favour by 'Y' who is also a customer of the branch, the accounts of the two customers will be affected. On the other hand, if he deposits draft drawn on the branch, the draft account, an internal account of the bank will be debited. Likewise, on payment of interest on deposit accounts, the 'Interest Account' at the branch will be debited and many personal accounts credited.

Kinds of Vouchers

The debit as well as the credit operations in different accounts, either by customers or by the bank itself, are made by means of vouchers. There are two kinds of vouchers:

(1) Which evidence only debit or credit to an account, and

(2) Which contains both debit and credit to different accounts. The 2nd category of vouchers may be called 'composite vouchers'.

Types of Debit Vouchers

The debit vouchers are created out of the following transactions:

1) Cheques issued by the customers;

2) Cheques/pay orders issued by the bank;

3) Withdrawal forms received from the savings bank account holders;

4) Drafts issued by other branches, of the bank payable at the branch;

5) Drafts issued by other banks on the branch, in terms of an approved arrangement between the two banks;

6) Dividend/interest warrants issued by the bank's customers and payable by the branch in terms of an approved arrangement;

7) Traveller's cheques issued by any branch of the bank which are presented to the branch for payment;

8) Drafts/pay orders issued by the branch itself which are cancelled at the request of the customer and amount is refunded to him;

9) Instruments like traveller's cheques/gift cheques, etc., of other banks which are paid by the branch in terms of an approved arrangement;

10) Letters of authority signed by the customers, containing standing instructions;

11) Debit vouchers prepared by the branch on its printed stationary which are authorised by designated official of the bank and may also carry authority from the customers in some cases if the debit is to his account at the branch;

12) In respect of realization of collection instrument sent to other branches of the bank, a debit advice (which may be known by different names in different banks) prepared by the other branch may itself as a debit voucher.

13) In case of remittance of funds by one branch to the other by means of telegraphic transfer or a mail transfer. The bank may treat the advice of transfer itself as debit voucher or may prepare a separate debit voucher.

Credit Vouchers

The credit vouchers are created out due to the following transactions:

1) Pay-in-slips filled up the customers (depositors as well as borrowers) for deposit of amounts in their accounts. Generally, the pay-in-slips are in a standard format adopted by the bank but there may be cases of a special kind of pay-in-slips in respect of some customers pursuant to a formal agreement between the bank and the customer.

2) Applications for issue of demand drafts, mail transfers, telegraphic transfers, banker's cheques pay orders, gift cheques, traveller's cheques and other similar instruments. Some of these applications may be made on behalf of the branch itself for the payments it has to make.

3) Challans for deposits into the accounts of Central/State Government, e.g. on account of direct/indirect taxes or under schemes like public provident fund, etc.

4) Credit vouchers prepared by the branch on its printed stationery which are authorised by an official of the bank. Normally, these vouchers are signed on behalf of the branch only but there may be some instances where the customer concerned also signs on the voucher as evidence that the transaction actually pertains to him. Examples are: deposit of locker charges (credit to an income account of the bank), deposit of money with the bank for purchase of non-judicial stamps required for execution of documents in favour of the bank, etc.

5) On payment of collection instruments from other branches of the bank, a credit advice (which may be known by different names in different banks) or a copy of the collection schedule received from the other branch may itself be treated as a credit voucher.

6) In case of debits or credits of similar nature to a large number of accounts in the same ledger or group of ledgers (e.g. debit on account of periodic interest, inspection charges etc. or credit on account of periodic payment of interest to depositors), it is a common practice among banks to prepare a consolidated voucher on their stationery and enclose thereto a list containing details of accounts to be debited/credited and the amount of debit/credit.

Examples of Composite Vouchers

In addition to debit vouchers and credit vouchers, there is a category of 'composite vouchers' also. These vouchers record the particulars of both debit and credit accounts. Most of the transactions covered by composite vouchers pertain to the internal accounts of the bank, i.e. non-customer accounts.

Examples: Bills received for collection, letters of credit issued by the branch, guarantees issued by the branch, etc.

Such vouchers may also be prepared to rectify an error while debiting or crediting an account. For example, in case the current account is debited in general ledger instead of cash credit account by mistake, the composite voucher will show debit to cash credit account with a corresponding credit to current account.

Multi-level Authentication (checking): All entries in the personal ledgers and the summary sheets are checked by persons other than those who have made the entries. Most clerical errors are thus detected immediately.

Bankers' Books

According to Section 2 (3) of the Bankers' Books Evidence Act. 'Bankers' Books' include ledgers, daybook, cash books, account books and all other books used in the ordinary business of a bank. Generally the following books are maintained by bank to keep up-to-date records of its customers.

Cash Book: All cash receipts and payments are recorded in the receiving cashier's cash book and paying cashier's cash book respectively. After this, on the basis of pay-in-slips received by the receiving cashier and cheques and withdrawals slips by the paying cashier, these transactions are entered first in the accounts of customers and after that Day Books are written. This is called the 'Slip System' of posting.

Ledger Book: General Ledger contains the total accounts of each ledger. Besides the GL, the following ledger books are maintained:

1. Current Accounts Ledger
2. FD Accounts Ledger
3. RD Accounts Ledger

4. Loan Ledger
5. Investment Ledger
6. Bills Discounted and Purchased Ledger

Other Books

1. Clearing Register
2. Securities Register
3. Draft Register
4. Bills for Collection Register
5. Safe Deposit Vault Register
6. Dishonoured Cheques Register
7. Letter of Credit Register

Checking of Vouchers: All entries in the personal ledgers and the summary sheets are checked by persons other than those who have made the entries. Thus, clerical errors are detected immediately.

Balancing of Books: A trial balance of the personal ledgers is prepared periodically, usually every two weeks, and agreed with general ledger control accounts. In banking parlance, this exercise is referred to as 'balancing of books'.

Accounting Systems of Different Banks

1. Accounting systems of different banks vary in terms of hardware configuration, software capabilities, levels of hardware and software security, and nature of transactions processed.

2. The accounting system in a bank is designed keeping in view the nature and volume of operations and information needs of various interested parties.

Every big bank has customized banking-software as per its own requirement and as such, the accounting systems differ amongst different banks.

TEST YOURSELF

1. In accounting, the __________ is used which implies that every credit/debit accounting entry should have one or more corresponding debit/credit entry.
   (a) Single entry system
   (b) Double entry system
   (c) Triple entry system
   (d) Any of the above

2. Normally in banks entries are first recorded in the ______accounts concerned and then in the ________.
   (a) Ledger, Journal
   (b) Journal, Ledger
   (c) General Ledger, Journal
   (d) Cash Book, Journal

3. Total of various items of summary sheet is posted to the respective control account in the __________.
   (a) Journal
   (b) General Ledger
   (c) Subsidiary Ledger
   (d) Day Book

4. In banks, the general ledger trial balance is prepared ________.
   (a) Every Day
   (b) Every Friday
   (c) Every Month
   (d) Every Year

5. Which are the features of banking transactions?
   (a) Transactions in a bank are of two types, cash and non-cash.
   (b) Non cash transactions, are also called 'Transfer Transactions'.
   (c) In transfer transactions, one or both of the accounts concerned may be of the customers or the internal accounts of the bank.
   (d) All of the above

6. Voucher is a very _____ accounting record which shows the authenticity of the transactions.
   (a) Primary
   (b) Secondary
   (c) Tertiary
   (d) None of the above

7. There are two types of transactions in a bank, cash and non-cash. The non-cash transactions also called __________.
   (a) Secondary Transactions
   (b) Subsidiary Transactions
   (c) Transfer Transactions
   (d) Additional Transactions

8. Vouchers which contain both debit and credit to different accounts may be called ______________.
   (a) Consolidated vouchers
   (b) Composite vouchers
   (c) Special vouchers
   (d) Complex vouchers

9. For which of the following transactions, a composite voucher is prepared?
   (a) Bills received for collection

(b) Letter of credit issued by the bank
(c) Bank Guarantee issued by the bank
(d) All of the above

10. If bank wants to rectify an error, which type of voucher will be created?
(a) Credit voucher
(b) Composite voucher
(c) Debit voucher
(d) Complex voucher

11. According to Section 2 (3) of the________. 'Bankers' Books' include ledgers, daybook, cash books, account books and all other books used in the ordinary business of a bank.
(a) NI Act
(b) Indian Contract Act
(c) Bankers' Books Evidence Act
(d) Company Act

12. All cash receipts and payments are recorded in the receiving cashier's cash book and paying cashier's cash book respectively. After this, on the basis of pay-in slips received by the receiving cashier and cheques and withdrawals slips by the paying cashier, these transactions are entered first in the accounts of customers and after that Day Books are written. This is called the ________ of posting.
(a) Slip System
(b) Accounting System
(c) Voucher System
(d) Ledger System

ANSWER

1	2	3	4	5	6	7	8	9	10
(b)	(a)	(b)	(a)	(d)	(a)	(c)	(b)	(d)	(b)

11	12
(c)	(a)

OPERATIONAL ASPECTS OF
HANDLING CASH & CLEARING

INTRODUCTION

In India, the payment and settlement systems are regulated by the Payment and Settlement Systems Act, 2007 (PSS Act) which was legislated in December 2007. The PSS Act as well as the Payment and Settlement System Regulations, 2008 framed thereunder came into effect from August 12, 2008.

OPERATIONAL ASPECTS OF HANDLING CLEARING

Important Operations Conducted at a Bank Branch: Cash, collection of local and outstation instruments and remittances on behalf of the customers.

Instruments Submitted by Customers for Collection: Cheques, drafts, pay orders, trade bills, dividend and interest warrants, NSCs, postal orders, term deposit receipts, tax refund orders, etc.

Type of Instruments: The instruments payable locally are collected through the clearing house. The instruments payable outside are sent by the bank for collection.

Settlement of inter-bank Transactions among the Local Banks: Done through clearing house. Post offices may also be members of the clearing house. There may be separate clearing houses for MICR (Magnetic Ink Character Recognition) and non-MICR instruments. The accounts of all member banks are maintained by the clearing house.

Management of Clearing House: It is done by RBI, State Bank of India or any other bank nominated by RBI.

Nodal Branch: If a bank has many branches within the area of a clearing house, it nominates one branch to act as the nodal branch of that bank. Nodal branch handles the instruments to be presented by other branches also.

Electronic Clearing Service (ECS)

It is in addition to regular clearing. ECS is of two types- ECS credit or ECS debit.

ECS (Credit): ECS (credit) is a new method of payment introduced by Reserve Bank of India which provides customers an option to collect their monthly/ quarterly/half yearly/yearly interest/dividend/salary/ pension directly through their bank accounts. The customer's bank account would be credited through the new payment mechanism, on the due date. In this system payment instruction would be issued by the bank electronically through the banker to the Clearing Authority and the Clearing Authority would supply credit reports to the bank with which customer maintains the specified account. The branch will credit the customer's account and indicate the credit entry as 'ECS' in his passbook/ statement of account.

ECS (Debit): In this scenario, the Reserve Bank of India has implemented an off-line electronic funds transfer system allowing paperless direct debit and credit transactions by banks, viz. Electronic Clearing Service.

After successful implementation of ECS-Credit scheme, Reserve Bank of India initiated the ECS-Debit, a facility of payment of pre-authorised debits through ECS. This ECS allows customer to pay their monthly/quarterly/half yearly/yearly utility bills like telephone, electricity, loan instalments, insurance premium etc. directly through their bank accounts. The customer's bank account would be debited through the new payment mechanism right on the due date. The customer would be advised in the usual manner to pay the bill.

Speed Clearing

Speed clearing refers to collection of outstation cheques (a cheque drawn on non-local bank branch) through the local clearing. It facilitates collection of cheques drawn on outstation core banking enabled branches of banks, if they have a networked branch locally. Speed clearing covers all transaction codes, other than those relating to government cheques.

Remittances

Remittances involve transfer of funds from one place to another. The common modes of remittance of funds are Drafts, RTGS, NEFT etc. Drafts are issued by one branch of the bank and are payable by another branch of the bank. In case there is no branch of the bank at that place, the draft is issued at the branch of another bank with which the issuing bank has entered into necessary arrangement. RTGS and NEFT are other modes of remittance which facilitate almost instantaneous transfer of funds between two centres.

CHEQUE TRUNCATION SYSTEM

Truncation is the process of stopping the flow of the physical cheque issued by a drawer at some point by the presenting bank en-route the paying bank branch. In its place an electronic image of the cheque is transmitted to the paying branch through the clearing house, along with relevant information like data on the MICR band, date of presentation, presenting bank, etc. Cheque truncation thus obviates the need to move the physical instruments across bank branches, other than in exceptional circumstances for clearing purposes. This effectively eliminates the associated cost of movement of the physical cheques, reduces the time required for their collection and brings elegance to the entire activity of cheque processing.

CTS thus brings elegance to the entire activity of cheque processing and clearing. The benefits from CTS could be summarized as follows:

- Shorter clearing cycle;
- Superior verification and reconciliation process;
- No geographical restrictions as to jurisdiction;
- Operational efficiency for banks and customers alike;
- Reduction in operational risk and risks associated with paper clearing;
- No collection charges for collection of cheque drawn on a bank located within the grid.

COLLECTION OF INSTRUMENTS (RBI GUIDELINES)

RBI Cheque Collection Policy

Keeping in view the technological progress in payment and settlement systems and the qualitative changes in operational systems and processes that have been undertaken by the individual banks. As per Cheque Collection Policy, banks are obliged to disclose their liability to customers by way of compensation/interest payments due to delays for non-compliance with the standards set by the banks themselves. The customer has to be compensated by way of compensation/ interest payment even if no formal claim is lodged to the effect.

Local Cheques

Local cheques are payable within the jurisdiction of the clearing house and will be presented through the clearing system prevailing at the center. Credit arising out of local cheques shall be given to the customer's account as indicated in the Cheque Collection Policy (CCP) of the concerned collecting bank.

Notwithstanding to the CCP of concerned collecting bank, ideally, in respect of local clearing, banks shall permit usage of the shadow credit afforded to the customers' accounts immediately after closure of the relative return clearing on the next working day or maximum within an hour of commencement of business on the third working day from the day of presentation in clearing, subject to usual safeguards.

Under grid-based Cheque Truncation System clearing, all cheques drawn on bank branches falling within the grid jurisdiction are treated and cleared as local cheques. The grid clearing allows banks to present/receive cheques to/from multiple cities to a single clearing house through their service branches in the grid location.

If there is any delay in credit, beyond the period specified above, customer is entitled to receive compensation at the rate specified in the CCP of the concerned collecting bank. In case, no rate is specified in the CCP for delay in realisation of local cheques, compensation at savings bank interest rate has to be paid for the corresponding period of delay.

Outstation Cheques

Maximum timeframe for collection of cheques drawn on state capitals/major cities/other locations are 7/10/14 days respectively. If there is any delay in collection beyond this period, customer is entitled to receive compensation at the rate specified in the Cheque Collection Policy (CCP) of the concerned bank. In case the rate is not specified in the CCP, interest rate on Fixed Deposits for the corresponding maturity to be paid. Banks' cheque collection policy also indicates the limit up to which outstation cheques are given immediate/instant credit.

Cheque Drop Box Facility

Banks are required to provide both the cheque drop box facility and the acknowledgement facility at their collection counters. No bank branch can refuse to give an acknowledgement to the customer if the latter asks for the same while tendering cheque for collection at the bank branch's counter. No bank can refuse to accept outstation cheques deposited for collection or refuse to offer its products to customers.

Collection of Account Payee Cheque - Prohibition on Crediting Proceeds to Third Party Account: As per RBI guidelines, Banks should not collect account payee cheques for any person other than the payee constituent. This has been done keeping in view the intent of the NI Act, to protect the banks from liabilities arising out of unauthorized collections, and in the interest of the integrity and soundness of the payment systems. These instructions shall also extend to drafts, pay orders and bankers' cheque.

Account payee cheques deposited with the sub-member for credit to their customers' account can be collected by the member bank (referred to as the sponsor member) of the Clearing House. However, there should be clear undertaking that the proceeds of the account payee cheque will be credited to the payee's account only.

Payment of Cheques/ Drafts/Pay Orders/Banker's Cheques

With effect from April 1, 2012, banks should not make payment of cheques/drafts/pay orders/banker's cheques if they are presented beyond the period of three months from the date of such instrument.

CASH OPERATIONS

Cash Transactions: Branch has to deal with custody as well as inter office movement of cash, involving the aspects of security, misappropriation and frauds.

1. **Cash and its Custody:** The Cash and Small Coin Balances must be kept in the Strong Room in the joint custody of the Head Cashier/Cashier and an authorised Supervising Official. No member of staff other than the Cashier/Teller should receive money over the counter from depositors.

2. **Strong Room/Safe:** The Strong Room or Safe must be under the double lock of the Cashier and the Supervising Official in charge of cash. Both officials must be present when the Strong Room/Safe is opened. All receptacles in the Strong Room used for storing Cash and Small Coin balances must also be under the double lock of the Cashier and the Supervising Official, except receptacle used for the Cashier's hand balance.

3. **Cash Balance of the Bank:** Bank has to follow the following guidelines:

   a) The bulk of the Cash Balance should always be in the Strong Room/Safe under joint custody. Only cash sufficient for the day's requirements will be withdrawn in the morning from joint custody.

   b) Cashier's Hand Balance left with the Head Cashier/Cashier during the day for the day's transactions will be kept as low as conveniently possible.

   c) The amounts of all notes and coins withdrawn from, or deposited in, the joint custody portion of the bank's Cash Balance (i.e. excluding the Head Cashier's/Cashier's hand balance) will be entered immediately in the Reserve Cash Register under the initials of the joint custodians.

   d) The Reserve Cash Register must always remain in the Strong Room.

   e) The amount will be recorded in the Cash Balance Book, which will be checked and signed by the Head Cashier/Cashier and the Supervising Official.

Automated Clearing House (ACH)

An automated clearing house (ACH) is an electronic funds-transfer system run by the National Automated Clearing House Association (NACHA). This payment system deals with payroll, direct deposit, tax refunds, consumer bills, tax payments and many more payment services.

TEST YOURSELF

1. Management of Clearing House is done by:
   (a) RBI
   (b) State Bank of India
   (c) Any other bank nominated by RBI
   (d) Any of the above

2. If a bank has many branches within the area of a clearing house, it nominates one branch to act as the ______ of that bank.
   (a) Nodal Branch   (b) Clearing Branch
   (c) Lead Branch   (d) Collecting Branch

3. Full form of ECS is:
   (a) Electronic Clearing System
   (b) Electronic Clearing Service
   (c) Electronic Collection Service
   (d) Essential Clearing System

4. ________ is a new method of payment introduced by Reserve Bank of India which provides customers an option to collect their monthly/quarterly/half yearly/ yearly interest/dividend/ salary / pension directly through their bank accounts.
   (a) ECS (Credit)   (b) ECS (Debit)
   (c) Speed Clearing   (d) Auto Clearing

5. ECS (Debit) allows customer to pay their monthly/ quarterly/half yearly/yearly utility bills like ______ etc. directly through their bank accounts.
   (a) Recharge prepaid mobile
   (b) LPG bill amount
   (c) Electricity bill
   (d) All of the above

6. ________ refers to collection of outstation cheques (a cheque drawn on non-local bank branch) through the local clearing.
   (a) ECS (Credit)   (b) ECS (Debit)
   (c) Speed Clearing   (d) Auto Clearing

7. Truncation is the process of stopping the flow of the physical cheque issued by a drawer at some point by the presenting bank en-route the ________.
   (a) Paying bank branch
   (b) Collecting bank branch
   (c) Clearing house
   (d) Nodal branch

8. Which are not the benefits from CTS?
   (a) Shorter clearing cycle
   (b) Superior verification and reconciliation process
   (c) No geographical restrictions as to jurisdiction
   (d) None of the above

9. Maximum timeframe for collection of cheques drawn on state capitals/major cities/other locations are ______ days respectively.
   (a) 5/10/14   (b) 7/14/21
   (c) 7/10/14   (d) 7/10/21

10. If there is any delay in collection beyond this period, customer is entitled to receive compensation at the rate specified in the Cheque Collection Policy (CCP) of the concerned bank. In case the rate is not specified in the CCP, interest rate ______ to be paid.
    (a) of Savings Bank Account
    (b) on Fixed Deposits for the corresponding maturity
    (c) of OD Account
    (d) on Fixed Deposits for one year

11. Which is the correct statement regarding RBI Cheque Collection Policy?
    (a) The customer has to be compensated by way of compensation/interest payment even if no formal claim is lodged to the effect.
    (b) Banks are required to provide both the cheque drop box facility and the acknowledgement facility at their collection counters.
    (c) No bank branch can refuse to give an acknowledgement to the customer if the latter asks for the same while tendering cheque for collection at the bank branch's counter.
    (d) All of the above

12. With effect from April 1, _____, banks should not make payment of cheques/drafts/pay orders/banker's cheques if they are presented beyond the period of three months from the date of such instrument.
    (a) 2010   (b) 2012
    (c) 2014   (d) 2016

ANSWER

1	2	3	4	5	6	7	8	9	10
(d)	(a)	(b)	(a)	(c)	(c)	(a)	(d)	(c)	(b)

11	12
(d)	(b)

CHAPTER 23

OPERATIONAL ASPECTS OF DEPOSIT ACCOUNTS

INTRODUCTION

Bank is an important service sector organisation. Customers play the most significant part in bank. In fact, the customer is the actual boss in a deal and is responsible for the actually profit for the organization. Customer is the one who uses the banking products and services and judges the quality of those products and services. Hence, it's important for an organization to retain customers or make new customers and flourish business. To manage customers, organizations should follow some sort of approaches like segmentation or division of customers into groups because each customer has to be considered valuable and profitable.

For a bank it is advantageous to have different types of clients because, it will receive deposits and provide loans for both business and individuals. Banking relationship is a contract between the Bank and the Customer. Therefore, for establishing relationship with the customer, Bank has to ensure that the customer is legally capable of entering into a valid contract and he has applied to the Bank in the proper form (Indian Contracts Act, 1872).

Acceptance of Deposits

As per Section 5(b) of BR Act, definition of banking business is "Accepting for the purpose of lending or investment, of deposits of money from public, repayable on demand or otherwise, and withdrawal by cheque, draft, order or otherwise".

Bank accepts different types of deposits from public. Deposits may be classified as Demand and Time deposits. The deposit which is paid on demand such as Current Deposit Account and Savings Deposit Accounts are called Demand Deposits. While Time Deposits, like Fixed Deposit and Recurring Deposits are generally repayable after an agreed period. Regarding period of deposit and rate of deposit are the matters to be agreed between bank and depositor, subject to the any direction given by RBI in this regard.

TYPES OF DEPOSIT ACCOUNTS IN BANK

Bank accepts deposit from the public in its deposit accounts. Banks maintain mainly two types of deposit accounts:

1. **Demand Deposits:** The deposits which are payable on demand are called demand deposits. Current Account and Savings Account (CASA) are categorised as demand deposit accounts. It is also called Low Cost Deposit, because banks pay no interest in current account and less interest in savings accounts. Over due Term Deposit, Unclaimed Deposit and Credit Balance in CC/OD Accounts are also called Demand Deposits.

2. **Term Deposit:** The deposits which are fixed for a definite period are called Term Deposits or Time Deposits. Recurring Deposit, TDR etc. are the example of term deposit.

SALIENT FEATURES OF DEPOSIT ACCOUNTS

Current Account

- Current account is meant for Individuals/Institutions having large number/volume of transactions, mainly for meeting their day-to-day business and operational requirements for parking their operational fund balances.

- Accounts can be opened by Individuals, Sole Proprietary Concerns, Partnership Firms, Private/ Public Sector Companies, Clubs, Associations, Trusts, Executors, Administrators, Govt./Local Bodies, Cooperative Societies, Religious Institutions, Educational Institutions, Charitable Institutions, Registered/Unregistered Societies, etc.

- Minors, Purdanashin women, Illiterate persons, Blind persons cannot open current account.

- No interest is payable in the account except where it may be specifically permitted.

- No restriction on maximum balance/number and amount of transactions/withdrawal in a day/month.

- Withdrawal from account: only through cheques. However for standing instructions, account can be debited without cheques.

- Overdrafts in the account can be allowed.

Savings Bank Account

- Savings account can be opened in the name of individuals operating singly or jointly with other individuals, associations, clubs or similar other non-trading institutions;

- Minors above 10 years can open SB account operated independently;

- Savings account can also be opened in the names of institutions which are specifically approved by the RBI for maintaining savings bank accounts with banks. These accounts cannot be used for business or trading.

- **Organisations for which Savings Bank Accounts cannot be opened:** Savings Bank accounts are opened for savings and not for any business. Therefore, such accounts cannot be opened in the name of business concern.

- Further, as per RBI directives, Government Departments or Bodies who for performance of their functions depend on Budgetary Allocations cannot open Savings Bank Accounts. Thus, RBI has specifically asked banks not to open SB accounts in the name of:
  - (a) Govt. Departments,
  - (b) Municipal Corporations or Committees,
  - (c) Panchayat Samities,
  - (d) State Housing Boards,
  - (e) State Electricity Boards,
  - (f) Water and Sewerage Boards,
  - (g) State Text Book Publishing Corporations or Societies,
  - (h) Metropolitan Development Authorities,
  - (i) State/District Level Cooperative Housing Societies
  - (j) Any Bank including Land Development Bank.

- **Organisations for which Saving Bank Accounts can be opened:** The above prohibition is not applicable for the following organizations/agencies and therefore banks can open SB account in their names:

  (a) Companies licensed under section 25 of Companies Act, 1956 which are permitted not to add to their names the word 'limited' (i.e. Non-profit making companies). For example, Chamber of Commerce, Indian Bank Association, etc.

  (b) Societies registered under Societies Registration Act, 1860 or any other corresponding law in force in any State/UT.

  (c) Primary Cooperative Credit Society being financed by the bank (PACS)

  (d) Institutions other than those mentioned above and whose entire income is exempt from payment of income tax under Income Tax Act, 1961.

  (e) Government departments (Central as well as State Government)/bodies/agencies in respect of grants/ subsidies released for implementation of various programmes/schemes sponsored by the Central Government as well as State Government on production of an authorization to the bank from the respective Government departments certifying that the concerned Government department or body has been permitted to open savings bank account. Banks should keep on their record a copy of the authorization issued by the respective State Government departments. For example (i) Khadi and Village Industries Boards (ii) Agriculture Produce Market Committees (iii) Distt Rural Development Agency (DRDA) (iv) Integrated Tribal Development Agency (ITDA) (v) Draught Prone Area Development Programme (DPAP) (vi) Member of Parliament Local Area Development Authority (MPLADS) (vii) Small Farmers Development Agency (viii) Marginal Farmers and Agricultural Laborer's Agencies (ix) Nagar panchayats and palikas, Municipal Bodies for credit of subsidy amount. (x) District Development Agency (DDA);

  (f) Development of Women and Children in Rural Areas (DWCRA);

  (g) Self-help Groups (SHGs), registered or unregistered, which are engaged in promoting savings habit among their members;

(h) Farmers' Clubs-Vikas Volunteer Vahini (VVV);

(i) Clubs, Associations, Society, Educational Institutions

(j) Any other institution permitted by RBI provided it is a non-trading institution.

- **Interest rate on Saving Bank Accounts:** As per RBI guideline, it has been decided to deregulate the savings bank deposit interest rate with immediate effect. Accordingly, the following Guidelines will be effective from October 25, 2011. Banks are free to determine their savings bank deposit interest rate, subject to the following two conditions:

  1. First, each bank will have to offer a uniform interest rate on savings bank deposits up to ₹ 1 lakh, irrespective of the amount in the account within this limit.

  2. Second, for savings bank deposits over ₹ 1 lakh, a bank may provide differential rates of interest, if it so chooses, subject to the condition that banks will not discriminate in the matter of interest paid on such deposits, between one deposit and another of similar amount, accepted on the same date, at any of its offices.

  The above revised guidelines would be applicable to savings bank deposits of resident Indians only. Interest rate on Non-Resident (External) Accounts Scheme and Ordinary Non-Resident Deposit under savings account, which has been prescribed at 4 per cent per annum at present, will continue to be regulated until further review.

- With effect from 1.4.2010, interest rate on savings bank is payable on daily product basis. It can be credited at any interval. The interest should be calculated and provided for even in case of inoperative S.B. accounts.

- 1% additional rate of interest over the standard rate is allowed on deposits held individually or jointly with dependents in the case of employees of the bank/retired employees/widows of employees/ widows of retired employees etc. and on deposits of an Association or a Fund, all the members of which are the members of the bank staff.

- **Levy of penal charges on non-maintenance of minimum balances in savings bank accounts:** Banks should inform customers regarding the requirement of minimum balance in savings bank account and levy of penal charges for non-maintenance of the same at the time of opening the account in a transparent manner. Banks are not permitted to levy penal charges for non-maintenance of minimum balances in any inoperative account.

Further, no charge should be levied for non-operation/ activation of Basic Savings Bank Deposit Accounts (BSBDAs).

- **Transfer of Accounts:** At the written request of the customer his Savings bank account can be transferred from one branch to another branch of the bank free of any charges. The account opening form and specimen signature card must be transferred to the branch where the account is being transferred by retaining a Photostat copy in the branch.

Fixed Deposits

- Minimum period as per RBI is 7 days. Maximum period as per IBA is 10 years. However, term deposits in the name of minors or as per court orders can be opened for more than 10 years.

- Interest rate on term deposits is deregulated and is decided by Asset Liability Management Committee of the bank. Bank cannot discriminate among customers regarding payment of interest except for single deposits of ₹ 15 lac and above but the difference should be minimal.

- The interest is normally paid on quarterly basis.

- If due date of term deposit is on a holiday, banks will make payment on next working day or thereafter and will pay the interest for the holiday to depositor at contracted rate irrespective of when the payment is taken.

- Depositor can request for addition or deletion of names in the deposit but at least one of the original depositors must remain.

- As per Section 269 T of Income Tax Act, if the principal plus interest of term deposit is ₹ 20,000 or above, the payment should be made through credit to account or issuing account payee cheque or DD. It should not be paid in cash.

- 'Bulk Deposits mean deposits of ₹ 1 crore and above. Bank can refuse premature payment of Bulk deposits. In case of premature payment of FDR, penalty will be decided by the bank. However, penalty cannot be charged in case of premature payment in case of death of depositor.

- In case of death of depositor, interest for overdue period will be paid at saving rate if depositor died after maturity date. If depositor dies before maturity of FDR, interest for overdue period will be paid at FD rate as on date of maturity for the period overdue amount remained with the bank.

- The account holders are permitted to make premature encashment of such deposits. In such cases, the principal amount is paid along with interest as applicable for the period for which the deposit was actually with the bank, less some penalty on the applicable rate of interest, as per bank's policy.

- Loans against the Fixed Deposit may be given to the customers. The rules relating to margin and interest rate are decided by the bank.

Recurring Deposits

- In RD, fixed amounts are deposited by the depositor every month for a pre-determined period.

- Interest is generally cumulated at quarterly rests based on month-end balances in the account and pre-determined amount is fixed as payable at the end of the period of deposit.

- RD is not opened under FCNR (B) Scheme.

NOMINATION FACILITY IN BANKS

Section 45ZA to 45ZF of BR Act describes nomination facility in banks.

1) **Deposit Accounts:** Section 45ZA of BR Act provides Nomination for payment of depositors' money. Where a deposit is held by a banking company to the credit of one or more persons, the depositor or, as the case may be, all the depositors together, may nominate, in the prescribed manner, one person to whom in the event of the death of the sole depositor or the death of all the depositors, the amount of deposit may be returned by the banking company. Banks may extend the nomination facility also in respect of deposits held in the name of a sole proprietary concern.

2) **Safe Custody:** Section 45ZC of BR Act provides Nomination for return of articles kept in safe custody with banking company. Where any person leaves any article in safe custody with a banking company, such person may nominate, in the prescribed manner, on person to whom, in the event of the death of the person leaving the article in safe custody, such article may be returned by the banking company.

The banking company shall, before returning any articles under this section to the nominee or the person appointed under sub-section (2), prepare, in such manner as may be directed by the Reserve Bank from time to time, an inventory of the said articles which shall be signed by such nominee or person and shall deliver a copy of the inventory so prepared to such nominee or person. Banks should note that the facility of nomination is not available in case of deposit of safe custody articles by more than one person.

3) **Safety Lockers:** Section 45ZE of BR Act provides Nomination for Release of contents of safety lockers. Where an individual is the sole hirer of a locker from a banking company, whether such locker is in the safe deposit vault of such banking company or elsewhere, such individual may nominate one person to whom, in the event of the death of such individual, the banking company may give access to the locker and liberty to remove the contents of the locker.

If safety locker is hired by two or more individuals with operational instruction of 'either or survivor', then only one nominee is allowed. But where any such locker is hired from a banking company by two or more individuals jointly and under the contract of hire, the locker is to be operated under the joint signatures of two or more of such hirers, such hirers may nominate one or more persons (Maximum two as per IBA guideline) to whom, in the event of the death of such joint hirer or hirers, the banking company may give, jointly with the surviving joint hirer or joint hirers, as the case may be, access to the locker and liberty to remove the contents of such locker. Where the nominee is a minor, it shall be lawful for the depositor making the nomination to appoint in the prescribed manner any person to receive the amount of deposit in the event of his death during the minority of the nominee.

a) Unless the nomination is varied or cancelled, the nominee is entitled to all the rights of the depositors. Payment by a banking company in accordance with the provisions of this section shall constitute a full discharge to the banking company of its liability in respect of the deposit.

b) On the removal of the contents of any locker by any nominee or jointly by any nominee and survivors as aforesaid, the liability of the banking company in relation to the contents of the locker shall stand discharged.

c) Rule 2 to 4 of the Banking Companies (Nomination) Rules 1985 provides for the procedure and forms for making nomination in respect of commercial banks. In case of Co-operative banks, similar provisions are incorporated in the Co-operative banks (Nomination) Rules, 1985.

DIFFERENT TYPES OF CUSTOMERS

During the opening of accounts, the banker deals with different types of customers. The banker should acquaint himself with various laws governing different types of customers. The customers can be classified as follows:

1. **Personal Accounts:** Banker should take care and verify certain facts while opening of accounts of individual. As per Indian Contract Act 1872, a person is competent to enter into a valid contract and open a bank account provided:

   - Individual should be major, i.e. of 18 years of age.
   - He should be of sound mind,
   - He is otherwise not disqualified by any law,
   - He should not be an insolvent,
   - Drunken person is not legally competent to enter into a contract,
   - He should be in good sense while lending a loan and entering into a contract.

a) **Accounts of Single Individual:** This is purely a personal account in the name of an individual and is normally operated upon by the account holder himself. The account holder may authorise another person to operate on his account. For this purpose, he gives a Mandate or executes a Power of Attorney in favour of such a person.

   In order to avoid legal complications that may arise after the death of the account holder, it is desirable to suggest opening of a joint account in the names of two individuals (unless it is essential in certain circumstances to open an account in the single name only), and/or to obtain proper nomination.

b) **Joint Accounts of Individuals:** A joint account is opened in the names of more than one individual for convenience of operations and/ or to avoid legal complications upon death of one of the joint account holders. A joint account is neither a partnership nor a trust account. It is important to obtain clear and unambiguous instructions regarding the mode of operation and repayment of balance of a joint account in the event of death of one or more joint account holder(s). Different types of operational instructions are as under:

   (i) Jointly or Survivor   (ii) Either or Survivor
   (iii) Former or Survivor   (iv) Any one or Survivor

   One or more of the joint account holders can authorise operation on the account on his/their behalf by giving a Mandate or executing a Power of Attorney, but, such Mandate or Power of Attorney must be given by all the parties to the accounts. Addition/deletion of any name, material alteration, closure of account and operational instructions in the joint account can be changed by all the account holders jointly. However, in joint accounts with operational instructions "Former or Survivor", instructions can be changed/revoked only by Former.

c) **Illiterate Person:** Illiterate person is a person who cannot read or write. Such persons are competent to enter in to a valid contract. The account (other than Current Account) of such a person may be opened provided he calls on the Bank with a latest passport size photograph. Photograph is essential for identification. Thereupon, his thumb impression or mark should be obtained on the account opening form/card in the presence of the Bank's official. Such thumb impressions or marks affixed by illiterate persons on instruments are equivalent to their signatures. Any withdrawal/repayment of deposit amount and/or interest by way of withdrawal form or otherwise should similarly be affixed with the thumb impression or mark of the depositor.

d) **Blind Persons**: Blind Persons can operate the account in bank. Signature of Thumb impression of blind person in the A/c opening form to be witnessed by a person who should certify that contents of the A/c opening form were explained to the blind person in his presence. The sign may be authorised by bank officer and a witness known to both the bank and the blind person. He should always visit the branch for cash withdrawal. As per all banking facilities including net banking, ATM, Cheque Book, Locker facility, loans to be offered to visually challenged customers without discrimination.

e) **Minors' Accounts:** A minor is a person below the age of 18 years. A minor is under legal incapacity to contract by himself and, therefore, a guardian recognised by law along can deal with the person and property of the minor. The term "guardian" includes a natural guardian or guardian appointed by the Court of Law. Ordinarily, an account of a minor is opened and operated upon by the natural guardian of the minor or by the guardian appointed by the Court.

   According to RBI guidelines (RBI/2013-14/581 DBOD.No.Leg.BC.108/09.07.005/2013-14) with a view to promote the objective of financial inclusion and also to bring uniformity among banks in opening and operating minors' accounts, banks are advised as under:

   a. A savings /fixed / recurring bank deposit account can be opened by a minor of any age through his/her natural or legally appointed guardian.

   b. Minors above the age of 10 years may be allowed to open and operate savings bank accounts independently, if they so desire. Banks may, however, keeping in view their risk management systems, fix limits in terms of age and amount up to which minors may be allowed to operate the deposit accounts independently. They can also decide, in their own discretion, as to what minimum documents are required for opening of accounts by minors.

c. On attaining majority, the erstwhile minor should confirm the balance in his/her account and if the account is operated by the natural guardian/ legal guardian, fresh operating instructions and specimen signature of erstwhile minor should be obtained and kept on record for all operational purposes.

Banks are free to offer additional banking facilities like internet banking, ATM/ debit card, cheque book facility etc., subject to the safeguards that minor accounts are not allowed to be overdrawn and that these always remain in credit. It is permissible to open any type of deposit account in the name of and/ or to be operated upon by a minor within the framework of rules of business of the Bank as outlined hereunder, but no Current Account should be opened.

According to Section 26 of NI Act, a minor can draw, endorse or negotiate a cheque or a bill but he cannot be held liable on such cheques or bill. Minor can be admitted to the benefits of partnership with the consent of other partners but cannot be made liable for the losses. A minor may be appointed as an agent on behalf of his principal but legally he cannot be held responsible to his principal.

When the minor becomes major he has the sole right to operate the account and guardian's power ceases. The payment should be made to the erstwhile minor upon providing his identity. When the account is operated upon by the guardian on behalf of the minor a Balance Confirmation Letter duly signed by the erstwhile minor and verified by the guardian should be obtained. If account is operated by the minor himself, the erstwhile minor should be asked to sign a Balance Confirmation Letter.

2. **Hindu Undivided Family (HUF):** Hindu Undivided Family' otherwise known as 'Joint Hindu Family' property, business or ancestral estates and its common possession, enjoyment ownership is the basis of formation of HUF. As per Hindu law, the Hindus, Sikhs and Jains can form HUF.

    HUF is governed basically by two schools of thought. In Bengal, it is governed by Dayabhag Law. In other parts of India, it is governed by Mitakshara Law. The law governing Hindu Undivided Family is codified under Hindu Code and now, succession among Hindus is governed by Hindu Succession Act, 1956. Part of this Act was amended in 2005 by the Hindu Succession (Amendment) Act, 2005.

Creation of Hindu Law under which all major members of the family get right by birth in the ancestral property of the family.

HUF property is managed by senior-most major male member called 'Manager' or 'Karta'. Upon death of Karta, next senior male coparcener becomes Karta. Joint owner of HUF are known as coparceners. It consists of one common living ancestor and his all male & female (female from Sept. 2005) descendents up to three generations next to him. HUF cannot enter into a partnership as per Supreme Court judgement of 1998.

HUF account is operated by Karta. Karta has authority to borrow money for the family necessities & for ancestral family business. Documents are to be executed by Karta. All major coparceners are to be made guarantors. The liability of the 'Karta' is unlimited, whereas the liability of the coparceners is limited to their shares in the joint family estate.

3. **Proprietorship Firm:** Business is wholly owned by an individual. In law, there is no difference between proprietor & the firm. In all respects, it is an account in the name of an individual only except that it is operated upon by the proprietor on behalf of firm. The firm should have PAN or GST Number. Proprietorship letter in bank's Proforma is to be obtained. Proof of proprietorship may be obtained. Creditors have recourse not only against assets of the firm but also against private assets of the proprietor. Proprietor can authorize another person to operate the account through Mandate or Power of Attorney.

4. **Partnership Firm:** Partnership is the relation between persons who have agreed to share profits of business carried on by all or any one of them acting for all (Indian Partnership Act 1932). As per RBI instruction now Registration Certificate and Partnership deed to be obtained. As per Indian Companies Act 2013, Maximum number of partner can be up to 100 in a firm (Earlier number of partners was restricted to 20 for other businesses & 10 for banking business). Partnership is not a distinct legal person from the partners who have made partnership firm. HUF cannot enter into a partnership as per Supreme Court judgement of 1998. The firm should have PAN or GST Number. A partner cannot delegate his authority to operate the account.

A minor cannot be a partner, but he can be admitted for his benefit in an existing partnership firm. The particulars of minor partner, particularly the DOB should be properly recorded.

In case of death/retirement/insolvency of a partner account should be stopped, if the balance is in debit a fresh account should be opened after fresh sanction of limit. In case of dispute when one partner revokes the authority against the other partner, operation in the account should be stopped.

Dissolution of the Partnership firm can takes place by following ways:
a) By mutual consent;
b) Death/insolvency/retirement of a partner;
c) Operation of Law (insolvency of all partners, business becoming unlawful, dissolution by a competent court; and
d) In case of automatic dissolution.

5. **Limited Liability Partnership (LLP):** A limited liability partnership (LLP) is a partnership in which some or all partners (depending on the jurisdiction) have limited liabilities. LLP is governed by limited liability partnership Act 2008. Liability is limited to the extent of his contribution in the LLP. Minimum two designated partners and no limit on maximum number of Partners. A partner is not liable for another partner's misconduct or negligence, except in certain cases. LLP is a legal entity separate from its partner. It has own assets in its name. Since LLP contains element of both 'a corporate structure' as well as 'a partnership firm structure' LLP is called a hybrid between a company and a partnership. It has perpetual succession (death of a partner does not affect the existence of LLP). Partners have a right to manage the business directly. Firms and companies can get themselves converted into LLP. LLP cannot raise fund from public.

6. **Companies:** Companies are defined in Indian Company Act 1956. As per the provision of Company Act 2013 (implemented with effect from 1st April 2014), recognizes—a joint Stock Company is a legal person with perpetual entity and is distinct from its members. A company or association of persons can be created at law as legal person so that the company in itself can accept limited liability for civil responsibility. Because companies are legal persons, they also may associate and register themselves as companies otherwise it will be treated as illegal. Address of the registered office is compulsory. It is the address at which all the documents & notices may be served upon the company. Cheques favouring company are not to be credited to the personal accounts of the Directors or other officers of the company.

Following documents are required for account opening of a company:

a) **Certificate of Incorporation:** Issued by Registrar of Companies. It is conclusive proof for incorporation of the company & compliance of all formalities by promoters.

b) **Certificate of commencement of Business:** A company having share capital cannot commence business until it has obtained the certificate to commence business (COB) from the concerned Registrar of Companies. Certificate of commencement of business is not required by Private Ltd Company as its shares are closely held and it can commence business on its incorporation.

c) **Memorandum of Association:** Company's fundamental & unalterable law. Embodies Company's name, Authorized capital, Objectives of the company, Liability of shareholders.

d) **Articles of Association**: Regulations controlling internal management of the company. Rights & powers of the Directors, rules about conduct of company meetings & business, Procedure for borrowing & limit on borrowing etc.

e) **Copy of Board Resolution**: Certified copy of Board Resolution authorizing to borrow from the Bank with details of limit, security etc., Persons who are authorized to sign the security documents and operate the Bank Account, persons in whose presence Seal of the company will be affixed to the security documents.

f) **Company Common Seal**: Common seal if any, of the company available should be embossed on bank's documents. As per Companies (Amendment) Act, 2015 and RBI instruction, Company Common Seal is not necessary, if other documents available during current account opening.

Different Types of Companies in India

(i) **Private Company**: A Private Company has share holders with limited liability and its shares may not be offered to the general public. Private Limited Company having a no minimum paid-up share capital limitation now. (As per Companies (Amendment) Act, 2015, paid-up share capital of one lakh rupee or such higher paid-up share capital as may be prescribed is omitted now). It has minimum two members and maximum members restricted to two hundred and Minimum two directors and no maximum number of directors is restricted.

(ii) **Public Company:** Public company means a company which is not a private company and has no minimum paid-up share capital limitation now (As per Companies (Amendment) Act, 2015, paid-up share capital of five lakh rupee or such higher paid-up share capital as may be prescribed is omitted now). Shares are offered to the public and are listed on stock exchange. Minimum seven members, no limit of maximum number. Minimum 3 directors maximum 15 director limits. Provided that a company may appoint more than fifteen directors after passing a special resolution (As per Companies Act 2013, no Central Govt. permission required now). At least one-woman director shall be on Board. Certificate of commencement of business is must to do any type of business.

(iii) Government Company: "Government Company" means any company in which not less than fifty one percent of paid-up share capital is held by the Central Government, or by any State Government, or partly by the Central Government and partly by one or more State Governments and includes a company which is a subsidiary company of such a Government company.

(iv) One Person Company: The Companies Act 2013 Act introduces a new type of entity to the existing list i.e., apart from forming a public or private limited company, the 2013 act enables the formation of a new entity a 'one-person company' (OPC). An OPC means a company with only one person having a sole member [section 3(1) of 2013 Act]. An OPC can be formed only by an Indian Resident and citizen.

(v) Other Companies: As per Companies Act 1956, companies can be classified on the basis of time, place of incorporation and nature of working share capital as follows:

a) Foreign Company: It means a company incorporated outside India and having a place of business in India whether by itself or through an agent, physically or through electronic mode and conduct any business activity in India in any other manner.

b) Existing Company: A company which is established before the Company Act 1956 is called Existing Company.

c) Holding Company: A company is known as the holding company of another company if it has control over another company.

d) Subsidiary Company: A company is known as subsidiary of another company when control is exercised by the latter over the former. A company is to be deemed to be subsidiary company of another.

7. Trust: Trusts are governed by the Indian Trust Act, 1882. A trust is created when ownership of a property is transferred to someone for holding or managing it for benefit of another person(s). Trust may be public charitable trust or private trust (for benefit of private individuals). Trusts managed by trustees. Loan can be granted if it is for the purpose of the trust. Trustee is authorised to borrow as per the trust deed. Original Trust Deed to be examined before financing. Certificate of Registration under Public Trust Act to be examined and copy to be kept on record.

8. Clubs & Societies: Clubs & Societies are non-profit making organisation and represent a group of persons. These are normally incorporated under Cooperative Society Act. Clubs can be registered under Society Act 1860, or Company Act 1956. These get the status of a legal entity only after their incorporation in their own name. These are governed by rules & regulations (bye laws). Certified true copy of resolution. Cheques favouring society, club, association not to be collected in individual accounts of office bearers or employees.

TEST YOURSELF

1. As per Indian Contract Act 1872, who is not competent to contract?
(a) Minor
(b) Insolvent
(c) Insane
(d) All of the above

2. For opening of bank account, registration of a partnership firm is:
(a) Optional
(b) Compulsory
(c) Not required
(d) As per partnership deed

3. As per Indian Companies Act 2013, Maximum number of partner in a partnership firm can be:
(a) 10
(b) 20
(c) 100
(d) 200

4. If partnership deed is silent about operation of the account, then the account will be operated by:

(a) Any of the partner
(b) All partners jointly
(c) First partner as per deed
(d) As per instruction of the partners

5. If bank finance to the partnership firm, the liability of a partner for the loan is:
(a) Unlimited
(b) Limited to their share in the business
(c) Limited
(d) No liability of partners

6. In a Government company, number of shares held by the Government are at least:
(a) 50%
(b) 51%
(c) 75%
(d) 100%

7. HUF property is managed by 'Manager' or 'Karta'. Who becomes the 'Manager' or 'Karta'?

(a) Senior most major male member
(b) Senior most major female member
(c) Appointed by all major coparceners
(d) Any of the major coparceners

8. If bank finances the limited liability partnership firm, the liability of a partner for the loan is:
(a) Unlimited
(b) Limited to their share in the business
(c) Limited
(d) No liability of partners

9. Embodies Company's name, Authorized capital, Objectives of the company, Liability of shareholders are written in:
(a) Certificate of Incorporation
(b) Memorandum of Association
(c) Article of Association
(d) None of the above

10. A company which is established before the Company Act 1956 is called ______.
(a) Holding Company   (b) Subsidiary Company
(c) Existing Company   (d) Foreign Company

11. Which is the correct statement about 'Public Company?
(a) Its share is listed in stock exchange
(b) Minimum seven members and no limit of maximum number
(c) Minimum three directors and maximum no limit
(d) All of the above

12. As per Indian Contracts Act 1872, a person who is competent to enter into a valid contract:
(a) He is otherwise disqualified by any law
(b) He should not be a solvent
(c) Drunken person is legally competent to enter into a contract
(d) He should be in good sense while lending a loan and entering into a contract

13. Which is not correct about an Illiterate person?
(a) Illiterate persons are competent to enter into a valid contract
(b) Photograph is essential for identification
(c) Normally, Left Hand Thumb impression (LHT) of male & Right Hand Thumb impression (RHT) of female is to be obtained
(d) None of the above

14. Which is not correct about Proprietory firm?
(a) In law, there is no difference between proprietor and the firm.

(b) Creditors have recourse not only against assets of the firm but also against private assets of the proprietor.
(c) Bank insists that proprietor should execute the security documents in the capacity as Proprietor on behalf of the firm as well as in his individual capacity.
(d) Proprietor cannot authorize another person to operate the account through Mandate or Power of Attorney.

15. Which is not correct about limited liability partnership (LLP)?
(a) LLP is governed by limited liability partnership Act 2008.
(b) Minimum 3 designated partner and no limit on maximum number of Partners.
(c) LLP is a legal entity separate from its partner.
(d) LLP cannot raise fund from public.

16. Which is not necessary for financing a Private Company?
(a) Memorandum of Association
(b) Articles of Association
(c) Certificate of Commencement of Business
(d) Board Resolution

17. A company is known as the _________ of another company if it has control over another company.
(a) Holding company   (b) Existing company
(c) Other company   (d) Foreign company

18. Which is not a statutory company in India?
(a) Reserve Bank of India
(b) Tata Iron & Steel Company
(c) The Life Insurance Corporation of India
(d) The Food Corporation of India

19. Which is not correct about Trusts?
(a) Trusts are governed by the Indian Trust Act, 1982.
(b) A Trust may be public charitable trust or private trust (for benefit of private individuals).
(c) Loan can be granted if it is for the purpose of the trust. Trustee is authorised to borrow as per the trust deed.
(d) Certificate of Registration under Public Trust Act to be examined and copy to be kept on record.

20. While giving a loan to a club or society or school the bank should study:
(a) Bye-laws   (b) Copy of Resolution
(c) Rules & Regulations   (d) All of the above

ANSWER

1	2	3	4	5	6	7	8	9	10
(d)	(b)	(c)	(b)	(a)	(b)	(a)	(b)	(b)	(c)

11	12	13	14	15	16	17	18	19	20
(d)	(d)	(d)	(d)	(b)	(c)	(a)	(b)	(a)	(d)

OPERATIONAL ASPECTS OF LOAN ACCOUNTS

INTRODUCTION

Lending is an important activity of banking industry. Bank invests public deposit in the form of lending and earns profit. Quality of the advances indicates bank's image in the market. A banker should have a thorough knowledge of the requirement of the customer and should be in a position to cater to the needs of the customer. Credit facility is an agreement with bank that enables a person or organization to take credit or borrow money when it is needed.

RBI GUIDELINES FOR LENDING BY BANKING COMPANIES

Banks accept deposit for the lending and investment purpose. Section 21 of the BR Act explains the power of Reserve Bank to control advances by banking companies. Reserve Bank may determine policy regarding advances and issue suitable directions to the banks in the public interest or in the interests of depositors or in the interest of banking policy. The policy may be determined in relation to advances to be followed by banking companies generally or by any specific bank. All banking companies or the banking company concerned, shall be bound to follow the policy.

The Reserve Bank may give directions to banking companies, either generally or to any banking company or group of banking companies. Every banking company shall be bound to comply with any directions given to it on the following matters:

(a) The purposes for which advances may or may not be made;

(b) The margins to be maintained in respect of secured advances;

(c) The maximum amount limit of advances or other financial accommodation which, may be made by that banking company to any one company, firm, association of persons or individual;

(d) The maximum amount up to which, guarantees may be given by a banking company on behalf of any one company, firm, association of persons or individual; and

(e) The rate of interest and other terms and conditions on which advances or other financial accommodation may be made or guarantees may be given.

OPERATIONAL PROCESS OF LOANS

1. **Receipt of Loan Application:** The request is generally in a standard format of the bank. The applications are entered in a Loan Applications Received Register. Required documents are also submitted with application.

2. **Assessment of Viability and Credit Worthiness:** The degree of scrutiny depends largely on the amount of the loan. Following parameters are generally considered to ensure that it is technically feasible, economically viable and commercially acceptable:

    a) Experience, competence and profile of the promoters of the unit.

    b) Performance of the unit in comparison to its peers.

    c) Conduct of its accounts with the existing lenders, if any.

d) Technical feasibility of the proposed unit.

e) Availability of inputs for production and commercial viability of the proposed business.

f) Ratio analysis to check unit's growth, its financial position, liquidity and the stake of promoters.

g) Guarantees and collateral securities offered.

h) Unit's capability to achieve the projected cash flows.

i) CIBIL Report, RBI List of defaulters, Credit report from other banks.

j) Locational restrictions, Govt, policy about particular industry, etc.

3. **Sanction:** Loan is sanctioned within powers delegated to concerned officials. If proposal is found to be acceptable, appraisal note along with necessary supporting papers is put up to sanctioning authority with recommendations. Detailed terms and conditions are written in the sanction letter which are communicated to applicant and his consent sought.

4. **Disbursement:** Documents prescribed by the bank are obtained and charges are created. Bank's charge is noted with Registrar of Companies, CERSAI, Transport Authority, insurance company, land records authority, etc. and then the loan is released.

5. **Monitoring and Supervision:** Monitoring is done through inspection, review of conduct of account. Conducting ongoing monitoring of the business relationship including ensuring that the transactions being conducted are consistent with the knowledge of the customer, the business and risk profile, including, where necessary, the source of funds and ensuring that documents, data or information held are kept up-to-date.

6. **Inspections:** Personal visit to the Unit/ office/ residence of the Borrower/Guarantor is called inspection. Pre-sanction Inspection is done before the sanction of the proposal and Post-sanction Inspection is done after disbursement. Post-sanction Inspections should be done on regular basis for proper monitoring of the loan account. Purpose of Post-sanction Inspections are as under:

a) To ensure that the amount disbursed has been utilised for purposes for which the loan was sanctioned. To ensure that the borrower has not availed of finance from any other lender without bank's permission.

b) To check that the borrower has not acquired/ disposed-off any asset without bank's consent.

c) To ensure that the borrower has not availed of finance against unpaid stocks.

d) To cross-check the figures declared in the stock statements with the books and physical verification of stocks.

e) To check that the unit has been working at the projected levels.

f) To check that there is a regular turnover of stocks and the unit does not carry any obsolete, unusable stocks. Review of the conduct of the account: By scrutinising the stock statements and other relevant financial data periodically and analysing it.

TYPES OF CREDIT FACILITIES BY BANK

The business of lending is carried on by the bank by offering various credit facilities to its customers. On the basis of the security bank credit can be classified in two types:

1. **Secured Advance:** The advance which is secured by primary or collateral security is called Secured Advance. In the event of loan default, the lender can take possession of the asset and use it to cover the loan. e.g. Business loan, Housing loan etc.

2. **Unsecured Advances:** Unsecured advances don't have asset either primary or collateral. These are also called clean advance. Unsecured loans rely solely on borrower's credit history and his income to qualify for the loan. e.g. Credit Card, Clean personal loan, Education loan (small) etc.

All types of credit facilities may be classified into two groups on the basis of fund out flow:

1. **Fund Based Credit**   2. **Non-Fund Based Credit**

1. **Fund Based Credit**: Fund Based Credit is the credit facility which involves direct outflow of Bank's fund to the borrower. Various types of Fund Based Credit facilities are as follows:

a) **Loan:** A term/demand loan is simply a loan provided for meeting the capital expenditure need and business purposes that needs to be paid back within a specified timeframe along with interest. Loans are given for purchase of machinery, equipments or any fixed assets for starting a business or fulfilling personal needs. Repayment Schedule, period of the loan, mode of disbursement, rate of interest and other terms are predetermined terms.

The loan which is repaid up to three years is called 'Demand Loan' and If repayment schedule is more than three years is called 'Term Loan'. Loans can be classified in three types on the basis of repayment period:

(i) **Short Term Loan:** Usually short-term loans are repayable within one year.

(ii) **Medium Term Loan:** It is generally repayable between one and three years.

(iii) **Long Term Loan:** It is repayable in more than three years.

b) **Cash Credit:** For running the business, borrower needs working capital to meet day-to-day expenses, stock and book debt. It refers to credit facility in which borrower can borrow any time within the agreed limit for certain period for their working capital need. It is a running account facility where credit and debit both are permitted. It is secured by way of Hypothecation of Stock (goods), Debtors (Book Debts) and all other Current Assets of the business generated during the course of business. Cash credit can also be secured by way of mortgage of immovable properties (as collateral security).

c) **Over Draft:** An overdraft allows a current account holder to withdraw in excess of their credit balance up to a sanctioned limit. Overdraft may be permitted without any security as 'clean overdraft' for temporary periods to enable the borrower to tide over some emergent financial difficulty. 'Secured overdraft' facility is secured by way of Mortgage of immovable properties and pledge of F.D., Bonds, Shares securities, Gold & silver and all other current assets of the business generated during the course of business.

d) **Credit Card:** Credit cards serve many useful functions, including the ability to pay for purchases when you don't have cash on hand. The credit card issuer essentially loans you the money to make the purchase, and you will be able to repay that loan at a later date while being charged a certain interest rate. The credit limit of the Credit Card depends upon the credit history and regular income of the card holder.

e) **Bridge Loan:** Loans given to businesses who might be in need of instant cash flow to finance a project. Bridge loans are normally obtained while the borrower is waiting for long-term financing to go through. These loans are repaid out of the amount of term loan sanctioned or the fund raised in the capital market.

f) **Composite Loans:** It is a loan which is granted for both buying capital assets and to meet working capital requirements. Composite Loans are usually given to an MSME Unit, cottage industry, artisan, farmers etc.

g) **Retail Loan:** Retail loans are those loans which are given by the banks to meet personal needs. Retail loans are smaller in size as compared to corporate loans. Home loan, Vehicle loan, Education loan, personal loan, Vacation purpose, medical purpose etc are categorized as retail loans.

h) **Bill Finance:** Bill discounting is a major activity with some of the Banks. Under this type of lending, Bank takes the bill drawn by borrower on his (borrower's) customer and pays him immediately deducting some amount as discount/commission. The Bank then presents the Bill to the borrower's customer on the due date of the Bill and collects the proceeds. If the bill is delayed, the borrower or his customer pays the Bank a pre-determined interest depending upon the terms of transaction. The transaction is practically an advance against the security of the bill which is due for payment.

i) **Export Finance:** Banks grant export credit on very liberal terms to meet all the financial requirements of exporters. The bank credit for exports can broadly be divided in two groups as under:

(i) **Pre-Shipment advances/packing credit advances:** It is a credit facility which is sanctioned to an exporter in the Pre-Shipment stage. Such credit facilitates the exporter to purchase raw materials at competitive rates and manufacture or produce goods according to the requirement of the buyer and organize to have it packed for onward export.

(ii) **Post-Shipment Finance:** Post shipment credit is a working capital facility granted by a bank to the exporter of goods/services from date of extending credit after shipment of goods/rendering of services to the date of realization of export proceeds. As per the extant instructions, the maximum period prescribed for realization of export proceeds is 12 months from date of shipment.

2. Non-Fund Based Credit: Non-fund based credits are such facilities extended by banks which do not involve outgo of funds from the bank when the customer avails the facilities but may at a later date crystallise into financial liability if the customer fails to honour the commitment made by availing these facilities. The banker undertakes a risk to the amount on happening of a contingency. Different types of Non-fund based credit facilities are as follow:

(i) **Letter of Credit:** Letter of Credit is an undertaking issued by a Bank (Issuing Bank), on behalf of the buyer (the importer), to the seller (the exporter) to pay for goods and services provided that the seller presents documents which comply with the terms and conditions of the Letter of Credit, within a specified time. The banks follow the Uniform Customs & Practices relating to Documentary Credits 600 (UCPDC 600) framed by International Chamber of Commerce. LC issued by the banker is irrevocable and shall not cancel without the consent of both the buyer and the seller.

(ii) Bank Guarantee: A Bank guarantee is a promise from a bank that the liabilities of a debtor will be met in the event that debtor fails to fulfil your contractual obligations. It is a promise from a bank or other lending institution that if a particular borrower defaults on a loan, the bank will cover the loss. It may be Financial Guarantee, Performance Guarantee or Deferred Payment Guarantee.

(iii) Derivative Products: In addition to the traditional non-fund facilities, banks are now offering the derivative products to their clients to enable them to hedge their currency and interest rate risks.

(iv) Buyer Credit: It is a short-term credit available to an importer (buyer) from overseas lenders such as banks and other financial institution for goods they are importing. The overseas banks usually lend the importer (buyer) based on the letter of comfort (a bank guarantee) issued by the importer's bank.

First let us try to understand it from a layman's perspective: Suppose I have to buy a certain high-end mobile phone from Delhi, but I am not able to go to Delhi, for this purpose. I live in Patna, but one of my friends Mr. Sanjay studies there in JNU. I will ask the supplier to send me the mobile and I assure him that I will make arrangements to make the payment to him through my friend Sanjay. The shopkeeper couriers the mobile to me. Sanjay pays the bill to the shopkeeper. I, in turn, send an NEFT to Sanjay's account.

Now coming to the exact definition, in order to make the payment of import bills, the importer buyer, say, in India requests his banker, say, Bank of India to arrange credit for him in foreign currency from its correspondent bank, say, Bank of India in New York. Conceding to his request, Indian Bank arranges a loan to him, say, for $ 1 million from Bank of America and makes it available to the importer for making payment of import bills. Sometimes importer himself strikes a deal by negotiating with various banks to get buyer's credit at a very competitive rate, say LIBOR+0.80 or so. Later on the importer repays this amount either through their EEFC account, realization proceeds of export bills etc. Such arrangements are known as Buyer's Credit.

As the ROI of such loans are cheaper as compared to bill finance rates, now-a-days, importer customers prefer to adopt the route of Buyer's Credit instead of availing bill negotiating facility under Letter of Credit.

(v) Supplier Credit: Under such credit facility an exporter extends credit to a foreign importer to finance his purchase. Usually the importer pays a portion of the contract value in cash and issues a Promissory note as evidence of his obligation to pay the balance over a period of time. The exporter thus accepts a deferred payment from the importer and may be able to obtain cash payment by discounting or selling such promissory note created with his bank.

Let us first understand the concept from a layman's point of view: The milkman gives us milk daily for all 30/31 days of a month, but he asks for money only at the end of the month. So, all these 30 days he has been extending credit to us. Such type of credit extended by the seller or supplier to the purchaser is termed as Supplier's Credit.

Now coming to the precise definition, such type of credit is extended by the exporter supplier to the buyer or importer of the capital goods. The terms can be down payment with the balance payable in instalments. To finance the credit given to the importer under such arrangements, the exporter raises a loan from his banker under the export credit scheme in force.

DIFFERENT TYPES OF BORROWERS

Bank accepts deposits for lending and investment purpose. During the lending, the banker deals with different types of borrowers. The banker should acquaint himself with various laws governing different types of borrowers.

The borrowers can be classified as follows:

1. Individual
2. Hindu Undivided Family (HUF)
3. Proprietorship Firm
4. Partnership Firm
5. Limited Liability Partnership (LLP)
6. Companies
7. Statutory Corporation
8. Trust
9. Club & Co-operative Societies

1. Individual: Banker should take care and verify the certain fact while lending to an individual. As per Indian Contracts Act 1872, a person is competent to enter into a valid contract provided:

- Individual should be major, i.e., of 18 years of age.
- He should be of sound mind,
- He is otherwise not disqualified by any law,
- He should not be an insolvent,
- Drunken person is not legally competent to enter into a contract,
- He should be in good sense while lending a loan and entering into a contract.

Different types of individual borrowers are as under:

a) **Single Borrower:** This is purely a personal account in the name of an individual and is normally executed by the account holder himself. Banker must verify the identity, character, credential and capacity of the individual borrower, whether person is capable to repay the loan and has ability to enter into valid contract or not.

b) **Joint Borrowers:** Two or more persons or a group of individuals who do not constitute a registered body of association are called joint borrowers. All documents are signed by all jointly and severally. It means all are jointly liable plus each one of them is individually liable for repayment of Bank's dues. In case of death or insolvency of any one or more of joint borrowers, account showing debit balance is broken to determine liability of deceased joint account holder/s.

c) **Illiterate Person:** Illiterate person is a person who cannot read or write. Such persons are competent to enter into a valid contract. We use thumb impression for entering into an agreement with them. Normally, Left Hand Thumb impression (LHT) of male & Right-Hand Thumb impression (RHT) of female is to be obtained. Thumb impression must be authenticated by bank official. Photograph is essential for identification. While opening account and providing loans, evidence to be created that the person understood terms & conditions beyond doubt.

d) **Loan to Minor:** Person below the age of 18 under Indian Majority Act and 21 years if he is a ward, under the Guardians and Wards Act 1890 is considered a 'Minor' in the eyes of law. Under the law a 'Minor' is not capable of entering into contract and such contract entered into by a minor is null & void. It will not stand in law and the assets of the minor are not available to the Bank for appropriation. Even if an advance is granted to the minor against the guarantee of third party who is legally competent to execute guarantee, legal remedy to recover the dues from guarantor is not available to the Bank.

Exception for Financing to Minor: Normally Banks do not finance to the minors. However, there is an *exception* where finance can be made for the benefit of a minor. Security documents in such cases are executed by the Guardian of the minor. Indian Contract act (Sec. 26) permits "a minor can draw, endorse, deliver and negotiate instruments so as to bind all other parties except himself". Even a minor can be a partner and may make an agreement which will be binding on other partners but will not be binding on him.

2. **Hindu Undivided Family (HUF):** 'Hindu Undivided Family' otherwise known as 'Joint Hindu Family.' Property, business or ancestral estates and its common possession is the basis of formation of HUF. As per Hindu law, the Hindus, Sikhs and Jains can form HUF.

HUF is governed basically by two schools of thought. In Bengal, it is governed by **Dayabhag law,** in other parts of India, it is governed by **Mitakshara Law.** The law governing Hindu Undivided Family is codified under Hindu Code and now, succession among Hindus is governed by Hindu Succession Act, 1956. Part of this Act was amended in 2005 by the Hindu Succession (Amendment) Act, 2005. Creation of Hindu Law under which all major members of the family get right by birth in the ancestral property of the family.

HUF property is managed by senior-most major male member called 'Manager' or 'Karta'. Upon death of Karta, next senior male coparcener becomes Karta. Joint owners of HUF are known as coparceners. It consists of one common living ancestor and his all male and female (female from Sept. 2005) descendants up to three generations next to him. HUF cannot enter into a partnership as per Supreme Court judgement of 1998.

HUF account is operated by Karta. Karta has authority to borrow money for the family necessities and for ancestral family business. Documents are to be executed by Karta. All major coparceners are to be made guarantors. The liability of the 'Karta' is unlimited, whereas the liability of the coparceners is limited to their shares in the joint family estate.

3. **Proprietorship Firm:** Business is wholly owned by an individual. In law, there is no difference between proprietor and the firm. In all respects, it is an account in the name of an individual only

except that it is operated upon by the proprietor on behalf of firm. The firm should have PAN or TAN. Proprietorship letter in bank's Proforma is to be obtained. Proof of proprietorship may be obtained. Creditors have recourse not only against assets of the firm but also against private assets of the proprietor. Bank insists that proprietor should execute the security documents in the capacity as Proprietor on behalf of the firm as well as in his individual capacity. Proprietor can authorize another person to operate the account through Mandate or Power of Attorney.

4. **Partnership Firm:** Partnership is the relation between persons who have agreed to share profits of business carried on by all or any one of them acting for all (Indian Partnership Act 1932). As per RBI instruction now Registration Certificate and Partnership deed to be obtained. As per Indian Companies Act 2013, Maximum number of partners can be up to 100 (excluding minor) in a firm. (Earlier number of partners was restricted to 20 for other businesses & 10 for banking business). Partnership is not a distinct legal person from the partners who have made partnership firm. HUF cannot enter into a partnership as per Supreme Court judgement of 1998. The firm should have PAN or TAN. Partner in trading firm has power to borrow money on behalf of the firm and implied powers to sell or pledge any of the partnership property. Partners will sign on behalf of firm and also in their individual capacity. A partner cannot delegate his authority to operate the account. A minor cannot be a partner, but he can be admitted for his benefit in an existing partnership firm. The particulars of minor partner, particularly the DOB should be properly recorded.

In case of death/retirement/insolvency of a partner account should be stopped, if the balance is in debit and a fresh account should be opened after fresh sanction of limit. In case of dispute when one partner revokes the authority against the other partner, operation in the account should be stopped.

Dissolution of the Partnership firm can take place by following ways:
a. By mutual consent;
b. Death/insolvency/retirement of a partner;
c. Operation of Law (insolvency of all partners, business becoming unlawful, dissolution by a competent court, and
d. In case of automatic dissolution.

5. **Limited Liability Partnership (LLP):** A limited liability partnership (LLP) is a partnership in which some or all partners (depending on the jurisdiction) have limited liabilities. LLP is governed by limited liability partnership Act 2008. Liability is limited to the extent of his contribution in the LLP. Minimum 2 designated partners and no limit on maximum number of Partners. A partner is not liable for another partner's misconduct or negligence, except in certain cases. LLP is a legal entity separate from its partner. It has own assets in his name. Since LLP contains element of both 'a corporate structure' as well as 'a partnership firm structure' LLP is called a hybrid between a company and a partnership. It has perpetual succession (death of a partner does not affect the existence of LLP). Partners have a right to manage the business directly. Firms and companies can get themselves converted into LLP. LLP cannot raise fund from public.

6. **Companies:** Companies are defined in Indian Company Act 1956. As per the provision of Company Act 2013 (implemented with effect from 1ˢᵗ April 2014), recognizes—a joint Stock Company is a legal person with perpetual entity and is distinct from its members. A company or association of persons can be created at law as legal person so that the company in itself can accept limited liability for civil responsibility. Because companies are legal persons, they also may associate and register themselves as companies otherwise it will be treated as illegal. Address of the registered office is compulsory. It is the address at which all the documents and notices may be served upon the company. Cheques favouring company are not to be credited to the personal accounts of the Directors or other officers of the company.

Following documents are required for account opening and lending to a company:

a) **Certificate of Incorporation:** Issued by Registrar of Companies. It is conclusive proof for incorporation of the company and compliance of all formalities by promoters.

b) **Certificate of Commencement of Business:** A company having share capital cannot commence business until it has obtained the certificate to commence business (COB) from the concerned Registrar of Companies. Certificate of commencement of business is not required by Private Ltd. Co. as its shares are closely held and it can commence business on its incorporation.

c) **Memorandum of Association:** Company's fundamental and unalterable law. Embodies

Company's name, Authorized capital, Objectives of the company, Liability of shareholders.

d) Articles of Association: Regulations controlling internal management of the company. Rights and powers of the Directors, rules about conduct of company meetings & business, Procedure for borrowing & limit on borrowing etc.

e) Copy of Board Resolution: Certified copy of Board Resolution authorizing to borrow from the Bank with details of limit, security etc., Persons who are authorized to sign the security documents and operate the Bank Account, persons in whose presence Seal of the company will be affixed to the security documents.

f) Company Common Seal: Common seal, if any of the company available should be embossed on bank's documents. As per RBI instruction Company Common Seal is not necessary, if other documents available during current account opening.

As per Companies (Amendment) Act, 2015, the following proviso regarding Company Common Seal shall be inserted, namely:

"Provided that in case a company does not have a common seal, the authorisation under this sub-section shall be made by two directors or by a director and the Company Secretary, wherever the company has appointed a Company Secretary."

Different Types of Companies in India:

(i) Private Company: Private Company has shareholders with limited liability and its shares may not be offered to the general public. Shareholders of private companies limited by shares are often bound to offer the shares to their fellow shareholders prior to selling them to a third party. Private Limited Company having a no minimum paid-up share capital limitation now. **(As per Companies (Amendment) Act, 2015, paid-up share capital of one lakh rupee or such higher paid-up share capital as may be prescribed is omitted now).** It has minimum two members and maximum member restricted to two hundred and Minimum two directors and no maximum number of directors is restricted.

(ii) Public Company: Public company means a company which is not a private company and has no minimum paid-up share capital limitation now **(As per Companies (Amendment) Act, 2015, paid-up share capital of five lakh rupee or such higher paid-up share capital as may be prescribed is omitted now).** Shares are offered to the public and are listed on stock exchange. Minimum seven members and no limit of maximum number. Minimum 3 directors with maximum 15 director limit. Provided that a company may appoint more than fifteen directors after passing a special resolution (As per Companies Act 2013, no Central Govt. permission required now). At least one-woman director shall be on Board. Certificate of commencement of business is must to do any type of business.

(iii) The public limited company can be further classified as:

a) Limited Liability Company: Liability of the member is limited to their contribution of capital.

b) Unlimited Liability Company: An unlimited company is a company having no limit on the liability of its members.

c) Limited by Guarantee: It is a registered company in which the liability of members is limited to such amounts as they may respectively undertake by the memorandum to contribute to the assets of the company in the event of its being wound up. In the case of such companies the liability of its members is limited to the amount of guarantee undertaken by them.

(iv) Government Company: "Government Company" means any company in which not less than fifty one per cent of paid-up share capital is held by the Central Government, or by any State Government, or partly by the Central Government and partly by one or more State Governments, and includes a company which is a subsidiary company of such a Government company.

(v) One Person Company: The Companies Act 2013 Act introduces a new type of entity to the existing list i.e. apart from forming a public or private limited company, the 2013 act enables the formation of a new entity a 'one-person company' (OPC). An OPC means a company with only one person having a sole member [section 3(1) of 2013 Act]. OPC will be formed as a 'Private Limited Company'. Hence, minimum paid up capital will be ₹ 1,00,000/-. Memorandum of Association of such a company will mandatorily prescribe the name of the other person, who in the event of death or disability of the subscriber shall assume his position. An

OPC can be formed only by an Indian Resident and citizen.

(vi) Other Companies: As per Companies act 1956, companies can be classified on the basis of time, place of incorporation and nature of working share capital as follows:

   a) Foreign Company: It means a company incorporated outside India and having a place of business in India whether by itself or through an agent, physically or through electronic mode and conduct any business activity in India in any other manner.

   b) Existing Company: A company which is established before the Company Act 1956 is called Existing Company.

   c) Holding Company: A company is known as the holding company of another company if it has control over another company.

   d) Subsidiary Company: A company is known as subsidiary of another company when control is exercised by the latter over the former called a subsidiary company. A company is to be deemed to be subsidiary company of another.

7. Statutory Corporation: A company may be incorporated by means of a special Act of the Parliament or any state legislature. Such companies are called statutory companies; Instances of statutory companies in India are Reserve Bank of India, The Life Insurance Corporation of India, and The Food Corporation of India etc. These statutory companies are governed by the act under which they are established. The provisions of the Companies Act 1956 apply to statutory companies except where the said provisions are inconsistent with the provisions of the Act creating them. Statutory companies are mostly invested with compulsory powers.

8. Trust: Trusts are governed by the Indian Trust Act, 1882. A trust is created when ownership of a property is transferred to someone for holding or managing it for benefit of another person(s). Trust may be public charitable trust or private trust (for benefit of private individuals). Trusts managed by trustees. Loan can be granted if it is for the purpose of the trust. Trustee is authorised to borrow as per the trust deed. Original Trust Deed to be examined before financing. Certificate of Registration under Public Trust Act to be examined and copy to be kept on record.

Clubs & Societies

Clubs & Societies are non-profit making organisation and represent a group of persons. These are normally incorporated under Cooperative Society Act. Clubs can be registered under Society Act 1860, or Company Act 1956. These get the status of a legal entity only after their incorporation in their own name. These are governed by rules & regulations (bye laws). Cheques favouring society, club, association not to be collected in individual accounts of office bearers or employees.

TEST YOURSELF

1. Which is a non-fund-based facility?
  (a) Overdraft   (b) Bill Finance
  (c) Term Loan   (d) Buyer Credit

2. Which is a fund-based facility?
  (a) Bank guarantee
  (b) Bridge loan
  (c) Derivative products service
  (d) Supplier Credit

3. Loans based on the periods of repayment are classified into:
  (a) Short term loan
  (b) Medium term loan
  (c) Long term loan
  (d) All of the above

4. Loans given to businesses who might be in need of instant cash flow to finance a project. ________ are normally obtained while the borrower is waiting for long-term financing to go through.
  (a) Bridge loans   (b) Composite loan
  (c) Credit card   (d) Bill finance

5. Usually short-term loans are repayable within:
  (a) 3 months   (b) 6 months
  (c) 12 months   (d) 36 months

6. Which is not an un-secured loan?
  (a) Bill finance
  (b) Credit card
  (c) Clean personal loan
  (d) Small Education loan

7. Financing against stock and book debt, banks are generally provides:
  (a) Over draft   (b) Cash credit
  (c) Term loan   (d) Bill finance

8. Which is a correct statement regarding export finance?

(a) Bank finance for both Pre-Shipment /packing credit & Post Shipment credit advances

(b) Packing credit facilitates to the exporter for purchase raw materials and produce goods

(c) In the Post Shipment credit advances, maximum period prescribed for realization of export proceeds is 12 months from date of shipment

(d) All of the above

9. Which is a correct statement regarding letter of credit?

(a) It is issued by bank on request of the exporter

(b) As per UCPDC 600, all LC is irrevocable

(c) It is a non-fund credit facility

(d) All of the above

10. Limitation period for filling a suit in term loan is ___ years from date of default of instalments.

(a) 1 (b) 2

(c) 3 (d) 5

11. Which is not a type of Bank guarantee?

(a) Financial Guarantee

(b) Government Guarantee

(c) Performance Guarantee

(d) Deferred payment Guarantee

12. Clayton's rule is applicable in which of the following accounts:

(a) Cash credit (b) Overdraft

(c) Term loan (d) Both 'a' & 'b'

13. Which is not a type of bill?

(a) Demand bill (b) Sight bill

(c) Usance bill (d) None of these

14. Which is not a type of Retail loan?

(a) Home loan (b) SRTO loan

(c) Education loan (d) Personal loan

15. A loan which is granted for both buying capital assets and to meet working capital requirements is called _________.

(a) Bridge loans (b) Composite loan

(c) Credit card (d) Bill finance

16. Which of the following is the correct sequence for financing the loan?

1. Assessment of viability and credit worthiness
2. Receipt of loan application
3. Disbursement
4. Sanction

(a) 1, 2, 3, 4 (b) 2, 1, 3, 4

(c) 2, 1, 4, 3 (d) 1, 2, 4, 3

17. Which one of the following parameters are generally checked during economically viable of a new proposal of loan?

(a) CIBIL Report

(b) RBI List of defaulters

(c) Credit report from other banks

(d) All of the above

18. Which one of the following are not the correct statement regarding purpose of post-sanction Inspections?

(a) To check that the borrower has not acquired/disposed-off any asset without bank's consent.

(b) To ensure that the borrower has availed of finance against unpaid stocks.

(c) To cross-check the figures declared in the stock statements with the books and physical verification of stocks.

(d) To check that the unit has been working at the projected levels.

19. The loan which is repaid up to ______ is called 'Demand Loan'.

(a) one year (b) two years

(c) three years (d) five years

20. For running the business, borrower needs working capital to meet day-to-day expenses, Stock and book debt. This type of financing is called:

(a) Cash Credit (b) Demand Loan

(c) Bridge Loan (d) Composite Loan

ANSWER

1	2	3	4	5	6	7	8	9	10
(d)	(b)	(d)	(a)	(c)	(a)	(b)	(d)	(a)	(c)

11	12	13	14	15	16	17	18	19	20
(b)	(d)	(d)	(b)	(b)	(c)	(d)	(b)	(c)	(a)

OPERATIONAL ASPECTS OF CBS ENVIRONMENT

INTRODUCTION

Indian Banking sector is passing through a series of innovative changes and Core Banking Solution (CBS) is the word most repeatedly heard among the latest changes. Opening up of Indian Banking sector due to the shift in Government policies and the globalization and the subsequent liberalization process happened world over, are the main reasons for such changes happening in Indian Banking system. The implementation of CBS and introduction of other allied innovative products have caused for big changes in the business of banks, not only in deposits and advances but also in parameters like non-performing assets (NPA) management, interest income, non-interest income (other income), earnings per share (EPS) etc.

CORE BANKING SOLUTIONS (CBS)

Core Banking is the integrative approach that efficiently unites different banking systems in selling their products and services with the aid of information technology. Core Banking Solutions (CBS) is the process which is completed in a centralized environment i.e. Core Banking Solution under which the information relating to the customer's account i.e. financial dealings, profession, income, family members etc are dealt with. These informations are stored in the Central Server of the bank that is available to all the networked branches instead of the branch server. The word Core in Core Banking Solutions (CBS) stands for Centralized Online Real-time Environment.

CBS is networking of branches, which enables customers to operate their accounts, and avail banking services from bank on CBS network, regardless of where they maintain their account. Thus, CBS is a step towards enhancing customer convenience through "Anywhere and Anytime Banking".

Need for Core Banking Solution

CBS is the need of current banking scenario for modernisation in banking operations. CBS fulfils the following banking operation needs:

a) Improve operational efficiency;

b) Reduce cost of operations;

c) Improve customer service;

d) Comply with Anti Money Laundering/ Know Your Customer requirements;

e) Integrate with electronic payment systems.

Benefits of CBS

CBS provides the following benefits in banking operations:

a) Anytime and Anywhere banking (online mediums/ SMS);

b) Standardised, simple and automated processes;

c) Increase in quality of the service provided to the customers;

d) Timely and accurate information for management decision making;

e) Strong audit and internal controls;

f) Bring down the cost of transaction and thereby improving operational efficiency;

g) Paving way for new value-added services thereby generating additional revenue for the Department.

Objectives of CBS

The key objectives are as below:

a) To increase the number of customers;

b) To provide multiple delivery channels like internet, mobile banking, ATMs, thereby bringing access to financial services to the doorsteps of the customers;

c) To enable faster money fund transfers to reach out to more customers;

d) To become one stop solution for financial inclusion initiatives of the Government of India.

Flow of Transactions in CBS

Banks generally adopt the following flow of transactions in CBS environment in their branch.

a) The user has to log in to the system with his user id and password at the branch.

b) Once the user logs in, he will get access to the different modules for doing the transactions.

c) When the user logs in and does a transaction, the transaction will go through a maker checker functionality.

d) In case of maker checker functionality when a teller or user (Clerical/Cashier level) initiates a transaction, the transaction has to be authorised by a supervisory official if the transaction exceeds the authority of the teller who initiates the transaction.

e) When transactions hits the host, the system will validate the transaction and debit or credit the particular account and a message is sent back to the user at the branch as to whether the transaction is complete or not.

f) The system validates the account number, balance in the account, authority of the teller who does the transaction, authority of the officer who authorises the transaction, and other validations.

Operational Aspects for Password Control

Problems in maintaining the integrity of the Password:

a) Users, do not understand the importance of the password. They disclose it to others, write down at some place, or use easy passwords and do not change their passwords at regular intervals.

b) Passwords are not changed/deleted on the transfer/ retirement of the operator/officer in the Master Record of the System Software.

c) In Certain cases multiple passwords are required to be entered.

d) Staff disclose Passwords to others very frequently for the convenience of work.

e) Sometimes, System Software does not store password in the encrypted form.

Steps to be Taken to Ensure the Integrity of the Password

Passwords secrecy should be maintained by Branch Manager, System Administrator, Users, and Authorised Persons. The critical passwords, for accepting sensitive jobs like entering operating systems, taking back-ups, monitoring disk space creating/editing Master Records should be known only to Branch Manager or System Administrator. The Operating System Password should be under Dual Control of Branch Manager and System Administrator in a sealed cover and opened in the presence of at least two persons. It should be changed at once on being opened.

Transaction Control

All the transactions should be controlled by the branch in the following manners:

a) Date should be authorised either by Branch Manager or System Administrator.

b) There should be control in the software so that entries pertaining to current date only would be accepted.

c) There should not be any provision to feed backdated or futuredated entries.

d) In the case of non-usage of terminals, terminals should be logged-off.

e) Only for the physically present users the requisite terminal/user account should be enabled.

f) Special batch reports should be printed, checked, authenticated and duly filed.

Personnel Controls

Personnel transactions should be controlled by the branch in the following manners:

a) There should be segregation of duties among the bank employees.

b) Authorization for amounts entered by the operators should be clearly defined and documented.

c) The job rotation should be carried out at regular intervals.

Day End Activities

At the end of the banking transaction Day End Activity must be carried out by branch in following manners:

a) Day end activities are carried out by either the Branch Manager or System administrator.

b) Supplementary activities should be checked and special users should be deleted.

c) Functions (performed centrally) to be completed at the day end.

d) Shutting down of complete computer system.

Logical Access Control

Access of the systems should be controlled in following manners:

a) Available security features be implemented. A security officer should be appointed who would ensure that available features have been implemented.

b) There should be a process in place for granting access levels. Users should have only the minimum access level needed to do their job. Users' access should be restricted to specific applications, menus within applications, files, and servers. Access levels should be periodically reviewed by the internal auditor. Procedures should be implemented to limit access to work stations after normal working hours.

c) Maintenance should be restricted to a minimum number of persons and it should be properly approved.

d) The password file should be encrypted.

e) Modem access should be protected by a secure system and Modem numbers should be changed periodically.

Role and Responsibilities of the Bank under CBS

The bank should have:

a) Data processing and data interface under various systems.

b) Data integrity and data security.

c) Business Continuity Plans and Disaster Recovery Plans.

d) Accounting manual and critical accounting entries (including month-end and year-end)

e) Controls and recording of various e-banking and Internet banking products.

f) Manual processing of key transactions.

g) MIS reports being generated and the periodicity thereof.

h) Hard copies being generated and the periodicity thereof.

i) Process of generating information related to various disclosures in the financial statements and the involvement of the IT systems.

j) Major exception reports and the process of generation thereof.

k) Major IT related issues such as, data/system corruption, system break-down, etc., having bearing on the preparation and presentation of financial statements.

l) Significant observations of internal auditors, concurrent auditors, system auditors, RBI inspection and internal inspection, etc., related to computerised accounting and overall IT systems.

m) Customer complaints related to mistakes in transactions (interest application; balances, etc.).

To ensure that the technology deployed is being operated in a safe, secure, sound and efficient manner and as per the process flow submitted by the bank, banks are required to get a System Audit done by a firm of Chartered Accountants. The scope of the System audit would include evaluation of the hardware structure, operating systems and critical applications, security and controls in place, including access controls on key applications, disaster recovery plans, training of personnel managing systems and applications, documentation, etc.

TEST YOURSELF

1. Full form of CBS is:
   (a) Complete Banking Service
   (b) Core Banking Services
   (c) Core Banker Solution
   (d) None of the above

2. CBS fulfils which of the following banking operation needs?
   (a) Improves operational efficiency
   (b) Reduces cost of operations
   (c) Improves customer service
   (d) All of the above

3. CBS does not provides which of the following benefits in banking operations?
   (a) Anytime and Anywhere banking
   (b) Standardised, simple and automated processes
   (c) Bring up the cost of transaction
   (d) Increase in quality of the service provided to the customers

4. Which is not an objectives of CBS?
   (a) To restrict the number of customers
   (b) To provide multiple delivery channels like internet, mobile banking, ATMs, thereby bringing access to financial services to the doorsteps of the customers
   (c) To enable faster money fund transfers to reach out to more customers
   (d) To become one stop solution for financial inclusion

5. In the CBS environment, the user has to log in to the system with his user id and password at the branch. Once the user logs in, he will get access to the ______ for doing the transactions.
   (a) Single modules
   (b) Different modules
   (c) Restricted modules
   (c) Assigned modules

6. When the user logs in and does a transaction in CBS:
   (a) The transaction is locked at Data Centre
   (b) The transaction will be final and validated by Data Centre
   (c) The transaction will go through a maker checker functionality
   (d) Any of the above

7. Problems in maintaining the integrity of the Password in the CBS environment:
   (a) Users, do not understand the importance of the-password. They disclose it to others, write down at some place, or use easy passwords and do not change their passwords at regular intervals.
   (b) In Certain cases multiple passwords are required to be entered.
   (c) Staff disclose Passwords to others very frequently for the convenience of work.
   (d) All of the above

8. Personnel transactions should be controlled by the branch in which the following manners?
   (a) There should be segregation of duties among the bank employees.
   (b) Authorization for amounts entered by the operators should be clearly defined and documented.
   (c) The job rotation should be carried out at regular intervals.
   (d) All of the above

<table>
<tr><td colspan="8" align="center">ANSWER</td></tr>
<tr><td>1</td><td>2</td><td>3</td><td>4</td><td>5</td><td>6</td><td>7</td><td>8</td></tr>
<tr><td>(d)</td><td>(d)</td><td>(c)</td><td>(a)</td><td>(b)</td><td>(c)</td><td>(d)</td><td>(d)</td></tr>
</table>

______

BACK OFFICE FUNCTIONS & HANDLING UNRECONCILED ENTRIES IN BANKS

INTRODUCTION

The back office is the portion of a bank made up of administration and support personnel who are not client-facing. Back-office functions include settlements, clearances, record maintenance, regulatory compliance, accounting, and IT services. For example, a financial services provider like bank is segmented into two parts: the front office (e.g. banking business, marketing, and customer support), and the back office (administrative and support services).

The back office can be thought of as the part of a bank responsible for providing all banking business functions related to its operations. The term "back office" originated when early banks designed their offices so that the front portion contained the associates who interact with customers, and the back portion of the office contained associates who have no interaction with customers. Despite their seemingly invisible presence, back-office personnel provide functions essential for operations. Their roles enable and equip front-office personnel to perform their client-facing duties. The back office is sometimes used to describe all jobs that do not directly generate revenue.

ROLE OF BACK OFFICE IN BANKS:

1) Back office consists of administration and support personnel.

2) Back offices carry out various functions to support the front office activities.

3) In specialised functions like Treasury operations and Forex, the back offices perform the main stream role of directly supporting the trading room or front office by controlling confirmations and settlement transactions.

4) With the introduction of computerisation in the banks, many of the activities, which were previously performed by the front office, are now performed by the back office, resulting in cost savings and economies of scale as also freeing the time for the front office staff to focus on sales and servicing functions.

5) Computerisation has eliminated the need of back office being a part of the branch. Back offices may be located somewhere other than the bank branch or bank office. Many are in areas and countries with cheaper rents and lower labour costs.

6) One of the important functions of the back office is to reconcile the accounting entries specially the inter office entries.

FUNCTIONS PERFORMED BY THE BACK OFFICE

1. **Book Keeping and Accounting:** Transaction processing, maintenance of General Ledger and other books of account, balancing of branch accounts, reconciliation of entries and sub-systems, preparation of financial statements.

2. **Deposits:** Calculation and posting of interest in CBS, service charges, reminders for renewals of

term deposits, nature of operation of account—single/jointly etc.

3. **Loans:** Centralised processing of loan proposals or any aspect of loan servicing, NPA management, calculation of EMIs, calculation and posting of interest, penal interest, processing fee, commission and prepayment charges, operational limits, risk management etc.

4. **Regulatory Compliance:** Identifying KYC gaps, customer grievance redressal system etc.

5. **E-banking:** Handling transactions through internet, mobile banking or ATMs, card based payments etc.

6. **Other Functions:** Clearing, collection, remittances etc.

RECONCILIATION FUNCTION IN BANKS

Reconciliation is an important function of banks. Banks have to follow guidelines issued by RBI and reconcile all their books on regular basis. Reconciliation function in banks can be classified as under:

1. Reconciliation of accounts for payments involving intermediaries
2. Reconciliation of accounts with correspondent banks
3. Reconciliation of bank accounts with RBI and other banks and institutions
4. Reconciliation of intra branch entries and sub-systems
5. Reconciliation of inter branch/office entries

1. **Reconciliation of Accounts for Payment Involving Intermediaries:** Account reconciliation process for various payment intermediaries are as under:

   a) The use of Electronic/Online Payment modes for payments to merchants for goods and services like bill payments, online shopping, generally involves the use of intermediaries like aggregators and payment gateway service providers. In arrangements involving such intermediaries, the payments made by customers (for settlement of e-commerce/m-commerce/bill payment transactions), are first credited to the accounts of these intermediaries and then transferred by these intermediaries to the accounts of the merchants in final settlement of the obligations of the paying customers.

   b) Any delay in the transfer of the funds by the intermediaries to the merchants account will entail risks to the customers and the merchants and also impact the payment system.

   c) To ensure that the payments made by customers are remitted by the intermediaries to the accounts

of the merchants without delay, RBI guidelines for opening and operation of accounts and settlement of payments for electronic payment transactions involving intermediaries should be followed.

   d) Further, management of ATMs is being assigned by banks to vendors who collect the amount from bank and load the same in the ATMs as well as collect the amount deposited by customers from ATMs and depositing with the bank.

   e) Banks normally centralize the process of monitoring ATM balances and monitor balance as per the books and balances as per ATM machines (commonly termed as Switch balance) and their reconciliation and ensure timely adjustment of reconciliation entries.

2. **Reconciliation of Accounts with Correspondent Banks:** For settlement of foreign exchange transactions, banks normally maintain accounts with their overseas branches/correspondents which are called Nostro accounts. Banks are required to reconcile the entries that have passed over an account with a correspondent bank against those that are passed internally in the books of the bank to a Nostro account. After reconciliation, the unmatched items in both accounts represent entries that have not been responded to or have been responded differently in either the books of the bank or its correspondent.

3. **Reconciliation of Bank Accounts with RBI and Balances with RBI:** Banks maintain a current account and other accounts with RBI to facilitate transactions relating to CRR, Repo and Reverse Repo, Clearing/RTGS, Currency Chest transactions through select branches. These branches having account with RBI, should reconcile the balances in these accounts. The maker checker concept is used for preparation of the reconciliation statement. Following items appearing in the reconciliation statements need closer attention:

   (a) Cash transactions remaining un-responded;

   (b) Revenue items requiring adjustments/write-offs;

   (c) Old outstanding balances remaining unadjusted for a significant period.

In case of purchase and sale of security transactions, the banks periodically reconcile the security balance in the bank's book vis-a-vis the balance in the custodian account (i.e., Subsidiary General Ledger or Demat account). As per RBI, investment balances as per bank's book should be reconciled at quarterly intervals with the balances in the Public Debt Office's books.

4. **Balances with Other Institutions and Banks Other than RBI:** Accounts may be maintained for the purpose of clearing/collection, investments, money at call and short notice. The process adopted for reconciliation of balance with RBI is adopted for reconciling the balances with banks other than RBI. No debit for charges or credit for interest should remain outstanding and all revenue should be accounted for in the same year. No cheque sent or received in clearing should remain outstanding. Any cheque returned unpaid should be accounted for on the same day on which they were sent in clearing or on the following day. All bills or outstanding cheques sent for collection and outstanding as on the closing date should have been credited subsequently.

5. **Reconciliation of Inter Branch Entries:** Balancing of Books/Reconciliation of control and subsidiary records balancing of the books of account means that the primary books of account have been tallied and the general ledger is balanced. At a particular point of time, the balance shown in a particular control account in the GL of the branch and the total of balances in all the folios of the subsidiary ledgers, pertaining to that control account, should be same. In the manual system of recording, balancing was an acute problem for branches having a large number of accounts. With computerisation, the original entry in the account is automatically posted in all the books and balances derived and therefore no problem of balancing.

Sundry/Suspense Account

The problem relating to reconciliation in suspense and sundry accounts has not been resolved by computerisation. Suspense account is used to temporarily record certain items like;

(a) Amounts the precise nature thereof which is yet to be determined or pending transfer thereof to the appropriate head of account;

(b) Debit balances arising from payment of interest warrants/dividend warrants pending reconciliation of amounts deposited by a company;

(c) Losses caused due to frauds and awaiting adjustment.

If entries in suspense account are not reconciled quickly, there may be frauds by passing debit entries in the account and siphoning off the amount. Details of old outstanding entries in suspense account, along with narrations, should be prepared periodically and decision on each entry is taken including provision/write off for old outstanding items. Outstanding entries in 'Sundry Deposits' or 'Sundries Account' should also be reconciled quickly. However, probability of fraud in such credit entries is relatively less.

RBI GUIDELINES ON INTER OFFICE RECONCILIATION IN BANKS

1. Banks should reconcile the entries outstanding in their inter branch accounts within a period of six months.

2. Banks should segregate the credit entries outstanding for more than five years in inter-branch accounts and transfer them to a separate Blocked Account which should be shown in the balance sheet under the head 'Other liabilities and provisions-Others' (Schedule 5). While arriving at the net amount of interbranch transactions for inclusion in the balance sheet, the aggregate amount of Blocked Account should be excluded and only the amount representing the remaining credit entries should be netted against debit entries.

3. Any adjustment from the Blocked Account should be permitted only with the authorisation of two officials, one of whom should be from outside the branch concerned, if the amount exceeds a particular amount.

4. Beginning April 1,1999, banks should maintain category-wise (head-wise) accounts for various types of transactions put through inter-branch accounts so that the netting can be done category-wise. Banks should make 100% provision against the net debit balance in the inter-branch account in respect of entries outstanding for more than six months. Banks should arrive at the category-wise position of unreconciled entries outstanding in the inter-branch accounts for more than six months as on March 31. While making provision, the credit balance in the Blocked Account should also be taken into account and the net debit in one category is not setoff against net credit in another category.

5. Banks should segregate inter-branch transactions relating to demand drafts from other interbank transactions.

6. Banks should introduce the system of segregating DD transactions, with reconciliation at weekly intervals and close monitoring of large amounts.

7. Banks should restrict originating debits to head office account to cash/funds transfer, purchase of securities/capital assets, withdrawals from Provident Fund, advances to inspection and other staff members.

RECONCILIATION SET UP AND PROCESS AT THE BANKS

1. The reconciliation work of inter-office accounts is normally centralised at the reconciliation department. When banks are working under CBS, they centralise this reconciliation work at the IT department at HO.

2. The inter-branch accounts are normally sub-divided into segments or specific areas, e.g., 'Drafts paid/payable', 'inter-branch remittances', 'H.O. A/c' etc.

3. Each branch has to send a daily statement of Inter Office account to the Central Reconciliation Department (CRD). If there is no transaction in this account, a NIL statement has to be sent by the branch. Based on these daily statements, the computer system matches the originating entries with the responding (reversal) entries for a particular day/period. If there remain any unreconciled entries, it could be due to - Nature of the entry i.e. there is a time lag involved in some entries like the draft issued entries; mistakes in one or more of the daily statements sent by the branches; frauds like payment of a forged draft.

The system will generate the report of unreconciled entries for any particular day or period in any format, age wise, amount wise, branch wise, category wise etc. as per the requirements of the Reconciliation Department. All the unreconciled entries in the statement generated by the system have to be examined.

TEST YOURSELF

1. The _______ can be thought of as the part of a bank responsible for providing all banking business functions related to its operations.
   (a) Front Office
   (b) Back office
   (c) Branch
   (d) Audit Office

2. Which is the function of back office in a financial services provider like bank?
   (a) Banking business
   (b) Marketing
   (c) Support services
   (d) Customer support

3. Which is the role of back office in banks?
   (a) Back office consists of administration and support personnel.
   (b) Back office carry out various functions to support the front office activities.
   (c) In specialised functions like Treasury operations and Forex, the back offices perform the mainstream role of directly supporting the trading room or front office by controlling confirmations and settlement transactions.
   (d) All of the above

4. _______ may be located somewhere other than the bank branch or bank office. Many are in areas and countries with cheaper rents and lower labour costs.
   (a) Front Office
   (b) Back office
   (c) Forex Branch
   (d) Treasury branch

5. Which of the following is the work of front office?
   (a) Calculation and posting of interest in CBS
   (b) Levy of service charges in the account
   (c) Opening of locker account
   (d) All of the above

6. The banking works like handling transactions through internet, mobile banking or ATMs, card based payments, and customer grievance redressal system are done by:
   (a) Back Office
   (b) Front Office
   (c) Zonal Office
   (d) Nodal Office

7. Which is not classified as Reconciliation function in banks?
   (a) Reconciliation of accounts for payments involving intermediaries
   (b) Reconciliation of accounts with correspondent banks
   (c) Reconciliation of bank accounts with RBI and other banks and institutions
   (d) Reconciliation of interbank entries

8. For settlement of foreign exchange transactions, banks normally maintain accounts with their overseas branches/correspondents which are called _______ accounts.
   (a) Vostro
   (b) Nostro
   (c) Loro
   (d) Overseas branch

ANSWER

1	2	3	4	5	6	7	8
(b)	(c)	(d)	(b)	(c)	(a)	(d)	(b)

MOCK TEST

Accounting & Finance for Bankers

MOCK TEST-1

1. Formula for calculation of compound interest if interest is paid Quarterly.
   - (a) $P(1 + r)$
   - (b) $P(1 + r/2)^2$
   - (c) $P(1 + r/4)^4$
   - (d) $P(1 + r/12)^{12}$

2. The difference between simple and compound interests compounded annually on a certain sum of money for 2 years at 4% per annum is ₹ 1. The sum (in ₹) is:
   - (a) ₹ 625
   - (b) ₹ 630
   - (c) ₹ 650
   - (d) ₹ 680

3. The least number of complete years in which a sum of money put out at 20% compound interest will be more than doubled is:
   - (a) 4 years
   - (b) 5 years
   - (c) 6 years
   - (d) 7 years

4. Difference between face value of bond and call price of bond is considered as:
   - (a) Call premium
   - (b) Call provision
   - (c) Discount premium
   - (d) Discount provision

5. The principal of which is linked to an accepted index of inflation with a view to protecting the principal amount of the investors from inflation. These bonds are called:
   - (a) Inflation Index Bonds
   - (b) Fixed Rate Bonds
   - (c) Capital Indexed Bonds
   - (d) Zero Coupon Bonds

6. If a 7% coupon bond is trading for ₹ 975, it has a current yield of ___ per cent.
   - (a) 6.63
   - (b) 6.85
   - (c) 7.03
   - (d) 7.18

7. A sound Capital Budgeting technique is based on:
   - (a) Cash Flows
   - (b) Accounting Profit
   - (c) Interest Rate on Borrowings
   - (d) Last Dividend Paid

8. Risk in Capital budgeting implies that the decision-maker knows ___________ of the cash flows.
   - (a) Variability
   - (b) Probability
   - (c) Certainty
   - (d) None of the above

9. Decision-tree approach is used in:
   - (a) Proposals with Longer Life
   - (b) Sequential Decisions
   - (c) Independent Cashflows
   - (d) Accept-Reject Proposal

10. Find out annual cash inflow and pay-back period from the following data:
    Cost of plant: ₹ 15,00,000. Life of plant: 10 years, Salvage Value of the plant: ₹ 1,00,000. Annual earnings before depreciation and tax: ₹ 2,00,000. Assume tax rate: 40%
    - (a) ₹ 1,86,000 and 7.523 years
    - (b) ₹ 1,76,000 and 8.523 years
    - (c) ₹ 1,80,000 and 8.123 years
    - (d) ₹ 1,66,000 and 7.523 years

Case Study

ABC Limited Profit and Loss Account for the year ended 31.03.2019 is given below:

Turnover - 7300	Cost of Sales - 4234	Distribution Costs - 1320
Admin Expenses - 480	Interest - 200	Tax - 372
Dividend - 400		
Balance Sheet as on 31.03.2019		
Fixed Assets		
Plant and Machinery - 3960	Current Liabilities = 890	
Current Assets = 2430	Trade Creditors – 200	
Stocks - 1392	Proposed Dividend - 400	
Debtors - 800	Taxation - 170	
Bank - 238	Accruals - 120	
Net Current Assets - 1540		
10% Debenture - 2000	Ordinary Shares - 900	
Financed by - 3500	Retained Profit - 2600	

Calculate question number 11-20 based on the above details.

11. Gross profit
   (a) 1266   (b) 3066
   (c) 4234   (d) 7300

12. Operating profit
   (a) 294   (b) 694
   (c) 1066   (d) 1266

13. Profit before tax
   (a) 294   (b) 694
   (c) 1066   (d) 1266

14. Profit attributable to shareholders
   (a) 294   (b) 694
   (c) 1066   (d) 1266

15. Retained profit
   (a) 294   (b) 694
   (c) 1066   (d) 1266

16. Gross profit margin
   (a) 17.34%   (b) 23.02%
   (c) 33.33%   (d) 42%

17. Operating margin
   (a) 17.34%   (b) 23.02%
   (c) 33.33%   (d) 42%

18. Return on capital employed (ROCE) ratio
   (a) 17.34%   (b) 23.02%
   (c) 33.33%   (d) 42%

19. Current Ratio
   (a) 1.17:1   (b) 2.73:1
   (c) 1:1.17   (d) 1:2.73

20. Acid test/Quick ratio
   (a) 1.17:1   (b) 2.73:1
   (c) 1:1.17   (d) 1:2.73

21. The main objective of providing depreciation is:
   (a) To allocate true profit
   (b) To show the true financial position in the balance sheet
   (c) To reduce tax burden
   (d) To provide funds for replacement of fixed assets

22. Depreciation is a process of:
   (a) Valuation
   (b) Allocation
   (c) Both valuation and allocation
   (d) None of these

23. Which of the following is not true?
   (a) Depreciation is an expense charged to the P&L a/c
   (b) Depreciation is not a part of the operating costs
   (c) Assets that are depreciated are tangible assets
   (d) Depreciation is like an insurance expense

24. Machinery worth ₹ 82000 is purchased and the firm spent ₹ 8000 on its installation. Its effective commercial life is estimated as 10 years and scrap value ₹ 10000. What will be written down value at the end of 3rd year, under straight line method?
   (a) ₹ 68000   (b) ₹ 66000
   (c) ₹ 62000   (d) ₹ 70000

25. Gap between ____________ and ____________ dates make a forex trade as cash/tom/spot trade.
   (a) Value Date and Settlement date
   (b) Trade date and T+1
   (c) Trade Date and T+2
   (d) Trade Date and value date

26. Which of the following is a direct quote in India?
   (a) 1 Pound sterling = US $ 1.70
   (b) 1 US $ = ₹ 48.90
   (c) ₹ 100 = US $ 2.10
   (d) both (a) and (b)

27. ________ is the simultaneous buying and selling of foreign currencies or an asset with intention of making profits from the difference between the exchange rate prevailing at the same time in different markets.
   (a) Swap   (b) Cross rate
   (c) Forward   (d) Arbitrage

28. The forward points = 0.011500 and spot rate 1US $ = 44.00. If the forward period is 180 days and number of days in a year are assumed at 360, calculate the interest differential.
   (a) 5.23%   (b) 5.43%
   (c) 5.85%   (d) 6.23%

29. Which is not a correct statement about the nature of accounting?
   (a) Accounting is a service activity
   (b) Accounting is very much a profession
   (c) Accounting is an Art not a Science
   (d) Accounting is the language of business

30. GAAP stands for:
   (a) Governmental Accepted Accounting Principles
   (b) Generally Accepted Accounting Principles
   (c) Governmental Adopted Accounting Principles
   (d) Generally Adopted Accounting Principles

31. ________ involves court and litigation cases, fraud investigation, claims and dispute resolution, and other areas that involve legal matters.
   (a) Internal auditing   (b) Forensic accounting
   (c) Cost accounting   (d) Inflation accounting

32. Accounting was practiced in India twenty-three centuries ago as is clear from the book named "_____" written by Kautilya, King Chandragupta's minister.
(a) Arthaniti
(b) Arthashastra
(c) ChanakyaNiti
(d) Arthatantra

33. Under the money measurement concept the following will not be recorded in the books of account of the business: (i) Value of furniture (ii) Quality of company goods (iii) Bad health of managing director.
(a) Only (i) and (ii)
(b) Only (ii) and (iii)
(c) Only (i) and (iii)
(d) (i), (ii) and (iii)

34. The system of recording business transactions based on dual aspect concept is called ___________.
(a) Double account system
(b) Double entry system
(c) Single entry system
(d) All of the above

35. This concept speaks about recording of only those transactions which are actually realized.
(a) Accrual concept
(b) Entity concept
(c) Dual aspect concept
(d) Realisation concept

36. The language of accounting is:
(a) Money
(b) Transactions
(c) Business
(d) None of these

37. The book, which contains all accounts permanently, is called:
(a) Journal
(b) Ledger
(c) Trial balance
(d) Balance sheet

38. Cash book records___________.
(a) All cash receipt
(b) All cash payment
(c) All cash receipt & payments
(d) All type of transactions

39. Consignee's account is a:
(a) Real a/c
(b) Personal a/c
(c) Representative personal a/c
(d) Nominal a/c

40. Nominal accounts relate to _______.
(i) incomes (ii) expenses (iii) assets (iv) liabilities
(a) (i) to (iv) all
(b) (i) and (ii) only
(c) (ii) and (iii) only
(d) (i) and (iii) only

Case Study

ABC Limited had the following balances on 31.03.2018.

Current Liabilities = 5,00,000	Current Assets = 7,00,000
Total Liabilities = 8,00,000	Total Assets = 16,00,000
Cash Provided by Operations = 9,00,000	Net Income = 3,60,000
Capital Expenditures = 2,00,000	Preferred Stock Dividends = 50,000
Cash Dividends = 1,00,000	Average Common Shares Outstanding = 100,000 shares

Calculate the question number 41 to 45 based on the above details.

41. What is the amount of working capital?
(a) 2,00,000
(b) 4,00,000
(c) 6,00,000
(d) 8,00,000

42. What is the current ratio?
(a) 0.5
(b) 1.2
(c) 1.4
(d) 1.8

43. What is the debt to total assets ratio?
(a) 0.5
(b) 1.2
(c) 1.4
(d) 1.8

44. What is the amount of free cash flow?
(a) 2,00,000
(b) 4,00,000
(c) 6,00,000
(d) 8,00,000

45. What is the amount of Earnings per share (EPS)?
(a) 1.10 per share
(b) 2.10 per share
(c) 3.10 per share
(d) 4.10 per share

46. Bank reconciliation statement is:
(a) Ledger account
(b) Part of the cash book
(c) A statement showing difference between the balance in the pass book and cash book
(d) A statement of position of balance of two books

47. From the books of Mr. Niraj it was observed that cheques amounting to ₹ 2,40,000 were deposited in the bank, out of which cheques worth ₹ 20,000 were dishonoured and cheques worth ₹ 40,000 are still in the process of collection. The treatment of this while preparing Bank Reconciliation Statement is:

   (a) Deduct 60,000 from overdraft balance as per pass book

   (b) Add 20,000 and deduct 40,000 from overdraft balance as per cash book

   (c) Deduct 60,000 from bank balance as per pass book

   (d) Add 60,000 from overdraft balance as per pass book

48. Benefits of preparing Bank Reconciliation Statement include:

   (i) It brings out any errors committed in preparation of Cash book/Bank Pass Book

   (ii) Highlights under delay in clearance of cheques deposited but not credited

   (iii) Help know actual bank balance

   (a) Only (i) and (ii)   (b) Only (i) and (iii)

   (c) Only (ii) and (iii)   (d) (i), (ii) and (iii)

49. Bank Reconciliation Statement is prepared by:

   (a) Creditor   (b) Debtor

   (c) Customer   (d) Bank

50. A Bank Reconciliation is prepared, so that the difference in the under noted balances is reconciled:

   (a) The difference in the balance in the cash column and bank column of the Cash book

   (b) The difference in the balance in the pass book at the beginning and at the end

   (c) The difference in the cash book and pass book balances as on the date

   (d) The differences in the bank ledger and pass book

What would be the impact of the following errors (in Qs. No. 51-54) on the Trial Balance?

51. A copy of a sales invoice for ₹ 10,000 is not recorded in the Sales Day Book.

   (a) Excess credit ₹ 10,000

   (b) Excess debit ₹ 10,000

   (c) No impact

   (d) None of the above

52. A supplier's invoice for ₹ 2,000 is posted to the debit of the Trade Payable's account.

   (a) Excess credit ₹ 2,000

   (b) Excess debit ₹ 4,000

   (c) Excess debit ₹ 2,000

   (d) None of the above

53. The daily total of the Sales Day Book is stated as ₹ 345,000 instead of ₹ 315,000 (i.e.overcast by ₹ 30,000).

   (a) Excess credit ₹ 30,000

   (b) Excess debit ₹ 30,000

   (c) No impact

   (d) None of the above

54. A purchase invoice is recorded in the Purchases Day Book as ₹ 14,500, without taking account of 10% of that amount offered as trade discount.

   (a) Excess credit ₹ 1,450

   (b) Excess debit ₹ 1,450

   (c) No impact

   (d) None of the above

55. Cost of replacement of defective parts of the machinery is ___________.

   (a) Capital expenditure

   (b) Revenue expenditure

   (c) Deferred revenue expenditure

   (d) None of these

56. Which transaction is a capital receipt?

   (a) cash received from sale of inventory

   (b) bank interest received on deposits

   (c) premises rent received from the tenant

   (d) proceeds of sale of equipment

57. The difference between selling price and present book value of machinery is called:

   (a) Capital income   (b) Revenue income

   (c) Revenue receipt   (d) Capital receipt

58. On the last date of his food truck business, A food truck owner sold snacks worth ₹ 2,500 and sold his truck for ₹ 20,000. How should these receipts be treated in his business books?

   (a) Capital Receipt - 0, Revenue Receipt - 22500

   (b) Capital Receipt - 2500, Revenue Receipt - 20000

   (c) Capital Receipt - 20000, Revenue Receipt - 2500

   (d) None of the above

59. For a bank, Rebate on bills discounted is an item of ___________.

   (a) an income

   (b) an expenditure

   (c) an accrued income

   (d) an income received in Advance

60. Which of the following parties in a bill of exchange do match?

   (a) Drawer—the person who orders the other person to make payment

   (b) Payee—the person who is to make payment

   (c) Drawee–the person who is to receive the payment as per order of the drawer

   (d) None of the above

61. The facility to get bill of exchange discounted puts them into the category of ______.

(a) Fixed assets   (b) Intangible assets
(c) Wasting assets   (d) Current assets

62. Which of these is not an essential feature of a bill of exchange?
(a) Conditional
(b) The drawer, drawee and payee must be certain
(c) In writing
(d) It should be properly stamped

63. The entry regarding payment of the bill will be passed in the books of the drawer if the bill is ___________.
(a) retained
(b) endorsed
(c) discounted
(d) retained or sent to bank for collection

64. Find the Correct equation:
(a) Assets = Equities (total claims)
(b) Liabilities = Assets – Capital
(c) Capital = Assets – Liabilities
(d) All of the above

65. _________ means the amount which the owner of business has invested in the firm and can claim from the firm.
(a) Capital   (b) Liability
(c) Assets   (d) Revenue

66. Which is not an Intangible asset?
(a) Loss   (b) Goodwill
(c) Patent   (d) Copy Right

67. A _________ is an account into which all gains and losses are collected, in order to ascertain the excess gains over the losses or *vice-versa*
(a) Trading Account   (b) Profit & Loss A/c
(c) Balance Sheet   (d) Cash Book

68. Trading account is a:
(a) Personal A/c   (b) Real A/c
(c) Nominal A/c   (d) None

69. Depreciation account appearing in the trial balance is shown in ________.
(a) Profit & Loss A/c
(b) Trading A/c
(c) Deducted from the concerned Assets A/c
(d) Shown on the liability side

70. Which of the following is a statement of revenues and expenses for a specific period of time?
(a) Trading Account   (b) Profit & Loss A/c
(c) Balance Sheet   (d) Trial Balance

71. Balance Sheet is a statement of _________.
(a) Assets   (b) Liability
(c) Capital   (d) All of the above

72. Which one is not the use of Accounting Ratios?
(a) Facilitate Inter-Firm comparison
(b) Facilitate Intra-Firm comparison
(c) Help in Planning
(d) None of these

73. Which is not a Solvency Ratio?
(a) Debtor's Turnover Ratio
(b) Current Ratio
(c) Debt-Equity Ratio
(d) Liquidity Ratio

74. The accounts and Balance Sheet together with the Auditor's report shall be published in the prescribed manner and ______ thereof shall be furnished as returns to the Reserve Bank within three months from the end of the period to which they refer.
(a) one copy   (b) two copies
(c) three copies   (d) four copies

75. Section 30(1(B) of BR Act, 1949 define:
(a) Audit of accounts
(b) Special audit
(c) Submission of annual accounts
(d) Copies of balance-sheets

76. Format A is the Balance Sheet of the bank. It contains _________ schedules.
(a) nine   (b) ten
(c) eleven   (d) twelve

77. In Form A, Investments are bifurcated into six segments in Balance Sheets, which are not in the segments?
(a) Government Securities
(b) Other approved Securities
(c) Shares
(d) None of the above

78. A company incorporated outside India but has a place of business in India, is termed as:
(a) Statutory Company
(b) Foreign Company
(c) Holding Company
(d) Subsidiary Company

79. Rights shares mean the shares which are:
(a) Issued to directors of the company
(b) Issued for a consideration other than cash
(c) Offered to the existing shareholders
(d) Issued to promoters of the company for their services.

80. The provisions regarding issues of shares at a discount are contained as per:
(a) Section 56 of Companies Act 1956

(b) Section 79 of Companies Act 1956
(c) Section 90 of Companies Act 1956
(d) Section 125 of Companies Act 1956

81. Discount allowed on issue of shares is shown in:
(a) Credit side of P & L a/c
(b) Liabilities side of Balance Sheet
(c) Debit side of P & L a/c
(d) Assets side of Balance Sheet

82. The major objectives of computerisation in banking are to improve:
(a) Customer service
(b) Housekeeping
(c) Productivity and profitability
(d) All of the above

83. Computerisation at the branch level can be used to:
((a) Provide better and speedy customer service
((b) Generation of various reports
((c) Analyze the branch-level data for decision making
((d) All of the above

84. Core banking applications provide anywhere, anytime ______ non-stop services, which is not possible with traditional localized branch automation systems.
(a) 12 by 7   (b) 24 by 6
(c) 24 by 7   (d) 12 by 6

85. As per Section 6 of the Banking Regulation Act, 1949, banks can engage in certain classes of business which are incidental to the business of banking like:
(a) Lockers
(b) Safe custody
(c) Collection of cheques
(d) All of the above

86. Punishment for non-adherence of the PML Act 2002 would be rigorous imprisonment for not less than ______ years but up to ______ years.
(a) 3, 5   (b) 3, 7
(c) 5, 7   (d) 5, 10

87. BCSBI Code is not applies to the products ________.
(a) Current accounts, savings accounts, term deposits
(b) Banking services related to Government transactions
(c) Demat accounts, Equity, Government bonds
(d) None

88. Which are the key elements of KYC policy?
(a) Customer Acceptance Policy (CAP)
(b) Risk Management (RM)
(c) Customer Identification Procedure (CIP)
(d) All of the above

89. Which is not categorised as Medium Risk Customer?
(a) NBFC
(b) Bullion Dealers
(c) Builders
(d) Stock Brokers

90. If a bank has many branches within the area of a clearing house, it nominates one branch to act as the ______ of that bank.
(a) Nodal Branch   (b) Clearing Branch
(c) Lead Branch   (d) Collecting Branch

91. ________ is a new method of payment introduced by Reserve Bank of India which provides customers an option to collect their monthly/quarterly/half yearly/yearly interest/dividend/salary/pension directly through their bank accounts.
(a) ECS (Credit)   (b) ECS (Debit)
(c) Speed Clearing   (d) Auto Clearing

92. If partnership deed is silent about operation of the account, then the account will be operated by:
(a) Any of the partner
(b) All partners jointly
(c) First partner as per deed
(c) As per instruction of the partners

93. Company's name, Authorized capital, Objectives of the company, Liability of shareholders are written in:
(a) Certificate of Incorporation
(b) Memorandum of Association
(c) Articles of Association
(d) None of the above

94. Which is not correct about limited liability partnership (LLP)?
(a) LLP is governed by limited liability partnership Act 2008.
(b) Minimum 3 designated partners and no limit on maximum number of partners.
(c) LLP is a legal entity separate from its partner.
(d) LLP cannot raise fund from public.

95. Which is a fund based facility?
(a) Bank Guarantee
(b) Bridge Loan
(c) Derivative Products Service
(d) Supplier Credit

96. Which is not an un-secured loan?
(a) Bill Finance
(b) Credit Card
(c) Clean Personal Loan
(d) Small Education Loan

97. CBS fulfils which of the following banking operation needs?
   (a) Improves operational efficiency
   (b) Reduces cost of operations
   (c) Improves customer service
   (d) All of the above

98. In the CBS environment, the user has to log in to the system with his user id and password at the branch. Once the user logs in, he will get access to the _______for doing the transactions.
   (a) Single modules
   (b) Different modules
   (c) Restricted modules
   (c) Assigned modules

99. Which is the function of back office in a financial services provider like bank?
   (a) Banking business
   (b) Marketing
   (c) Support services
   (d) Customer support

100. For settlement of foreign exchange transactions, banks normally maintain accounts with their overseas branches/correspondents which are called _______ accounts.
   (a) Vostro
   (b) Nostro
   (c) Loro
   (d) Overseas branch

ANSWER

1	2	3	4	5	6	7	8	9	10
(c)	(a)	(a)	(a)	(c)	(d)	(a)	(b)	(b)	(b)

11	12	13	14	15	16	17	18	19	20
(b)	(d)	(c)	(b)	(a)	(d)	(a)	(b)	(b)	(a)

21	22	23	24	25	26	27	28	29	30
(a)	(b)	(b)	(b)	(d)	(b)	(d)	(a)	(c)	(b)

31	32	33	34	35	36	37	38	39	40
(b)	(b)	(b)	(b)	(d)	(a)	(b)	(c)	(c)	(b)

41	42	43	44	45	46	47	48	49	50
(a)	(c)	(a)	(c)	(c)	(c)	(a)	(d)	(c)	(c)

51	52	53	54	55	56	57	58	59	60
(c)	(b)	(a)	(c)	(b)	(d)	(a)	(c)	(d)	(a)

61	62	63	64	65	66	67	68	69	70
(d)	(a)	(d)	(d)	(a)	(a)	(b)	(c)	(a)	(b)

71	72	73	74	75	76	77	78	79	80
(d)	(c)	(a)	(c)	(b)	(d)	(d)	(b)	(c)	(b)

81	82	83	84	85	86	87	88	89	90
(d)	(d)	(d)	(c)	(d)	(b)	(d)	(d)	(b)	(a)

91	92	93	94	95	96	97	98	99	100
(a)	(b)	(b)	(b)	(b)	(a)	(d)	(b)	(c)	(b)

MOCK TEST-2

1. Calculate the EMI of a loan of ₹ 100,000 given @ 9% p.a. for 12 months.
   (a) ₹ 8745   (b) ₹ 8845
   (c) ₹ 8620   (d) ₹ 9215

2. In this arrangement, the amount of EMI increases during the term as the repayment progresses from being lowest in the first year and increasing steadily thereafter.
   (a) Regular EMI   (b) Step-up EMI
   (c) Step-down EMI   (d) Balloon EMI

3. When difference between compound and simple interest for three years is ₹ 122 at 5% rate per annum, the principal is ______.
   (a) ₹ 15800   (b) ₹ 16000
   (c) ₹ 18000   (d) ₹ 17600

4. A bond holder of a company has one of the following relationships with it. Identify:
   (a) shareholder   (b) depositor
   (c) creditor   (d) employee

5. A coupon bond that pays interest annually is selling at par value of ₹ 1000, maturity in five years and has a coupon rate of 9%. The yield to maturity on this bond is:
   (a) 9.0%   (b) 8.1%
   (c) 7.2%   (d) 9.6%

6. The face value of a bond is ₹ 10000, its coupon rate 10% and time to maturity is 4 years. If the YTM is 10% it falls by 1% what will be the percentage change in price of the bond?
   (a) 2.3%   (b) 4.1%
   (c) 3.2%   (d) 2.6%

7. Which of the following investment rules does not use the time value of the money concept?
   (a) The payback periods
   (b) Internal rate of return
   (c) Net present value
   (d) All of the above use the time value concept

8. Which of the following is a risk factor in capital budgeting?
   (a) Industry specific risk factors
   (b) Competition risk factors
   (c) Project specific risk factors
   (d) All of the above

9. Consider the following data on a proposed investment: Investment required: ₹ 160,000, Annual cash inflows: ₹ 40,000, Life of the investment: 6 years, Salvage value: 0 and Discount rate: 10%. Based on the above data, what is the payback period of the proposed investment project?
   (a) 0.25 years   (b) 3 years
   (c) 4 years   (d) 5 years

10. The cost of a project is ₹ 15,00,000. Its working life is 15 years and salvage value of ₹ 50,000. Annual income before depreciation and after tax ₹ 250,000. Assume tax rate 50%. Find out payback period, Post pay-back profit and Post pay-back Profitability index.
    (a) 6 years, ₹ 24,00,000 and 150.33%
    (b) 5 years, ₹ 25,00,000 and 153.33%
    (c) 6 years, ₹ 23,00,000 and 153.33%
    (d) 5 years, ₹ 25,00,000 and 150.33%

Case Study

ABC Limited Profit and Loss Account for the year ended 31.03.2019 is given below:

Turnover - 8030	Admin expenses - 600	Dividend - 320
Cost of Sales - 4818	Interest - 200	
Distribution Costs - 1606	Tax - 286	
Balance Sheet as on 31.03.2019		
Fixed Assets (Plant & Machinery) - 4000	Current Liabilities = 1100	
Current Assets = 2800	Trade Creditors - 520	
Stocks - 1800	Proposed Dividend - 320	
Debtors - 960	Taxation - 160	
Bank - 40	Accruals - 100	
10% Debenture - 2000	Net Current Assets - 1700	
Financed by - 3700	Ordinary Shares - 900	
	Retained Profit - 2800	

Calculate question number 11-20 based on the above details.

11. Gross profit:
(a) 1006
(b) 2206
(c) 3122
(d) 3212

12. Operating profit:
(a) 200
(b) 520
(c) 806
(d) 1006

13. Profit before tax:
(a) 200
(b) 520
(c) 806
(d) 1006

14. Profit attributable to shareholders:
(a) 200
(b) 520
(c) 806
(d) 1006

15. Retained profit:
(a) 200
(b) 520
(c) 806
(d) 1006

16. Gross profit margin:
(a) 12.53%
(b) 17.65%
(c) 33.33%
(d) 40%

17. Operating margin:
(a) 12.53%
(b) 17.65%
(c) 33.33%
(d) 40%

18. Return on capital employed (ROCE) ratio:
(a) 12.53%
(b) 17.65%
(c) 33.33%
(d) 40%

19. Current Ratio:
(a) 1:0.91
(b) 1:2.55
(c) 0.91:1
(d) 2.55:1

20. Acid test/Quick ratio:
(a) 1:0.91
(b) 1:2.55
(c) 0.91:1
(d) 2.55:1

21. The XYZ purchases a new equipment. The selected data is given below:
Cost of equipment: ₹ 25,000, Useful life of equipment: 5 years, Tax rate: 30%.
If equipment is depreciated using straight line method, what is the depreciation tax shield associated with the new equipment?
(a) ₹ 5,000
(b) ₹ 1,500
(c) ₹ 3,500
(d) ₹ 7,500

22. Which are the advantages of Straight-Line Method?
(a) Simple and easy to understand
(b) The book value of an asset can be reduced to Zero
(c) A fair evaluation of an asset each year on the balance sheet
(d) All of the above

23. Which is not a disadvantage of Written Down Value Method?
(a) In subsequent years the original cost of the asset is completely lost sight of.
(b) The asset can never be reduced to zero.
(c) Income-tax authorities recognize this method.
(d) This method requires elaborate book-keeping. The determination of correct rate of depreciation is a complex task.

24. A firm purchased machinery worth ₹ 76000 on January 01, 2019 and its life is expected to be 8 years, with scrap value at the end ₹ 12000. What is amount of depreciation?
(a) ₹ 11000 per annum
(b) ₹ 9500 per annum
(c) ₹ 9000 per annum
(d) ₹ 8000 per annum

25. An Indian importer with foreign currency payables enters into a forward contract. His expectation is __________.
(a) Indian Rupee to Depreciate
(b) Indian Rupee to Appreciate
(c) Foreign Currency to Depreciate
(d) None of the above

26. A person wants to remit Euro and there is no quotation with the bank for Euro. Bank works out the rate through ₹/$ rate and $/Euro rate. This is called:
(a) bid rate
(b) offer rate
(c) cross rate
(d) floating rate

27. Forex rate in Delhi is 1 US $ = 68.80/90. In London the 1 US $ = 0.70 Euro. What is the buying rate for Euro/Rupee rate?
(a) 48.16
(b) 98.42
(c) 98.29
(d) 98.34

28. Forex rate in Delhi is 1 US $ = ₹ 48.80/90. In London the 1 Euro = US $ 1.60/65. An exporter wants an export bill of Euro 50000 to be purchased by the bank. How much amount will be given to the exporter in domestic currency?
(a) 3851000
(b) 3882500
(c) 3904000
(d) 3896000

29. Who frames the accounting standards in India?
(a) Reserve Bank of India
(b) The Institute of Chartered Accountants of India
(c) Ministry of Company Affairs
(d) SEBI

30. The Institute of Chartered Accountants of India, recognizing the need to harmonise the diverse accounting policies and practices at present in use

in India, constituted an Accounting Standards Board (AS(B) on 21st April, _____.
(a) 1949   (b) 1965
(c) 1977   (d) 1981

31. The major differences between IFRS and GAAP is the specification of the way inventory is accounted regarding for:
(a) LIFO Inventory
(b) Costs of Development
(c) Write-Downs
(d) All of the above

32. The ______ means pricing of goods and services within a multidivisional organisation, particularly with regard to the cross-border transactions.
(a) Selling price
(b) International transfer pricing
(c) Transfer pricing
(d) Arm's length price

33. This accounting convention states that once a particular accounting practice, method or policy is adopted to prepare accounts, statements and reports.
(a) Convention of Conservatism
(b) Materiality Convention
(c) Convention of Consistency
(d) Convention of Full Disclosure

34. The concept that recognizes the distinction between the receipt of cash and the right to receive the cash is called ______________.
(a) Accrual Concept
(b) Cash Concept
(c) Materiality Concept
(d) Full Disclosure Concept

35. Accounting to the______________, account should report only what is material and ignore insignificant details while preparing the final accounts.
(a) Convention of Conservatism
(b) Convention of Materiality
(c) Convention of Consistency
(d) Convention of Full Disclosure

36. Which of the following is a journal?
(a) Purchase book   (b) Creditor a/c
(c) Debtor a/c   (d) Capital a/c

37. Transaction is first recorded in the______ and they are posted to the______.
(a) Ledger, journal   (b) Journal, ledger
(c) any of the above (d) none of these

38. Debit means:
(a) an increase in asset
(b) an increase in liability
(c) an increase in the proprietor's equity
(d) a decrease in asset.

39. Which of the following accounts will be credited on giving cash donations?
(a) Cash account
(b) Donation account
(c) Purchase account
(d) None of the above

40. A ledger is called a book of:
(a) Primary entry
(b) Secondary entry
(c) Final entry
(d) None of the above

X Ltd., has a current ratio of 3.5:1 and quick ratio of 2:1. If excess of current assets over quick assets represented by inventories is ₹ 24,000, calculate ...

41. Current liabilities:
(a) ₹ 16,000   (b) ₹ 36,000
(c) ₹ 56,000   (d) ₹ 76,000

42. Current assets
(a) ₹ 16,000   (b) ₹ 36,000
(c) ₹ 56,000   (d) ₹ 76,000

Given the following information:
Total assets = ₹ 3,00,000
Non-current Liabilities = ₹ 80,000
Shareholders' Funds = ₹ 2,00,000
Non-Current Assets:
Fixed assets = ₹ 1,60,000
Non-current Investments = ₹ 1,00,000

43. Calulate Current Assets
(a) ₹ 20,000   (b) ₹ 30,000
(c) ₹ 40,000   (d) ₹ 50,000

44. Calulate Current Liabilities
(a) ₹ 20,000   (b) ₹ 30,000
(c) ₹ 40,000   (d) ₹ 50,000

45. Calulate Current Ratio
(a) 1 : 1   (b) 1 : 2
(c) 2 : 1   (d) 2 : 1.5

46. As per cash book there is overdraft of ₹ 520, Bank recovers interest of ₹ 50. What shall be the balance in the pass book?
(a) ₹ 520   (b) ₹ 50
(c) ₹ 570   (d) ₹ 470

47. As per the cash book there is an overdraft for ₹ 16,000, Bank charges interest of ₹ 800 and a commission of ₹ 250. What shall be the balance in the pass book?

(a) ₹ 16,800   (b) ₹ 16,250
(c) ₹ 17,050   (d) ₹ 16,550

48. In a current A/c there is a balance of ₹ 8,000, bank recovers folio charges of ₹ 150. What shall be the balance in the pass book?
(a) ₹ 8,150   (b) ₹ 7,750
(c) ₹ 7,850   (d) None of these

49. Overdraft balance as per cash book of the customer is ₹ 5,500. Bank charges an interest of ₹ 60 and a cheque has been issued for ₹ 1,350 but it is not presented for payment. What will be the balance in the bank pass book?
(a) 4,210   (b) 4,150
(c) 4,090   (d) 5,440

50. Which is not the correct statement regarding Need of Bank Reconciliation Statement?
(a) It does not help to understand the actual Bank balance.
(b) It helps to identify the mistakes in the Cash Book and the Pass Book.
(c) It helps to detect and prevent frauds and errors in recording the Banking transactions.
(d) It helps to incorporate certain expenditures/income debited/credited by Bank in the books of accounts.

51. Errors of part omission do not permit ______________.
(a) Correct totalling of the Balance sheet
(b) Correct totalling of the Trial Balance
(c) The Trial Balance to agree
(d) Preparation of Final Accounts

52. Trial balance remains untallied due to errors. Various types of errors can be:
1. Error of omission
2. Error of commission
3. Errors of principal
4. Intentional errors
(a) 1, 2 and 3 only   (b) 1, 3 and 4 only
(c) 2, 3 and 4 only   (d) 1 to 4 all

53. XYZ had purchased certain goods from ABC firm, but these were not recorded in the purchase journal. This is error of _________. It will (affect/not affect) the trial balance
(a) Omission affect
(b) Compensating, not affect
(c) Principle, affect
(d) Omission, not affect

54. The closing stock given in the Trial Balance is transferred to which of the following accounts ______________.
(a) Trading Account

(b) Profit and Loss Account
(c) Manufacturing Account
(d) Balance Sheet

55. Which is a capital receipt for the owner of the bicycle shop?
(a) purchase of bicycle delivery vehicle by cheque
(b) sale of old bicycle delivery vehicle for cash
(c) sale of bicycles for cash
(d) purchase of bicycles by cheque

56. Sale of machine of machine merchandising business __________.
(a) Capital receipt
(b) Capital income
(c) Revenue income
(d) Revenue receipt

57. For a bookshop owner, which of the following item is a capital receipt?
(a) Receipt of sales commission from the publisher
(b) Cash discount from a supplier of stationery
(c) Proceeds from the disposal of old bookshelf
(d) Cash from sale of notebooks

58. An expenditure charged to P&L a/c over a period of 5 to 6 years is an example of:
(a) Revenue expenditure
(b) Capital expenditure
(c) Deferred revenue expenditure
(d) All of the above

59. A draws a bill on B for 50,000 for 3 months. Before the due date B sends 1/5th of the amount to A. B requested A to draw a new bill for the balance amount plus interest @ 12% p.a. for 3 months. Find the amount of the new bill.
(a) 5,210   (b) 4,150
(c) 4,120   (d) 5,820

60. On 1.3.2018 X draws a bill on Y for 3 months for ₹ 40,000. On 4.5.2018 Y pays the bill to X at 12% discount, the amount of discount will be____.
(a) ₹ 200   (b) ₹ 400
(c) ₹ 600   (d) ₹ 100

61. The following is (are) the current liability (ies):
(a) Bills payable
(b) Outstanding expenses
(c) Bank overdraft
(d) All of the above

62. B drew a bill of ₹ 20,000 for 2 months on A for mutual accommodation. It was decided that the proceeds would be shared equally. How much amount would be received by A if the bill was discounted @12% p.a.?
(a) ₹ 18,600   (b) ₹ 9,800
(c) ₹ 10,000   (d) ₹ 10,200

63. A draws a bill on B for ₹ 4,500 for mutual accommodation in the ratio 2:1. A got it discounted at ₹ 4,230 and remitted 1/3rd of the proceeds to B. At the time of maturity, how much amount A should remit to B such that B can pay off the bill?
(a) ₹ 3,000
(b) ₹ 2,880
(c) ₹ 2,920
(d) ₹ 3,010

64. It means the amount which the firm owes to outsiders. Long term liabilities are those liabilities which are payable after a long term. Current liabilities are those liabilities which are payable in near future (generally within one year):
(a) Capital
(b) Liability
(c) Assets
(d) Revenue

65. Which is correct statement regarding Fixed assets?
(a) Fixed assets are those assets which are purchased for the purpose of operating the business but not for resale.
(b) Fixed assets which are kept for short term for converting into cash or for resale.
(c) Fixed assets is a part of Intangible assets.
(d) All are correct statements.

66. _____ means the amount which, as a result of operations, is received by the business.
(a) Capital
(b) Liability
(c) Assets
(d) Revenue

67. The closing stock of the last year becomes the opening stock of the current year. Opening Stock will include which of the following?
(a) Opening Stock of Raw Material
(b) Opening Stock of Semi-finished goods
(c) Opening Stock of Finished goods
(d) All of the above

68. Closing stock appearing in the Trial Balance is shown in __________.
(a) Trading A/c and Balance Sheet
(b) Profit & Loss A/c
(c) Balance Sheet only
d. Trading A/c only

69. Goods costing ₹ 10,000 were damaged by fire. Insurance company admitted a claim of ₹ 8,500. Profit & Loss a/c will be debited with...
(a) ₹ 10,000
(b) ₹ 8,500
(c) ₹ 5,500
(d) ₹ 1,500

70. If depreciation is not charged, Profit & Loss a/c will show:
(a) More profits
(b) Less profits
(c) Nominal profits
(d) Original profits

71. At the end of each financial year all accounts of ...... and ...... are transferred to Trading and Profit & Loss account, called closing entries.
(a) Assets, liabilities
(b) Income, liabilities
(c) Expenses, assets
(d) Income, expenses

72. Those financial ratios which measure the long-term solvency and capital structure of the firm is called:
(a) Turnover Ratios
(b) Leverage Ratios
(c) Liquidity Ratios
(d) Profitability Ratios

73. Which one is also called as "Liquidity Ratios"?
(a) Profitability Ratios
(b) Turnover Ratios
(c) Long-term Solvency Ratios
(d) Short-term Solvency Ratios

74. In Format A, Schedule _______ form Liability Side of the Banks Balance Sheet and Schedule _____ on the Asset side of the Balance Sheet.
(a) 1 to 5, 6 to 12
(b) 1 to 6, 7 to 12
(c) 1 to 4, 5 to 12
(d) 1 to 7, 8 to 12

75. In Form A, details of Contingent Liabilities are given in:
(a) Schedule 3
(b) Schedule 5
(c) Schedule 8
(d) Schedule 11

76. In a Bank Balance Sheet, Figures should be rounded-off to the nearest_______.
(a) Rupee
(b) Hundred rupees
(c) Thousand rupees
(d) Lakh rupees

77. Which of the following can be included in the category of voucher in a bank?
(a) Pay-in-slip
(b) Cheque
(c) Withdrawal form
(d) All of the above

78. Profit on re-issue of forfeited shares is transferred to:
(a) Profit and Loss a/c
(b) Capital Reserve a/c
(c) Share Capital a/c
(d) General Reserve a/c

79. Rights shares mean the shares which are:
(a) Issued to directors of the company
(b) Issued for a consideration other than cash
(c) Offered to the existing shareholders
(d) Issued to promoters of the company for their services

80. Expenditure incurred on issue of equity shares is:
    (a) Revenue expenditure
    (b) Capital expenditure
    (c) Deferred capital expenditure
    (d) None of the above

81. A public company having a share capital:
    (a) Must issue a prospectus
    (b) Cannot file a statement in lieu of prospectus
    (c) Doesn't need prospectus
    (d) May file a statement in lieu of prospectus

82. What is the meaning of UPS?
    (a) Uniform power system
    (b) Unchanged power system
    (c) Uninterrupted pressure system
    (d) Uninterrupted power system

83. Which are the leading Causes of Data Loss:
    (a) Natural Disasters
    (b) Human Errors
    (c) Software Malfunction
    (d) All of the above

84. 'Resume' and 'Love letter' are which type of Virus?
    (a) Dangerous   (b) Childish
    (c) Ineffective   (d) Effective

85. Banks are increasingly using outsourcing as a means of:
    (a) Reducing cost
    (b) Accessing specialist expertise
    (c) Both of the above
    (d) None of the above

86. The BCSBI has been established on the recommendation of __________.
    (a) R V Gupta Committee
    (b) S. S. Tarapore Committee
    (c) Narshimham Committee
    (d) V K Nair Committee

87. As per KYC policy, Bank has to open account to which of the following name?
    (a) Anonymous name
    (b) Fictitious name
    (c) Political party
    (d) Criminal background

88. Which is categorised as Low Risk Customer?
    (a) Statutory Bodies
    (b) Trust
    (c) Charities
    (d) Non-resident customer

89. The Director of FIU-IND is vested with the power of a _______ under the code of civil procedure.
    (a) Civil Court   (b) High Court
    (d) Supreme Court   (d) CBI Court

90. Which are not the benefits from CTS?
    (a) Shorter clearing cycle
    (b) Superior verification and reconciliation process
    (c) No geographical restrictions as to jurisdiction
    (d) None of the above

91. With effect from April 1, ______, banks should not make payment of cheques/drafts/pay orders/banker's cheques if they are presented beyond the period of three months from the date of such instrument.
    (a) 2010   (b) 2012
    (c) 2014   (d) 2016

92. Which is the correct statement about 'Public Company'?
    (a) Its share is listed in stock exchange
    (b) Minimum seven members, no limit of maximum number
    (c) Minimum three directors, maximum no limit
    (d) All of the above

93. As per Indian Contracts Act 1872, a person who is competent to enter into a valid contract:
    (a) He is otherwise disqualified by any law
    (b) He should not be a solvent
    (c) Drunken person is legally competent to enter into a contract
    (d) He should be in good sense while lending a loan and entering into a contract

94. A company is known as the ____________ of another company if it has control over another company.
    (a) Holding company   (b) Existing company
    (c) Other company   (d) Foreign company

95. Which is not a type of Retail loan?
    (a) Home loan   (b) SRTO loan
    (c) Education loan   (d) Personal loan

96. Limitation period for filling a suit in term loan is ___ years from date of default of instalments.
    (a) 1   (b) 2
    (c) 3   (d) 5

97. Which is not an objective of CBS?
    (a) To restrict the number of customers
    (b) To provide multiple delivery channels like internet, mobile banking, ATMs, thereby bringing access to financial services to the doorsteps of the customers
    (c) To enable faster money fund transfers to reach out to more customers
    (d) To become one stop solution for financial inclusion

98. When the user logs in and does a transaction in CBS:
    (a) The transaction is locked at Data Centre

   (b) The transaction will be final and validated by Data Centre

   (c) The transaction will go through a maker checker functionality

   (d) Any of the above

99. Which is the role of back office in banks?

   (a) Back office consists of administration and support personnel.

   (b) Back offices carry out various functions to support the front office activities.

   (c) In specialised functions like Treasury operations and Forex, the back offices perform the mainstream role of directly supporting the trading room or front office by controlling confirmations and settlement transactions.

   (d) All of the above

100. The banking works like handling transactions through internet, mobile banking or ATMs, card based payments, and customer grievance redressal system are done by:

   (a) Back office

   (b) Front office

   (c) Zonal office

   (d) Nodal Office

ANSWER

1	2	3	4	5	6	7	8	9	10
(a)	(a)	(b)	(c)	(a)	(c)	(a)	(d)	(c)	(c)
11	**12**	**13**	**14**	**15**	**16**	**17**	**18**	**19**	**20**
(d)	(d)	(c)	(b)	(a)	(d)	(a)	(b)	(d)	(c)
21	**22**	**23**	**24**	**25**	**26**	**27**	**28**	**29**	**30**
(b)	(d)	(c)	(d)	(a)	(c)	(c)	(c)	(b)	(c)
31	**32**	**33**	**34**	**35**	**36**	**37**	**38**	**39**	**40**
(c)	(b)	(c)	(a)	(b)	(a)	(b)	(a)	(a)	(b)
41	**42**	**43**	**44**	**45**	**46**	**47**	**48**	**49**	**50**
(a)	(c)	(c)	(a)	(c)	(c)	(c)	(c)	(a)	(a)
51	**52**	**53**	**54**	**55**	**56**	**57**	**58**	**59**	**60**
(c)	(a)	(d)	(d)	(b)	(d)	(b)	(c)	(c)	(b)
61	**62**	**63**	**64**	**65**	**66**	**67**	**68**	**69**	**70**
(d)	(b)	(a)	(b)	(a)	(d)	(d)	(c)	(d)	(a)
71	**72**	**73**	**74**	**75**	**76**	**77**	**78**	**79**	**80**
(d)	(b)	(d)	(a)	(d)	(c)	(d)	(b)	(c)	(c)
81	**82**	**83**	**84**	**85**	**86**	**87**	**88**	**89**	**90**
(d)	(d)	(d)	(a)	(c)	(b)	(c)	(a)	(a)	(d)
91	**92**	**93**	**94**	**95**	**96**	**97**	**98**	**99**	**100**
(b)	(d)	(d)	(a)	(b)	(c)	(a)	(c)	(d)	(a)
